DATE DUE

SEP 06 '94 RET'D			
OCT 31 '94 RET'D			
FEB 11 '99			

A FINE WILL BE CHARGED
FOR EACH OVERDUE BOOK

Life, Liberty, and the

The Plunder of Early America

Pursuit of Land

Daniel M. Friedenberg

Prometheus Books • Buffalo, New York

Published 1992 by Prometheus Books

96 95 94 93 92   5 4 3 2 1

Library of Congress Cataloging-in-Publication Data

Friedenberg, Daniel M.
    Life, liberty, and the pursuit of land : the plunder of early America / by Daniel M. Friedenberg.
        p.   cm.
    Includes bibliographical references and index.
    Summary: Examines the methods of acquiring and using land that developed in colonial America as a means to gain economic and political power.
    ISBN 0-087975-722-1 (cloth)
    1. Public land sales—Great Britain—Colonies—History. 2. Public land sales—United States—History. 3. Land grants—Great Britain—Colonies—History. 4. Land grants—United States—History. 5. Land companies—England—History. 6. Land companies—United States—History. [1. Land tenure. 2. United States—History—Colonial period. 1600–1775. 3. United States—History—Revolution, 1776–1783. 4. United States—History—1783–1800.] I. Title.
HD194.F75   1992
333.3′0973—dc20   91-42160
                                                                             CIP
                                                                              AC

Printed on acid-free paper in the United States of America

To

ANNE FREMANTLE

and

JOSEPH T. SHIPLEY

Thank you.

"[Historians] those romance-writers . . . where, facts being set forth in a different light, every reader believes as he pleases, and, indeed, the more judicious and suspicious very justly esteem the whole as no other than a romance in which the writer hath indulged a happy and fertile invention . . . though these widely differ in the narrative of facts, some ascribing victory to the one, and others to the other party; some representing the same man as a rogue, while others give him a great and honest character; yet all agree in the scene where the fact is supposed to have happened, and where the person, who is both a rogue and an honest man, lived."

Henry Fielding, *Joseph Andrews,* Bk. 3, Chapter 1

Contents

8   Contents

List of Illustrations

Preface

The United States is the world superpower of the second half of the twentieth century. In the seventeenth century there were only small English settlements scattered along the Atlantic coastline from what is now North Carolina to Massachusetts. In the early eighteenth century they rolled up to the Allegheny Mountains, and then later in the century drove west of the mountains and to the Gulf of Mexico. By the nineteenth century, settlers were surging toward the Pacific coast, swallowing one-third of Spanish Mexico, and after two unsuccessful invasions of British Canada, they bit off what is now Oregon and Washington in the northwest, and hopped over Canada to acquire Alaska. This swelling of America's borders did not stop within the land limits of the two oceans, but leapt through Caribbean waters to Puerto Rico and the Virgin Islands; and through Pacific waters to Hawaii, Guam, and American Samoa.

Thus, in a fundamental sense, the history of the United States is land munching in every direction to create a great empire. Since this pattern was set from the earliest settlements, it is useful to look back to see if the devices created in order to foster this explosive growth can help explain how American society later developed.

Prince Otto von Bismarck, the first chancellor of the united Germany, a man not noted for levity, remarked that there was a special providence for drunkards, fools, and the United States. Surely chance was indeed kind to pick as the neighbor to loot a decaying Spanish empire with an enormous but sparsely populated territory. Even more fortunate, the North American continent was occupied by a people, the Indians, both ill-equipped in military might and divided in warring factions that would not unite. The white man's diseases were a great ally in conquest. And the one truly formidable enemy that could have blocked American growth (and did, to the north in British Canada) was the mother country in tongue and religion, where mutual bonds of common ancestry prevented war from rotting into fratricide.

The study of the first stumbling steps in the rise of American empire is the purpose of this book, what Thomas Jefferson might more properly have called, when writing the Declaration of Independence, the inalienable rights of Life, Liberty, and the Pursuit of Land, rather than the Pursuit of Happiness. An ironic observer might avow that that is what Jefferson meant, knowing his fellow Virginian plantation grandees did indeed equate land with happiness. This pursuit of land, based on killing the redskin natives and enslaving the blackskins snatched from Africa, was not only the deep piling on which the first American structure set; it also molded a political and social system better to fit the needs of the aggressors. The great success of this system produced certain national traits that still exist and can be briefly noted: a view of land divorced from its function as part of nature, and seen as a consumer throw-away product to be abused without regard for the future; the conviction that influence to acquire land, and other forms of wealth later, rested on control of the political process; and a tendency to greed and self-righteous arrogance that created a false sense of omnipotence. Since these traits developed early, an analysis of the American child, and in particular its methods of seizing and using the land, leads to an understanding of the adult, which is us today.

Part One

The Formation of the Colonies

1

The Period of Exploration

"Gold rules everything. Its power is such that it is able to deliver souls from Purgatory or open to them the gates of Paradise."

Letter of Columbus to King Ferdinand

It is difficult to state one prime motive for the European push into the New World. The Christian desire to save souls was surely a factor, and some historians have emphasized the pressure of population growth as a reason for the expeditions. The need to find new trade routes to the Far East, "the Indies," was also a strong passion, as was rampant greed for gold and silver, with open or secret tithing to the monarchs. In addition, there was the desire to own land, and through it to gain economic and political power. Land was sought by individuals as a sign of personal wealth, and by nation-states as the right of imperial expansion. The New World can justly be called a real estate—a royal estate—venture.

To balance these various factors and see which threads were most strongly sewn into the future tapestry of the United States, a brief detour must be taken through the structure of European society, particularly England, in the period before the first explorations. America was a child of England, and the explorers, followed by the colonists, brought English traditions and habits of thought with them.

The European culture out of which Christopher Columbus sailed was a feudal Catholic entity in decay. The Albigensian and Hussite heresies

17

had sown their seeds: the Protestant Reformation was in the air. The Renaissance had destroyed the cultural unity of the Middle Ages, and the Lombards, the "pope's usurers," were already stage props for capitalism. Feudal society, on the decline since the close of the thirteenth century, was being replaced by the knitting together of nation-states. Everywhere the minds of men in the late fifteenth century were buffeted by new ferment.

The spiritual legacy of the feudal system had been sharply defined by class relations based on the land. The root was the fief, a body of land of varying size, the holder of which swore fealty to one of a group of greater and lesser lords. The hierarchy extended to the monarch. Fealty meant military service, and in return for this the holder of the feudal estate was supreme within his small domain. Provided he performed his duty, he was rarely bothered by the nebulous central authority.

The power of the fief-holder rested on his control over labor. Though there were in some countries a small group of freemen, the greater part of the rural population consisted of villeins and serfs. The villeins, who were in a minority, were perpetual tenants with a tenure fixed by custom. The rest were serfs, a French derivation of the Latin *servus* or slave. Bishop Adelberon in the eleventh century gave a clear definition of the two classes in European society. The first consisted of two subgroups: the clergy, who prayed, and the seigniors, who fought. The second worked to support the first.

At the end of the Middle Ages the monarchies began to assume more power. To do this they had to break the power of the barons, who were the linchpins of the feudal structure. The struggle inflamed Europe for hundreds of years. In England Edward IV won in 1471 when "the last of the barons lay gory in his blood on the field of Tewkesbury," the final drama in the Wars of the Roses. Henry VII tore another hole in the feudal order by freeing the fief-holders of the need to maintain their private armies. Their power base destroyed, the nobles were reduced to mere royal courtiers.

This measure by Henry VII had other fearsome results. Since the nobles no longer needed to maintain small farmsteads, each supplying its quota of armed men, it was in their interest now to obtain the highest money rent possible. This meant clearing the land of people to raise sheep to supply the expanding woolen industry. Vagrancy on an unparalleled scale took place. Every important historian of the period has linked this change with a series of violent catastrophes for the peasants, leading to the rise of modern capitalism in England and the growth of empire caused by a flood of miserable wretches from the home country moving in any direction in order to survive.[1]

Henry VIII added fuel to the fire when he turned Protestant. To build up internal support, he distributed Catholic Church lands to favorite cronies, who then had everything to lose if the anti-papist policy was crushed. The property of the abbeys came into the market after 1536, followed by those of the guilds and the chapels. The new owners promptly drove out the peasants from the former church lands in order to create sheep pasture. By 1696, when the first reliable statistics were published on England and Wales, the arable land was estimated at eleven million acres, while pasture and meadow combined accounted for almost the same, another ten million acres.[2]

With so much land removed from the plow, famine became endemic. The 1600s were the worst period in all of English history for widespread hunger. The five years from 1647 to 1651, the four years from 1658 to 1661, and the seven years from 1692 to 1698 were terrible epochs of mass starvation.[3] A massive shift from rural to urban centers took place, increasing the misery, as evicted serfs and villeins poured into the cities. Drunkenness, prostitution, theft, and murder were the inevitable results, which led to still more repressive laws. It has been asserted that, during his reign, Henry VIII hanged some seventy-two thousand persons. Richard Hakluyt the younger's preface to *Diverse Voyages Touching the Discovery of America* (1582) captured the atmosphere that set the stage for mass English migration, even before the settlements of Jamestown and Plymouth:

> Yea, if we would behold with the eye of pity how all our prisons are pestered and filled with able men to serve their country, which for small robberies are daily hanged up in great numbers, we would hasten and further, every man to his power, the deducting of some colonies of our superfluous people into those temperate and fertile parts of America.[4]

We know why the English poor came to colonial America, as indeed they later fled to or were dumped on Australia. What were the motives of the English kings? The early documents indicate a variety of reasons, but the unifying element was imperial land expansion. Giovanni Caboto (John Cabot) was a Genoese navigator hired by Henry VII to explore the Westward passage. Cabot's touching the mainland of North America was the legal basis for all later English claims. Raimondo di Soncino wrote a long letter to the Duke of Milan dated December 18, 1497, referring to this trip. "Having obtained royal privileges securing to himself the dominions he might discover, the sovereignty being reserved to the Crown . . . ," then continuing, "and having wandered thus for a long time, at length he hit upon land, where he hoisted the royal standard, and took possession for his Highness." The voyage was obviously made for territorial reasons. Trade was also an important factor. "And it is said that before long his Majesty will arm some ships for him and will give him all the malefactors to go to that country and form a colony, so that they hope to establish a greater depot of spices in London than there is in Alexandria." Showing the mentality of the time, Raimondo di Soncino comments toward the end of the despatch: "I have also spoken with a Burgundian . . . who affirms all this, and who wishes to return because the Admiral Cabot has given him an island, and has given another to his barber of Castione."[5]

The English did not follow up this first exploration, and almost a century passed before Sir Humphrey Gilbert sailed west again. Edward Hayes, commander of the only ship to return to England from this expedition, began his *Sir Humphrey Gilbert's Voyage to Newfoundland* in 1583 with the pious statement that a prime purpose of the trip was finding a right way "of planting a Christian habitation." But Hayes also wrote, "When first Sir Humphrey Gilbert undertook the western discovery of America, and had procured from Her Majesty [Elizabeth] a very large commission to inhabit and possess at his choice all remote and heathen lands not in the actual possession of any Christian prince. . . ."[6] In fact, Gilbert's patent of colonization gave him full territorial rights over all land within six hundred miles of the spot where he settled.

Very shortly thereafter, Richard Hakluyt the younger wrote a great work of propaganda for Sir Walter Raleigh to give Queen Elizabeth. Here, he presents his three prime "Reasons for Colonization." In order, they are: the glory of God by planting of religion among infidels, the increase of the force of the Christians, and the possibility of the enlarging of the dominions of the Queen's Most Excellent Majesty. Amusingly, Hakluyt concludes with a list of men useful in colonizing, and though it is long— including fishermen, husbandmen, construction men, and soldiers—somehow he forgets to include Anglican ministers. Likewise, the First Charter of Virginia, granted by King James I in 1606, states the purpose in the third clause: "propagating of Christian religion to such people, as yet live in Darkness and miserable Ignorance of the true knowledge and Worship of God." However, the king sagely reserves the right to a fifth of any gold or silver found, and the land is given "in free and common Soccage,"[7] that is, as freehold and not outright. The monarchs were careful to mix their Christian resolve with trade and imperial expansion.

As the smell of Mexican and Peruvian gold and silver wafted north, English unction went through its own alchemy. The tale of Gilbert's voyage to Newfoundland is still medieval in feeling. Sir Francis Drake and Sir Walter Raleigh show a different mentality. Brief quotes from Drake and Raleigh will demonstrate the shift in values.

Sir Frances Drake Revived, published in London in 1626 from notes that Drake himself had reviewed, carries the subtitle "Calling upon this dull or effeminate Age, to follow his noble steps for gold and silver." The late Elizabethan reader might shake his head in approval at pious sentiments such as "conclude with me, that the LORD only, can do great things!" but many Englishmen were far more titillated when on its third voyage (1572) Drake's band entered Nombre de Dios, the Caribbean port of Spanish Panama, and, after feathering the enemy with arrows and breaking skulls with the butt ends of pikes, came to their objective. The writer almost drools as he describes what they found in the governor's house:

> We saw a huge heap of silver in that nether room; being a pile of bars of silver of, as near as we could guess, seventy feet in length, of ten feet in breadth, and twelve feet in height, piled up against the wall, each bar was between thirty-five and forty pounds in weight.[8]

Sir Francis Drake carried away as much as thirty tons of gold and silver from these expeditions. To avoid the sack of all Cartagena, the Spaniards gave him a ransom of £110,000 in ducats "for that which was yet standing" (the ducat was then valued at five shillings, sixpence sterling). Since Drake did not consider the abbey of Cartagena, located a quarter of a mile below the town, as part of the agreement, he squeezed out another large sum in ransom. The Drake expedition had been funded in part by £5,000 supplied by a corporation in which Queen Elizabeth held a large interest. A £600,000 profit was made and the queen received about £275,000 as her cut.

Sir Walter Raleigh, the cynosure of English Renaissance gentlemen, was equally frank. His work entitled *The Discovery of Guiana* (undertaken in 1595), did indeed represent a more frank and less "dull or effeminate Age." The New World was a place for spoils and not much more: ore was what counted, and to get gold and silver it was proper to ruin peoples and countries. Raleigh sums up his views after the tale: "To conclude, Guiana is country that hath yet her maidenhead, never sacked, turned, nor wrought: the face of the earth hath not been torn, nor the virtue and salt of the soil spent by manurance. The graves have not been opened for gold, the mines not broken with sledges, nor their images pulled down out of their temples."

This was not to be endured. Raleigh made a rousing pitch to Queen Elizabeth: "Her Majesty may in this enterprise employ all those soldiers and gentlemen that are younger brethren, and all captains and chieftains that want employment, and the charge will be only for the first setting out in victualling and arming them; for after the first or second year I doubt not but to see in London a Contraction-House of more receipt for Guiana than there is now in Sevilla for the West Indies."[9] Raleigh is here referring to the fact that the entire trade of Spanish America passed through the Casa de Contración at Seville in Spain.

The lust for loot wheezed and then coughed to death as evidence mounted that the English colonies did not have gold and silver. Raleigh failed in his efforts to find it during two expeditions to Virginia (the name for all English North America at the time). He was sent to the Tower of London, first by Elizabeth and then by King James I. Freed by the latter monarch in 1616 expressly to find the gold of Guiana (Venezuela) he failed again. In 1618, Raleigh was separated from his head on charges of treason, the more simple reason being he never found the gold and silver promised.

From our time it is difficult to understand how sincere Christians, and decent men, could act with such rapacity in the New World.[10] But this is because we tend to paint the values of today on another age. The tough leaders of sixteenth- and early seventeenth-century American expeditions operated within the only code they knew, that of the crumbling citadel of post medieval Europe. But those values had little relation to the American experience. The terrain was obviously different. Yet more important than unexplored forest and jungle, than vast spaces and mighty rivers, was the fact that the natives consisted of red-skinned heathens with an alien culture.

Before the Protestant Reformation and the rise of capitalism, most white European Christians shared certain common standards. Sometimes violated, they were recognized as standards nonetheless.[11] Those values had already been dealt a severe body blow by the ferocious wars, declared and undeclared, set off by the Reformation. They were completely set aside when it came to exploring the New World. Many explorers were honest men in their own eyes: but the American Indians were not Christians; they practiced "abominations" (which in specific areas, such as Mexico, was certainly true) and they were seen as outside the pale of known civilization. Discovering a new land occupied by a heathen people meant valid seizure to Europeans, as did Christian duty enjoin saving their souls. The monarch who sent the explorer not only owned the land, but could deed this land and its inhabitants to anyone even before it was discovered, as was done in the cases of Columbus, Cabot, and Humphrey. The knightly ideal SOLI • DEO • HONOR ET GLORIA still embraced God and Glory, but Honor no longer meant the same thing. Francisco de Vitoria, a Dominican professor at the University of Salamanca, was four centuries ahead of his time when he lectured to incredulous students that Christian rulers had no rights over infidels and that the extension of empire was not a just cause for war.

The division of feudal society into two classes, a military aristocracy and a toiling peasantry, also left its psychological mind print. It was only natural that the martial admirals and adventurers, as well as many of the later colonists, dreamed of becoming aristocrats. This could only be done through seizing land and precious metals. It did not occur to the new-comers that the natives had any "human rights" in the modern sense, for the society from which Europeans came treated the peasants much like slaves. Any restraint based on church and custom was not operative in heathen regions.

The only group of early colonists who took up cooperative work for themselves on the soil, rather than seizing booty, was the Puritans, particularly the extreme wing called Separatists. The ideal for these Puritans —who were the dangerous radicals of their age—was to re-establish the rather mythical communal life of rural Christian brotherhood that pertained to the small fiefs of England before the fourteenth century. Following this ideal, their land at Plymouth was at first tilled in common and the livestock held as communal property. Only later, for a very brief period indeed, were the land and animals apportioned.

With this exception, the early conquerors and colonists came from the same mold and were dominated by similar ideas. They shared an obsessive desire to succeed, prodded forward by burning memories of hunger or social abasement at home. They felt free of the constraints of Europe but, paradoxically, wanted to succeed in establishing values that were imitative of Europe. The medieval concept of the seignior was still in important ways their beacon. Riches and nobility were the visible proof of this high estate, and the most obvious badge of aristocracy was ownership of land. Dealing with a culture alien in religion, social structure, and skin color, they practiced any violence and deceit to achieve their goal. The hammer blows of this legacy, despite the passage of centuries, were dented so sharply into the New World, they are still with us today.

2

Sacking Indian Lands

*"**ABORIGINES**, n. Persons of little worth found encumbering the soil of a newly discovered country. They soon ceased to cumber; they fertilize."*

Ambrose Bierce, *The Devil's Dictionary*

The English beached in what had been a well-populated country on the Atlantic seaboard.[1] The accounts of early explorers sailing along the coast from the present Hudson River north to Maine teem with reports of a coastline and nearby islands bright with fires at night. Everywhere the voyagers met friendly Indians.

We have little accurate information on population density. The first reports of white men are general in tone. The explorer Giovanni da Verrazzano, who in 1524 worked his way up the Atlantic coast from what is now North Carolina to Canada, noted how "well-peopled" was Block Island; in the next century the actual count was 109 persons to the square mile. Slightly to the east, Martha's Vineyard had at the same count 27 persons to the square mile. One of the early settlers in Massachusetts estimated the Narragansetts at some 30,000 tribesmen. Daniel Gookin, supervisor of the mission reservations in Massachusetts, queried old Indians in 1674 as to the tribes of lower New England a half-century earlier. From these admittedly provisional figures, the data indicates a range of 72,000 to 90,000 Indians in that area alone. Northern New England running to western Connecticut may have had a population of as many as 144,000 persons in 1600. In 1656, Adriaen Van der Donck wrote that the Indians in New Netherlands told him they had been ten times as numerous before the arrival of the white men.

The first records known of the lethal effect on the Indians of the English invasion come from farther south. Arthur Barlowe in 1584 found the Carolina Algonquins to be "marvelously wasted, and in some places, the country left desolate." Thomas Harriot noticed in a report from 1588 that "the people began to die very fast" after the English visited Indian towns. In 1608 a "strange mortalitie" was reported by Jamestown colonists to have smitten "a great part of the people" on the Chesapeake Bay.

A shipborne plague, smallpox or typhoid, swept through New England from 1616 to 1619. It was concentrated along the coast from Narragansett to the Kennebec River (now southern Maine) and some thirty miles inland. A little more than a decade later a smallpox epidemic struck the Saint Lawrence region killing tens of thousands of Iroquois. We have actual witnesses to these devastations. When the Pilgrims landed in December of 1620 at Plymouth, there were no living persons: starvation had finished off what the plague had left of the Patuxet tribe. In 1619, Thomas Dermer visited coastal New England and found "ancient plantations, not long since populous, now utterly void." Near Boston Bay, Thomas Morton observed, "For in a place where many inhabited, there hath been but one left alive . . . and the bones and skulls seemed to mee a new found Golgotha."

Fairly accurate figures are known of the havoc. Some 12,000 Powhatans greeted the English in 1607. By the end of the century there were fewer than 1,000 left. The Narragansetts declined from 5,000 warriors to barely 1,000. The Wamesits, who had fielded 3,000 men, were shriveled to some 250. Daniel Gookin was told that the Pequots could "raise four thousand men, fit for war" before the English came, but that only 300 were left in 1674. The old surviving Indians also gave Gookin accounts of populations before 1600 that added up to 18,000 warriors in the five great Indian confederacies; this was more fighting men than in the American army during most of the years of the Revolution. But by 1674 the Indians in lower New England were reduced to less than 9,000 persons.

Francis Jennings,[2] reviewing these figures, notes the decline to be almost 90 percent, a figure that he states is in harmony with the decreases established for Spanish America. Jennings adds that it took the white men the entire seventeenth century to bring back the population to what it was before his arrival: what Jennings calls, therefore, a resettlement, not a settlement. For while that demographic catastrophe was wiping out the Indian, the colonists in Massachusetts had swollen to nearly 20,000 in 1646; and New England alone at that time harbored at least 50,000 Englishmen.[3]

It is said that statistics don't bleed. We are fortunate to have an eye-witness account of this death stalk from the Aztecs, the most advanced Indian people on the North American continent in the sixteenth century. The account is worth quoting if only because it puts in better perspective the seeming miraculous conquest of the Aztec empire by Hernán Cortés:

> When the Spaniards left Tenochtitlan [now Mexico City], the Aztecs thought they had departed for good and would never return. . . . While the Spaniards were in Tlaxcala, a great plague broke out in Tenochtitlan. It began to spread during the thirteenth month and lasted for seventy days, striking everywhere in the city and killing a vast number of our people. Sores erupted on our faces, our breasts, our bellies; we were covered with agonizing sores from head to foot.
>
> The illness was so dreadful that no one could walk or move. The sick were so utterly helpless that they could only lie on their beds like corpses, unable to move their limbs or even their heads. They could not lie face down or roll from one side to the other. If they did move their bodies, they screamed with pain.
>
> A great many died from this plague, and many others died of hunger. They could not get up to search for food, and everyone else was too sick to care for them, so they starved to death in their beds. . . . The first victims were stricken during the fiesta of Teotlecco, and the faces of our warriors were not clean and free of sores until the fiesta of Panquetzaliztli.
>
> And now the Spaniards came back again. . . .[4]

This unexpected germ warfare was a delight to the English colonists.[5] The first page of Reverend Increase Mather's book *A Brief History of the Warr With the Indians in New-England* states, "That the Heathen People amongst whom we live, and whose land the Lord God of our Fathers hath given to us for a rightful Possession. . . ." It was the Lord's will that the Indians should be weakened first by plague and then by war in order for the New Englanders to inherit the land. King James I himself called the 1616–1619 devastation the "wonderfull Plague."[6] The Reverend Cotton Mather, son of Increase Mather, considered the most competent colonial writer of the late seventeenth century, simply dismissed the native inhabitants as "miserable *Animals*."[7]

In Virginia, God's pedal could be accelerated. The Indians rose up against the intruders in 1622. This was greeted with joy by the whites, who embarked on a campaign of extermination. As Edward Waterhouse exulted, "Our hands which before were tied with gentlenesse and faire usage, are now set at liberty. . . . Now their cleared grounds in their villages (which are situate in the fruitfullest places of land) shall be inherited by us, whereas heretofore the grubbing of woods was the greatest labour."[8] To lull the natives, the English signed peace treaties to surprise them, and the Virginia Council even boasted of this treachery. One negotiator carried a butt of poisoned sack to a parley and encouraged the Indians to drink. He estimated with pride that he managed to kill two hundred of them.[9] Englishmen at Jamestown threw Indian children in the water and shot out their brains.[10]

This attitude continued into the eighteenth century, when the English leaders were supposed to have gained in sophistication. Lord Jeffery Amherst, after whom a respected New England college is named, controlled native affairs. He loathed Indians and wrote to Colonel Henry Bouquet, military commander at Fort Pitt, asking if it were possible "to send the Small Pox among those dissatisfied tribes." Bouquet replied he would try to distribute germ-laden blankets, adding "as it is a pity to expose good men against them, I wish we could make use of the Spanish method, to hurt them with English dogs . . . who would, I think, effectively extirpate or remove that vermin."[11]

The real purpose in reducing the Indian was to take his land. This created a quandary for the best legal minds in both England and the colonies. It is an interesting aspect of English civility that it can never nakedly despoil but must find a respectable basis for action, real estate being no exception. In fact, one might make the general statement that the codifiers of property law dealing with Indian land tussled during the first centuries of the conquest with the momentous problem of how to make legal that which was manifestly illegal; that is, how to assimilate legitimately what had been stolen.[12]

As was previously noted, European monarchs claimed ownership of land by the right of discovery. This was in reality a flimsy doctrine, for it could only be maintained by force. No English king, for example, dreamed of sending a sea captain to China to claim the land even though the inhabitants were not Christians and had a different skin color and alien culture. The claim to the land, therefore, was not an argument between the right of discovery and the right of prior occupancy but rather the question of who could kill the other more effectively. Having muskets rather than bows and arrows, the British argued that the right of discovery made the whole of North America an English protectorate and that all rights in land were vested in the Crown. It followed, therefore, that these rights could only be acquired through royal grants; indeed, even the Indians, who had roamed the land from time immemorial, could only hold it by grants from the Crown. In the proprietary colonies that were to follow, the proprietor claimed the same right.

THE USE OF "LARGE, STRONG, AND FIERCE" DOGS AGAINST THE INDIANS. Woodcut from *Regionum Indicarum Per Hispanos olim devestatarum accuratissima descriptio*, by Bartolome de Las Casas, Heidelberg, 1664.

A doctrine so absurd in practice must bend. Settlers advancing on strange soil had to find ways to quiet the Indian claims. This was not apparent at first, because the early plagues had wiped out almost all of the coastal Indians, but as the English pushed forward it had to be resolved. As a general statement it may be said that the colonists tended to regard all land not occupied by Indian farms or houses as open territory to be taken at will, while some token form of payment was required elsewhere.

The difference in the way white men and Indians viewed the land also was a serious problem. To the Indians, like the sky above and the waters below, the earth was a commonwealth for all men and could not be owned or traded. The value of land lay in its use and not otherwise. Each tribe did occupy a loosely defined area, usually respected by neighbors. Some allotted garden plots or recognized hunting reserves to preserve fur-bearing animals. They would also "give" part of their land in return for presents, but this was thought of as mutual gift-giving and not alienation. There were minor exceptions. The Delawares and Powhatans had well-defined private hunting areas in the eastern region. But for the larger tribes, such as the Iroquois and the Creek, the emphasis was always on the tribal ownership of hunting territory.[13]

The root difference in attitude between the white man and the red man made conflict inevitable. When a colonist came to "empty" land, he claimed it and considered the stake permanent. "Their land is spacious and void, and there are few and [they] do but run over the grass, as do also the foxes and wild beasts," the Reverend Robert Cushman wrote.[14] And it followed that the New England natives "inclose noe Land, neither have any settled habytation, nor any tame Cattle to improve the Land by," and so were devoid of any legal claim to their territory.[15]

Where the Indians were numerous and therefore still a threat, the English dispensed with theory and sought to purchase the land even though it took the Indians many years, given the different perspectives, to understand quite what was happening. The doctrine of right by discovery was therefore modified. Though ultimate title to the land was in the English sovereign, that title was subject to a right of occupancy by the Indians. Therefore, purchase of the land extinguished the right of occupancy. Indeed, purchases from the Indians were regularly upheld by the local courts in Massachusetts; the necessity for acquiring the Indian title came to be uniformly recognized.[16] In time this attitude spread throughout New England and crystallized in the statement of Chancellor Kent that "the people of all the New England colonies settled their towns upon the basis of a title procured by fair purchases from the Indians with the consent of Government except in a few instances of lands acquired by conquest after a war deemed to have been just and necessary."[17]

The distance between the eloquent legal theory expounded by Chancellor Kent and the vile suggestion of Lord Amherst is shorter than it seems: the views merely reflect the training in the first case of a lawyer and in the second of a military officer. Marshall Harris, the historian of the American land tenure system, wrote the most careful study of this problem. In his quiet way the writer pinpoints the real meaning. "It seems clear that the acquisition of land from the Indians cannot be studied as if the purchases were free barter and sale transactions between equal parties. . . . It can be said that the resulting system of land tenure would have been no different if the territory occupied by the thirteen original colonies had been completely uninhabited by human beings."[18]

3

America as a Land Speculation

"Land was the fundamental source of wealth in provincial America. . . ."

Leonard Woods Labaree, *Conservatism in American History*

The first attempts at colonization were financed by men like Gilbert and Raleigh, with backing from the Crown. Their resources were limited, and it wasn't long before companies took their place. These companies were organized for private profit, with settlement being secondary. The shift from individual to group financing is curiously illustrated by the change in meaning of the word *adventurer* over three centuries. Originally French, referring to the taking of a chance, the word stood for a gamester in the fifteenth century, a soldier of fortune in the sixteenth, and an investor in company shares in the seventeenth.

In 1606, two groups of merchants from rival commercial centers set themselves up as shareholders. Those in London called themselves the London Company, while shareholders from the port cities of Bristol and Plymouth were referred to as the Plymouth Company. The two groups eventually went their separate ways through a series of reorganizations, though there were overlapping investment interests by certain persons in both entities.

The London Company, whose name eventually changed to the Virginia Company because of its close public identity with the Jamestown colony, counted among its subscribers a group of the leading noblemen and merchants of the kingdom. Shares were sold at £12.5 each, the total capital amounting to some £200,000. The leading shareholders were Sir Thomas Smith (also spelled Smythe), a founder and first governor of the East India Company and among the top merchants of the time; Sir Edwin Sandys, son of an Anglican archbishop, who had interests in the East India Company and the Moscovy trade; the prominent financier John Ferrars; Sir Robert Rich, nephew of the Earl of Essex and himself later the Earl of Warwick, a man who backed freebooters in the earlier style of Elizabeth's time; Sir George Calvert, later to become Lord Baltimore and proprietor of Maryland; Sir Thomas Gates; Sir George Somers; Lord De La Warr (from whose name came Delaware); and the Earl of Southampton, friend and ally of Essex, a picaresque nobleman who was Shakespeare's patron. Obviously, these men had the ear of King James I, who himself looked for personal gain: in this period kings were expected to administer the government in part from their own resources, which pushed them to squeeze the highest possible return from such participations.

The London Company received an enormous land patent, with loans to the king from the company's capital as an added inducement. The patent covered from the 45th to the 38th degrees north latitude and in theory stretched westward to the "South Sea" (the Pacific Ocean). It covered the entire strip along the Atlantic seaboard from Nova Scotia to what is now Virginia. In December of 1606 the company sent three ships to America, all of which were filled to capacity with men, there being no women passengers. This was the group that founded Jamestown in Virginia, the first permanent English settlement in America.

The purpose of the expedition was to find precious ore and stones through mining or plunder. But the "fool's gold" or worthless glistening metal that Captain Christopher Newport brought back to England indicated that false hopes had been aroused. In 1609, and then again in 1612, the company reorganized under new charters; more capital was raised by holding popular lotteries. But corporate expenses, mismanagement, internal strife, and little income from the struggling settlement brought home the sad fact that Virginia, unlike the richer Spanish colonies, was a land of malaria and dysentery rather than gold, silver, or precious stones. The Virginia Company, teetering on the edge of bankruptcy, had its charter revoked in 1624. Virginia was thereafter a royal colony.

The merchants of Bristol and Plymouth, who operated the Plymouth Company, were the less important of the two investing groups. They had two leaders: the first being John Popham, chief justice of England; and the second, Sir Ferdinand Gorges. Gorges, of Spanish descent but a loyal Anglican, had been a protégé of Lord Essex, embroiled in his plots, and then turned state's evidence in Elizabeth's time.

Their land patent, conferred by James I, was from the 41st to the 34th degree north latitude, provided that no colonies would be within one hundred miles of those of the London Company. The Plymouth Company attempted in 1607 to establish a settlement at the mouth of the Kennebec River. Because of the harsh weather and bad management, the attempt failed. Beset by financial problems, in 1620 the company reorganized after an infusion of new capital and became known first as the New England Company and then the Massachusetts Bay Company.[1]

This was the background for the settlement of the Massachusetts Bay Colony. Actually, a radical group of Puritans had already set up a colony at Plymouth in 1620. But these Separatists,[2] now calling themselves Pilgrims in the New World, were poor and lacking in influence. The moderate wing of the Puritan movement, which had a nominal affiliation with the Church of England, was led by men with greater financial resources and connections than the Separatists. These were the men who received a land grant in 1629 to colonize at Massachusetts Bay. In the same year, this group obtained a royal charter confirming their rights and allowing a government resident in America, which was to be nominally subordinate to the company. Three hundred-fifty settlers were sent over, and later that same year the financial interest of the company, whose investment policy was still controlled by Puritans or their sympathizers, was transferred to the colonists. This internal coup was managed by the shrewd John Winthrop.

In the 1630s another group of Puritans obtained a grant of land in the Connecticut Valley, an area of rich pasture to the southwest of the Massachusetts settlement. Although the Connecticut patentees shared the aims and views of the Massachusetts leaders, some conflict ensued. But in 1638, three townships in the Connecticut Valley declared themselves a commonwealth and Massachusetts Bay acceded to the secession.

It should be emphasized that these settlements, whether in Virginia or New England, were financed for private profit. We tend to look back upon these events as though the English settled and developed the New World by conscious plan, which is incorrect. The shareholders of the various corporations were trying to repeat the Spanish success. Dazzled by the reports of gold, silver, and jewels pouring out from Mexico and Peru, the subscribers hoped their part of the New World would also contain precious mines or Indian cities and graves to sack. The plantations were organized for those purposes; the physical presence of the colonists was incidental. To this rule, the Puritan communities were a partial exception in the sense that the religious factor also entered. But even in New England ideology was subordinate to capital return. For example, a London subscriber to the *Mayflower* expedition who owned one hundred shares, each capitalized at £10, would have a right to as large a return on the net earnings as one hundred men at work in the colony.[3]

The Virginia and New England land speculations were only part of a large capital movement spreading from England into the bourgeoning British Empire. It must not be forgotten that North America was only one region of activity. English lords and merchants were speculating, English soldiers killing, and English colonists invading, not only North America, but Ireland, the West Indies, and, somewhat later, India. Sir Walter Raleigh, the paragon of the English renaissance, treated the Irish serfs like the English Virginian planters treated the Indians, and with the same aim: to reduce their numbers and seize their land and possessions. Of some seventy-five thousand persons who left Britain in the first part of the seventeenth century, only one-third went to what would become the United States.

The clique surrounding King James I, as has been indicated, included men with great lusts for land and money. Sir Ferdinand Gorges received a Crown grant in 1639 for what is now the entire state of Maine, part of his reward for betraying Lord Essex. Sir William Alexander received Nova Scotia in its entirety, and Sir George Calvert picked up Maryland. A secretary of state, Calvert also was a shareholder of the Virginia Company and of the Council of New England; he had extensive land grants in Ireland as well. Sir Thomas Smith and Sir Edwin Sandys, investors in Virginia, had leading positions in the nascent penetration of the Far East. The Earl of Warwick was involved in both Virginia and New England.

The coterie surrounding King Charles I worked the same way. Sir William Berkeley was a royal commissioner for Canada; in 1641, he was appointed governor of Virginia, where he gave himself thousands of acres. Sir William was one of the eight titled Englishmen to receive the grant of the Carolinas. His brother, Lord John Berkeley, another proprietor of the Carolinas, was also given western New Jersey. Sir George Carteret, branded as a pirate by Parliament during the Civil War, was a great favorite of the royal household. In 1667, he became a member of the council handling trade and plantations, the nest of the speculators. Sir George was also a proprietor of the Carolinas and shared New Jersey with Lord Berkeley, taking the eastern part. Anthony Ashley Cooper, who was to become First Earl of Shaftsbury, had great colonial interests, including investments in Barbados, the Bahamas, and Bermuda. Involved in the Hudson's Bay Colony, he was likewise a patentee in the Carolinas. Sir John Colleton was a proprietor of the Carolinas and had estates in Barbados. The Earl of Clarendon, the architect of the Restoration, whose daughter married the Duke of York, also sat on the council handling trade and plantations and became a patent holder in the Carolinas. Clarendon received his main rents from Irish grants (his son, Edward Hyde, was appointed head of the combined provinces of New York and New Jersey in the early eighteenth century and milked them dry in an unusually brief period). Allied with these men were two immensely powerful political figures, the Duke of Albermarle and the Earl of Craven.

In the corrupt period of the Restoration, the sky was the limit. The Duke of York, brother and successor to Charles II, was the leading stockholder of the Royal African Company, which smashed the Dutch monopoly in the slave trade and then established its own monopoly slaving in the New World. This was done by writing a restrictive clause into the peace treaty with Spain after that country was humbled in the War of the Spanish Succession in 1713: one-quarter of the profits, however, were reserved for each of the kings of England and Spain. In 1669, Charles II gave an enormous grant in Virginia—larger than all of Massachusetts— to several favorites, and in 1673 he turned over the entire colony to Lords Culpeper and Arlington; the latter, not so coincidentally, was in charge of foreign policy at the time. Through debt settlement and royal patronage, William Penn, son of Admiral Sir William Penn, received from the Crown what later became known as the states of Pennsylvania and Delaware.

These lords and rich merchants—sometimes operating alone through royal patronage, sometimes in groups using influence or spending cash where it counted—manipulated for personal gain the English possessions as though they were private fiefs in the feudal period and did so with total disregard for the settlers in North America, who had now begun to raise children with an outlook no longer merely a carbon copy of the Old World system of values.

4

The Southern Colonies

" 'Oh! there is an aristocracy here, then?' said Martin. 'Of what is it composed?'
'Of intelligence, sir,' replied the colonel; 'of intelligence and virtue. And
of their necessary consequence in this republic. Dollars, sir.' "

Charles Dickens, *Martin Chuzzlewit*

Virginia

Colonial Virginia is the story of land jobbery based on the Siamese twins
of tobacco and slavery. The obsession of Virginians for land began early:
In order to encourage immigration the Virginia Company had allotted fifty
acres of land to proprietors for every person they brought to the colony.
The practice was continued by the Crown after the company lost its charter, and freemen paying their own passage were also entitled to fifty acres,
plus an additional fifty for a wife and each child. This allotment was called
a "head right." The system was subject to flagrant abuse by means of issuing head rights to nonexistent persons, and by 1650 estates of many thousands of acres were appearing. That of Lord De La Warr, an early governor,
was probably the largest.

In 1704, the period before the development of large plantations, there
were twenty-five Virginians who owned at least 5,000 acres. Then the size
of estates began to expand. By 1750, when the average land holding was
about 750 acres, important planters owned estates ranging in size from

30,000 and 100,000 acres. It has been estimated that in this first half of the eighteenth century the Virginia royal governors and councils had given almost 3 million acres to the controlling elite in a manner shortly to be discussed. It may be added that although the records kept in Virginia are much more detailed than those for other plantation colonies, the same conditions prevailed throughout the south.

The reason for this brush-fire spread of large plantations was tobacco. The immense popularity in Europe of tobacco made it an excellent cash crop in the warmer part of the English colonies. It was particularly ideal in Virginia for a variety of reasons: the natural fertility of the soil, the network of tidal rivers and creeks that gave every planter his own landing-stage with direct contact to the ocean trade, the ease of confiding the routine operations of a single crop to ignorant gang labor, and the cheapness of land, thus eliminating the need to rotate crops.

The bedfellow of tobacco was slavery. In 1619, a Dutch privateer put into the James River and disembarked 20 Africans to be sold as slaves. In 1649, there were some 300 blacks out of the total population of 15,000; by 1670 the blacks constituted five percent of the population, about 2,000 out of 40,000. The slave part of Virginia jumped to 6,000 in 1700, and by 1730 blacks formed over a quarter of the colonial population (30,000 out of about 114,000 persons). At the time of the American Revolution, blacks constituted nearly 40 percent of the Virginia population.[1]

The slave trade was actually a two-way profitable business for British capital, not only for the purchasers but also for the sellers, who were now English. As was previously pointed out, through war the Royal African Company had been granted the exclusive right to trade in slaves with the British possessions. Thus, some of the same group of English aristocrats who were proprietors in colonial America made money as stockholders selling slaves, and as landowners receiving quitrents[2] when the slaves tilled the land. The largest landowner of all was Thomas Lord Fairfax, who had married Catherine, granddaughter of Lord Culpeper, one of the two leading patent holders from King Charles II. Lord Fairfax held some five million acres.

It was only through land grants and land speculation that a native planter aristocracy developed in Virginia.[3] The real origins of those families thus lay in slavery. Thomas Jefferson, for example, the son of a wealthy planter, was married to the daughter of a much wealthier planter, who left the young couple at his death forty thousand acres of land and 135 slaves.[4] This brought Jefferson's slave gangs and house retinue to some 200, including half-sisters and brothers of his wife. With all due credit to the many-faceted genius of Jefferson, it was the slaves working his fields

"STAGES IN THE CULTURE AND MARKETING OF TOBACCO": (a) a common tobacco house, (b) hanging the leaf on a scaffold, (c) prizing, (d) tobacco hanging to cure, (e) public warehouse, (f) inspecting tobacco in the warehouse, (g) conveying tobacco by a double canoe. From William Tatham, *An Historical and Practical Essay, etc.,* London, 1800.

who gave him the opportunity to write his abstract theory against slavery; in practice, he increased his slave holdings both during the Revolution and while he was president.[5]

The early aristocrats had estates not much larger than 5,000 acres. The Randolph family founder, William Randolph, was one of the most powerful men in colonial America. Yet he only acquired 10,000 acres in his lifetime. The Lee family of Virginia is considered by many Americans as equal in prominence to the Adams family of Massachusetts. The first of the line, Richard Lee, came to Virginia in 1640 and was the largest landowner by the time of his death; he owned 13,000 acres. The Byrd dynasty was created by William Byrd the elder, a hard-working tobacco planter, slave dealer, fur trader and speculator. He willed an estate of some 26,000 acres—cutting off two daughters with a few hundred pounds in order to leave intact the plantation—to his son, William Byrd II. This second Byrd, to whom Americans owe a great deal for his fascinating diaries —the most entertaining picture we have of our early eighteenth century— increased the estate through political intrigue and speculation till, at his death, it amounted to almost 180,000 acres of the best land in Virginia.

The eighteenth century saw the full fruit of a political-economic nexus based on influence and social standing.[6] Robert Carter, dubbed "King Carter" because of his power and arrogance, became manager for the estate of Lord Fairfax. As land agent with an inside position, he began his own purchases. From the connections he made, Carter moved to the political sphere. In 1724 alone he arranged to receive 86,978 acres in the present counties of Fauquier and Prince William. In 1730, Carter patented 50,212 acres on the banks of the Shenandoah River. When he died in 1732, he owned some 300,000 acres. There are many such examples: William Fitzhugh acquired through political friendship 54,000 acres in a short period.

To the west, beyond tidewater, grants of estates of 20,000 to 40,000 acres were not infrequent. The opening of the Shenandoah Valley made even these land grants seem small. In 1736, William Beverley acquired a grant of 118,491 acres in the valley. A few years earlier, Jost (or Joist) Hite received a huge tract farther up the valley. The most fantastic of all, the series of grants received by Benjamin Borden from 1734 to 1749 through his friendship with Governor Gooch, totalled some 600,000 acres in the same region.

Virginia, before the creation of new states out of its western part as an aftermath of the Revolution, was larger than all of New England with Delaware tossed in. The enormous Northern Neck land grant owned by Lord Fairfax was only a part of the tidewater area. The rest of the province was available to those who knew how to manipulate the political system to their advantage. A knowledge of this system is necessary.

COLONEL WILLIAM BYRD, 2ND, OF WESTOVER (1674–1744). Oil on canvas. Courtesy of the Virginia Historical Society.

The administrative structure of Virginia as a royal colony was the same as all the other royal colonies. The governor was picked by London and the legislative branch consisted of an appointed council and an elective assembly. The council was usually a tool supporting the governor. The assembly, the "popular voice," was also under the control of rich colonists. In the southern colonies these were large planters; to the north the merchants had more of a voice. Everywhere the vote was restrictive. Furthermore, votes were taken by show of hands (the secret ballot was a late development) and it boded trouble to reject publicly the great landlord's candidate or the leading local politico.

Since the legislative branch had control over the salaries of the royal governors, it was to the mutual advantage of all concerned to work together. The councilors and assemblymen were provincials who viewed politics less as a source of prestige than as a money-making business, which is still true today. Most governors were poor-cousin aristocrats whose sole aim of office was to get rich quickly and return to England. With rare exceptions, that meant to hustle on the main boulevard of wealth, which was land grants. This required subservient councilors and assemblymen, and the way to control them—and to assure prompt payment of their salaries—was to distribute the spoils. The structure of the rich landed families, and the continued use of land grants to increase their wealth, was thus the political story of Virginia, as indeed it was of most of the colonies.

The assembly in Virginia usually followed the council, as smaller fish follow big fish to feed off the remnants they discard. Usually consisting of twelve councilors, this upper house of the legislature (which also served as the supreme court of the colony) was the place of residence for the top aristocracy. The spoils system of the ruling class, whether in land or appointment to lucrative offices such as judges, sheriffs, provincial secretaries, and treasurers, came through council membership. Thus, a study of the council choices explains most clearly who ruled colonial Virginia and for what purpose this rule was used.

Leonard W. Labaree[7] made a careful study of the councilor system in Virginia. His conclusions are striking. Labaree analyzed Virginia personnel from 1680, when complete records began, up to the Revolution. Ninety-one men received council appointment in this period of nearly a century. Of these, fifty-seven family names are represented, but nine names account for slightly less than a third of the total appointments—including five Pages and three each from the Burwell, Byrd, Carter, Custis, Harrison, Lee, Ludwell, and Wormeley families. Contributing two councilors each were fourteen other families, including such names as Fairfax and Randolph. Labaree concludes that over 60 percent of the places on the council were occupied by members of only twenty-three families; and for any one time during this period, a roster of the Virginia council showed from a third to a half of the members were closely related to one or more other councilors and more distantly connected by blood or marriage with various others. Indeed, the system became increasingly closed as time went on, and at the outset of the Revolution ten of the twelve members of the council were related to one or more of their colleagues and all but two were sons or grandsons of former councilors.

The domination of the councils by this plantation class was devoted to three aims: acquisition of new land, evasion of quitrents, and avoidance of land taxes. The first aim was by far the most important: in the recorded proceedings of the Virginia council, land grants occupied more space than all other subjects combined.[8] Indeed, this sometimes led to conflicts with the royal governors, which gave the appearance of "democracy" and misled some historians as to the meaning of Virginia's later resolute adherence to the Revolution. For there were natural antagonisms bred between the governor and the council, largely based on the opposition of native plantation owners to land control by absentee English aristocrats. The governor, anxious to return to London quickly with a fortune, under official pressure to collect the quitrents upon which his salary depended, and sometimes sincere in his duty to parcel out land in order to increase immigration, often collided with the plantation lords who tried to monopolize land grants. Two royal governors, Colonel Sir Edmund Andros and Francis Nicholson, were driven from office because the wealthy councilors pulled strings in England.

Often, however, the matter was resolved by mutual greed. Governor Alexander Spotswood, for example, attempted to limit land grants to the large planters and enforce payment of quitrents. He met with concerted opposition from the plantation leaders William Byrd II and Colonel Philip Ludwell, both of whom were highly indignant at the thought of having to pay such fees. Then Spotswood brought action against Ludwell but was stopped in the General Court for lack of a quorum because half of the attending councilors who composed that body were Ludwell's relatives and so were disqualified from sitting on the case. The governor was blocked by what he called a "hereditary faction of designing men." It was then that Spotswood decided to stay in the colony and become a great plantation lord himself. All differences were shortly resolved. By agreement with the council, he made himself a series of grants, mostly through dummies (blank patents transferred back to him after assignment), and left his position of governor as owner of some 85,000 acres.[9]

The Virginia system was based on collusion, which by the time of the Revolution had extended the power of these elite landed families from the council to political control of nearly every office. The collectors and sheriffs in the various counties found it convenient not to question the extent of the property holdings of these men, and no one would dare prosecute them. There existed a gentleman's agreement that despite the rivalry for council membership, no faction would expose another.

To protect their tight control on one side against any demands on the part of the poor white "rabble"[10] and on the other against payment of quitrents to absentee lords in England, the Virginia plantation owners devised an elaborate system of intermarriage. This became more intwisted as time went by, parallel to the growing exclusive control of the Council. Examples at the top level illustrate this process. Colonel Philip Ludwell, who was well rewarded with large land grants for supporting the tyrannical Governor William Berkeley, married Benjamin Harrison III's sister. Colonel Daniel Parke married a daughter of Colonel Philip Ludwell. One of the daughters from that joining married William Byrd II and another John Custis, whose son was the first husband of Martha Washington. Benjamin Harrison III married Colonel Lewis Burwell's daughter—President William Henry Harrison was a direct descendant. Their son, Benjamin Harrison IV, married one of Robert ("King") Carter's daughters. Richard Lee II's son, whose direct descendant was General Robert E. Lee, married Benjamin Harrison IV's first cousin, whose mother was Colonel Philip Ludwell's granddaughter. Mann Page, who built Rosewell (the largest and grandest house in all Virginia), married another daughter of Robert Carter. Lawrence Washington, half-brother of George, married the daughter of William Fairfax, the cousin of Lord Fairfax. Peter Jefferson, father of Thomas Jefferson, married Jane Randolph. John Marshall was a Randolph descendant.

The negative aspects of this system were early apparent. The most obvious was the drop in white freeholds. At least 80,000 indentured servants were brought to Virginia in the seventeenth century, a process which then radically decreased and finally died out altogether with the development of slavery after 1680. Edward Randolph was asked by the Board of Trade as early as 1696 to find out why Virginia, the earliest settled area, was not growing at the same rate as the northern colonies. His report struck at the heart of the matter: Randolph stated that the reason servants were no longer willing to come to Virginia was that the members of the council engrossed all the land for themselves. The flight of disgruntled whites from Virginia, which peopled western Carolina and Maryland as well as Delaware and Pennsylvania, further increased the percentage of blacks in the Old Dominion. The properties of these seventeenth-century yeomen were absorbed into larger and larger estates until

STRATFORD, WESTMORELAND COUNTY, VIRGINIA. Built by Thomas Lee about 1725, and the birthplace of Robert E. Lee. Courtesy of the Library of Congress.

enormous land holdings became the order, with the "plantation economy" fully defined. The small freehold farmer who remained did not understand this process and felt that the slave was his enemy. Instead of turning his hatred toward the shareholder in the slave trade and the large planter, the small farmer reacted against the black and became thus an ally of the large plantation slaveholders. Unlike New England, education was likewise restricted to the small elite class, thus closing the circle whereby ignorance reinforced racism, and racism was used to perpetuate ignorance. Though exact statistics are not available, it would appear that secondary education in Virginia was not available to more than a thousand students each year, while perhaps a tenth of this number went on to higher education.[11]

It has often been noted that of the five urban centers of colonial America, namely, Boston, Philadelphia, New York, Newport, and Charles Town, none were in Virginia. The dependence on English goods—more readily understood as an element in the balance of trade with a cash crop like tobacco—meant little trade within the colony itself. The plantations manufactured the necessities they could not or did not buy in England. Soon every large estate had its own smith, carpenter, cooper, etc., as can be seen today by visiting the outhouses of Mount Vernon, George Washington's landed property, which stretched ten miles along the Potomac River. The great planters, without a counterbalancing mercantile class, lived almost as medieval lords. Insulated from the world of common-sense compromise and daily struggle by absolute control over slaves and dominating the smaller white planters, they developed a contempt for commerce.[12] This was the reverse side, but unfortunately in some ways the logical projection, of the elitist society that produced Jefferson, Madison, Marshall, and Randolph.

Maryland

Sir George Calvert, a friend and favorite of both King James I and his son, Charles I, was raised to the peerage as Lord Baltimore. King James had given Baltimore estates in Ireland and in the southeastern part of Newfoundland, but when His Lordship visited the American property, he complained that it was cold and inhospitable. Upon ascending the throne, King Charles allowed Baltimore in 1632 to switch his patent to the land now known as Maryland, though by charter at least a part of it belonged to Virginia.

Lord Baltimore died before the grant was signed, and his son, the second Lord Baltimore, took over his father's patent. The second lord never visited America but sent over his brother as governor.

Sir George received a grant the like of which had never appeared in any English area before or since. His Lordship was free to grant baronies and manors as he pleased, exactly as the king of England. Lord Baltimore personally controlled all branches of the government; no distinction was made among the executive, legislative, and judicial. As in medieval fiefs, ownership of the soil was invested in the lord proprietor. Refusal to recognize the absolute power of the Baltimore family meant confiscation of all goods, loss of land, or death; and edicts were passed punishing seditious speeches by "fine, banishment, boring of the tongue, slitting of the nose, cutting off of both ears, whipping, or branding on the hands or forehead."[13] Coins were struck in England under the second Lord Baltimore for use in the colony. In effect, a separate absolute hereditary monarchy was established.

The first Lord Baltimore was a convert to Catholicism. This was no problem insofar as Charles I was concerned, since he himself had like sympathies. However, it did cause difficulties in the New World, where the settlers were strongly anti-Catholic. But the Baltimores were both discreet and intelligent. Though welcoming Catholics to Maryland, they chose Protestants to deal with the resentful Virginians and also invited Puritans to settle as a foil against their large Anglican neighbor.

The real interest of the Baltimores was money, which came both from quitrents and duties on tobacco exports. A cheap land policy was therefore adopted. The holders of large estates likewise wanted their land grants to rise in value and agents were sent to the German Rhine Valley, wasted by the Thirty Years' War, who sang the song of virgin land in a golden climate. Many thousands listened and, prospering, sent word back home of the good news. As early as 1700, Maryland had the third largest population among the colonies, some 32,000 persons, only being surpassed by Virginia and Massachusetts Bay. The income to the Baltimores (paid sometimes in specie and sometimes as an initial tobacco duty) ran from between £5,000 and £8,000 a year.

The position of proprietor's agent was the key to land grants. Charles Carroll, who had been Baltimore's solicitor and register in the land office, in 1712 was elevated to this post. He was so "liberally rewarded for his services"[14] that he carved out a great fortune by distributing favors to others and land to himself. When John Adams met Charles Carroll, Jr., in 1774 at the First Continental Congress, he noted in his diary that Carroll was "of the first fortunes in America" and that "his father has a vast estate which will be his." In western Maryland the leading speculator was Daniel Dulany the elder. Rising to power in the inner circle of government, he secured large grants in the 1720s and 1730s, creating the town of Frederick on his land in Frederick County. According to the land office records, the average grant in this period was 28,535 acres.[15] Besides Charles Carroll and Daniel Dulany, the major Maryland freeholders were Richard Bennett, the Lloyd family (David Lloyd was another agent of the proprietor), William Paca, Benjamin Tasker, Thomas Johnson, and Thomas Lee Sims. All these men occupied important positions under the lord proprietors and their land grants were scattered throughout several counties.

Students of the American Revolution will note that many of these men (or their descendants), who owed so much to the patronage of the Baltimores, were also among the leading revolutionaries. There is a sound reason. As in Virginia, through friendship and mutual logrolling, "two, three, five, and even ten times as much land was sometimes included in the survey as was called for in the grant."[16] Charles P. Gould in *The Land System in Maryland* also points out other methods of acquiring large plantations. Quitrents were avoided by taking out land warrants (in effect future options), and not patenting the land until buyers came or it rose in value. Leasing was another device, with the rent set to cover the quitrent; when the land increased in value, the lease was terminated. Since the quitrent was set at between seven and twelve percent of the rental value of the land, and the land was also subject to a poll-tax, one can see the size of the stakes.

The first five proprietors were indifferent as long as regular income came in. But Frederick, sixth Lord Baltimore, was a spendthrift who, in the 1740s took an active interest in his inheritance. Pushing to increase the revenues, he investigated the various practices and brought suit to compel restitution in matters of land fraud and accurate payment of quitrents. This united both branches of the legislature, the rich landholding councilors as well as the usually turbulent assembly.[17] The Maryland plantation grantees were terrified of any searchlight beaming on the source of their land grants and were as reluctant to pay quitrents as their Virginia peers. The fear of losing their land and of the imposition of quitrents was an important factor that brought the rich landlords of Maryland to revolutionary thinking.

The Baltimores had their ups and downs in colonial history, usually with a quick finger to the breeze. They naturally lost power when Oliver Cromwell ruled England, but popped up again after the Restoration. When the Catholic James II was dethroned in 1688, Maryland was made a Crown colony, though William and Mary left unimpaired the revenue for the Baltimores. Then in 1715, the family having become Protestant, Maryland was given back to them. The colony continued as a private fiefdom until the American Revolution.

The Carolinas

To the south of Virginia and the north of Spanish Florida lay a vast region stretching between the 31st and 36th parallels north latitude, an area whose length equalled that of the New England and middle colonies put together. Claimed by the Spanish as the province of Chicara, and explored by French Huguenots as a possible haven in the 1560s, it was also coveted by the English. In 1629, King Charles I granted the entire territory to Sir Robert Heath, later chief justice, who in gratitude named his gift Carolina after the king. The Heath patent, however, was later voided and in 1663 Charles II gave the same land to eight favored English lords, of whom the most noted were the Earl of Clarendon and the Duke of Albemarle.

The proprietors of the Carolinas drew up an absolutist charter, which has a curious history. John Locke, the noted philosopher of government whose influence on the principles of the American Revolution was enormous, was physician to the Earl of Shaftesbury, one of the eight patentees. Through his patron, Locke was appointed secretary to the standing committee that became the Council of Trade and Plantations. He thus held a position somewhat similar to that of John Stuart Mill about two centuries later at the despotic British East India Company, whose job and consequent income likewise did not seem to war with his advanced political ideas.[18] For it was John Locke who drew up the Fundamental Constitutions, a feudal document that was to be the governing body of law for the Carolinas. The eight grants were divided into seigniories, each consisting of twelve thousand acres, governed by a lord proprietor. A lord palatinate ruled over all. Titles of nobility were accorded, the major ones being landgrave, taken from medieval Germany, and cacique, the Indian title for a tribal chief. As in England, the structure was thus tied to the amount of land held—all this in a vast malarial stretch. There was even a provision for "leetmen" or serfs, a class ultimately filled by black slaves.

The Fundamental Constitutions provided the major source of profit for lord proprietors through quitrents on land sales. "Commoners" would initially buy land from the proprietors and their feudal nobility (the landgraves and caciques created by the proprietors), and could subinfeudate (in turn grant) this land themselves. An exception was made for the initial settlers, freemen arriving before 1670, who were entitled to 150 acres; this was then extended until 1679, the allowance for the latter period being 100 acres. The proprietors also granted about 800,000 acres to the landgraves and caciques, mostly before 1700. Several leading figures in colonial American history settled in the Carolinas: Thomas Pinckney appears in 1710, the

Rutledges somewhat later, and the Calhouns toward the end of the first decades of the eighteenth century.

The absurd feudal mishmash called the Fundamental Constitutions collapsed in no time, an important factor being the inclusion of a local assembly: John Locke, as Plato, was better at theory than practice. Settlers came in from New England, Virginia, Barbados, as well as the home country. They soon objected, through the assembly, to the payment of quitrents. The proprietors, more properly to control the situation, divided their colony into two parts. In 1691 the two territories were reunited until 1712; and thereafter separated again, to become known as North and South Carolina.

Shortly before 1700 the introduction of rice into South Carolina led to a tremendous increase in the slave population. Rice, like tobacco in Virginia, was an easy crop to grow and only required gang slave labor under an overseer. From an export of 2,000 barrels of rice in 1700, production jumped to some 15,000 barrels in 1715. As a result, by 1708 the number of blacks almost equalled the whites; and shortly thereafter there were more blacks in the colony than whites. A slave revolt in 1739 led to a severe tightening of controls and South Carolina soon became known as a dreaded slave colony.

In South Carolina there were intermittent wars with the Spanish and the Indians. The assembly attempted to raise money to pay militia by selling land, but the proprietors vetoed the action. The crisis was brought to a head by a major outbreak of Indian warfare on the southern border, after whi h the absentee lords made the major mistake of reserving all the conquered lands for themselves. The entire colony united in protest in 1719, with the assembly petitioning the king to make South Carolina a royal province. The Privy Council agreed. In 1729 a similar situation occurred in North Carolina, which also became a royal colony. The lord proprietors, after years of legal action, settled their claims for £25,000, which sum included arrears of quitrent.

The concentration on rice production, grown and harvested almost exclusively by slaves (later followed by that of indigo), also created an elitist planter economy in South Carolina. In the early days, aside from the holdings of the lord proprietors, land was rather evenly distributed. But the Spanish and Indian wars entailed higher taxes at the same time the smaller planters were losing ther competitive struggle against cheaper slave labor.[19] The Virginia picture was thus duplicated, since the great plantation holders, who could put up their estates and slaves as collateral against loans during hard times, then bought out at very low prices the land of the smaller planters. By 1730, the slave population was about double that of free men and most

INGIDO CULTURE IN SOUTH CAROLINA. From a map of the parish of St. Stephen in Craven County, etc., after a drawing by Henry Mouzon. The scene supposedly depicts Mulberry, a plantation on the Cooper River. Courtesy of the Charleston Library Society, Charleston, South Carolina.

of the white community was poor. A small elite of rice-growing plantation owners controlled the economic wealth.[20]

The buyout by the Crown eased many problems. There was, however, one exception. Lord Carteret, better remembered as Lord Granville, was probably the aristocrat with the shrewdest grasp of foreign affairs in the England of his time. Out of the eight original proprietors, he was the only one who took land in lieu of a cash payment when the patentees sold. Then he succeeded in fixing his land claim, known as the Granville Grant, on a strip of land at least sixty miles wide in North Carolina, along the Virginia border, and on which was settled the larger part of the population. As a close friend of King George II, it became apparent that special influence lay behind this arrangement. It was an error on the part of the royal government and led to endless trouble.

Under the former lord proprietors, North Carolina settlers were in constant discord. The Granville Grant heightened this tumult. Unlike Lord Fairfax in neighboring Virginia, whose son came to live in that province, Granville only regarded the proprietary as a milking station and acted through agents whose interest was as much in lining their own pockets through land grants to themselves as in land sales and quitrent collections for their lord. Matters grew worse after Granville's death, with his heir being even more delinquent. The land office was closed in 1766 and many persons, unable to secure titles, merely settled on Granville land as squatters. The slightest rumor that the proprietor would assert his rights led to civil commotion, for the quitrents were already worth £6,000 annually, if they could be collected. It was no accident that at the outbreak of the Revolution a clause was incorporated into the North Carolina state Constitution declaring that the soil belonged to the people. It may be added that the British Commission on American Loyalist Claims eventually awarded the Granville heirs a large sum in compensation for their losses.

There is an interesting sidelight to the Granville Grant that casts much light on the inner wheels of the land system at the highest level. Henry McCulloh, supervisor of the royal revenues and land grants in North Carolina, in 1737 feathered his nest by granting to himself, with some associates, a patent of 1.2 million acres—almost the size of Delaware. However, close to 500,000 acres of this grant lay in the area formerly given to Lord Granville. (The British monarchs had very clumsy ideas of American territory; a half-million-acre gift one way or the other was a trifling error.)

A ferocious dispute broke out between McCulloh and Granville, both of whom had high connections. Lawsuits were filed. Finally, a compromise was reached involving cash, division of acreage, and adjustment of quitrents.

In all this, the settlers working the soil—or in reality, their slaves—had as much to say as the mosquitoes hovering overhead.

The land purchased by the Crown from seven of the eight lord proprietors became a part of the public domain and thus fell under the control of the royal governors and councils. The same picture presented itself here as elsewhere, with the governors and councils either in conflict with e ach other or in mutual greed allotting the best land to themselves, their families, and friends. Leonard W. Labaree[21] made a study of the South Carolina council system similar to the one he made of Virginia. The same concentration among a small group of individuals was evident. Seven interrelated families accounted for a quarter of all the royal council members during the period from 1719 to 1776. The council aristocracy seemed to involve hereditary passage of membership. As a leading example, William Bull, his son, and grandson were all councilors. Three daughters of William Bull married into families that provided seven more councilors. The great majority were wealthy planters but, unlike Virginia, some were also rich merchants from Charles Town (later Charleston) who had made most of their money on the import of black slaves.

In North Carolina the royal governors dominated the council. Henry McCulloh worked with Arthur Dobbs, a large-scale speculator and associate. McCulloh's influence was strong enough to secure the appointment of Dobbs as governor in 1752. Dobbs wound up owning a 300,000-acre plantation in the southern part of the colony.[22] Governor Richard Everard issued patents for 400,000 acres in which the amount of the land, the description of the boundaries, the sums paid, and the name of the patentees were left blank. Depending on who paid how much, the names and acreage were then filled in. Gabriel Johnston, another governor, granted 104,700 acres in a very brief period in a similar way. By the use of these blank patents, the Moore and Moseley families, with partners, obtained title to some 500,000 acres.[23] By the time of the Revolution, the largest part of the good farming land had been thus bestowed, except that located in the extreme west near the mountains.

5

The Middle Colonies

"This hunger after Land seems very early to have taken rise in this Province, & is become now a kind of Epidemical madness, every Body eager to accumulate vast Tracts without having an intention or taking measures to settle or improve it."

Peter Wraxall writing in 1754 in New York

New York

Holland, after winning its independence from the Spanish in a ferocious and prolonged war involving most of Europe, turned to commerce for survival. Its navy became the most formidable then known, and behind the navy sailed its merchant fleet.

The Dutch West India Company, chartered in 1621, was a purely commercial enterprise. "Its prime object was to earn dividends for its stockholders by trade. It was to carry on large mercantile operations in the Atlantic basin, prey upon Spanish commerce, conquer Brazil, carry slaves to American plantations, reap profits from traffic in furs and establish settlements."[1] It did well from the start and the use of the phrase "Dutch treat" from earliest colonial times is a measure of how canny were the Dutch traders. The first order of business in the early days was Spanish plunder, meeting with spectacular success: for the original capital was 7.2 million florins, and within a few years the cargoes of captured ships from

53

the Spanish silver fleets brought in 90 million florins. The second order of business was black gold, and in the seventeenth century the Dutch company was the greatest slave-trading body in the world.

Rather far down among the list of priorities was the fur trade, for which purpose New Amsterdam was founded. Sacking, slaving, and the conquest of Brazil relegated the tiny settlements of Fort Orange (Albany) and Manhattan to a position of little importance.

The Dutch Atlantic coastline settlement was based on the 1609 discovery of the Hudson River by Henry Hudson, an English navigator sailing under the flag of Holland. The population of New Amsterdam increased so slowly the company in 1629 declared that any member who brought in fifty adult settlers would receive vast river estates in "perpetual fief of inheritance," with juridical lordship over the estate tenants.

Six men, called patroons, originally signed up but only one actually persisted. He was Kiliaen Van Rensselaer, a wealthy jeweler from Amsterdam who never set foot on his New World property. The Rensselaer patroonship covered some 700,000 acres, including what are now the counties of Albany and Rensselaer, a part of Columbia County, and a strip of Massachusetts. Besides the pledge of settlement, it was acquired in 1630 for "certain quantities of duffels, axes, knives and wampum." Kiliaen Van Rensselaer then obtained a slick agent who made three more purchases of land so vaguely defined that the patroonship, called Rensselaerwyck, encompassed about one million acres—one-quarter larger than the entire present state of Rhode Island.

The leasing system created by the patroons who followed was the Dutch equivalent of quitrents. However, its terms were more severe. The usual English quitrent was a shilling per hundred acres, more often than not unpaid. In New Amsterdam it was settled at two shillings and six pence per hundred acres; dispossession quickly followed nonpayment because the landlords, unlike the absentee London aristocrats who worked through dilettante agents, eventually came to live on the estates themselves. These harsh terms led to continual tenant agitation and revolt.

By 1650 the flood of English settlers began to drown the Dutch; when Charles II decided to take over the colony, the English settlers to the north and south were tenfold more numerous than the Dutch, and the Dutch themselves in New Amsterdam province were close to minority status.

Charles II based his 1664 invasion, which was in violation of the peace then reigning with Holland, on the fiction that all North America belonged to England because of John Cabot's voyage in 1497. The Dutch thus claimed New Amsterdam because of an Englishman and the English claimed it because of an Italian! Charles then handed over the territory to his brother, the Duke of York, later King James II. The Dutch militia surrendered to the British fleet without resistance; from their point of view, which was reasonable, the difference between English Protestant traders and their own countrymen was small and, without a voice in the management of the province, they had little to lose. As noted before, the Duke of York gave away that part now known as New Jersey to two favorites, Lord John Berkeley and Sir George Carteret, two of the eight English lords who had earlier received the Carolinas. Naming the rest of the area after himself—that is, New York—he ruled as proprietor until he ascended the throne in 1685. At that time, New York became a royal colony.

The feudal patroon system was left intact by the English, who adopted the same approach: where before there had been only Dutch patroonships, thereafter there were Dutch and British. They were now called manors.

After New York became a royal colony, the governors started to grant huge patents for a variety of reasons ranging from gambling debts to the grossest venality. One authority states that the rule of thumb for most governors was to reserve for themselves one-third of each grant as their share.[2] Some of the royal governors were so corrupt they even brought upon themselves investigation, a rarity among the eighteenth-century English peerage. A brief view of the successive administrations is possible because of accurate records.

Colonal Thomas Dongan ruled under King James II from 1682 to 1688. He was friendly with Robert Livingston, to whom he gave 160,000 acres (called Livingston Manor), as well as 90,000 acres to Frederick Philipse (called Philipsborough Manor). After a brief interlude, Colonel Benjamin Fletcher was sent in 1692 and remained in power until 1698. It has been claimed that in these six years Fletcher gave away half of the available land in the colony to some thirty persons. Fletcher gave Stephen Van Cortlandt 86,000 acres (called Cortlandt Manor). He gave Adolph Philipse 205,000 acres (called Philipse's Highland Patent). Henry Beekman received a patent from Fletcher of a tract sixteen miles in length in Dutchess County, followed by another running twenty miles along the Hudson River and eight miles inland. These combined holdings were called the Beekman Patent. Colonel William Smith received from Fletcher an estate of fifty square miles in Nassau County on Long Island. Smith was also appointed chief justice of the colony. A survey in 1697 indicated that four families—the Van Cortlandts, the Philipses, the Livingstons, and the Van Rensselaers—owned some 1.6 million acres, comprising much of the present counties of Westchester, Dutchess, Albany, Putnam, Columbia, and Rensselaer.

Colonel Fletcher was succeeded in 1698 by Richard Coote, Earl of Bellomont, an Irish peer who died in office in 1701. Bellomont was an

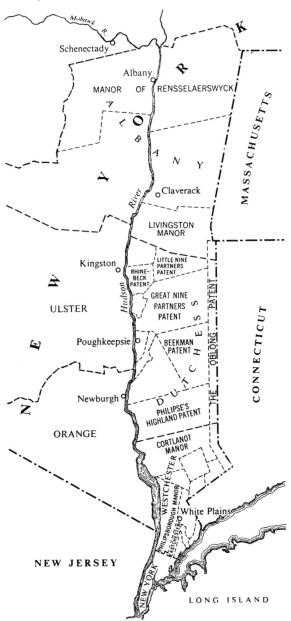

COLONIAL GRANTS IN NEW YORK STATE. From *A Factious People: Politics and Society in Colonial New York,* by Patricia U. Bonomi, New York, 1971. Courtesy of Columbia University Press.

imperial sport, an honest man who even insisted on dealing fairly with the Indians. Appalled by the give-aways of the public land, the governor notified the home government that the development of the colony was being slowed down because immigrants went to other areas where land could be acquired outright rather than in tenancy. He suggested that all land patents over one thousand acres be broken. This induced the most violent hostility on the part of the landed aristocracy, the opposition leaders, of course, being Stephen Van Cortlandt, Robert Livingston, and William Smith. It is here that we see the first stage of the resentments leading to later support for the American Revolution. It is best demonstrated in the case of the Dellius Patent.

Perhaps the most notorious land grant made by Governor Fletcher was to Godefridus Dellius, the Dutch minister at Albany, with several associates. The fine hand of Peter Schuyler, one of those associated, was behind this grant. The Dellius Patent was for 620,000 acres, with an annual quitrent of a raccoon's skin. The land was actually swindled from the Wapping Indians (who fought with the English against the French) according to a deposition made before an investigation on the part of Lord Bellomont in 1698. In fact, though the grant involved was unusually large, this was rather a typical case in which the Indians had been stupefied with drink and then persuaded to sell their tribal lands to agents of the Crown for additional rum of a value of thirty beaver skins and sundry other goods, whereupon it was conveyed by Governor Fletcher to Dellius for an unrecorded monetary consideration.[3]

The Earl of Bellomont attempted to void the Dellius Patent (as well as the Evans and Bayard patents) on the basis of fraud. The colonial aristocrats were frightened, not so much for the specific cases but because the implications would extend to their own land grants. They marshalled their political influence so effectively that the assembly repealed its initial vacating of the Dellius grant. But the Crown, supporting the position of Bellomont, refused to accept the repeal and confirmed the forfeiture. This aroused much colonial indignation in the name of local government and home rule.[4] What the colonial manorholders really wanted was the freedom to corrupt ignorant Indians in order to seize their land by the time-honored methods of bribery, whiskey, and misreading boundary terms.

The appointive judiciary was an ally or more properly an extension of these families. In the case of the Wappings, the Indians could not get a New York lawyer to take their case since all had been "previous Retained on the other Side." Even the Crown lost a case before the New York Supreme Court when it tried to protect a bonus of land to a veteran of the French and Indian War. The opposing party was a Van Rensselaer.[5]

With Bellomont safe in his grave, Edward Hyde, the Viscount Cornbury, was sent over as governor. Ruling from 1702 to 1708, he modeled himself on Fletcher. After the revelations of Bellomont, New York governors were instructed to give land patents of no more than 2,000 acres, but the new governor set out instead to repeal a bill of Bellomont's vacating a number of land patents. Hyde claimed that they had been granted before the new limitation went in effect. Then he worked with so many dummies (the long-established technique to bypass land restrictions) that he actually issued to a group of his partners a patent of some 2 million acres. Schuyler and his associates obtained another, fifty miles long, in the Mohawk Valley.

Viscount Cornbury was the last of the most venal governors simply because land was running out. Except for upper New York, land belonging to the Six Nations,[6] there was little left to patent. William Cosby (1732–1736) and George Clarke (1736–1743), however, employed all the old tricks on a smaller scale. Clarke was particularly clever. Appointed secretary and deputy-auditor of New York through a powerful relation, he became a council member and then lieutenant-governor. He "dominated" Governor Montgomerie and was "first minister" to Cosby.[7] Clarke arranged for his son George, Jr., to become secretary of New York and also a councilor, while his second son, Edward, served as Indian commissioner, "thus facilitating the purchase of land from the Indians."[8] Clarke owned 118,000 acres when he returned to England, with an estate worth £100,000 at the time of his death.

Victory in the French and Indian War (1754–1760) altered the picture, for now new northern spoils lay open. The first beneficiary was Lieutenant-Governor Cadwallader Colden, who formerly had been a chief critic of colonial greed. When his turn at the honey pot came in the 1760s, however, "In less than one year he granted some 174,000 acres; over the next few years approximately a million acres including the Princeton patent of 1765 that went to James Duane and some of his friends."[9] These last patents are important in American history because they were the root of the conflict that later led to the saga of Ethan Allen and the creation of Vermont as an independent state. But Colden's activities pale before those of William Johnson.

Among the land barons of eighteenth-century America, Peter Warren and his nephew William Johnson deserve special consideration. Sir Peter, vice admiral in His Majesty's naval forces, was commander of the American station and the idolized hero of the spectacular capture of Louisburg, the French fortress in Nova Scotia, in 1745. With an enormous sum in prize money, seated in the finest New York City house at No. 1 Broadway and a country house in Greenwich Village, Peter Warren

EDWARD HYDE, LORD CORNBURY, THIRD EARL OF CLARENDON (1661–1723), delicately described as "in feminine attire." Oil on canvas, unidentified artist. Courtesy of the New York Historical Society, New York City.

cemented his position in colonial society by marrying Susannah DeLancey, daughter of Stephen DeLancey and Anne Van Cortlandt, whose father was Stephen Van Cortlandt.

Like almost all rich and well-connected men in his time (as well as our own), Sir Peter speculated in real estate. Having acquired land in the Mohawk Valley, which was considerably upstate from his city residence, Warren summoned his nephew William Johnson from Ireland, who came to America in 1738 at the age of twenty-three.

William Johnson, later Sir William, Baronet, became an even more idolized military figure on land than his uncle at sea. Hero of Lake George, conqueror of Fort Niagara, and colonel of the Six Nations in the French and Indian War, Johnson was then appointed superintendent of Indian affairs for the colonies north of Maryland. He built the baronial center of Johnson Hall in Johnstown, enlarged his land holdings, and begat children with equal zest. With his Indian concubines, his half-breed litters, a personal physician, a dwarf as jester, a secretary, a tailor, a butler, and a large retinue of servants, the wenching, hard-drinking Irish warrior baronet dominated Upper New York in feudal absolutism that can only be compared with Hernán Cortés two hundred years earlier in the Oaxaca Valley of Mexico.[10]

Tied by blood relations to the richest and most powerful families in the New York Colony, supported by the British in London for his undoubted loyalty and Indian connections, Sir William Johnson indulged to the full his passion to own land.

In 1739, the first year after his arrival in America, Sir William made a land purchase in the Mohawk Valley. From there he moved to the Susquehanna Valley. Then he started acquiring acres between the branches of the Delaware and the Susquehanna rivers. In 1751 Sir William bought Onondaga Lake and the land around it. From Governor Clinton he acquired title to one-sixth of the Arent Stevens patent, some 20,000 acres. In 1766 he was a principal of the Illinois Company, with a one-eighth share, in which Governor William Franklin of New Jersey—through his father, Benjamin Franklin, operating as agent in London—tried to gain title to 1.2 million western acres. This scheme was blocked but it became part of another story intimately related to the American Revolution.

Never daunted, Sir William engineered a land grant from the Crown in 1769 for his services in the French and Indian War. Either 80,000 or 99,000 acres, depending on the source, the annual royal quitrent was set at two beaver skins. Shortly before this gift, Sir William—with his partners General Thomas Gage, Lord Holland, and Sir Henry Moore (then governor of New York)—bought from the Oneidas 123,000 acres on the north bank

SIR WILLIAM JOHNSON (1715–1774). Oil on canvas (ca. 1751), by John Wollaston. Collection: Albany Institute of History and Art. Gift of Laura Munsell Tremaine, in memory of Joel Munsell.

of the Mohawk River. In this same period, Sir William's share in another partnership brought him 27,000 acres on Schoharie Creek. In 1770 he acquired a tract twenty miles long and one mile deep on both sides of the Charlotte River. In the northeast, he extended his holdings to the far bank of the Sacandaga and along that river to its junction with the Hudson.

This obsession with land on the part of a war hero with the highest social and political connections led to the most enormous personal landholding in colonial America outside the Lord Halifax grant in Virginia. In 1772, Sir William lumped it together and arranged for his private empire to be made a separate political unit, called Tryon County after his friend and confederate, Governor Tryon of New York. The political rewards followed. Through this creation Sir William automatically picked two assemblymen; his influence was so great that he could direct the election of two Albany members and the Schenectady member as well. He thus controlled the election of five of the twenty-seven New York assemblymen. Perhaps better for himself, in July of 1774, almost two years to the day before the Declaration of Independence, Johnson died of too much living.

The leading families of New York Colony were enmeshed through marriage, politics, landholdings, and commerce in a net that imitated the feudal pattern of European countries. This maze of family relations became so intertwined that most of the third generation of the seven main families could look back on one or more common grandparents. The chart in figure 1 (pages 64–65) illustrates this maze. The intrabreeding continued beyond the time limits set by this analysis, as can be shown briefly. Colonel Robert R. Livingston, grandson of the original Robert Livingston, married Margaret Beekman. Another in this direct line, Walter Livingston, married Cornelia Schuyler, and their daughter married Robert Fulton of steamboat fame. Lieutenant Colonel William Johnson, grandson of Sir William Johnson, married Susan DeLancey; her brother Lord Wellington's quartermaster-general, was killed at the Battle of Waterloo.

Equally significant are the other marriages within these families involving top mercantile interests or lesser landed estates. James DeLancey, son of the patriarch Stephen, married Anne Heathcote, daughter of the patentee of Scarsdale Manor, in Westchester County. Peter DeLancey, another son, married Elizabeth Colden, daughter of the politically powerful Cadwallader Colden. (The 1775 double portrait, by Matthew Pratt, of Colden with his grandson Warren DeLancey—named after Peter Warren—is a valuable early American painting at the Metropolitan Museum of Art in New York City.) Still another brother, Oliver DeLancey, married Phila Franks, of the rich Jewish merchant family: the site of their house is now Fraunces Tavern, the historic inn and museum in downtown New

CADWALLADER COLDEN (1687/88–1776) AND WARREN DELANCEY (1761–1842), his grandson. Courtesy of the Metropolitan Museum of Art, Purchase, 1969, Morris K. Jesup Fund (69.76).

Figure 1

Names	Interlocking Family Relations	Political Positions	Land Acquisitions	Related Facts
Oloff Van Cortlandt	Oloff married Anneke Lookermans. One son, Stephen, married Gertrude Schuyler, sister of Peter Schuyler. Another son, Jacobus, married Eva DeVries, step-daughter of Frederick Philipse.	Oloff was twice burgomaster of New Amsterdam. His son Stephen was an assemblyman. His son Jacobus was mayor of New York City.	Stephen was granted 86,000 acres centered at Cortlandt, in Westchester County. His brother Jacobus acquired adjacent lands at Bedford and Katonah, as well as what is now known as Van Cortlandt Park in New York City.	Oloff was described as the fourth richest man in the colony in 1674. He was a partner in ventures with Frederick Philipse. His son Stephen received Cortlandt Manor from Gov. Fletcher.
Frederick Philipse	Frederick first married Margaret Hardenbroeck and then Catherine Van Cortlandt, by whom he had Philip and Adolph, with Eva DeVries a step-daughter.	Son Adolph was the main party strategist of the Governor's Council. Philip's son, Col. Frederick (II), after an assembly career, was appointed to the Supreme Court.	Frederick received a patent covering 90,000 acres in Westchester County. His son Adolph received 205,000 acres, now the whole of Putnam County (called the Highland Patent).	Frederick was the richest man in New York in 1674. He was a close friend of Gov. Fletcher, who confirmed his patent, originally granted by Gov. Dongan. Adolph continued this relation, receiving the Highland Patent.
Stephen DeLancey	Stephen married Ann Van Cortlandt, daughter of Stephen Van Cortlandt. Their daughter, Susannah, married Commodore Peter Warren, later vice admiral.	Stephen was an assemblyman. His son James was a councilor, chief justice, and lieut. governor of New York. DeLancey dominated 18th-century New York politics.	Stephen was greatly involved in New York City real estate. His son James speculated in large Mohawk Valley and other upriver lands.	Fraunces Tavern, where Washington said farewell to his troops in Lower Manhattan, was original DeLancey property. DeLancey Street in New York City is named after the family realty property.

Henry Beekman	Henry first married Janet Livingston and then Gertrude Van Cortlandt.	Henry was an assemblyman.	His land holdings dominated the northern part of Dutchess County.	Henry was a colonel in the militia.
Sir William Johnson, Baronet	Sir William was a nephew of Commodore Peter Warren, married to Susannah DeLancey.	He was superintendent of Indian affairs for the northern dept. and colonel of the Six Nations. He was also a councilor and one of the most powerful political figures in the northern New York colony.	He received the larger part of northern Albany County, centering on the Mohawk River. This was expanded by grants and purchases to create one of the largest individual landed estates in all the colonies.	Sir William was feudal lord of upper New York Indian country, with close ties to the Iroquois. The upriver Johnson, with his downriver DeLancey cousins, controlled New York politics.
Robert Livingston	Robert married Alida Schuyler Van Rensselaer, sister of Peter Schuyler and widow of Nicholas Van Rensselaer. Robert's son, Gilbert, married Cornelia Beekman.	Robert was an Indian commissioner and an assemblyman. Immediate descendants included a Supreme Court judge, a speaker of the assembly and the first chancellor of New York State. In 1758 four Livingstons sat in the Assembly.	He was patentee to 160,000 acres in Dutchess and Albany counties (called the Livingston Manor), as well as a substantial part of Ulster County.	Robert was a close friend of Governors Dongan and Hunter, from whom he received and had confirmed his land patents.
Peter Schuyler	Peter first married Engeltie Van Schanck and then Marie Van Rensselaer, granddaughter of the original patroon. Peter's brother's son, John Jr., married Cornelia Van Cortlandt.	Peter was mayor of Albany and councilor; then senior councilor and acting governor. His nephew, Myndert, was an assemblyman and also mayor of Albany.	Peter was a grantee in the 620,000 acre Dellius Patent, later cancelled, and a one-seventh partner in the Saratoga Patent, greatly supplemented through later purchases.	He was a close friend of Gov. Fletcher, from whom he received his interest in the patents. The Philipses, Van Cortlandts, and DeLanceys worked at New York City, while the Schuylers represented upstate, centered at Albany.

York City. Mary Philipse, a great-granddaughter of Frederick Philipse, married Roger Morris, of the Manor of Morrisania, a smaller Westchester County patent. Lewis Morris III, third generation from the patriarch of this family, married Sarah Gouverneur, descendant of Abraham Gouverneur, an early successful merchant. Somewhat later, Alexander Van Rensselaer married Sarah Drexel, tying in the eighteenth-century aristocrats with the rising nineteeneth-century plutocrats.

The relation of the landed interest to the appointive councilors is instructive. Of the seventeen families with the largest estates, thirteen of them had family members on various councils. Between 1691 and 1775, these landed aristocratic families averaged at least a quarter of the total membership on the councils. The families were Bayard, DeLancey, DePeyster, Heathcote, Johnson, Livingston, Morris, Nicoll, Philipse, Schuyler, Smith, Van Cortlandt, and Van Rensselaer. The strong influence of this tightly-knit elite of council members was a formidable bloc in patenting the enormous land grants.[11]

The oligarchic influence of this group became even sharper as time went on. Between 1750 and 1776, twenty-five of the twenty-eight councilors "bore the names of conspicuously large landowning families."[12]

The manor system greatly slowed up the development of the New York Colony. There was no reason an immigrant should become a feudal vassal when freehold land was available in nearby provinces. Furthermore, unlike Virginia and Maryland, whose land systems were similar to that of New York but where there were no cities, the Hudson River fur trade created a burgher aristocracy in New Amsterdam (later to be named New York City), which matched in pomp and power the river lords. The development of the New York Colony, as a result, created a monied aristocracy based on a fusion of urban and rural rich rather than that of a plantation economy. The long hard winters, prohibiting the cultivation of tobacco, rice, and indigo, likewise impeded the creation of an aristocratic caste resting on slave labor. The political development of New York was somewhat unique because of this complex interplay of factors.[13]

It should also be noted that by the last half of the eighteenth century many of these manors were broken up through family division or profligacy, as was also occurring in Virginia. Rensselaerwyck, Livingston Manor, Philipsborough, Morrisania, and Cortlandt Manors survived, as did the large grants to the Beekmans and the Schuylers. The American Revolution destroyed Tory land holdings, such as those of the DeLanceys and the Johnsons. What remained intact ¡more han the actual holdings, however, was the imprint of an economic structure in which personal advancement was often seen as a consequence of control or corruption of the political process.[14]

Pennsylvania

William Penn is among the most interesting figures in American history. He was the son of a very wealthy family with a military background. Indeed, his father was a noted admiral who, in 1655, seized the island of Jamaica, which, under slave labor, became the most valuable English tropical colony. At the age of eighteen William Penn converted to pacifism and the new Quaker religion, for which faith he was twice briefly imprisoned. Despite his zealous faith, Penn contrived throughout his life to be a personal friend of both King Charles II and King James II. "Penn never ceased to be cavalier when he went Quaker, or gentleman when he became democrat. His instincts and tastes were those of the English aristocracy; he appreciated a thoroughbred horse, a well-built ship, good food, drink, and handsome women."[15]

William Penn agreed with Charles II to wipe out a large debt that the Duke of York, the king's brother (later James II), owed Penn's father by taking instead land in the colonies to serve as a refuge for the persecuted Quakers. The Pennsylvania charter was narrower than that received by Lord Baltimore, and in addition to giving the king veto power over the colonial assembly, it also permitted Parliament to tax the settlers. These restrictions were due to Charles II's irritation with Massachusetts Bay, which had supported Oliver Cromwell in the Civil War. In fact, Charles looked with a certain favor on the Quakers because they had been the only dissenting body which, due to pacifist principles, had not fought against the monarchy.

In 1682, Penn himself came to America with some one hundred Quakers. He established good relations with the Indians, a policy that continued throughout his life, and was unique among English settlers. This led to the ironic remark of Voltaire that Penn's first step "was to enter into an alliance with his American Indian neighbors; and this is the only treaty between those people and the Christians that was not ratified by an oath and was never infringed."[16]

William Penn preceded Benjamin Franklin as being America's first great advertising copy-writer. To push land sales, he wrote an *Account of the Province of Pennsylvania,* published not only in English but also in French, Dutch, and German, which eulogized the beauties and bounties of his province. Besides giving special discounts to Quakers, Penn, out of conviction, also set the quitrent at such a low charge that it angered Lord Baltimore next door. Maintaining paid agents in the Rhine Valley, so many thousands of German settlers were attracted that what is called the "Pennsylvania Dutch" (from "deutsch" or German) made up almost

WILLIAM PENN IN ARMOUR, AGE 22. Courtesy of the Historical Society of Pennsylvania.

half the population within a score of years. However, Penn did insist on two features that caused much tension in the next century; namely, that ten percent of all land sales be retained by the family and that Penn lands were forever free of taxation.

Penn's promotion was a great success. The colony grew as much in three years as had New Netherlands under the Dutch in forty years. Oddly, William Penn himself lost money despite his advertising genius because, believing in the natural goodness of all men, he was swindled by almost all his governors and agents: indeed, one of the latter substituted his name for that of Penn on a sale deed of the entire province, which William Penn signed without reading, and so almost lost the colony as a result.

Much has been made of the amity that existed between the Lord Proprietor and the Indians. This was true during the life of William Penn. It was no longer true under William's three sons: Thomas, John, and Richard. In addition to their own debts, they inherited other financial obligations from their overtrusting father. Though the sons owned by charter a feudal domain of enormous size, William Penn's refusal to cheat or kill the Indians had left them in treaty possession of less than five percent of the province. Besides, the settlers on this small part of the land held back paying quitrents. "The Penns were land poor, living on pretense, agility, and great expectations. Their only appreciable income came from the purchase money laid down for large tracts at the moment of sale. And the only open spaces large enough to accommodate such tracts were over the Indian line."[17] By 1729 the heirs sold twenty-thousand acres in Indian territory. In 1734 they adopted the fraudulent techniques used in other colonies, signing blank land warrants and sending them to their agents.

In 1737 the wheel came full turn and William Penn's heirs acted in a way no different from other colonial proprietors and governors. The best example is the Walking Purchase.[18] Thomas Penn, the second Lord Proprietor (who, giving up the Quaker faith, had become Anglican), pressed an alleged Indian sale to his father in 1686 (though the document was not signed by either party) of a tract of land "as far as men can go in a day and a half." A good trail was cleared through the wilderness and the proprietor hired the three best runners in the province. Paced by horseback, with Indians to record the event, the three men dashed forward. One quit, a second drowned in a creek, but the third went the whole course till the appointed time, covering sixty-four miles. The Penn family added a half-million acres of Indian land to their province in the Minisink region north of the Lehigh River. When the Delawares, who lived there, refused to leave, the Six Nations were bribed through William Johnson to drive them out. It has been estimated that by this and other chicanery the second and third generations of the Penns built up the quitrents, collecting more than £63,000 in the eighteenth century before they lost the province.

The Quakers, a minority sect before long in Pennsylvania, would have soon lost political power if it had not been for the gratitude of the Pennsylvania Dutch to the Penn family for bringing them to the province. The council was easiest to dominate, since it was appointed by the proprietor. The assembly was controlled for years by a system of rotten boroughs (the 16,000 voters in the three eastern counties having twice as many members in the assembly as the 15,000 voters in the five western counties), but eventually the Quakers were unseated by the combined hostility of the Scotch-Irish Presbyterians on the western frontier who resented the Quaker refusal to kill off the Indians and make available new land, and by farmers in the more settled regions who objected to the quitrents and the Penn family's exemption from taxes. A leader of the anti-Penn coalition, whose political career dated from this conflict, was Benjamin Franklin, called by the colony's Chief Justice Allen "that Disturber of the Peace" and a "grand Incendiary": attacks supported with a degree of serenity by Franklin since he enjoyed the lucrative printing business at the assembly's command. Franklin was sent to England in 1764 by the assembly to ask for the abolition of the proprietary system; less known was his role as agent to promote land speculation in western Indian territory.

As noted, the Quakers maintained their pacifist principles after the death of William Penn, drawing down upon themselves the hatred of their fellow colonials in both the French and Indian War and the Revolution. Consistently Tory, John Penn, the grandson of William Penn, ruled Pennsylvania for the English throughout the Revolution.

New Jersey and Delaware

Lord John Berkeley and Sir George Carteret were the two courtiers given New Jersey by the Duke of York when he took over New Amsterdam. The two absentee noblemen, only interested in quitrents, set up such an elaborate tax system that the settlers revolted. Berkeley, unable to draw the income he had hoped for, sold his western part of the province to two Quakers in 1674, who in turn sold it to a Quaker group headed by William Penn. Another group of twenty-four investors bought the remaining eastern part from the Carteret family in 1682.

The Quakers who held West Jersey, facing persistent anger on the part of the settlers over quitrents, bit by bit gave up their undoubted legal right to collect this unpopular tax. The situation in East Jersey was different. The proprietors would not yield their stubborn claim to quitrents, and the freeholders, many of whom were from New England where the soil was free of this incumbrance, were equally determined not to pay. This was especially true around Elizabethtown, where there was constant commotion.

In 1702 the proprietors of both Jerseys ceded their political rights to the Crown and the area became a royal province. They did not give up their proprietary rights, however, and thus still claimed payment in East Jersey. The riots continued.

Governor Robert Hunter attempted to impose strict order in 1713 by setting up a policy of appointing proprietors or agents of the proprietors to the council in order to subdue the rebellious assembly. The policy was followed by subsequent governors: the combined power of the governors and councils led to a "stranglehold" by the landed interests.[19] The curious part was that the victory of the landed party was Pyrrhic: the law called for payment of quitrents, and the judiciary supported the law, but the collections were almost nonexistent. Sometimes the governors were actually bribed by rich landowners who were not proprietors to thwart the collection; more often the sheriffs and other enforcement agents, sympathetic with the popular party, made no attempt to enforce the law. The proprietors were divided themselves: the practice of collecting quitrents was given up in West Jersey, and many proprietors even in East Jersey abandoned the struggle. The result was confusion: with adjacent areas being subject to different rules, the quitrents charged being of varying amounts, and the enforcement at times severe and at times delinquent. Beverley Bond, Jr., summed it up: "In their first concessions, the proprietaries in East Jersey made a serious mistake in demanding an excessive quit-rent. Had they been willing to reserve only the moderate rate that was customary in New York, they might have avoided the fatal controversy with the Elizabethtown settlers, for these determined opponents of the quit-rents would then have been without any possible legal pretext to support their claims. Later, the proprietaries by their refusal to compromise aroused the settlers, with New England traditions, to make the persistent defiance that ended in a virtual victory."[20] East New Jersey was a rare example of successful colonial defiance against an antiquated feudal law.

Delaware, the most southerly of the middle colonies, had originally been claimed by Maryland under Lord Baltimore's charter. However, King Charles II also gave this area to his brother the Duke of York, together with New Jersey after seizing New Amsterdam. The reason was that the

Dutch, shortly before, had in their turn taken Delaware from the founding Swedes. Such confused and overlapping claims were common and the king himself probably could not have indicated where Delaware and New Amsterdam were on a map of the time. William Penn desired a seaport for his province of Pennsylvania and arranged in 1682 to purchase the area from his friend the Duke of York, with the assent of Charles, thus extinguishing the Baltimore claim.

The Penn family ruled the two provinces together, though the dispute as to whether Delaware belonged to the Penns or to the Baltimores continued all the way to 1767, when the present line between the colonies was adopted. Thus the Quakers, a very small sect in Delaware and the Jerseys and a minority even in Pennsylvania, controlled these provinces throughout most of the colonial period. After the Revolution, Penn's heirs received £130,000 to release all claims, an enormous sum for the time.

6

The Northern Colonies

"They [the Bay Puritans] have a depraved appetite after . . . great portions of land, land in this wilderness, as if men were in as great necessity and danger for want of great portions of land, as poor, hungry, thirsty seamen . . . after a long and starving passage."

Roger Williams to Major Mason, June 22, 1670

Massachusetts and Connecticut

Those dissenters from the Church of England who called themselves Puritans were unhappy in the England of King James I and his son Charles I. They were mainly yeomen and tradesmen, the middle ranks in English society forming the new class that would explode a few short years later under Oliver Cromwell and wipe out forever the unlimited power of kings. In this earlier period, however, fretting against religious restrictions and unsure of their future, some looked across the ocean for a place to site a New Jerusalem on earth.

The first group to come to the New World were the Separatists, the most radical wing of the Puritan movement, who had already tried to maintain a colony in Holland. Their leaders made a business deal with the Virginia Company in 1620 to settle along the Chesapeake Bay. The captain of the *Mayflower,* however, ran too far north and, encountering dangerous seas and shoals when trying to sail south, gave up and anchored

73

in what is now Provincetown harbor. The Pilgrims complained but the captain refused to continue, and after exploring the area for some five weeks, the group settled where Plymouth now stands.

The London merchants who put up the £7,000 to finance the expedition had insisted on a contract whereby the colonists agreed to work for seven years and put all the net earnings into a common fund from which the shareholders would be paid, with a certain amount set aside to feed and clothe the colonists. But by 1623, slightly more than two years after settlement, there were so many objections to the communal holdings (a form of organization that the Pilgrims had originally supported) that Governor Bradford breached the contract and gave out individual land plots, settling with the London backers for a payment of £1,800. In 1691, when there were 7,000 persons in Plymouth, the settlement was merged into the larger colony of Massachusetts Bay.

Massachusetts Bay Colony was established in 1630 as an outgrowth of the Plymouth Company, which had gone through several reorganizations. The shareholders were all wealthy Puritans or sympathizers. This group was unique in that not only did it establish separate company headquarters in the colony, but most of the shareholders lived there—a significant reason for its thriving. Though Massachusetts Bay recognized the authority of the king and called for harmony with the laws of England, in practical terms the colony was independent. By 1643 the population had reached 16,000 persons, more than all the other English colonies in America put together.

The Reverend Thomas Hooker left Massachusetts Bay in 1636 with a group of friends and founded what is now called Connecticut. The new settlement, composed also of Puritans, lived in harmony with its mother colony. The freeholders formulated what they called Fundamental Orders and the government was modeled on that of Massachusetts Bay.

By a historic fluke, Connecticut just missed becoming a proprietary similar to Pennsylvania and Maryland. In 1635, the year before Reverend Hooker emigrated to the Connecticut Valley, the Council of New England, a company successor to the Old Plymouth Company, had granted this area to James, Marquis of Hamilton. His daughter Anne, Dutchess of Hamilton, claimed after the Restoration that her father had been prevented by the Civil War from taking possession. She petitioned the Crown to restore the proprietary and force the inhabitants to pay her quitrents.

Fitz-John Winthrop, son of Connecticut Governor John Winthrop, Jr., went to England and defended the colonists. With biting sarcasm he noted that despite the honor of being placed under the patronage of the Hamilton noble family, the people of Connecticut had a "strange notion and fright of the word, quit-rent . . . and, besides, how all mankind in this country think themselves happy in the one understanding, that they have a just and firm title to their lands by purchase from the natives. . . ."[1] The case dragged along for many years, a final petition being made by Anne's son, the Earl of Arran. The decision went against the claimants because the Crown felt that a revival of all such claims "would lead to unspeakable disturbance and confusion."[2]

Governor John Winthrop, who ruled Massachusetts Bay from its start, wrote in a frank moment that one reason he came to the New World was that his estate had greatly diminished; he could no longer live in his accustomed style. He defined democracy as the "meanest and worst of all forms of government,"[3] and believed in a "mixt aristocracy"[4] in which only freemen who lived on their own land (or professional men or merchants) were allowed to vote. Winthrop further narrowed this definition by restricting the vote to Congregational Church members, controlling through his working alliance with Reverend John Cotton, leader of the clergy, those who were eligible. The church and state in the Massachusetts Bay Colony and in Connecticut were thus more rigid than Anglican England, against which the Puritans had so protested.

The doors to both provinces were, in their Truth, bolted to nonbelievers. Governor William Bradford of Plymouth Colony, in righteous indignation, suppressed a vote on a measure in 1646: "The sum of it was, to allow and maintain full and free tolerance of religion to all men that would preserve the civil peace, and submit unto Government; and that there was no limitation or exception against Turk, Jew, papist . . . or any other."[5] Quakers were a particular source of rabid hatred.

History presents the ludicrous situation of a Royal Commission, set up in 1662 after the Restoration, which had to press New England to be less autocratic. One point was "that they [the Puritan leadership] permitt such as desire it, to use the Common prayer [of the Anglicans]," to which Massachusetts Bay refused to agree. Another request of the commission was "that all freeholders may have the voets in Election of officers civill and Military," and it, too, was rejected by the Puritan leadership. Perhaps most piercing of all statements of the Royal Commission was that "No Colony hath any just right to dispose of any lands conquered from the natives, unless both the cause of the conquest be just and the land lye within the bounds which the king by his charter hath given it, nor yet to exercise any authority beyond these bounds."[6] This threw a shadow over all the land acquired in the local wars against the Wampanoags, Narragansetts, and the Pequots.

In effect, the royal commissioners had become the champions of the rights of both the English freeholder and the Indians against what the foremost authority on America's colonial period called "the oligarchical rule of the magistrates."[7] It can be seen how the earliest seeds for independence were planted in the zealous souls of the leaders in New England. As with the plantation aristocrats of Virginia, their resentment against the mother country was motivated more by the resolve to retain power than by any vision of individual liberty.

The thin poor soil, rocky hills, and harsh climate of New England made farming less attractive than fishing or trading, but land was still both a symbol and reality of wealth. There were significant examples of the relation between political power and land grants from the very beginning of Massachusetts Bay Colony. In 1634 there was a revolt against the oligarchy when the enfranchised (a very small group itself) voted that the governor should abide by the rules of the original charter that gave to the whole body of freemen the right to participate in the making of the laws. A very important feature of this struggle was the desire of the freemen to share in the partitioning of lands. Governor Winthrop had graciously given himself 1,800 acres, and his cohorts Dudley and Saltonstall 1,700 and 1,600 acres respectively. The lesser-connected men were afraid that "the richer men would give the poorer sort no great proportions of land." Thus, the first revolt against the Puritan leaders was sparked by monopoly control of the land.

The power of granting was closely tied up with the theological state. When the clergy of Massachusetts Bay wanted to expel Roger Williams for his dissenting religious views, Williams's home town of Salem, where he was the minister, refused to sanction the move. It was only when Salem was told that needed land would not be given to the town that the magistrates succeeded in evicting Roger Williams. Probably an added factor was Williams's effrontery to state that the whites had no proper title to Indian lands.

Though the Puritan townships were created by free grants of land to approved settlers, as time went by, political influence began to control unappropriated land. The "eastern men of property" and the pioneers of the frontier became separate classes.[8] The settlers moving west were not given equal shares but rather shares according to their wealth. In Windsor, Connecticut, for example, the wealthiest 10 percent of the settlers received 41 percent of the land; the poorest 20 percent, a mere 3.5 percent.[9] Furthermore, a system that seemed equitable, namely, sale by public auction, in fact was an extension of the same approach. Money was so scarce in New England that, in a practical sense, many of the men who controlled the political mechanism, and instituted the auctions, were the only ones who could buy the land. Thus, Connecticut in 1715 auctioned off 105,793 acres and the whole tract was purchased by William Pitkins, one of the committee appointed to sell the land.[10]

The very important historian Frederick Jackson Turner, in developing his famous theory of the ever-advancing frontier to explain American uniqueness, used many examples of land-grant favoritism from early Massachusetts and Connecticut to explain the new frontier mentality.[11] Several follow.

The settlement of Salisbury was established on the basis of land grants to a dozen proprietors (including the younger Dudley), only two of whom settled there. Dunstable and Lancaster (Nashaway) fit in the same category. Mendon settlers asked for relief from public work charges on the grounds that the actual residents, a minority of the proprietors, were carrying the total cost; while Deerfield settlers complained that the best land belonged to proprietors "never like to come to a settlement amongst us." The most notorious case was Leicester, where the twenty-two land holders included two sons of the governor, a father of a late governor, and a son of the chief justice. Not one settled in Leicester. Turner concludes that by 1762, "the transfer from the social-religious to the economic conception was complete, and the frontier was deeply influenced by the change to 'land mongering.' "

An important distinction did exist between the New England land-grant system and that operative elsewhere, namely, the enforcement of the regulations. Land in every sale had to be reserved for the support of a minister and a town school; and each grantee had seven years to build a house of specified size and clear land for cultivation. Even though influence modified these provisions, the worst evils of absentee speculation were softened in both Massachusetts Bay and Connecticut.

Following the report of the Royal Commission, and open defiance as to its recommendations, King Charles II—who despised the Puritans —annulled the Massachusettts Bay Company charter and made the province a Crown colony. This meant a royal governor, a council, and, worst of all, the possibility of land grants leading to quitrents. Familiar with Charles's gift of all Virginia to two of his aristocratic cronies, the colony was in an uproar. The small farmers, united with their religious leaders, were in no mood to accept landlords and quitrents.

The colony did receive a governor and council, and these men did try the same game as elsewhere. Actually, the practice preceded the royal takeover. In 1677, Edward Randolph, in an inquiry, stated that Richard Wharton, the president of Governor Dudley's Council, with several others, had engrossed large tracts in the Narragansett County. But this activity quickened with the sending over of the hated royal governor Colonel Sir Edmund Andros. Reverend Increase Mather, spiritual leader of the colony, accused Andros of irregularities in land grants in Charlestown, of giving away to favorites the commons belonging to several towns, and of Andros himself taking possession through a dummy of an island off Plymouth.[12] When the Catholic James II was overthrown in 1688, Governor Andros was promptly jailed. Massachusetts laid its case before William and Mary, the new monarchs, and in 1691 a charter was issued that vested the original title to the soil in the hands of the settlers.

Only one other conflict involving a patent occurred and this was marginal to the colony. A certain Colonel Dunbar in 1729 attempted to settle a group of Irish Catholics on his newly granted proprietary on the east bank of the Kennebec River. The colonel maintained that Massachusetts Bay had no control over his land, which fell under the jurisdiction of Nova Scotia. Under continued protest from the Puritans, and no doubt influenced by the religion of the prospective settlers, the Privy Council voided the Dunbar patent. The Puritans, so magnificent in fighting to protect their own interests, were bigots in all else.

Rhode Island

Roger Williams, the Salem minister, preached religious tolerance and separation of church and state. The children of the men who had preached the same message when a despised minority in England, now secure in their own theocracy, brought Williams up on charges in front of the General Court and sentenced him to be sent back to England. Williams escaped to the more tolerant Indians and, buying some of their land at Narragansett Bay, settled there in 1636. A few friends joined him and they called the settlement by the name of Providence. So many people began to pour in, most of them fleeing the religious tyranny of Massachusetts Bay, that Reverend Williams went to England in 1644 and obtained a charter from the Long Parliament, governing during the Civil War. After the Restoration, to humble Massachusetts, King Charles II in 1663 confirmed the charter.

The Rhode Island settlement was considered "that sewer"[13] and when the first New England Confederation was formed, Williams was snubbed and excluded. Massachusetts indeed tried to snuff out its life by an economic boycott. The small province was the home of "a heterogeneous collection of men and women who held many sorts of religious and social opinions and who sought a refuge there for conscience's sake and other reasons, because they were unable to live anywhere else"[14]—individuals like the visionary Roger Williams and that cantankerous threesome, Anne Hutchinson, William Harris, and Samuel Gorton, as well as groups of Anglicans, Quakers, Unitarians, Roman Catholics, and Jews. There were, of course, some with more typical greeds, and the famous colonial city of Newport only escaped by a hair's breadth of becoming a separate feudal property. William Coddington, the wealthy and worldly wise founder, tried to create a small independent proprietary, with the people becoming his tenants. Coddington went to England in 1649 and received a patent from the Council of State, which appointed him governor for life with control over the island of Narragansett Bay equal to proprietors like Baltimore and Penn. He failed only because of a revolt of his tenants, who sent delegates to England and succeeded in voiding the patent.

Maine and New Hampshire

The provinces of Massachusetts, Connecticut, and Rhode Island were small areas and quickly settled. There was relatively little opportunity for the hanky-panky involved in large land grants and the resultant formation of hereditary elites. This was less true in the great terrain stretching north to the French frontier, a vast forested waste into which the three southern New England colonies could be dropped and vanish with space to spare. Like the western part of Virginia and the northern part of New York, such areas were ideal for speculation. Maine, which was not one of the thirteen original colonies, will be touched on, while New Hampshire will be reviewed in more detail.

The separate development of Maine from the Massachusetts Bay Colony was a direct outcome of the personal ambitions of Ferdinand Gorges, a prime promoter of the Plymouth Company. Sir Ferdinand, a Church of England supporter often in conflict with the Puritan sympathies of most of the Plymouth and Bristol merchants backing the Plymouth Company, obtained in 1622, with Captain John Mason, an enormous grant of land north of the Massachusetts Bay Colony. Then in 1629, the two partners received a land grant in what is now Maine from the Plymouth Company, though the records are not clear as to whether the grant was a confirmation of the earlier one or an enlargement of a separate 1626 grant. Gorges, Mason, and associates called the territory—which extended through Maine, New Hampshire, and as far west as Lake Champlain—by the name of Laconia and set up the Laconia Company, with its first settlement at Portsmouth, to merchandise the land.

In 1635 the Council of New England[15] was about to surrender its charter. The directors apportioned among themselves various land holdings, Mason taking what is now New Hampshire and Gorges taking what is now Maine. Sir Ferdinand then secured his position in 1639 by obtaining a royal proprietary charter, framing an elaborate constitution for the unpopulated wilderness. He founded Gorgeana (now York) which thus became in 1641 the first chartered English city in the New World.

If time had been on the side of Sir Ferdinand, Maine would have become, like Maryland and Pennsylvania, a proprietary colony under the rule of his family. But the Civil War broke out in England. Sir Ferdinand, a rabid monarchist, took up arms for the king, fought, and was taken prisoner. Shortly thereafter he died. His heirs under the Commonwealth made no claim to Maine, probably fearing expropriation, and a chaotic period ensued. The few inhabitants declared themselves a separate body in 1648 and then, in 1652, surrendered authority to the Massachusetts Bay Colony.

After the Restoration, the Gorges family reasserted its claim to Maine, meeting with encouragement on the part of Charles II. The Crown's attorney upheld the Gorges's petition and a royal proclamation ordered the people of Maine to recognize the proprietorship. Ferdinand Gorges, grandson and namesake of the original patentee, was short of money and, recognizing the difficulties of setting up a quitrent system in a wilderness peopled by few and hostile people thousands of miles from England, sold his position in 1677 to John Usher, a Boston merchant. Usher, however, came under tremendous pressure from the Massachusetts Bay authorities, and the next year was forced to deed the purchase to his home colony. Most of the settlements, which were mainly on the southern limit of Maine as we know it now, were then incorporated into the Massachusetts Bay Colony and remained as such until Maine attained its separate status as an independent state in 1820 as part of the Missouri Compromise.

New Hampshire came into existence through the same process. When the Council of New England surrendered its charter in 1635 and the directors allocated the various land holdings, Captain John Mason took that territory which he named New Hampshire after Hampshire in England, a position confirmed by the Crown. He died shortly thereafter and, with the Civil War and the subsequent Commonwealth, the Masons did not press their proprietary claim. After the Restoration, however, Captain Mason's heir, Robert Mason, attempted to revive the proprietary rights, indeed with far more persistence than the Gorges heirs to Maine. First in 1661, and then again in 1674, the Crown's attorneys reported in favor of Robert Mason. If it were not for his intemperate pressing of quitrent claims against the settlers, sometimes even against the wording of the judgment in his favor—for the proprietary title was confirmed as to all vacant tracts but the Crown requested conciliation where land was already settled—Mason probably would have become a northern Lord Baltimore. Coercing the royal officials, spreading agents through the province, attempting to seize town commons (which were then used to pasture cattle and procure firewood), Mason aroused the ire of the populace. The local courts would not enforce Mason's eviction notices. Finally, growing weary of the struggle, Robert Mason in 1690 sold his claim to Colonel Samuel Allen of London. Allen, who then declared the colony his personal property, appointed himself governor in 1692.

The greed of Colonel Allen—who established quitrents of £22,000 a year as his due—was so marked, the settlers rose in revolt. Because of the civil commotion, the Earl of Bellomont, then governor of Massachusetts Bay Colony, was asked to investigate. Bellomont, whom we have met before as one of the few honest men in this period of history, denounced Allen's title as defective even though he reported an offer was several times made to him of a bribe of £10,000 if he would hold in Allen's favor.[16] The Privy Council, annoyed with the constant tumult, backed Bellomont and in 1705 refused to reopen a suit appealed from a naturally anti-Allen New Hampshire court. The Allen claim dragged on until his position was sold some forty years later to a number of local persons who dropped all pretense to quitrents.

The history of New Hampshire takes a curious turn at this point, for it became, in effect, though technically established as a royal colony, the personal domain of a single family. Where the Masons and Allens had failed, the Wentworth family succeeded. As is often the case, home oligarchy was more acceptable than that of absentee rulers.

The Wentworths were early New Hampshire settlers and soon took a prominent position in the colony. John Wentworth became lieutenant-governor in 1717. Massachusetts and New Hampshire at that time shared the same governor for military reasons, the French border being so close, but the northern colony was separately administered. This meant that Wentworth was in effect the real governor in all internal matters. He used his position to fill his own pocketbook and those of family and friends. The main source was through land grants and marked-down land purchase prices. This was done, as usual, through control of the Royal Council.

When John Wentworth assumed office in 1717, three persons connected with him by marriage were then council members. Three more relatives joined the council during his term of office, giving him control of the twelve-man council.

The regime of John Wentworth was relatively free of scandal in comparison with that of Benning, his eldest son, who had been a councilor and then became the first separate governor of New Hampshire in 1741, holding his appointment for twenty-five years. Benning Wentworth's regime was marked by land grants for personal gain. His was as extensive and far more obviously fraudulent than any other colonial governor. Benning Wentworth's control over the council through family appointments was even more overt than that of his father. Six Wentworths, by name or through marriage, were councilors initially; during his stay in office, he added a brother and two nephews.

The Wentworth family under Benning's administration treated New Hampshire as a poacher's paradise. Mark, Benning's brother, was one of the dozen land magnates—and second largest shareholder—who in 1746 purchased the remaining Allen claim to unsettled land holdings in the colony. Benning himself disdained paying any money at all. During his term of office he distributed two hundred large tracts of land to various groups of persons, in each case reserving for himself a personally selected lot of five hundred acres, always located in the most valuable corner.[17] The governor thus acquired some 100,000 acres of New Hampshire land at no cost, scattered in such a way that he would participate in the colony's growth and development no matter what the area.

The land acquisition was only part of the picture. The royal governor received a percentage fee for every land grant and thus put new townships on the block to the highest bidder. But Benning Wentworth was insatiable and, running out of New Hampshire soil, started to grant land west of the Connecticut River, that is, land outside the colony's clearly determined borders. The conquest of Canada in 1760 opened up new vistas. A wild scramble for land started in the conquered area directly north, and in the one year of 1761 Benning Wentworth granted eighty new townships.[18] All this, of course, was only possible by packing the royal council; yet "One can only marvel that the Privy Council allowed this family to continue its monopoly of the government."[19]

The value of these land grants, both for Benning Wentworth and for his cronies, must be placed in the context of the rise in population, and hence land values, during this period. In 1766 the population of New Hampshire was approximately 50,000; by 1775 there were more than 80,000 residents.

The land grabbing of the governor and his councilors became so overt that London started to take notice. But the Wentworth family influence —and money—was so powerful, it took years before anything was done. In 1766, Benning Wentworth was allowed to resign and the next year his

FRANCES DEERING ATKINSON, LATER LADY JOHN WENTWORTH (1738–1815), AGE 27. Oil on canvas (1795), by John Singleton Copley. Collection of The New York Public Library, Astor, Lenox and Tilden Foundations.

nephew John—the son of Mark Wentworth, who had acquired a large slice of the Allen land claim and become one of the richest men in New England—was appointed royal governor. That the younger John was a chip off the old block can be seen by the fact that his first important business deal after graduating from Harvard was to participate with his brother (obviously a tip-off through the family connection) in the syndicating of a thirty-six mile purchase on the northwest frontier of the province— the new township of Wolfborough. As is apparent from the accompanying illustration, his taste in women was as acute as his grasp of land values.

John Wentworth, heir-apparent to one of the top land and mercantile fortunes in New England, was only twenty-nine when he became governor of New Hampshire. He packed the Royal Council as had his uncle. He renewed all the old family appointments and added an uncle, another uncle by marriage, a first cousin once removed, a step-cousin, and the husband of a cousin. Eight of the twelve council seats were occupied by family, and in 1773 he added a ninth.

The Revolution unseated John Wentworth too soon for him to equal his uncle's record in land jobbery. In 1777 the New Hampshire legislature confiscated lands of Loyalists absent from the state, including, of course, the former royal governor. Thus ended the dynasty.

7

The Quitrent Thorn

"It being only land they come for."

Thomas Woodward, writing of colonists in the 1660s

The main discontent among white male settlers in colonial America, whether puffed up by anti-black or anti-Indian or anti-papist or even anti-British prejudice, had as its base the land: the getting hold of land, the cost of crops and sale profit, and land taxes. The tax that most often aroused the spirit of revolt was the quitrent.

The quitrent was originally a release for money of certain villein feudal obligations, such as laboring for the lord a certain part of the week or giving him a part of the crop. The person paying was thus "quit" of those obligations to the overlord of the soil. This evolved into the theory that the original landlord, the baron or the king, had a perpetual interest in the land even after sale. As long as the quitrent was paid, the title remained with the purchaser; if not, it reverted to the original owner. The lords proprietors themselves who received entire provinces as grants from the Crown, were subject to quitrents; and though only symbolic, the Penns, the Baltimores, and the Duke of York tendered Indian arrows or beaver skins as token quitrent to their overlord, the king.

Quitrents covered all colonial lands except the colonies of Massachusetts Bay, Connecticut, and Rhode Island, where none had been called for by the original charters. When Massachusetts Bay was made a royal colony, the Lords of Trade in London informed the newly appointed royal governor, Edmund Andros, in 1686, to provide for quitrents on all land grants. Such a great uproar resulted, the issue was permitted to die quietly. Elsewhere the Crown or the proprietors were the overlords and the quitrent was the symbol of the bond between the lord and the land.

Though the quitrents paid by the proprietor to the Crown were merely symbolic, those which the proprietors demanded from the freeholders in their proprietaries were often quite heavy. In most colonies the annual quitrent was ultimately set at two shillings for each hundred acres, though certain proprietors tried to push the rate as high as four shillings. The proprietors in East Jersey and Lord Granville in North Carolina met with the most tenant resistance. The Baltimores in Maryland and Lord Fairfax in Virginia (in the earlier period) also faced great discontent. William Penn charged less than the others, but after his death Pennsylvania quitrent caused endless tumult in the assembly. On the other hand, the Crown in Virginia and New York[1] received meagre returns. Governor Robert Dinwiddie of Virginia complained that there were at least one million acres that had been settled without ever having been entered on the rent rolls.[2] The problems of the Earl of Bellomont in New York have already been touched on. It should be emphasized that normal land taxes were paid in addition to quitrent; and since the manor and plantation grandees often avoided these taxes through their control of the sheriffs, the burden fell most heavily on the freehold farmers.

One mitigant was evasion, which was possible even in the proprietary colonies. This was because the absentee proprietors had agents and auditors who not only could be bribed but whose natural sympathies were often on the side of their fellow colonials. Maryland, which supposedly had the most efficient collection system, could gather only about one-third of the amount due. In Pennsylvania, though the staggering sum of £180,000 due on quitrents was shown as a total on the books between 1701 and 1776, the percentage collected was about the same as in Maryland. In North Carolina collections ran at a fifth of what was owed.[3]

In the royal colonies, the income from quitrents was not as significant a factor for the Crown as it was in the individual proprietaries, where, as with the Baltimores and Penns, it was their main livelihood. The plantation and manor aristocrats often avoided payments by the various tactics discussed, mainly through connivance between the royal governors and the legislative bodies for their mutual self-interest: as we have seen, the fortunes of Crown representatives, such as Fletcher in New York, Spotswood in Virginia, and McCulloh in North Carolina were built on such methods. The Crown attempted to enforce quitrents by basing the salaries of royal governors and other appointees on their collection; but getting huge land grants through logrolling was more of an incentive than the prompt payment of salaries. Furthermore, the sting of quitrents in the royal colonies was soothed by using the revenue for popular improvements, such as building roads or by reducing other taxes when applying part of the money to the ordinary expenses of government.

There was another important reason working for the colonials, which quieted the worst effects of the quitrent system in the royal colonies. This was the conversion in the eighteenth century of the office of auditor-general into a sinecure in England for a royal favorite. William Blathwayt held the office from 1680 to 1717; though a tactful and intelligent man, his insistence on quitrent collections caused much resentment. Under Horatio Walpole, from 1717 to 1757, and more especially under the Reverend Robert Cholmondeley, from 1757 until the outbreak of revolution, the system worked better from the point of view of the Americans because it was badly enforced. Walpole dutifully audited all accounts sent from the colonies but did not press when reports were infrequent, as from New York, and did not demand general reports on colonial revenue, as Blathwayt had done. Cholmondeley simply viewed his office as a life annuity and paid little attention to his duties. As a result, where quitrents had already been made part of the system, they continued to be paid; where there was evasion, they continued to be evaded; and where they were due but not pursued, they were ignored. The evils of the sinecure system thus worked to the advantage of the colonials.[4]

It should be noted that the British government after 1763 began to plan vast changes in the quitrent system, of which leading provincial figures were well aware. In 1766 the Earl of Shelburne sent a circular letter to the governors of all the royal colonies in America asking for a full account of the methods by which they levied the quitrents and any arrears due, the number of patents, the names of the patent holders, and the date of such patent grant. Panic ensued in certain high circles, as can be imagined, when the governors of New York and North and South Carolina responded that there were many land grants not recorded, that the quitrent laws were not enforced, and the collections were poor.

The bureaucracy worked slowly but surely. In 1774 the Board of Trade gave instructions for a thorough reform in the system of land grants, with a new uniform method established for all the royal colonies. In each colony the administration was directed to survey all Crown lands and to divide each tract into lots of not less than one hundred or more than one thousand acres, and to offer them for public sale with a purchase price of not less than six shillings, and a quitrent of a half-penny per acre, all to be rigorously enforced without exception.

Though it is apparent that influential colonial figures pulled strings in London and prevented any retroactive punitive action against illegal holdings or unpaid quitrents, it was also obvious that the British had determined to put an end to any such future actions. The gild was off the lily for the big land speculators. This directive of 1774, combined with previous prohibitions on speculation in western lands taken from France after the French and Indian War (a matter which will be analyzed in greater detail in a later chapter), were important milestones in the movement toward the Revolution. For quitrent payments were one subject that united all Americans in bitterness, from those imitation English lords, the southern Anglican plantation owners, to the poorest Scotch-Irish Presbyterian on the Appalachian frontier. Twin colonial children grew up together: land speculation and hatred of quitrents; and when they joined hands against Britain, the Revolution was not far off. Charles M. Andrews, considered the leading scholar on the American colonial period, summed it up by stating that quitrents "probably had more actual influence in bringing about independence than had some of the widely heralded political and constitutional doctrines of the pre-Revolutionary period."[5]

8

The American Child Is Born

"As Mark Twain recalled hearing from a slave in Hannibal [Mo.], 'You tell me whar a man gits his corn pone en I'll tell you what his 'pinions is.' "

By 1733 the thirteen original colonies were formed and the thin strip along the Atlantic coast from Maine to Georgia was occupied by persons with certain well-defined traits and ways of life. These can be briefly noted.

The thirteen colonies can be divided into three standard categories. The smallest colonies were the two self-governing provinces of Connecticut and Rhode Island. Their autonomy had its roots more in the Crown's hatred of the Puritans from Massachusetts Bay than in any desire to encourage self rule. There were three proprietary colonies (Maryland, Pennsylvania, and Delaware), while the remaining eight were royal colonies directly governed by the monarch.

At the turn of the eighteenth century, Massachusetts Bay, with some 80,000 inhabitants, was the largest province in population. Virginia followed with about 55,000 persons; Maryland, New York, and Connecticut each had approximately 30,000 people; New England as a region consisted of some 130,000 persons; the Chesapeake colonies had over 87,000; while there were some 65,000 persons in the middle colonies.

The shareholder companies, which had originally founded Virginia and Massachusetts Bay for private profit, had lost their charters and the two colonies were taken over by the Crown. The fortunate proprietors, the Penns in Pennsylvania and Delaware and the Baltimores in Maryland, had,

89

to a large extent, surrendered their political power as the eighteenth century advanced, but held on to their economic interests. With the exception of Lord Granville in North Carolina and Lord Fairfax in Virginia, the original proprietors of the Carolinas, the Jerseys, and New Hampshire lost both political and economic control. The Duke of York gave his proprietary of New York to the Crown when he became King James II. The last colony, Georgia, was turned back to the Crown when the founders tired of their philanthropic experiment. The political outlines of the various provinces were thus early formed.

Another way of describing the thirteen colonies is by dividing them into those founded for religious, proprietary, or solely commercial reasons.[1] In general, one might state that the group dominated by Massachusetts Bay (Massachusetts, Connecticut, Rhode Island, and New Hampshire) were stained to a greater or lesser degree by the Puritan influence: The proprietaries had their origin in the economic self-interest of the proprietors, though Pennsylvania and Delaware under William Penn reflected a religious factor as well. Provinces like New York and Virginia were dominated by business interests. As early as 1676, according to a report of Edward Randolph, there were thirty merchants in Boston worth between ten and twenty thousand pounds. Most of these fortunes were made in the slave trade, with Rhode Island's distillation of rum a strong runner-up. Plantation lords in Virginia—such as the Byrds, the Randolphs, the Lees, and the Carters —sat on wealth extracted by the sweat of forced labor, the slaves mainly being bought from the New England shipowners. Southern landed estates were kept intact by entailment and primogeniture. In New York and Pennsylvania the land-rich stood side by side with merchant capital built upon the fur trade down the Hudson River to New York City and on water and land routes into Philadelphia. On the eve of the American Revolution, Philadelphia was the largest city, with over 30,000 persons; New York was second, with 20,000; while Boston trailed with some 15,000 persons. But the seven largest cities had only 5 percent of the population, while at least 90 percent of the colonists were farmers.

Obviously, such divisions also have subclasses: the coastal strip can be distinguished from inland; flatland from piedmont or mountain area; well-watered loam from drier rocky soil; and the national origin of different peoples, with the English settlers dominating the coastline, while the Scotch-Irish and Germans settled farther west. The so-called cavalier origin of certain tidewater Virginians is an excellent example of how myth can bind tighter economic, and hence social, control of the coast over the hinterland; this was perhaps even more true in North Carolina.

The climatic range between north and south was in many ways the prime factor shaping provincial society. Until the eighteenth century there was little regional difference among the colonies. The unit size of farms in Virginia and Massachusetts Bay before the introduction of slavery was about the same and over 60 percent of the southern plantations were still small enough to be tilled by the owners themselves. The seed of the divergence lay in the fact that northern soil and climate produced a system relying on diversified crops, whereas the raising of a single staple crop—because ignorant forced gang labor could be easily introduced where the work was simple and uniform—was more profitable south of Pennsylvania. Tobacco, rice, and indigo fitted this formula well and were excellent cash crops for overseas trade. Furthermore, indentured white laborers worked usually no more than five to seven years to fulfill their contract and were then, with their children, free; but slavery was lifetime, and children of slaves, being owned by the master, were a supplementary cash flow.

Within a matter of decades, the southern and northern land systems went their separate ways and created societies with quite diverse features. Yet there were basic similarities as well. Leonard W. Labaree[2] analyzes the colonial epoch by dissecting the attitudes and deeds of the upper crust: "In spite of local differences the aristocratic position typified by the provincial councilors was basically the same throughout the colonies, whether it was that of the great land-owners of Virginia or New York, the rich merchants of Boston or Charles Town, or the Puritan magistrates of Connecticut. In varying degree and with varying emphasis, the ruling families everywhere upheld the religious, social and political, as well as the economic, views of the conservative governing class of colonial America."

Above all, it was land hunger that shaped these elites. Even the urban rich, including New Englanders, found most attractive the lordship of great domains. They were not only seeking the prime form of American wealth but, consciously or not, trying to imitate the English aristocratic mode of life. As Carl Bridenbaugh described it so well: "Nearly every rich Charlestonian sank his surplus wealth in land and slaves, turning planter as well as business man. Samuel Wragg bought Lord Shaftesbury's thirty thousand acre barony, and the Pinckneys, Manigaults and others followed his lead. At Boston Elisha Cooke and Samuel Waldo not only acquired lands, but became extensive speculators. Edward Shippen and Peter Boynton of Philadelphia maintained country estates and dabbled in western lands and the fur trade. Rare indeed was the Newport merchant who did not own an estate on Rhode Island or in the Narragansett country. But by far the most famous connection between counting house and broad acres existed at New York, where large holdings became notorious."[3]

As land mixed with blood among the elite in each colony through a network of intermarriages, so the two found hearth in politics. These men ran provincial affairs for their direct interest. The councilors, of course, were appointed by the governors or proprietors, but even on the lower levels—the judges, sheriffs, naval officers, auditors, secretaries, and treasurers —the appointments came from the ranks of the class of gentlemen. Before the early decades of the eighteenth century, the lesser aristocracy, not directly supping at the governor's table, ran the provincial assemblies. As these families enlarged their power, they controlled elections from behind the scenes much as in England at the same period the great Whig families, whose heads sat in the House of Lords, controlled elections to the House of Commons. "No matter how 'democractic' the suffrage might be, the voters were usually offered a choice on election day, when offered any choice at all, between men picked by the aristocratic leaders from among their own number."[4]

It can thus be stated that of more importance than the land jobbery that created estates larger in several cases than the entire bulk of European countries was the social and political structure that became fixed in the thirteen colonies as a result. Critics have stated that this view ignores the economic flexibility as well as the great opportunity afforded to ambitious immigrants. It is true that some of the huge land patents were dissipated by sloth and indifference while others were taken over by men more hard-working and tenacious. But what a distinguished historian called the "little groups—'oligarchies' or 'aristocracies' which dominated politics and society alike,"[5] survived the changing fortunes of individuals. An economist might label this system as government promotion and development of the state through legal and illegal corruption for the benefit of favored individuals.

Under the welter of facts and what seem to be contrary views, the colonial period had stamped on it certain earmarks. There was patrician rule of society based to a large extent on land acquired through grants or speculation, with power exercised by means of appointed councils and controlled assemblies.[6] And this power was used to hold down land taxes,[7] evade quitrents, and enlarge the land holdings of the elite. The revolts over quitrents and arrogant British governors were not so much against arbi-trary authority as they were opposed to its use for the benefit of absentee English landlords rather than colonial ones. The growing dissatisfaction with the role of the Crown in many respects was a desire to hold on to local power, based on what had already been seized by home-grown aristo-crats, and had little to do with theoretical arguments about popular gov-ernment and the so-called rights of man.

Part Two

Land and the American Revolution

9

Preamble

"One generation passeth away and another generation cometh, but the earth abideth forever."

Ecclesiastes

Humankind is a tall pine tree thrusting from earth, and where each crop of cones may fall, one can never know. This was more true of the eighteenth century than most others, for what Americans call the French and Indian War, and Europeans call the Seven Years War, then followed by the American Revolution, were spasms in a long-term rivalry between England and France. The German military writer Karl von Clausewitz defined peace as an interval between wars, and never was the definition more true than at that time. Starting in 1689 and lasting till 1815, with four wars already fought before the Napoleonic period, this violent upheaval has been called the Second Hundred Years War by some historians.

That phase known as the Seven Years War, from 1756 to 1763, was fought in Europe, North America, India, the Atlantic coastline of Africa, the islands of the Caribbean, and even as far away as the Pacific Ocean. Its result was British control over the farthest reaches of a growing empire and, with great import for the future, England established Prussia as a foremost European power. Though the nominal start was a battle between English troops and the French along with their Indian allies in the Ohio Valley, this was only the match put to the dry wick of English and French gunpowder that exploded worldwide two years later. Beneath the sanguinary skins bubbled intense national pressures. In England the Tories and Whigs struggled for control.[1] Buried still farther under the political maneuvering for party power built the torque of a new class of workers opposed to factory bondage under the Industrial Revolution. Territorial acquisition, national conflict, party strife between land-rich nobles and money-rich merchants, as well as class strife between capital and labor, all splashed in fluid chaos and out from the ladle poured the French Revolution, which changed society forever.

In the North American aspect of this conflict an important factor was the disproportion between the English and French populations. Figures vary but it is certain that by 1750 there were less than 90,000 whites in French Canada while there were at least 1.25 million settlers in the thirteen colonies.[2] France, with a homeland of some 20 million persons, saw an emigration of a meagre 200 persons a year on average to Canada from 1608 to 1760, whereas about 200,000 Englishmen came to North America during the first century of colonization.[3] This figure does not include Germans and Scotch-Irish.[4] The local fighting power to draw from, the auxiliary support forces and the taxing ability, were overwhelmingly in favor of Britain. Indeed, it was only due to their Indian allies (who mainly supported the French for the very fact that they were no threat as settlers) that France kept the war effort in the New World going as long as it did.

As to the internal picture of the American provinces during this period, the colonial fever for land speculation was as strong as the imperial itch on the part of their masters. English and French kings strove for conquest of nations and continents; the local aristocrats in the colonies, backed by their partners in London, passionately sought great private estates.

Yet no period in American colonial history is more difficult to penetrate than that which began with the forming of several Virginian western land companies in the 1740s and ended with the American Revolution a generation later. So many forces and counterforces were involved both in America and England, so much silent influence is not part of the record, we are left with a sense of confusion after all the available facts are put together. It was a wide panorama centered on the impotence of the Indians before masses of white settlers moving westward; the clash of Pennsylvania and Virginia interests; and the desire of English lords, against official British policy, to suck the fruit of land speculation. Many of the great American revolutionary leaders were involved, especially George Washington, Patrick Henry, and Benjamin Franklin.

The structure of most colonial society, as has been pointed out, was based on land acquisition. At one sweep, as a result of the French and

Indian War, an enormous territory—many times the size of the seacoast colonies—was dangled before the avid eyes of the colonial leaders, who were already well seasoned in the ways of seizing land. Their greed, however, was blocked by the Proclamation of 1763, a result of the end of the French and Indian War, which clearly defined the eastern slopes of the Appalachian Mountains as the limit of settlement. To get around this wall some of the best minds of colonial America and imperial England bent their efforts.

As a separate factor, the conflict between Pennsylvania merchants involved in the Indian trade and Virginia speculators interested in western land came to a head, with actual armed clashes; it seemed at times to exceed the passions fired by warfare with the Indians.[5] Border problems added fuel to the fire. The frontiers of the northern colonies (aside from some dubious western claims on the part of Connecticut) were rather clearly defined. But those of the central and southern colonies were indefinite to the west and unclear each with respect to the others.

Within each colony there were competing factions as well. In Virginia the Loyal Company, led by Dr. Thomas Walker and rooted in the piedmont counties, was a rival of the Ohio Company, a tidewater speculation in which the Washington family was prominent. In Pennsylvania the Penn proprietary collided with the forces headed by Benjamin Franklin, the Whartons, and Joseph Galloway. Sir William Johnson of New York, superintendent of Indian affairs for the northern colonies, used his connections with the Indians of the Six Nations not only to enlarge his personal empire but also to obtain land concessions for certain speculative companies. The fur traders, who had suffered losses in the French and Indian War and the subsequent Indian uprising under Chief Pontiac, combined in a pressure group, self-styled the "Suffering Traders," to lobby for western lands as compensation. Some fur traders opposed all white settlement beyond the Alleghenies as detrimental to their business. To complicate matters further, in all the factions there were highly placed individuals who were quite willing to shift position in return for personal share participation in speculative companies.

Overriding the colonials were the English lords, anxious to repeat their earlier successes in obtaining for a pittance vast tracts of American land by commanding the king's ear. Sometimes working with the royal governors, sometimes with powerful individual colonists, often against government policy expressed in the 1763 Proclamation, the influences brought to bear on the British Board of Trade and the Privy Council were enormous and often self-contradictory.

In this vast welter of events, private letters are a surer guide than official policy statements. With rare exceptions, we can only chart by one clear star and that is self-interest. A key to power and money in the eighteenth century was land and, lacking a hereditary noble class, this was even more true in colonial America than in Europe. The proudest English aristocrat and the most radical American libertarian were united in their passion to obtain the fertile western acreage that had fallen, so to speak, from heaven as a result of the French defeat in the Seven Years War.

The forces lining up for the American Revolution threw their dark shadows in these maneuvers to acquire land. The poor white settlers, "illegally" streaming west of the Alleghenies, viewed the land companies with as much dread as did the Indians, and conceived freedom as free land title. The great speculators felt thwarted by the 1763 Proclamation, and defined independence as the right to scheme for enormous tracts. The English Privy Council saw unhindered westward movement as American insolence, not only disloyalty to Crown policy but also a grave danger to British control of trade and manufacture. Those colonists who were stirred by traditional loyalties or too conservative to be swayed by abstract political doctrines blowing in from French intellectuals, supported England; many of those who did not, tried to ride the gravy train or straddle the fence. Western land speculations, thus, are a very important radar to trace the coming American Revolution.

10

The Ohio Company and the French and Indian War

"The neighborhood of the French to our North American colonies was . . . the greatest security for their dependence on the mother-country, which I feel will be slighted by them when their apprehension of the French is removed."

The Duke of Bedford

The aristocracy of Virginia depended on constant new injections of fertile land to replace the soil wasted by tobacco production, as well as for speculative resale to immigrants. Since Virginia, by the terms of its original grant, stretched to the "South Sea" or indefinitely westward, the interlocking executive and legislative oligarchy satisfied this need by successive land grants until the colony advanced through the Shenandoah Valley and up the crests of the Alleghenies. The problem at this point was that the French, backed by the Indians,[1] asserted that the land beyond the mountains was their territory. This was the immediate cause of the French and Indian War.

The area involved, the Ohio Valley, was claimed by both England and France though ordinary intelligence would assume it belonged to the Indians, who had inhabited it for thousands of years before the arrival of the white man. England based its right on the discoveries of Cabot and, more directly, on the 1713 Treaty of Utrecht by which the Iroquois and their territory came under British protection. The French argued from prior discovery, strengthened in their case by actual occupation. Given Eu-

EUROPEAN CLAIMS IN NORTH AMERICA, 1750. From *A New History of the United States*, by William Miller, New York, 1958. Reproduced by permission of Virginia Miller.

ropean terms of reference, the Gallic claim was stronger. In fact, Governor James Glen of South Carolina in 1753 admitted that the area belonged to the French. However, as in most such matters, the military power of the stronger established ultimate "legitimacy."

In 1743, James Patton, a well-connected Virginian, petitioned the council for 200,000 acres of land "on three branches of the Mississippi and the waters thereof," based on settling one family for each thousand acres. This was a typical speculative land deal, except for the novelty of the location, which was technically in territory claimed by France. The Virginia council, after two years of mulling, granted Patton 100,000 acres,[2] an action that probably had no legal basis. The other 100,000 acres in Patton's petition were given to John Robinson and a group of his associates on the council. This was obviously a logrolling deal.

John Robinson, at the time of the patent, was treasurer of the colony and speaker of the House of Burgesses[3] from 1738 to 1766, two of the most powerful political positions in Virginia after the governor. The Robinsons were related to the Randolphs by marriage and the two families formed a most important political axis. (As an aside, we get a better view of the background of the monies changing hands in such land grants through the unexpected death of John Robinson in 1766, when it leaked out that his account as treasurer of the colony was short by £102,000, an enormous sum. So many of the top men of Virginia were involved in this defalcation that a public investigation was quashed.)

Thomas Lee, of the patrician Lee family, was a member of the council (and later president) when the patents were given to Patton and Robinson. He must have immediately seized on the rich potential, for within two years Lee, with the frontiersman Thomas Cresap and Lawrence Washington (the older half-brother of George Washington), started to campaign for a grant of 500,000 acres to a new land company named the Ohio Company.

Sir William Gooch, the acting governor of Virginia, was hesitant as to whether his power included the right to grant land west of the Alleghenies, a hesitancy strengthened by his support of a faction of the Virginia oligarchy opposed to that of the Lees. He wrote to the Board of Trade in England for an opinion. A very rich London Quaker tobacco merchant, John Hanbury, was then given shares in the newly formed company, and directly petitioned the board, stating that the aims of the company were to settle the Ohio country and extend British trade among the Indians living beyond the Alleghenies. Lawrence Washington was also dispatched to London to gain the support of the Fairfax contacts, into whose family he had married.

After resolving certain points and receiving approval from the Privy Council, in March of 1749 the Board of Trade instructed Sir William Gooch to make the grant, stipulating that a fort should be built and that after two hundred families were settled on the initial patent of 200,000 acres of land, an additional 300,000 acres would then be given on similar terms.

The Ohio Company shares were owned by the cream of Virginia society: Fairfaxes, Lees, Carters, Harrisons, and Masons were in the forefront. Three Washingtons were included (young George being one), twenty shareholders were burgesses, nine served on the council, two became presidents of the council, and one became acting governor. Of the non-Virginians, four were top London merchants, one was lieutenant-governor of North Carolina, and five were leading men of Maryland. The Ohio Company shareholders, thus, were among the richest and most powerful men of the Chesapeake colonies in alliance with English commercial interests.

The French were gravely concerned. Backed by such men, supported by an official act of the Privy Council in London, and dedicated to settle lands in what was considered French territory, the Ohio Company of Virginia was correctly viewed as an arm of imperial British policy, whose aim was to drive a wedge between French Canada and its Louisiana Territory. The French reacted by seizing all English traders in the Ohio country and then built a chain of forts in what is now western Pennsylvania.

Robert Dinwiddie had replaced Sir William Gooch as acting governor of Virginia in late 1751. Dinwiddie, also an Ohio Company shareholder and a great partisan of the company interests, reacted in outrage. He sent a message to the French ordering them to depart from the disputed area. The messenger was another company shareholder, young George Washington, who first stepped onto the stage of history at this point. The message, rejected by the French, was in fact the start of the French and Indian War.

The rest is history. The fort that Governor Dinwiddie built in the contested region was overrun by the French. General Braddock, sent by the British to punish the French, was routed. Hostilities commenced along the entire frontier, though the main action of the war in America was fought in the north. In two years, the conflict spread to Europe and then became the first incontestable world war in which England, Prussia, and Hanover eventually defeated France, Austria, Russia, Sweden, Spain, and Saxony.

It would be specious to state that the speculative activities of the Ohio Company were the sole reason for a war that devastated several continents. However, without a doubt the mellow combination of pocketbook and patriotism of Virginia's governor and his fellow aristocratic Virginian shareholders did initiate this famous war. Kenneth P. Bailey strains to be objective in *The Ohio Company of Virginia,* the classic account. But the facts overwhelm him.

> The Ohio Company, including Dinwiddie's activities as a member, had been under suspicion in Virginia for some time. As has been pointed out, every act of Dinwiddie's which had to do with the west was met with apprehension on the part of the public, particularly the lower house. Most of his efforts to build up an army for the defense of the west met with stubborn resistance from this legislative body. Nor was the opposite to be expected. The house had no desire to push the interests of a speculative company from which they derived no benefits. . . . If the war were fought over economic causes, it seems to have been really for the economic interests of the very few. . . . There was too much danger that it would result in "a rich man's war and a poor man's fight."[4]

It may be added that except where specific Ohio Company shareholders were involved, the aggressive actions of Governor Dinwiddie were discouraged by the other colonies as well. Pennsylvania, whose fur traders feared an Ohio Company dominance, opposed Dinwiddie. Maryland refused to assist Virginia until the progress of the war aroused patriotic vigor. North Carolina, under the governorship of an Ohio Company shareholder, naturally gave aid. Governor James Glen of South Carolina felt the English position was unsound, and New York shared these doubts. In Virginia itself the war was unpopular for reasons just quoted. Kenneth P. Bailey concludes: "On the whole it seems fair to suggest that the recalcitrant position of the colonies was due in part to their animosity toward the Ohio Company. They could see no reasons for sending men and money to advance the personal business of these speculators."

What no one except a few prescient European diplomats realized was that in removing the barrier of the French from the Ohio Valley, the Americans no longer needed British protection. The American Revolution in fact began with victory in the French and Indian War.

11

The Proclamation of 1763

"Secure some of the most valuable lands in the King's part, which I think may be accomplished after a while, notwithstanding the proclamation, that restrains it at present, and prohibits the settling of them at all. . . ."

George Washington to his land agent, William Crawford, 1763

At the end of the Seven Years War the British were triumphant but broke. William Pitt, much loved by the bankers and merchants for his reckless spending, had piled up a colossal debt. Though by the terms of the Treaty of Paris in 1763 (which actually followed three years after the end of fighting in North America) the French gave up all American soil east of the Mississippi River except the city of New Orleans, the Indians were still in control of all land west of the Alleghenies.

Pontiac, chief of the Ottawas, was aghast at the doom he so clearly foresaw for his people. In 1763, seeing the colonists push forward without end in overwhelming numbers, now no longer held back by French counterweight, he organized a heroic defense, called Pontiac's Conspiracy in the double-tongue of history. Rallying all the tribes east of the Mississippi, except the Iroquois—though even one tribe of the Six Nations joined—Pontiac attacked and took every English outpost except Fort Pitt (now Pittsburgh) and Detroit. In this most formidable Indian uprising in all colonial history, General Amherst—a soldier more blundering, if possible, than General Braddock—lost at least five hundred regulars while over two thousand colonists were killed. Since the Indians did not write chronicles, we do not know their losses. The inevitable result was captured in the felicitous words of a typical American historian: "At last the savages, becoming, as always, disunited and straitened for supplies, sullenly made peace; and at the call of the rich and now free Northwest, caravans of English immigrants thronged thither to lay under happiest auspices the foundations of new States."[1]

This most happy result was not seen in quite the same way by either the Indians or the British. The last thing the Exchequer in London wanted, with a doubled national debt of £140 million sterling at the conclusion of the peace treaty, was a draining series of Indian wars. The land speculations of rich colonials and the need for virgin tobacco fields were smaller factors to them than the cost of Indian conflict. This position was sharpened by British resentment over what it considered the poor colonial contribution, both in men and money, during the French and Indian war.

The shift in English policy regarding western lands in fact preceded Pontiac's war by several years. The first sign appeared in 1758 when by the Treaty of Easton the colony of Pennsylvania, where Quaker policy anticipated the British attitude, pledged the Shawnee and Delaware tribes that no settlements would be made west of the Alleghenies without Indian consent. This was confirmed the next year by George Croghan, deputy to Sir William Johnson in northern Indian matters, followed by Colonel John Stanwix and General Monckton. In 1761, Colonel Henry Bouquet, the Swiss-born hero who had relieved Fort Pitt during Pontiac's War, backed up the accord signed at Easton by issuing, with the approval of his superiors, a proclamation that enlarged the Pennsylvania agreement to all lands west of the Alleghenies: "This is therefore to forbid any of his majesty's subjects to SETTLE or hunt to the WEST of the ALLEGHENY mountains on any pretence whatever," and stipulating that court martial would result if the order were violated.

The Proclamation of October 7, 1763, repeating this wording as official British policy, was in reality only recognition of what had become guiding principle, making official the Treaty of Easton and Bouquet's proclamation. The sole exceptions, which then became very important in later speculative land schemes, were valid titles already given in Virginia (as well as those held by the French) to land lying west of the proclamation line. England, in taking over France's American territory, besides picking up an estimted 150,000 to 200,000 hostile Indians, had also inherited some 70,000 Frenchmen, many with extensive estates.

The British ministers, on learning of the Indian uprising under Pontiac, admitted that the 1763 Proclamation had been too long delayed. It

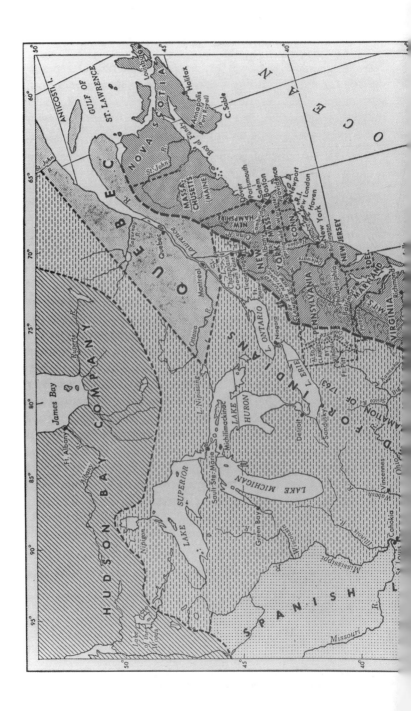

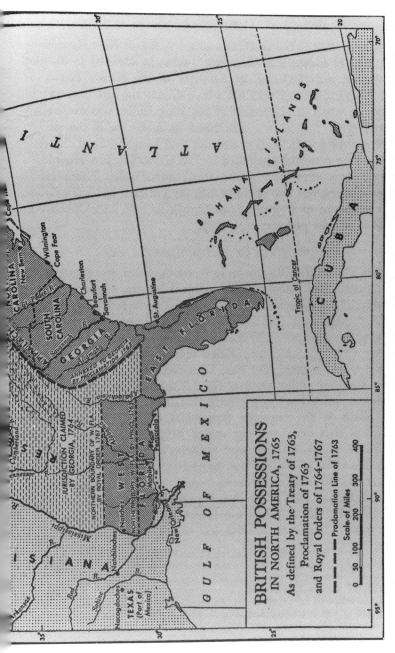

BRITISH POSSESSIONS IN NORTH AMERICA, 1765. As defined by the Treaty of 1763, the Proclamation of 1763, and Royal Orders of 1764-67. From *The Coming of the Revolution, 1763–1775*, by Lawrence H. Gipson, New York, 1954. Reproduced by permission of HarperCollins Publishers.

must not be assumed, however, that this solution was viewed as permanent and congealed policy; the initial thought was to reassure the Indians in order to reduce the heavy cost of frontier garrisons, to protect the fur trade, and, gradually, to extend the old colonies or create new ones.

Though sincerely issued by the English government, at best the 1763 Proclamation could only hold back but not prevent westward movement. The colonial population was doubling every twenty to twenty-five years and "Canute might as well have commanded the waves not to advance as for the British government to forbid the Americans, in their distress [because of the post-war depression], to seek new fortune across the mountains. . . ."[2] It has been estimated that in three years alone, from 1765 to 1768, some thirty thousand whites ignored the proclamation. The removal of the French, and the impotence of the Indians, meant that nothing but armed force could restrain the pioneers; and many of the British officers and colonial militia were too actively involved in land speculation to put into effect the terms of the hated order. The real question, given the impossibility of enforcing the proclamation, was whether the land would be given over to small freeholders or patented to syndicates of rich colonials and British lords for marking up at great profit in resale to settlers.

The general colonial view of the 1763 Proclamation, after the initial shock of disbelief, was that it was a ruse to lull the Indians. The reaction of George Washington, who continued his speculations as though nothing had happened, was typical of upper-class southern provincials.[3] More worldly persons such as Benjamin Franklin knew, and acted on the knowledge, that by means of the 1763 Proclamation the lords of England were buying time to organize their own patents. The best connected colonists, as a result, rushed to use influence both with their royal governors and with their friends in England in order to get in on the ground floor of a new spate of land speculations.

This was the genesis of such partnerships, to mention only the most prominent, as the Mississippi Company, the Illinois Company, the Indiana Company, and the Vandalia Colony. Putting aside their individual success or failure, the origins, share interest, and business methods of the men behind these speculative projects tell much about the tensions leading up to the Revolution and the subsequent evolution of American politics.[4]

12

Evading the 1763 Proclamation: The Land Companies

"The government consists of a gang of men exactly like you and me. They have, taking one with another, no special talent for the business of government, they have only a talent for getting and holding office. Their principal device to that end is to search out groups who pant and pine for something they can't get and promise to give it to them. Nine times out of ten, that promise is worth nothing. The tenth time it is made good by looting A to satisfy B. In other words, government is a broker in pillage."

H. L. Mencken

The Ohio Company Whelps the Mississippi Company

The Ohio Company of Virginia, which had been launched with such golden hopes, soon ran into problems. The long years of the French and Indian War paralyzed all activity, preventing the company from meeting the terms of a grant that called for settling two hundred families. Also, the internal politics in Virginia was hostile to the company, not only because of public ire against its role in starting the war, but also because of party politics.

This hostility requires some explanation. Although the aristocratic class formed a united front when its collective privileges were threatened, internally it was divided (as was true of New York Colony in this same period)

109

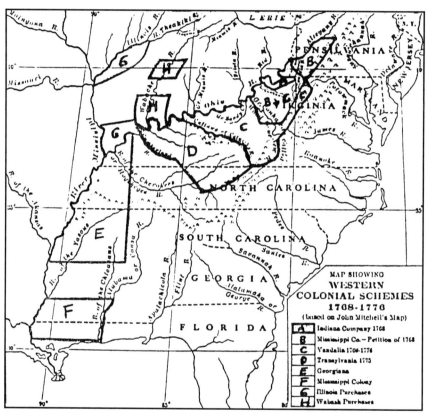

MAP OF THE MAJOR LAND COMPANIES, 1768–1776.

into two competing factions. One might be called the Tidewater or Northern Neck clique and the other the Albemarle and Shenandoah clique; or plantation owners living north or south of the Rappahannock River. Though not so sharply defined, it was also the older aristocracy against the new blood. The Ohio Company was dominated by old Virginians from the tidewater area. The newly rich group from the southwestern part of Virginia was composed of more aggressive men, with the outstanding exception of George Washington. The Loyal Company and the Greenbrier Company, new partnerships created by Piedmont speculators, were thus rivals of the Ohio Company.[1]

The power of each faction ultimately depended on its influence with the governor, whose cooperation was necessary not only to receive land patents, but also to set the terms. Under Sir William Gooch, acting governor in the 1740s, the Ohio Company was out of favor. In fact, in order to receive its original grant, the shareholders of the Ohio Company had to appeal to influential interested parties in London to put pressure on the Virginia government to act: as mentioned, that was the reason for Lawrence Washington's trip to England in 1748. The Ohio Company charter was only secured due to the influence of the Duke of Bedford, who received a share as reward, rather than by the Virginia council.

Things changed when Colonel Thomas Lee, a leading member of the Ohio Company, became pro tem governor after the departure of Sir William; and the fortunes of the company were definitely up when Robert Dinwiddie, whose interest in the Ohio Company preceded his arrival in America (as is known by correspondence between Lawrence Washington and Dinwiddie while the latter was still in London), was appointed to the top Virginia office in 1751.

The relation of the Ohio Company to the French and Indian War has been noted. In 1757, Dinwiddie resigned because of ill health and returned to England. The position of the company then weakened. During the years of the war the shareholders, who by their own statement had spent over £10,000 to advance the undertaking, believed, with reason, that after the eviction of the French their patent would be renewed. The change in British policy, culminating in the 1763 Proclamation, came as a tremendous blow.

Another problem the company faced was that the partners, though among the leading aristocrats of colonial Virginia, had little influence on the lords controlling British policy in London. Benjamin Franklin and his colleague Samuel Wharton, who were far more astute in such matters, knew where to apply pressure and whom to corrupt. The Virginia autocrats, in their private cocoon of black slaves and small white planters and mechanics, reacted with rage when they could not have their way: that rage transformed itself into a colony whose aristocrats were united in revolution a few short years later. At this earlier point of time, however, their inability to break through the rules established by the 1763 Proclamation left them unable to pursue their speculative activities. Losing favor in Virginia itself after the departure of Governor Dinwiddie, the Ohio Company shareholders were paralyzed.

One possible solution was another grant. The leading lights of the company felt they might improve their chances by making a claim to a new area. Much of the same group holding Ohio Company stock—including George Washington and his half-brother, John Augustine Washington; four Lees; Presley Thornton; and William and Henry Fitzhugh—organized a new scheme called the Mississippi Company, which, after originally exploring the possibility of a grant farther west, petitioned in 1768 for an area running on the far side of the Alleghenies from western Pennsylvania to what is now Kentucky. The original petition for a million acres in the Mississippi Valley was then enlarged to two and a half million acres. The group requested that the king forego quitrents, fees, and taxes for twelve years, in return for which they would attempt to establish two hundred families on the land. Arthur Lee, whose father had been the initial sponsor of the Ohio Company, was in London and acted as agent.

The Mississippi Company made little headway. The truth was that the Virginians behind this new company did not have sufficient influence and, as will be seen, another group of colonials, mainly from Pennsylvania, were in this same period on the point of achieving a great coup in land speculation. As a final note, Washington recorded his total loss in the venture as a little more than £27.[2]

Some evidence seems to indicate that the Mississippi Company was formed as a diversion to give more weight to the Ohio Company claims. Clarence W. Alvord, whose two-volume study entitled *The Mississippi Valley in British Politics* is the lodestar from which all other ore of the period must be mined, speculates that the Virginia group hoped that by avoiding a frontal attack on the more powerful Pennsylvania syndicate (whose project, first called the Indiana Company, then the Walpole Company, and last Vandalia, overlapped the area desired by the Mississippi Company), more consideration would be given as a sop to their Ohio Company.

There appears to be some truth in this analysis, as shown by later events. The British ministry rejected entirely the petition of the Mississippi Company, one in which no English lords or merchant princes participated. However, to buy off pressure from shareholders of the Ohio Company, which had some British participation, two shares of the total of seventy-two shares in Vandalia were given to Ohio Company members. Colonel George Mercer, the company agent in London, also got an extra share for his "cooperation." To quiet the claims of the veterans of Washington's 1754 Virginia regiment in the French and Indian War, the Vandalia sponsors also assigned these men a total of 200,000 acres from their much larger patent, of which Washington ended up with 40,000. The future first president was not happy since his shares in the Ohio Company and the Mississippi Company were larger than his land claim under the veterans' bonus. But most of the other persons involved accepted the settlement with varying degrees of resignation.

The Greenbrier and Loyal Companies

It will be recalled that the Virginia council in 1745 made two grants each for 100,000 acres: one to James Patton and the other to John Robinson. Several years after his patent, John Robinson formed the Greenbrier Company to market the acreage. The company took its name from the Greenbrier River on which the grant lay, the area involved being the first lateral river bank beyond the Alleghenies. Eventually the Greenbrier Company became a satellite of a much larger speculation created by Robinson and his friends.

When the Ohio Company was about to receive its charter by means of pressure from London, Speaker Robinson and his legislative cronies decided to organize a still more ambitious scheme. Called the Loyal Company, it was launched and received both council approval and the governor's sanction without trouble. The grant was for 800,000 acres along the western frontier of Virginia. In terms of present geography, most of the Ohio Company patent fell in West Virginia, as well as a part of western Pennsylvania; while the Loyal Company patent fell mainly in what is now Kentucky.

The Loyal Company was backed by the newer aristocrats from the Piedmont. The more prominent were Peter Jefferson, father of Thomas Jefferson and the wealthiest squire in Albemarle County; Dr. Thomas Walker, a practicing physician and surgeon without medical degree; John Lewis, whose family enters prominently in Revolutionary annals; five Merriwethers, who were related by blood to almost anyone of importance in western Virginia; Francis Thornton; and Edmund Pendleton. Most of these men were members of the council or assembly. Pendleton was the front man for the John Robinson interests, Lewis represented the Shenandoah Valley and the others were mainly from Albemarle County. The older aristocrats were not completely excluded: for example, Francis Thornton and Thomas Nelson were members of both the Loyal Company and the Ohio Company. In general, however, there was a clear line separating the two competing cliques.

In contrast to the Ohio Company patent, the Loyal Company was not required to settle any families. The grant was made solely as a speculation and, put simply, was a present that the leaders of the legislature, with the governor participating, made to themselves. This elicited a complaint to the Crown from George Mercer, representing the Ohio Company in London. Listing the various land patents to the dominant political faction in the Virginia legislature, he wrote, "No less than 1,350,000 acres of land were granted by the governor and council to borrowed names and private land-mongers who were incapable of making effectual settlements. . . ."[3] The complaint was true but had no ring of pure silver, for it was the whine of one group of hungry speculators preempted by another.

Dr. Thomas Walker, the heart and brains of the Loyal Company, deserves special notice. Agent of the Loyal Company for some forty-one years, Dr. Walker had his finger in every official land activity in Virginia during the second half of the eighteenth century. Like similar top Virginians, a dazzling marriage inaugurated his career. It was to Mildred Thornton, widow of Nicholas Merriwether, whereby he acquired the Castle Hill estate, some 11,000 acres in Albemarle County. Mildred Thornton was also a cousin to George Washington and, though Walker and Washington were antagonists in the feud between the Ohio Company and the Loyal Company, they were partners in other projects, such as the Great Dismal Swamp venture. Walker was also the bosom friend and neighbor of Peter Jefferson, and became guardian of Thomas Jefferson after his father's early death. Through the force of his personality and a web of family ties, Walker's faction dominated the land grants of the Virginia council for decades. Dr. Walker also had that charming ability to siphon personal interest into official appointments, a characteristic of great success everywhere. It was due to his Machiavellian hand that the Loyal Company succeeded where the Ohio Company failed.

The French and Indian War suspended development plans and in 1763 the Virginia council, under direct orders from London, notified company officials that the Loyal Company patent was not to be renewed, because of the proclamation forbidding settlement west of the Alleghenies. The reaction of company shareholders was not what might be thought from loyal colonists, for Walker and his associates of the Loyal Company went ahead in open violation of the proclamation. Going one step further, the company, in 1766, assured of the support of William and Thomas Nelson of the council and, it would seem, the governor himself, urged all who had quitted their claims during the war to return to them on pain of forfeiture—an entirely illegal action.[4]

By winking an eye the Virginia government could overlook those subrosa actions, but the Crown still stood in the way. The difficult solution to this problem would be to move the boundary farther west by treaty agreement with the Indians. It would seem that only a miracle could achieve such an aim in view of the 1763 Proclamation, but Dr. Walker set to work.

The first step was to be sure that Virginia commissioners at Indian treaties involving land changes would go along. The Virginia legislature dutifully chose two men to represent the colony at such treaties: Colonal Andrew Lewis, son of John Lewis and head of the Greenbrier Company, and Dr. Thomas Walker, head of the Loyal Company! Like Dinwiddie and Washington representing both government policy and their own pocketbooks as shareholders in the Ohio Company, Lewis and Walker could now proceed with unclouded vision.

After the Treaty of Fort Stanwix in 1768, which established the boundary lines to the north of Virginia, Lord Shelburne in London was anxious to settle the entire western frontier in order to avoid Indian wars. He ordered John Stuart, superintendent of Indian affairs for the southern department, to fix the frontier to the south. Lewis and Walker, the Virginia commissioners, wanted to move the boundary as far west as possible in order to make legitimate the claims of the Greenbrier and Loyal companies. John Stuart, however, agreed with the Cherokee chiefs that the line of the boundary should run to the mouth of the Great Kanawha River in what is now West Virginia, rather than farther west to the Ohio River alongside what we now call Kentucky. The Virginia commissioners worked through their political friends and the House of Burgesses passed a request that Stuart move the boundary to the Ohio River. The royal governor, however, had no choice but to back the superintendent of Indian affairs and, with the reluctant signatures of Lewis and Walker appended, the Treaty of Lochabar, South Carolina, in 1770, established the line at the Great Kanawha.

Then an odd thing happened. By agreement with the Cherokee chiefs, for "a promise of £500 that was never paid,"[5] the line was moved west to the Ohio River after treaty signing. It was obvious that much rum flowed. John Stuart did not object since the change was made with the consent of the Cherokees themselves. It is not difficult to guess who offered the money to the Cherokee chiefs, for the line of the Loyal Company claim now was extended even beyond the original grant.

Dr. Walker, apparently in fear of reversal by the Privy Council, went to work immediately. By December 16, 1773, some 980 surveys were made, on which basis 201,554 acres of land, slightly more than one-quarter of the original grant, were sold. Thomas Walker had succeeded, unlike the Ohio Company shareholders, in thwarting the declared policy of the British Crown. This was due to his close contacts with the Virginia legislature, many of whose members had a personal interest in his success. Indeed, the Virginia council was so subservient to Walker that when settlers established themselves on land that the Loyal Company no longer owned, after the revocation of the patent in 1763, the sheriff was ordered to remove the offenders unless they purchased their land from the company. In effect, settlers who by Virginia law had a preemptive right to fifty acres, were forced to buy land they had already improved from a company whose charter had lapsed. This would have been impossible, the evidence indicates, if it were not for the fact that Governor Dunmore in Virginia and William Legge, Earl of Dartmouth in England (who had succeeded to the office of colonial secretary) both were personally involved in the speculation.[6]

It almost goes without saying that Dr. Thomas Walker in 1775 represented Albemarle County in the Virginia assembly as a member of the Revolutionary Convention. Patriotism and land thirst were blood brothers in the Virginia planter aristocracy.

The Trader's Company, the Illinois Company, the Indiana Company, and Vandalia

Pennsylvania and Virginia were ferocious rivals in the West. The renowned merchants of Philadelphia were more interested in the fur trade than in land settlement, which would hurt their business. They attempted to block speculation in western land to the point that they became in effect allies of the Indians against the Virginia planters seeking new land. Then the long years of war, followed by the struggle of Pontiac against the in-rushing white tide, ruined their affairs. Perhaps worse, the secondary conditions of the 1763 Proclamation forbade all trade with Indians in rum and rifles. Only licensed traders, confined to designated posts, could continue as before.

A group of the most powerful Pennsylvania merchants pressed for compensation. These "Suffering Traders," as they called themselves, banded together and set up the Trader's Company. Their ambitious scheme required support from the highest political level. The chosen head was William Franklin, illegitimate son of Benjamin Franklin, who by influence through his father had been appointed governor of New Jersey in 1762 (against the violent opposition of the Penn family). It was understood, however, that William Franklin could not be known as a leading shareholder since the shift in British policy made such private lobbying contrary to public office. The "inside man" in London would be Benjamin Franklin, who had been sent there in 1764 by the Pennsylvania assembly to attempt to revoke the proprietary of the Penns. At the start, George Croghan was sent as liaison between the Trader's Company in Philadelphia and Benjamin Franklin in London. Croghan was a famous Indian trader with the invaluable asset of a Mohawk wife and a daughter married to Chief Joseph Brant of the Mohawks. It may be added that Croghan also acted as an independent agent for Sir William Johnson (with whom lived Molly, the sister of Chief Brant), who had separate instructions to make legal a huge grant of land in upper New York Colony that Sir William had wheedled out of his friends in the Iroquois confederation. Other Trader's Company shareholders were Joseph Galloway, Benjamin Franklin's closest business associate and the richest merchant of Philadelphia (who later was one of the prominent Tories); and the Philadelphia Indian traders of the firm of Baynton, Wharton, and Morgan, then teetering on the edge of ruin because of its war losses. Benjamin Franklin was doubly interested in the success of the project because he also had a financial interest in this firm.

Croghan and Franklin made little progress with Lord Hillsborough, appointed by the Crown to supervise Indian affairs. Hillsborough, who apparently could not be "touched," resolutely adhered to the terms of the 1763 Proclamation and took the irritating position that if colonial interests had been hurt during the Seven Years War, the Indians had likewise suffered.

George Croghan returned to America and met with Sir William Johnson in upper New York, where the two discussed a very clever way of getting around the proclamation. Many Frenchmen in the period of French control had acquired legal titles to large tracts of western lands, which were left undisturbed by the peace treaty. The new approach would be to purchase these titles.[7] Croghan wrote a long letter to Sir William on March 30, 1766, after returning to Philadelphia, parts of which clarify the strategy:

> Soon after My Return hear from your Honours I Wrote you about the Scheme of purchasing what Ever grants the French was posesed of in the Illineois Cuntry and Informed your honour that Governor Franklin with some other Gentlemen hear had formed the Same Scheme. . . .

itt is Likewise preposed to aply for a Grant of 1200000 acerrs of Lands to the Crown in that Cuntry and to Take into this Grant two or three Gentlemen of fortune & Influence In England, and Governor franklan and those other Gentlemen Desier to know whome your honour would Chouse ther to be Concerned. . . .

the Sooner your honour Considers this plan & Writes to Governor franklin the Beter as one half of England is now Land Mad & Everybody there has thire Eye fixt on this Cuntry. . . .[8]

It is clear from this letter that though George Croghan had a very uneducated grasp of English spelling, he had a Ph.D. in Human Nature.

The Illinois Company was organized with the dual aim of purchasing French grants and applying for a new land grant. It was thus, like the Virginian ploy of spinning the Mississippi Company from the Ohio Company, a rebirth of the Trader's Company with the same shareholders. These men had, previous to the new entity's formation, bought out the lesser fry of the "Suffering Traders" for about thirty cents on the dollar. Now Sir William Johnson formally joined the group, though he, too, like Governor William Franklin, and for the same reason, insisted that his name not be made public. William Trent, speaker of the New Jersey assembly and chief justice thereafter, for whom the city of Trenton is said to be named, acquired an interest. Sir Henry Moore, royal governor of New York, accepted a piece as well. The intent was to make the Illinois Company appear to be a project of large colonial interest rather than a mere vehicle for reimbursement of war losses. The key positions of the new shareholders also would help speak to the right ears in London.

A formal proposal was made to the Crown for a land grant of 1.2 million acres lying between the Illinois and Mississippi rivers and as far north as the Wisconsin, an area much farther west than previous patents granted and now located in the state of Illinois. A proprietary colony was projected, owned by the shareholders with Sir William Johnson to be the future governor.

The heavy artillery was wheeled forward. Sir William wrote to British Secretary of State Henry S. Conway, enclosing the plan "at the request of several Gentlemen of fortune & character," emphasizing the benefits that would accrue but not mentioning his own personal interest. The royal governors of New York and New Jersey, both silent shareholders, roundly endorsed the project. Benjamin Franklin only criticized the small scope of the proposal since "there would [should] be nearly 63,000,000 acres—enough to content a large number of reasonable people"[9]: this from the man who had been sent to London by the Pennsylvania assembly to break the power of his own colony's proprietor to patent land and collect quit-rents. Benjamin Franklin, in letters written at the time, was optimistic about Shelburne's reaction but very concerned with Hillsborough.

The less than homespun philosopher was right. Lord Shelburne, in 1767, convinced the Privy Council of the utility of the proposal, which was then submitted to the Board of Trade. Lord Hillsborough, president of the board, dissented. At this time American affairs were growing more complex and the office of secretary of state for the colonies was created in 1768. Hillsborough was appointed to the position and then denied the petition. The Illinois Company died soon after childbirth.

"But Franklin and his friends had more than one string to their bow."[10] Another string related to the Earl of Shelburne's desire to fix the boundary line along the western edge of the colonies to avoid future Indian wars. Sir William Johnson, as superintendent of Indian affairs for the northern department, had this responsibility in his zone. Sir William, like Dr. Thomas Walker farther south, knew who to approach and how to get what he wanted, both officially and unofficially. The boundary treaty to be signed at Fort Stanwix (present site of Rome, New York) in 1768, was carefully planned. Trent and Wharton spent most of the summer with the Six Nations of New York distributing presents among the chiefs; then Sir William assembled the Iroquois leaders at Fort Stanwix after having conveyed there twenty boatloads of additional presents, as well as quantities of food and rum.[11]

Sir William proposed to the Indians that the border should be rectified to compensate the "Suffering Traders." The Iroquois gratified their friend by giving away a tract of land of some 3.5 million acres, bounded by the Ohio River on the west, the Allegheny Mountains on the east, and the Little Kanawha River on the south: that is, northern West Virginia. It should be pointed out that the Six Nations more readily assented because the area was the hunting grounds of Indian tribesmen tributary to the Iroquois but did not include their own lands.

Two days later, after more eating and drinking, the chiefs of the Six Nations willingly pocketed £10,460 for another enormous tract to the south and west, including areas in present-day Ohio and Kentucky. Here the fraud was even more overt, for the area was never a subject of the British arrangement for the western frontier and the lands definitely belonged to the Shawnee and the Huron, along with the Cherokee claiming a part as well. Sir William Johnson had no authority to buy the land, and the land did not belong to the seller. Sir William knew, however, that the other tribes were so terrified of the Iroquois that they might be forced to accept the concession. The "Suffering Traders" now really had their hands on something with which to barter.[12]

The Trader's Company, alias the defunct Illinois Company, now assumed a new form called the Indiana Company. The exact same shareholders were involved at first. In 1769, the year following the Treaty of Fort Stanwix, Samuel Wharton and William Trent went to London to plead the cause of this new company. They immediately ran against the rock that had shipwrecked all the colonial speculative deals, namely, Lord Hillsborough.

It is necessary to touch on the internal political situation in England at this time to understand the implacable opposition of Lord Hillsborough to American land speculation.

There was a split in the Whig party in the early days of King George III, most simply categorized by the phrases "Old Whigs" and "New Whigs." The split was between the older mercantile attitude and the new imperialist attitude. Mercantilism was an economic system of values based on exporting the largest possible quantity of a country's products and importing the least possible in order to establish the most favorable balance of trade. Colonial America had waxed fat on this system before 1763, the crucial date of a changing British system, for as part of the English bloc it was protected from foreign competition. As long as the colonists were content to raise tobacco, indigo, rice, and hemp; to catch fish; and to cut timber for masts, they were guaranteed the British market. In return, they could not manufacture and had to buy their finished products in the home country. Mercantilism was an article of faith in the eighteenth century and even a man as sympathetic to the Americans as William Pitt affirmed in his famous speech on the repeal of the Stamp Act, "that if the Americans should manufacture a lock of wool or a horse shoe, he would fill their ports with ships and their towns with troops."

The 1763 Peace of Paris, following the French defeat in the French and Indian War, had brought another school of thought to high places. Mercantilism also implied the protection of the colonies at the expense of the home country. Why, certain eminent men wondered, should not the colonies help to maintain a system so much for their benefit? Why should they not be taxed to pay for some of the costs of the Seven Years War and for the protection of empire?

The conflict of attitude betweeen the Old Whigs (the mercantilists) and the New Whigs (the imperialists) filtered down to every level. Lord Shelburne, who had issued the 1763 Proclamation, was an imperialist. His view was flexible and apparently foresaw a gradual enlargement of American empire, lulling the Indians while creating new provinces west of the Appalachians. This view, of course, was shared by the speculators, who wanted to receive large land grants cheaply and then sell them at great profit, and by the settlers as well, who hoped, under the preemptive laws of the various colonies, to get free land.

Lord Hillsborough, to the contrary, was the epitome of the Old Whig. In the gossipy words of Nathaniel William Wraxall, a contemporary: "The Earl of Hillsborough was a man of elegant manners and wanted neither ability nor attention to public business, but his natural endowments, however solid, did not rise above mediocrity."[13] Hillsborough was an aristocrat, an English lord with an Irish peerage; what made him so formidable, and quite eccentric in the eighteenth century, is that he was incorruptible. The basis of his sharp opposition to westward expansion is contained in a report he approved when president of the Board of Trade:

> We take leave to remind your Lordships of that principle, which was adopted by this Board, and approved and confirmed by his Majesty, immediately after the treaty of Paris, viz., the confining of the western extent of settlement to such a distance from the seacoast, as that those settlements should lie within the reach of the trade and commerce of this kingdom, upon which the strength and riches of it depend, and also of the exercise of that authority and jurisdiction which was conceived to be necessary for the preservation of the colonies in due subordination to, and dependence upon, the mother country.[14]

What could be done with such a man? He would not yield. He could not be bought. And he had the support of the king.

It was Samuel Wharton—to whose brother Thomas we owe the prestigious Wharton School of Finance and Commerce at the University of Pennsylvania—who thought of the answer.[15] The technique was to corrupt everyone around Hillsborough to the point that he must sink. It was not put so crassly: it carried the name of share participation. Wharton realized that the only way to swing the speculation was to enlarge the partnership to include the English elite, who would then unite in self-interest to pull down Hillsborough. He met a fellow spirit in Thomas Walpole, the great London banker and member of Parliament, second son of Horatio Lord Walpole and nephew of Sir Robert Walpole. By July 24, 1772, a company had been organized. Its personnel was selected with shrewd care. There never had been in the history of colonial land speculation a company like the Walpole Company, whose name was later changed to the Grand Ohio Company and, when successful, to the Vandalia Colony.

Almost the entire top level of British society became shareholders. The Walpole Company included, at first or later, the following British persons: Lord Camden, lord chancellor; Lord Hertford, lord chamberlain and close to the king; Lord Gower, president of the Privy Council; the "dissolute and needy" Lord Rochford, member of the Privy Council and secretary of state for the northern department; Richard Jackson, counselor of the Board of Trade; George Grenville, from 1763 to 1765 first lord of the treasury and chancellor of the exchequer; Earl Temple, brother of George Grenville; Anthony Todd, postmaster-general and superior to Benjamin Franklin; Thomas Pitt, of the powerful Pitt family; Sir George Colebrook, director of the East India Company; Grey Cooper, a secretary of the treasury; Thomas Pownall, formerly governor in turn of New Jersey, Massachusetts, and South Carolina, and member of Parliament; and three Walpoles—Robert, Richard, and Thomas himself.

The most prominent American shareholders were, of course, the same group who had initiated and guided the venture: Benjamin Franklin and his son, Governor William Franklin; four Whartons, including Samuel and Thomas; Sir William Johnson; William Trent; Joseph Galloway; and George Croghan. The Philadelphia firm of Baynton, Wharton, and Morgan had gone into the hands of receivers in 1767, and their successors in interest were a new aggressive firm represented by the Franks brothers.

The final organization of the company, which took place in December of 1769, had seventy-two shares, with Thomas Walpole holding eight shares, Samuel Walpole five shares, William Trent four shares, and the others one or two shares each.

With so many mouths to feed, the first step was to follow the sage advice formerly given by Benjamin Franklin and enlarge the area requested. The Walpole Company petitioned for 20 million acres, including the land ceded by the Six Nations at the Treaty of Fort Stanwix and the purchase illegally made two days later, as well as land due southwest of it. For this, the petitioners graciously offered to pay £10,460 sterling, which was the cost of the bribe to the Iroquois at Fort Stanwix; and they further agreed to set a quitrent of two shillings for every hundred acres, to commence after the expiration of twenty years. Then the claim was enlarged to 30 million acres (as jubilantly reported in an extant letter written by George Croghan in 1772), the reason being that the Indians to the south had agreed, for an undisclosed sum, to cede an additional area to white settlement.

It seemed that the project could not fail. Its very tidal-wave sweep, however, began to set up counter eddies. Most of the claims of the other land companies were submerged under the proposed Walpole patent. It will be recalled that various American pleaders from these other companies were soliciting in London at this time. Colonel George Mercer was trying to resurrect the Mississippi Company, and the Ohio Company was still gasping. These Virginians also had their English allies, whose financial interests would be quenched, and they set up a concerted howl. The British ministry was bombarded by many personal pressures and claims, and the treasury sent back the issue to the Board of Trade for review.

This gave Lord Hillsborough a golden opportunity. Opposed to both the Pennsylvania and Virginia companies, and desiring to forbid all settlement beyond the Alleghenies, he conceived of a strategy. He asked Virginia for an opinion as to the Walpole Company, knowing full well the answer; it may be added that Norborn Berkeley, Lord Botetourt, governor of Virginia, was a protégé of Hillsborough and could be relied on to respond as directed.

The *opéra bouffe* for all but the hapless Indians continued in the next scene with the death of Governor Botetourt before he could answer. William Nelson, president of the Virginia council and acting governor until a replacement could be sent (himself, with his brother Thomas, involved in the land companies so threatened by the Walpole group), drew up a reply strongly backing, as was to be expected, the claims of the Ohio Company against the Walpole Company.

Seeing the resolute opposition put up by friends of the Virginians, the executive members of the Walpole group followed the ancient wisdom that the donkey responds better to the carrot than the stick. On May 7, 1770, an agreement was signed whereby the Walpole Company turned two shares of its company stock over to the Ohio Company "in consideration of the engagement of their agent Col. Mercer to withdraw the application of the said company for a separate grant within the limits of the said purchase." Mercer himself received an extra share for his cooperation (as has been indicated in an earlier chapter). One day later, the happy colonel wrote the Board of Trade withdrawing his former petitions as the Ohio Company representative and declaring his hope that the Walpole grant would be approved. In the same month, Arthur Lee, representative of the Mississippi Company, was bought off by the receipt of two shares.[16] With Virginia in their pocket, the way was clear for the Walpole patent if only Lord Hillsborough could be sunk.

The stubborn Hillsborough still opposed the grant. This led to an extraordinary split in the government, with the Committee of Council for Plantation Affairs, packed with Walpole shareholders, fighting for the grant; while the Board of Trade, under the presidency of Hillsborough, stalled. The king solved the problem by the time-honored method of kicking Hillsborough upstairs, making him an earl, and asking for his resignation.

Lord Hillsborough retiring from office under protest, on August 1, 1772, the Board of Trade approved the Walpole patent, assented to by the Privy Council. Shortly thereafter, Benjamin Franklin wrote a letter to his son William, which started with the triumphant line, "At length we have got rid of Lord Hillsborough. . . ."[17] In May of 1773 the draft for a proprietary charter for the Vandalia Colony was submitted, the name being chosen because the queen was said to be descended from the royal line of the Vandals, then a greater honor than we might consider today. Walpole's group decided on a more appropriate name, the Grand Ohio Company, as patentees of the colony. Their work was aided by the appointment of Lord Dartmouth to Hillsborough's post, the news of which filled Franklin with great joy. Dartmouth, stepbrother of Lord North, the prime minister, was as venal as his predecessor was honest.[18] Very interested in colonial land speculation, he had obtained a personal grant in 1770 of 40,000 acres in East Florida and was an active partner in other Virginia schemes.

But history is inscrutable. This brilliant project, backed by the mightiest men in England and now supervised by a sympathizer, ran into a delaying action. In July of 1773, two months after the submission of the proprietary charter, the king's attorney and the solicitor-general requested a clearer definition of the boundaries. Despite enormous pressures, the matter dragged on for almost two years.

What had happened was that the weights and counter-weights caused this delay. Virginia shareholders in the Ohio Company, including George Washington, repudiated Colonel Mercer's sellout and continued, through their friends, to oppose Vandalia. General Thomas Gage, British commander in America, took a strong stand against the new colony, agreeing with Hillsborough that it was against England's interest to have colonials so far removed from the arm of the home government. British lords with interest in the fur trade fought against westward expansion. Courageous voices in His Majesty's opposition referred to the patentees as "consisting of Many Noble Lords & all the Secretaries in office, in Colours of no agreeable Hue."[20] Intelligent Britains and Americans were also uneasy that at least sixty thousand persons had already settled on the land to be given to the absentee owners, with the inevitable civil commotions that must accompany their expropriation. As troubles in India tied up the Privy Council, Benjamin Franklin, the prime colonial supporter, operating in England, was revealed—in the famous incident of the Hutchinson letters —as involved in quasi-treasonable activities and dismissed as deputy postmaster-general for the colonies.[21]

In spite of all these setbacks, the power of the Walpole group was too great to prevent Vandalia from being rejected. In May of 1775 a draft of the royal grant for the new colony was completed and submitted by

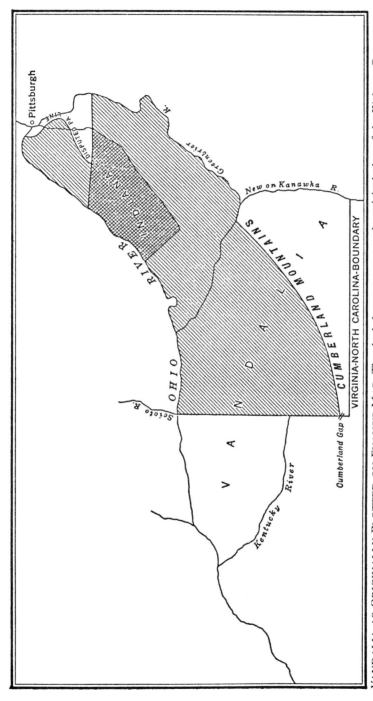

VANDALIA AS ORIGINALLY PLOTTED ON EVANS'S MAP. The shaded area represents the original plan of the Walpole Company for a proprietary colony, December 27, 1769. The unshaded area represents the revised plan of May 6, 1773, for the colony of Vandalia, the proprietary area remaining unchanged.

the solicitor-general. Its execution was suspended, however, by the Boston Tea Party, which threw the British ministry into a rage against Americans and American projects. The final settlement of the grant and victory came just a few weeks too late. Indeed, as in Greek mythology, even the gods are subject to Fate.

The Illinois and Wabash Land Companies

It was European creed that the king owned his domain and therefore he—directly or through such agents as the royal governors—could alone grant land. In 1757, Charles Pratt the English attorney-general (later the Earl of Camden, lord chancellor), with Charles Yorke, the solicitor-general, issued a legal opinion referring to India: "In respect to such places, as have been or shall be acquired by treaty or grant from the Grand Mogul or any of the Indian princes or governments, your Majesties letters patents are not necessary, the property of the soil vesting in the grantees by the Indian grants."

This legal opinion was discovered by William Trent when in London, who made out a copy eliminating the words "the Grand Mogul" so it might seem to apply to "Indian princes" in America rather than India. Lord Camden, by this time a leading member of the Walpole Company, probably tipped off Trent as to the implications.[22] Another version is that Samuel Wharton, while in London, requested the opinion from Lord Camden, who then twisted the earlier decision to apply to Indians in America.

Regardless, the implications were explosive. It meant that when individuals, whether Englishmen through agents or colonists themselves, would negotiate land purchases from Indian chiefs, title was valid and therefore the 1763 Proclamation no longer applied.

Trent forwarded the opinion to George Croghan with a letter signed by Thomas Walpole, Samuel Wharton, Lord Camden, and a certain Lord G. presumed to be Lord Gower, instructing Croghan to use it as authority to purchase land laying north of the Ohio River, Indian territory without question protected by the 1763 Proclamation and even beyond the limits of the Vandalia Colony then proposed. In effect three prominent Englishmen, two of them peers, and an eminent colonial, by use of a bogus opinion were conniving to violate the specific orders of the Privy Council.

Trent and Croghan, veteran frontiersmen, were then working with several Lancaster traders who were allied with Philadelphia merchants called David Franks and Company. Members of this latter company were the Franks and Gratz brothers, Jewish merchants associated with Scotch part-

MICHAEL GRATZ, PHILADELPHIA MERCHANT. Oil on canvas, by Thomas Sully.

ners. David Franks and Company was a commercial rival of Baynton, Wharton, and Morgan, which firm at this time was in perilous finances and apparently could not raise the money for such a speculation: it will be recalled that in the final organization of the Walpole Company, Baynton and Morgan had been replaced in interest by members of the Franks family. Croghan therefore went to David Franks with the legal opinion and accompanying letter. Franks resolved to act immediately.

In June of 1773, William Murray, western agent for David Franks and Company, arrived in the Illinois country and purchased from the Indians two large tracts of land, one at the junction of the Illinois and Mississippi rivers and the other at the confluence of the Ohio and Mississippi rivers. The partnership set up for this venture was called the Illinois Land Company, not to be confused with the Illinois Company formed by Benjamin Franklin with his Philadelphia friends.

The Franks-Gratz group had little political support in Pennsylvania, probably because of the connections of those excluded from the deal. They decided therefore to turn to Governor Dunmore of Virginia, a man known for his cupidity, notifying him that the company would recognize the authority of that colony.[23] Such a decision involved more than abstract love of Virginia. In October 1775, Murray purchased two additional large tracts of land on the Wabash River, north of the Ohio. Done in the name of the Wabash Land Company, Governor Dunmore headed its list of shareholders, followed by Governor Thomas Johnson of Maryland; Charles Carroll, the prominent landowner of Maryland; and merchants from Baltimore, Philadelphia, and London. The company must have been launched the year before, because it was at that time Lord Dunmore wrote a recommendation of acceptance to Lord Dartmouth without of course stating his personal involvement.

These crafty tactics were aborted by the storms of Revolution. Preparing for the future, however, the Illinois Land Company and the Wabash Land Company were reorganized under the combined name of the United Illinois and Wabash Land Companies, for which shares were sold during and after the war action. Among those who purchased shares were Robert Morris, called the financier of the Revolution; James Wilson, Philadelphia jurist who became a justice of the Supreme Court, and Silas Deane of Connecticut, agent of the Continental Congress in France. Following the Revolution, the company, aided by its prominent shareholders, brought its claims to the land before Congress. This story, however, is food for a future chapter.

Lord Dunmore's War for Land

John Murray, Earl of Dunmore, was sent to America as governor of New York and then transferred to Virginia in 1771. He was among the greedier of a very greedy tribe of Britons who came to the colonies to carve out a quick fortune. As can be expected, he dovetailed closely with many of the colonial leaders of these two royal colonies who shared his view that one hand washes the other. Clarence W. Alvord, dean of historians of British imperialism in the Mississippi Valley, called Dunmore "the greatest plunger of them all."[24] In Virginia, it was natural that Dr. Thomas Walker and Colonel Andrew Lewis became his closest associates. It may be added that Dunmore's reputation must have preceded his transfer, for the Scottish nobleman had already started to feather his nest in the New York Colony, where he had transferred several large land grants to himself in the western part of that province. Lord Dunmore was unusually protected from charges of corruption or irregularity, because his daughter was married to the Duke of Sussex, son of King George III.

Hemmed in by the proposed colony of Vandalia, which was now accepted as inevitable by the resentful Virginians, Dunmore and his speculative associates sought land that Virginia could still claim by charter right. The problem, of course, was the prohibition of all land grants west of the Alleghenies by the 1763 Proclamation. This difficulty the royal governor overcame by asserting that he thought the confirmation of the Cherokee boundary line, established by the treaty signed at Lochaber, South Carolina, in 1770, released him from the terms of the Proclamation. Lord Dartmouth replaced Hillsborough shortly thereafter as supervisor of American affairs, and graciously dozed while Dunmore made his plans.

The Shawnees, subordinate to the Six Nations, had accepted with sullen resignation Sir William Johnson's ceding of their lands in the present state of West Virginia. Their Kentucky hunting grounds were now being nibbled at by Dunmore and his speculator friends. From 1771 to 1773 the Shawnees attempted to form an eastern tribal confederacy similar to that created in 1763 by Pontiac to resist the white man; but through gifts to his Indian friends Sir William Johnson in the north restrained the Six Nations and the Delawares, while John Stuart did the same in the south with the Cherokees.

The evidence makes it quite clear that Dr. John Connolly, nephew of George Croghan and Lord Dunmore's western agent, desired to rouse the Shawnees to a desperate act, now that they were isolated, in order to break their power and seize their lands. It is known that Connolly, in April of 1774, sent an open letter to his land agents on the Ohio to be in readiness for war; and immediately thereafter groups of frontiersmen brutally murdered several Shawnee parties. The despairing Indians convulsively attacked in what history rightly calls Dunmore's War.

This indeed was what the speculators in western Virginian lands had waited for.[25] In urging volunteers, Colonel William Preston, commander of the militia of newly formed Fincastle County to the extreme west of settled Virginia, openly stated: "The Oppertunty we have so long wished for, is now before us."[26] The Virginia militia defeated the Shawnees on October 9, 1774, at Point Pleasant in one of the bloodiest battles of all the Indian wars, and the Shawnees acceded to the boundary line established at the northern line of the Ohio River. Lord Dunmore was now free to patent land to himself and his associates on the Ohio River in Kentucky.

There is documentary evidence of the maneuvers to foment this war. Patrick Henry met Thomas Wharton at Philadelphia in this same year when they were both delegates to the First Continental Congress. Wharton questioned Henry "& put some leading questions to discover if possible the real intentions of Dunmore for prosecuting this unjust war, and was happy enough to succeed . . . on which he (Henry) said, that he was at Williamsburg with Ld Dunmore when Doctor Connolly first came there, that Connolly is a chatty, Sensible man, & informed Dunmore of the Extream richness of the Lands which lay on both sides of the Ohio; that the prohibitory orders which had just been sent him relative to the Land on the hither side (or Vandalia) had caused him to turn his thoughts to the opposite shore, and that as his Lordship was determined to settle his family in America, he was really pursuing this war in order to obtain by purchase or treaty from the Natives a tract of territory on that Side."[27] The conversation took place only two weeks before the final battle at Point Pleasant when the Shawnee power was destroyed.

Transylvania

In the late 1760s, Patrick Henry, his brother-in-law Colonel William Christian, William Byrd III, and some associates formed a company to establish settlements in what is now western Kentucky. The stiff opposition of the British to western land speculation stopped them. Henry then heard of the opinion of Lord Camden and Charles Yorke—that a title to land was binding if bought from an Indian chief—and revived the Kentucky project in 1774, sending an agent to the Cherokee in order to negotiate a sale. For unknown reasons no purchase was made.

Richard Henderson and a group of seven North Carolinians, a competing group of speculators, pushed to success a similar project. At first called Richard Henderson and Company, later changed to Transylvania Company, on March 17, 1775, they bought from the Cherokee chiefs for the sum of £10,000 the land lying south of the Ohio River and between the mouths of the Great Kanawha and Tennessee rivers, an enormous expanse of about 20 million acres, nearly all of present Kentucky and a part of what is now northern Tennessee. The partners used as their model the previous Illinois Land Company purchases of David Franks and Company farther northwest. In this case we can safely assume that the Camden and Yorke legal opinion was a decisive factor, as it had been with the Illinois purchases, since Henderson had already sent out as agent Daniel Boone on his famous exploratory canvass in 1769 but was not able to act until there could be found some legal basis for purchase. Richard Henderson himself challenged the "absurd doctrine of Kings and Popes having right to claim and dispose of countries at their will and pleasure." He much preferred what he thought to be less absurd, that is, his having the same right.

Governor Dunmore of Virginia soon got wind of this purchase and, himself involved in speculative schemes relating to the area, denounced the "infamous Company of Land Pyrates," which from the royal view indeed they were. But this was March of 1775 and the days of British authority were numbered. Within the same week of Dunmore's condemnation, the Virginia convention (following Jefferson's *A Summary View of the Rights of British America,* published shortly before) denied the doctrine that all lands belonged to the king and rejected Dunmore's position. Henderson, who short years before would have been declared an enemy of the state, was now a hero.

In September of 1775 the Transylvania Company dispatched a representative to the Second Continental Congress, meeting at Philadelphia, asking for equal footing with the other colonies. The problem was sticky, since the Kentucky lands in question belonged to Virginia under its charter and, aside from natural pride of sovereignty, the Virginia speculators were unwilling to see such an attractive chunk of acreage slip through their fingers. The Virginia delegates to the Congress therefore insisted that their legislature approve any decision.

The outcome was a stalemate, which was in fact a victory for Henderson. Virginia's second convention, meeting shortly thereafter, did not take a position, mainly due to the influence of Patrick Henry. Since Henry himself had been interested in this same project, it has been inferred, and seems reasonable, that he and Henderson had a private understanding.

It was also at this time that George Rogers Clark made his first appearance as a land speculator, taking up patents under Henderson.

Trouble, however, was brewing at the Transylvania Company, that trouble which often comes to those with too quick a success when fishing in muddy waters. Transylvania had created a serious split among the Virginia speculators, for its boundaries included lands claimed by the Loyal Company and the Ohio Company. Thomas Abernethy points out that "Thomas Nelson and Richard Corbin belonged to the Loyal Company; Philip Ludwell Lee, John Tayloe and Robert Carter were members of the Ohio Company; while William Byrd, Ralph Wormeley and John Page had been associated with Patrick Henry in his unsuccessful plan to buy lands from the Cherokee in the spring of 1774."[28] Envy was bringing out the long knives; and Colonel William Preston, George Mason, and George Washington were particularly hostile.

Once independence was declared, the sympathy for Richard Henderson in Virginia evaporated. It was one thing to support the right to buy Kentucky land when the British Crown had sealed off the area from colonial speculation, but quite another when the Crown was out and the land bought by the Transylvania Company was within the charter of Virginia's border. The House of Delegates assembled in October of 1776 and the question of western lands was put on the agenda. Henderson himself was on hand to oppose the creation of a new Virginia county in the Kentucky country. Jefferson and Mason, however, fought for Virginia's interest; in the case of Mason, we can also assume he was fighting for his own private interests and those of his neighbor and colleague Washington as well, whose invisible influence was enormous as the new American commander-in-chief. In December, Kentucky was declared a new county of western Virginia. Though Henderson and his associates were deposed as independent proprietors, the question of who legally owned the soil was left open for a later date.

Though outside the limits of this immediate study, in 1778 the Virginia assembly decided to settle claims on the part of land companies, of which the Transylvania Company was one. By this time Henderson, a realist, was ready for compromise and declared his willingness to accept only a part of his company's original claim. Two hundred thousand acres were accordingly given on the Green River in Kentucky, not as good as almost the entire state but still a rather sizeable area of certain terrain for a man who, with his associates, had by luck picked the right historic moment to purchase lands declared off-limits by official British policy.[29]

Georgiana

General Phineas Lyman of Connecticut in June of 1763 organized the "Military Adventurers," a group of colonial officers from New England who—like George Washington and his regiment farther south—had served in the Seven Years War and were seeking western lands in the form of a veteran's bonus. General Lyman and his associates had taken over a former project conceived in 1755 by Samuel Hazard, a Philadelphia merchant who had proposed to the Crown that he receive a grant of land as lord proprietor of a colony running some one hundred miles west of Pennsylvania and Virginia. The new group, however, shifted their proposed patent much farther south, suggesting that it abut the northern limit of West Florida, thus blocking Spanish influence from the adjoining region west of the Mississippi River. General Lyman, who went to London to push his scheme, worked closely with Benjamin Franklin, the two attempting to persuade Lord Shelburne that a line of colonies, Franklin's Indiana Company (reborn later as Vandalia), and Lyman's project, would create a bulwark extending from the Great Lakes to the Gulf of Mexico.

Lyman, who strove to cultivate influential politicians in London for almost ten years, had neither the political savvy nor the monied connections of Samuel Wharton, who was petitioning there at the same time for what would become Vandalia. Lyman returned to Connecticut discouraged in 1772. Then news arrived of the fall of Hillsborough and the appointment of Lord Dartmouth. General Lyman, who had met Dartmouth and was well aware of that lord's avid interest in western land speculation, wrote and congratulated him, suggesting that the original idea of his colony be revived. He added that New England's population in general, and Connecticut's in particular, were growing so greatly that he could assure the new colony would be immediately populated.

A new name was proposed, Georgiana, to honor, and of course to flatter, George III. So sure of success was General Lyman—and though the records are not extant, we may be sure that Dartmouth himself would participate fully in the land grant—he sent out a committee to reconnoiter the region. This group chose the area to the north of newly settled Natchez. Some four hundred families from Connecticut and Massachusetts, including that of Lyman, began the journey to the new site with high hopes.

It was precisely then, namely October of 1773, that the British ministry determined to revise its method of land grants, a decision made on a higher level than that of Lord Dartmouth. As a result, squatters' rights were all that Lyman's company could obtain, and the idea of Georgiana went up in smoke.

Phineas Lyman stayed on despite this reverse. His is a sad story. Sixty-six-years old and of Tory sympathy, he and his followers rejected the Revolution. His wife died and in 1781 the Spaniards, who had joined the French in supporting the colonial cause—to break England and not in support of colonial liberty, it must be emphasized—invaded the pro-British area. Lyman died shortly thereafter. His supporters were driven out and made a five-month forced march, during which two of Lyman's daughters and many others perished, on the long trek across hostile Indian country to Savannah. This dire retreat through feverish swampland and tropical growth is one of the unsung epics of early Americana and deserves its troubadour.

West and East Florida

The two Floridas were taken over by the British as a result of the 1763 Peace of Paris. What was called East Florida is almost the same area as the present state of Florida. West Florida consisted of the present states of Mississippi and Alabama as well as a small corner of southeastern Louisiana to the east of the Mississippi River. The sole exception to this blanket acquisition was the city of New Orleans at the mouth of the Mississippi, which was left in French hands.

Monfort Browne was appointed lieutenant-governor of the vast area of West Florida, and then became the governor for a short while. History records that his main activity seemed to be patenting land to himself, as a result of which he owned long strips along the Gulf of Mexico. Governor Browne in 1771 then formed a company whose other two main shareholders were Lord Eglington and William Taylor, the latter having served as the military commandant of the southern district. The group then petitioned the Privy Council for the creation of a new proprietorship, the Mississippi Colony, covering an enormous region including the present state of Mississippi and the extreme western part of Alabama.

The Privy Council referred the matter to the Board of Trade, which was interested because such a proprietary might be used to bypass New Orleans as the emporium of trade for the furs collected throughout the Mississippi Valley. The final decision, however, was negative for much the same reason as Georgiana was turned down. The British ministry had come to a decision in 1773 that there should be a drastic revision in the method of disposing of the royal domain, and orders were given to hold up all land patents while the new rules were formulated. This decision swept away the speculative hopes of the shareholders of the Mississippi Colony, as it did those of Georgiana and the other flimsy proposed proprietaries.

During this same period an overflow from the seacoast colonies led to several significant grants of land in West Florida. A proposal for a settlement from New Jersey, initiated by Captain Amos Ogden, veteran of the Seven Years War, was favorably received. Captain Ogden was granted 25,000 acres near Natchez and an additional strip of 15,000 acres was reserved for the future colonists. Likewise Colonel Israel Putnam, also a veteran of the Seven Years War (whom we shall meet later as a master land speculator after the American Revolution), with some fellow officers, set up a Company of Military Adventurers from New England and petitioned the Crown for suitable land. Nineteen townships of some 23,000 acres each were reserved for the company, whose development was thwarted by the outbreak of the Revolution shortly thereafter. Another grant of 25,000 acres near Natchez was set aside for a minister from New Jersey by the name of Samuel Sweesy, who actually started a colony, which was also aborted by the Revolution. A New York group headed by a father and son, Jacques and Garrett Rapalje, received a similar promise of 25,000 acres. Pennsylvania and New Jersey immigrants under Thomas Hutchins, with partners, petitioned and received 25,000 acres under the proviso that the grant did not conflict with that already awarded to Colonel Putnam. Two tracts, each for 25,000 acres, were reserved for Peter Van Brugh Livingston and associates, who planned to bring in settlers from New York: Peter's kinsman, Philip Livingston, Jr., secretary to the royal governor, was without doubt a factor in the grant. Colonel Anthony Hutchins and company received 152,000 acres near Natchez for families from Virginia and the Carolinas.

It is apparent that the British ministry, until its review of 1773, had determined to set up settlements, mainly of 25,000 acres each, to encourage the development of West Florida. The matter was then held in abeyance until the outbreak of the Revolution, whereupon the outlying province was made an asylum for Loyalists fleeing the rebellious colonies. A new boom then started, with land grants generously being awarded to persons who gave proof they were friends of the mother country, with the majority of the refugees coming from Georgia, South Carolina, and Virginia. Among these was Thomas Taylor Byrd, son and heir of Colonel William Byrd III, one of the few Virginia aristocrats opting for Great Britain during the Revolution. The land grants were smaller in accordance with the new policy of the Board of Trade, usually running between 1,000 to 2,000 acres each. The designation of West Florida as an asylum for Loyalists, however, was set back by the Spanish conquest of the province in 1781.

East Florida, almost as isolated from the seaboard colonies by geography as West Florida, was at that time a swampy region more fit for copperhead snakes than human beings. The Spanish, before evacuating the region in 1763, had sold most of their land claims "to a shady pair of land speculators, a Gordon of Charlestown and a Fish of New York, who claimed 10 million acres but sold out to the Crown for £15,000."[30] If so, they were the only ones who made money in the region for a long time. There is on record a survey of holdings sent to Lord Dartmouth on October 23, 1773. Of less than 600,000 acres surveyed, the Earls of Beresford and Dartmouth held 40,000 acres each; Charles Turnbull held 33,000 acres; while 20,000 acres each were patented to the Earl of Besborough, the Earl of Cassilis, Grey Cooper, Sir William Duncan, William Fitzherbert, and Charles Townshend. Clarence W. Alvord[31] adds to this list other esteemed names, though it is not clear whether the list only refers to East Florida: those of Lords Eglington, Lord Holland, Lord Stirling, Lord Egmont, Lord Gordon, Lord Temple and his brother George Grenville, Thomas Pitt, and General Jeffrey Amherst. Lord Temple, George Grenville, Grey Cooper, and Thomas Pitt were also shareholders in the Walpole Company. It is apparent that Lord Dartmouth, who controlled such patents, simply gave away enormous tracts in this newly acquired territory to friends and colleagues.

13

The Quebec Act of 1774

"Chance and caprice rule the world."

La Rochefoucauld, Maxim 435

After William Murray purchased the two large western tracts of land on the basis of which the Franks-Gratz syndicate floated the Illinois Land Company, he registered the deed at Kaskaskia, the French settlement on the Illinois River. The English officer in charge notified General Thomas Gage, and the British commander in turn notified London. The flagrant violation of the 1763 Proclamation determined the Privy Council to resolve once and for all the question of colonial land speculation beyond the Alleghenies and at the same time to set forth the legal and religious rights of the conquered French in the Mississippi Valley as well as in Canada.

General Haldimand in Canada was instructed in early 1774 to issue a declaration reaffirming the 1763 Proclamation and explicitly stating that all land purchases from the Indians made since 1763 without royal license were "void and fraudulent." This has become known as the Quebec Act of 1774, sometimes referred to as the Proclamation of 1774, though by its terms it became effective one year later.

The restriction of white entry into the lands west of the mountains, set forth as a temporary measure by the Proclamation of 1763, was thus continued by the new act. The northern part of the territory east of the Mississippi River, taken from the French in the previous war, was brought

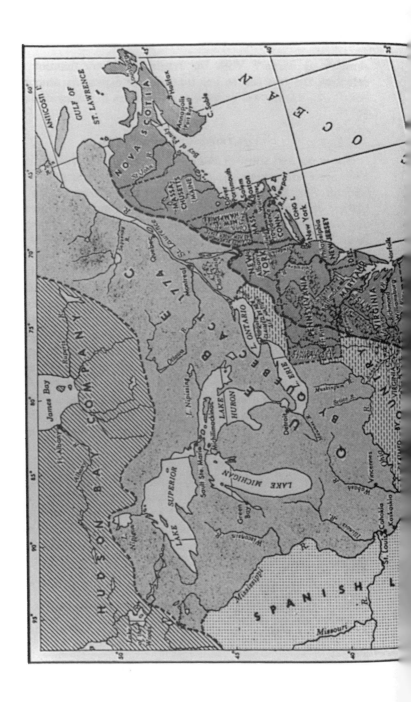

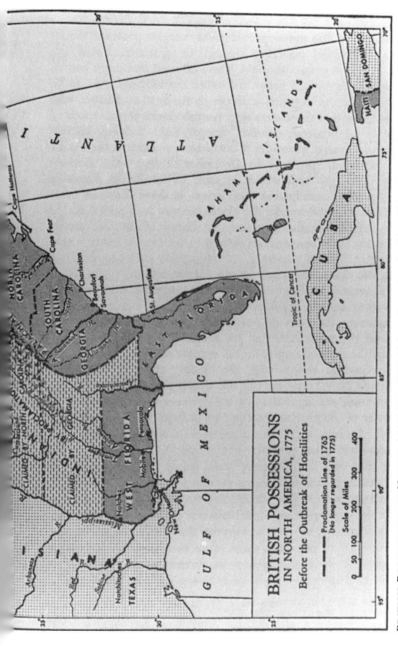

BRITISH POSSESSIONS IN NORTH AMERICA, 1775. Before the outbreak of hostilities. From *The Coming Revolution, 1763–1775*, by Lawrence H. Gipson, New York, 1954. Reproduced by permission of HarperCollins Publishers.

into the British political structure run from Quebec. The southern part of the territory was declared Indian country, with control flowing directly from the Crown. The borderline of these two enormous land masses was set at the Ohio River. Rather ironically from a historic point of view, this meant that the English finally accepted what had been the French claim that led to the French and Indian War, namely, that the southern boundary of Quebec extended to the Ohio River.

The other part of the Quebec Act of 1774 dealt in a realistic way with the problem of French Catholics. The British confirmed that Canadians were allowed to live according to their own religion and laws. This was no more than what the Protestants were doing in the Thirteen Colonies except that they had anti-papist laws, while all Protestants living in Canada enjoyed with Roman Catholics equal rights to exercise their religion.

It would be hard to imagine a declaration more calculated to infuriate the colonials and one, moreover, stabbing with equal force the south and north: the land issue in the Chesapeake colonies and the religious issue in New England. It was now evident to the leading southern and middle colony speculators, as well to ordinary immigrants desiring to enter western lands, that English policy was not, as George Washington had written to his agent William Crawford, merely a temporary restraint, but that Great Britain desired an iron curtain at the Alleghenies. It seemed obvious to both rich and poor that the English would govern the western territory from Quebec mainly for the benefit of the fur trade. The 1774 Proclamation thus succeeded in rousing the fury of ordinary people, who up to this point had no interest one way or the other in proclamations dealing with land.[1]

From an objective view the other answers set up by the Quebec Act of 1774 seem fair and equitable if one considers Indians and Catholics human beings entitled to equal rights with white Protestants. The fact is that the act was a catapult of the American Revolution. The provision dealing with religion pricked Massachusetts most of all. The First Continental Congress, then meeting, denounced the British for "establishing the Roman Catholic religion." Sam Adams in particular had a field day. All the wrath of his Puritan ancestry roaring through his bones, he raged against papist Britain, speaking and writing with vitriol that Catholics could now hold office and that Catholic influence would infiltrate from Canada throughout the colonies. General Gage wrote home with astonishment that the New England farmers were convinced that their religious liberties were endangered and "they cannot be made to believe the contrary." This propaganda inflamed the common people in a way that almost nothing before had done. "In the Quebec Act of June 1774, the mother country sealed its infamy

The Hon.ble *SAMUEL ADAMS*, Efq.r

Firft Delegate to Congrefs for Maffachufetts

J.Norman Sc.

SAMUEL ADAMS. Line engraving by John Norman (1748–1817). Courtesy of the Worcester Art Museum, Goodspeed Collection, Worcester, Massachusetts.

in the eyes of many Americans and gave colonial propagandists their juiciest plum since the Stamp Act. . . . Every provision of the act—however just or liberal—was turned against the British government with devastating effect by the American patriots."[2] In the following year, the Second Continental Congress addressed a letter to "The Oppressed Inhabitants of Canada" and when the French, now content with the guarantee of their rights, refused common cause with the Revolution, the colonies then voted six to five in October 1775 to invade that country.

The wild propaganda directed against the Quebec Act even found its sharp cry in the Declaration of Independence, where the charge was made that the British were "abolishing [in French Canada] the free system of English laws . . . establishing therein an arbitrary government, and enlarging its boundaries so as to render it a fit instrument for introducing the same absolute rule in the colonies." The Massachusetts patriots trumpeted that the Mississippi Valley would become a French-Catholic preserve aimed at penetrating New England and Virginia with Romish doctrines.[3]

History, of course, has different levels of meaning. The English made no effort to apply their new-found liberalism to Ireland, which indicated that religious tolerance was less of a factor than their desire to use the French Canadians as a check against the rebellious colonials. Given the time and place, however, the British ruling class had to be deaf and blind not to realize that nothing could stop the settlers by scores of thousands from pouring over the mountains into such a fertile land so thinly occupied. Their support of the fur traders, and those of Canada over the colonists, was very shortsighted. And mercantilism as an economic article of faith was sinking. The Quebec Act of 1774 thus was a clinker. "Ratifying the Proclamation of 1763, it decreed the persistence of Yesterday in an era already warm with Tomorrow's sun."[4]

14

The Influence of Land on the Revolution

"The success of this war depends upon a skillful steerage of the political vessel. . . . This can only be done on popular principles and maxims which are so abhorrent to the inclinations of the barons of the South, and the proprietary interests in the middle colonies, as well as to that avarice of land which has made upon this continent so many votaries to Mammon that I sometimes dread the consequences."

John Adams to Horatio Gates, March 23, 1776

The problems flowing from the British takeover of western lands after the victory over the French in the Seven Years War haunted their ruling class. An important group who rigorously followed mercantile theory was totally against taking the enormous land mass. The reason was based on two factors. The first was that the French sugar-producing islands in the Caribbean were more profitable as booty than Canada and the Mississippi Valley, with their long communication lines and hostile peoples. The second was that the unruly colonials, who had already caused many problems, would be even more difficult to keep down in a territory so removed from the seaboard. Some of this position came into focus in an anonymous pamphlet issued in the period immediately preceding the 1763 Peace of Paris. Bearing the provocative title *Reasons for Keeping Guadaloupe at a Peace preferable to Canada*, the case was well spelled out:

HIGH BRITISH MINISTRY OFFICIALS

1. WILLIAM PITT, EARL OF CHATHAM. Stipple engraving by J. Chapman (1809). Emmet Collection, Miriam & Ira D. Wallach Division of Art, Prints and Photographs, The New York Public Library, Astor, Lenox and Tilden Foundations.

2. THE EARL OF SHELBURNE. Engraving, anonymous. Print Collection, Miriam & Ira D. Wallach Division of Art, Prints and Photographs, The New York Public Library, Astor, Lenox and Tilden Foundations.

3. LORD ROCKINGHAM. Steel engraving in *The Political Register,* October 1771.

4. WILLIAM, EARL OF DARTMOUTH. Stipple engraving by William Evans after Gainsborough. Portrait File, Miriam & Ira D. Wallach Division of Art, Prints and Photographs, The New York Public Library, Astor, Lenox and Tilden Foundations.

I say the acquisition of Canada would be destructive, because such a country as North-America, ten times larger in extent than Britain, richer in soil in most places, all the different climates you can fancy, all the lakes and rivers for navigation one could wish, plenty of wood for shipping, and as much iron, hemp, and naval stores, as any part of the world; such country at such a distance, could never remain long subject to Britain.

The argument over what to do with the western lands was fought out in the highest councils of the ministry. Lord Egremont, secretary of state in 1763, opposed taking over the French territory. Settlers should be directed to Nova Scotia or Georgia "where they would be useful to their Mother Country instead of planting themselves in the Heart of America out of reach of Government." Lord Shelburne, president of the Board of Trade, was close to agreeing, yet he felt the chance should not be lost to seize such an enormous land area. Shelburne likewise felt that settlers should be directed to the underdeveloped coastal colonies where they would be under easy control and serve as a market for English exports.

It was William Pitt, the great war hero, who carried the argument for taking Canada and the West. Pitt felt—and persuaded the king—that the empire was flexible enough to expand into the interior without losing control.

A compromise was then reached in 1763 that led to the ceding of these lands to Britain at the Peace of Paris while at the same time issuing the Proclamation that forbad western settlement. In retrospect, we know this compromise was a disaster because it was based on contrary elements, but it seemed logical at the time. It may be added that William Pitt got sick shortly after these events and ceased to dominate English politics. If he had retained his health, and thence prime ministry, things might have been different, because with his great prestige, Pitt could have modified the 1763 Proclamation rather than allowing it to curdle into the Quebec Act of 1774.

There were astute men in high posts who saw the British error. Charles Gravier, Count of Vergennes, to whom the people of the United States owe a debt of gratitude for persuading Louis XVI of France to aid the Americans during the Revolution, was then French ambassador at Constantinople. He made a striking prophecy: "England will erelong repent of having removed the only check that could keep her colonies in awe. They no longer stand in need of her protection. She will call on them to contribute toward supporting the burdens they have helped to bring upon her, and they will answer by striking off all dependence." In England, William Burke, related to the famous conservative Edmund Burke, wittily remarked, refer-

COUNT DE VERGENNES

ring to the French Canadians: "A neighbor that keeps us in some awe, is not always the worst of neighbors."

The decisions taken in 1763 solved nothing. Whenever the British ministers seriously discussed the colonies, a burning question arose: how to handle the vast western region. Every ministry realized that this was a hydra-headed problem. How could there be a conciliation between the various interests clamoring for attention? The Indians' rights must be protected to avoid another costly uprising. The claims of various colonies to the West must be considered. The influence of the great land companies could not be ignored. There were the fur traders who opposed western colonization. And most of all, there was the imperial interest to conserve.

The conflict of interests ran like a gaping wound through the mouth of English policy. In 1772, for example, at a time when the Walpole Company had already organized the new colony of Vandalia and its approval was expected, the commissioners for trade and plantations reported that "the extension of the fur trade depends entirely upon the Indians being undisturbed in the possession of their hunting grounds and . . . all colonizing does in its nature, and must in its consequences, operate to the prejudice of that branch of commerce." Thus, like a person with a split personality, the English simultaneously backed opposing positions. Finally, in the Quebec Act of 1774, harassed by colonial truculence and twitching its tail, the British lion made the irrevocable decision to freeze the colonists out of the West.

The cleaved English policy was based on certain realities. Perhaps the major one was money, for money was needed to incorporate French Canada into the British Empire. Aside from bureaucratic costs, the settlers had to be kept out and the French and Indians pacified.[1] Appropriations to the colonies during the war years of 1756 to 1763 totalled over £1,150,000; while in December 1763 alone there was placed in the budget an item of £372,774 for the support of overseas garrisons, the major part being allocated for America. The British felt that the colonials, who had benefited so much from the war, should shoulder some of this crushing financial load.[2]

This problem of money led to a major cabinet crisis. Lord Barrington proposed the total abandonment of the West to the Indians. George Grenville asserted that if this were not done, the colonies shall be forced to bear some part of the imperial burden. Charles Townshend then declared that he would resign if the cabinet did not reach some decision on the subject so that he could lay before the House the opinion as to the maintenance of forts in the interior, the required military force, and the taxes on the Indian trade as well as those on imports. Lord Shelburne rejected the policy of abandonment and won the day. It was then decided to impose taxes on the colonies in

order to defray part of these expenses.[3] This was the background of the Revenue Act of 1764 (generally known as the Sugar Act), the extension of the
Stamp Act to the colonies in 1765, the 1767 Townshend Act, and the Tea
Act of 1773—the last leading to the Boston Tea Party. It can thus be seen
that the expense of military control of the western lands was a most important factor in creating the taxes that ultimately led to the American Revolution.

The hostile reaction of the Virginia aristocrats to the changed environment after 1763 is another key to understand the black clouds of
coming revolution. The plantation owners, with reason, resented higher
colonial taxes to maintain the western lands at a time when speculation
and settlement in these lands was stopped. As we have already shown,
the inner story of Virginia (as well as Maryland and the Carolinas to a
large extent) is one of land speculation tied to the twins of tobacco and
slavery. In a geographical sense Virginia is also the story of steady westward movement, from Tidewater to Piedmont and then to the bluegrass
country beyond the Alleghenies: and when this movement was blocked,
colonial history stopped and American history began. Understanding tobacco thus makes clear the history of the colonial South.

Tobacco growing eats up the life of soil and the land is stripped of
use after only three or four years. Ignorant of fertilizers and scientific
contouring, the large land owners simply shifted slaves to another part
of their estate when the soil could no longer support the crop. By 1750,
however, the woodlands began to be used up in the Tidewater, and the
center of tobacco production (as well as a similar shift in political power)
started to move west to the Piedmont.

The cultivation of the piedmont land in Virginia, with its deeper deposit
of humus, more than compensated for the exhaustion of the tidewater land,
leading to an increase in the volume of the tobacco exported. Between 1745
and 1754 this increase amounted to over seven million pounds of tobacco,
with almost forty-six million pounds exported in 1754 alone. The English
market became saturated, keeping the price of tobacco low. As a result, the
debt of the plantation owners to the English merchants steadily mounted.
The planters were further angered by their feeling that secret understand-
ings among the British importers kept prices at a depressed level. Another
factor in the reduced crop price was a considerable decrease in the consumption of pipe tobacco by the middle part of the eighteenth century.

A vicious cycle operated: increased production, coupled with lesser demand, lowered the price of tobacco. The rising debt of the planters compelled
them to seek richer western lands to grow even more tobacco in order to
compensate for the lower price. But when the additional tobacco was exported the large crop weakened the price even more. Tobacco was the cur-

rency that plantation grandees used to pay for imported cloth, coffee, tea, rum, madeira, silver, furniture, carpets, as well as their sons' education in English universities—and for more black slaves carried in the hulls of New England ships. The tobacco plantation homes "were richly furnished, in many cases, on advances made by English factors of tobacco or rice. In 1766 a committee of Parliament obtained evidence that the American debt due English merchants amounted to £4,450,000. More than nine-tenths of this sum was the indebtedness of Southern planters."[4] As Thomas Jefferson beautifully expressed the point: "These debts had become hereditary from father to son, for many generations, so that the planters were a species of property annexed to certain mercantile houses in London."[5] Indeed, by the time of the Revolution the tobacco harvest, already mortgaged before growth, amounted to more than one-half the total sum of colonial exports.

Economics in the eighteenth century was still a primitive science and the changing conditions evoked resentment rather than creative response. The southern aristocrats, caged in their glittering semi-feudal society, could not see that smashing the system would destroy their own cozy world as well. Their ideal, often achieved, was to live like English country gentlemen. It was a lifestyle based on large estates and mansions, house parties, gambling, horse-racing and fox-hunting. The basis of the system was a guaranteed market, cheap land, and cheap slaves. The last was to a certain extent solved by using black studs, men who were treated with enough care in the gracious climate to do their job well. The guaranteed market was built into the English mercantile philosophy. But cheap land, once the Piedmont and lateral valleys of the Alleghenies were settled, was blocked by the 1763 Proclamation and the 1774 Quebec Act.[6]

For every Washington, who endeavored to get the planters to switch from tobacco to grain; for every Jefferson, who invented the first scientific plough, there were ten proud and lethargic plantation aristocrats who seethed in righteous indignation over their inability to curry favor with the Virginia or Maryland or Carolina councils, as had their fathers and grandfathers, in order to procure western lands at no or little cost. They could not understand that planting more acreage only dropped the price of tobacco more because of the increased production. Fortunately for the future of an independent United States, these aristocrats were not able to foresee that through their revolt against the mercantile system that tied an agrarian America to an industrial England, they would not only destroy their own cherished way of life but also end up subjugated to the north, as they had been to the mother country.

The falling price of tobacco, accumulated debts, exhaustion of coastal soil, and prohibition of speculation in western lands had an ironic effect. It radicalized the southern aristocracy, which would normally have been the most conservative. Everywhere in the South, the elite was more uniformly revolt-minded than in the northern or central colonies. Their rebellion, however, was limited to throwing off the British yoke, as they conceived it, in order to return to the pre-1763 system, that is to be free of taxation and to be free to engross, through control of the political process, enormous tracts of western land either for rice and tobacco production or for speculative resale to the many thousands of land-hungry immigrants who were pouring into America.[7] They no more thought in terms of political democracy than did King George III, whom they detested.

When a leading aristocrat like Daniel Dulany of Maryland, whose land holdings in Frederick County were second only to the proprietary interest, wrote the radical pamphlet *Considerations on the Propriety of imposing taxes in the British Colonies*, he was lauded throughout New England for his violent denunciation of the Stamp Act. With all due credit to an American patriot, Dulany was very radical when it came to king and Parliament but just as conservative when it came to domestic policy. His aim was to pay out less money in taxes in order to have more money to enlarge his land holdings. But he could not do so because of the prohibition on western land speculation. Dulany's position mirrors almost the entire revolutionary stance of the southern aristocrats.[8] What indeed had the French and Indian War been fought for if not to take over the western land? Why should the colonists pay taxes to garrison a frontier to keep themselves out?

Thomas Jefferson reacted by expounding the extreme view, which denied that vacant land in America was part of the king's domain: "It is time for us to lay this matter before his majesty and to declare that he has no right to grant lands of himself."[9] Jefferson's thinking was even more interesting when he wrote into the Declaration of Independence a protest against the king's "raising the conditions of the new Appropriations of land." This was a burning issue in Virginia. George Washington's great-grandfather acquired land for next to nothing through a friendly agent of the Crown. Patrick Henry's father received land through the same process. Peter Jefferson, Tom's father, had done much the same. Why should Virginians now be blocked from the new western acreage?

From our point of view—which, of course, can be both a dangerous and an unreal way of looking at history—the issue has much irony. In effect Jefferson was stating that the British government was unjust in its efforts to protect the Indians; but speculative grants or purchases of land based on wiping out the Indians were just. It was tyranny to protect the rights of the weak who had occupied the land for untold generations; it

THOMAS JEFFERSON. Oil on canvas, by John Turnbull. Courtesy of the Library of Congress.

was liberty to seize this land, kill the natives, and then resell it at a profit to other white men who in many cases would then enslave blacks to farm it.[10]

The curb on speculation in western lands was only one facet feeding the widespread mood of revolt. Equally provoking, as Jefferson indicated in the previously-quoted sentence from the Declaration of Independence, was the British endeavor to create a more fair system of quitrents and land sales, a reform that hit many of the more northerly colonies as well. When we discussed the quitrent system, it was pointed out that from 1766 the administration in London was slowly working to reorganize this plan and that in 1774 the Board of Trade issued instructions to create a new uniform method of land grants. This reform was immediately branded as a despotic act in Virginia and elsewhere. In particular, the requirements of public notice and open auction meant that the councils would be stripped of their power to grant enormous tracts to members and favorites. Even poorer settlers felt threatened by this measure, which regularized and enforced quitrent payments as well.

Fuel was also dumped on the revolutionary fire by a fluke of history. During the first hundred years of settlement, as noted before, a typhoon of immigrants from the British Isles poured into the colonies. Then immigration slowed. However, western Europe had another population explosion in the middle of the eighteenth century, which was coupled with several serious crop failures. Local factors in Ireland and Scotland also contributed. The lord lieutenant of Ireland wrote in the summer of 1773 that rent gouging, landlord absenteeism, and the collapse of the linen industry were the reasons for the new massive European emigration that started around 1760. In Scotland during this period there was a disruption of the clan system and the same slump in the linen industry.[11] (As distinguished an immigrant as Tom Paine only arrived in 1774.) The result was that tremendous pressure for land built up in just the decade when the western acreage was cut off both from the speculators and the settlers.

It is apparent that the influence of land on the American Revolution was only one of a complex series of contributing events. In the northern colonies, aside from the religious question inflamed by the 1774 Quebec Act, new taxes and trade restrictions after 1763 were more provoking.[12] Though the Pennsylvania land companies also were gravely effected by the 1763 Proclamation and the 1774 Act, the speculators did not control the politics in that colony and had few popular roots in the people. But it is equally apparent that the Revolution never could have succeeded had it only been based on revolt in New England; indeed, that was the basic reason John Adams shrewdly manipulated the choice of George Washington, a Virginia plantation owner, to head the Revolutionary Army. For in the South, land was the decisive factor in opting for independence. The political theories and programs of the radicals, such as Sam Adams, Patrick Henry, and Tom Paine, as well as their more moderate brothers, Thomas Jefferson and Christopher Gadsden—enlarged voting rights, cheap money, less executive power and more opportunity for the poor—were of great importance, too. They did motivate men to fight, especially in New England; but the money and the power, the business and military leadership, came to a large extent from colonists whose deep financial interests were involved. In the South these men sprang from the class disaffected over land.

The southern grandees, whose rage had driven them to unite their interest with the merchant leaders of the middle and northern provinces, hoped for better days once the British blockade west of the Alleghenies would be removed. Many men, hungry for land in all the colonies, spun their plans and drove forward with their schemes, even after fighting broke out. An old-new face, Spain west of the Mississippi, a river now exposed to the revolting colonies, exerted its magnetism on the western plotters for large land grants. Another generation began to move into the limelight: men such as George Rogers Clark, William Blount, Robert Morris, and James Wilson. General Wilkinson, John Sevier and Aaron Burr, for better or worse, are inseparably linked with this new West; while Ethan Allen and his brothers created a new state, Vermont, almost solely due to the conflict of different groups of land speculators. And the common people, the faceless mass striving to find dignity in a new life in the hinterland— and without mercy hunting down the hapless foe, the Indian—pressed forward to make a new culture and a new nation on the silent and waiting land.

15

Some Eminent Patriots

Benjamin Franklin

"It is difficult to decide whether an upright, sincere, and straightforward course of action is the outcome of probity or worldly wisdom."

La Rochefoucauld, Maxim 170

Josiah Franklin, the father of Benjamin Franklin, was an English immigrant who, after trying out several small towns and various trades, settled in Boston and became a candlemaker. His wife, Abiah Folger Franklin, Benjamin Franklin's mother, was the daughter of one of the first settlers on the island of Nantucket.

The Franklins were a large brood, Josiah having married twice, with children from both wives. Benjamin was the last son of a father almost fifty years of age. His older brother, James, became the editor of the leading liberal Boston newspaper, *The New England Courant*. Apprenticed to his brother at the age of twelve, Benjamin, rowdy as a young man, quarreled with James after five years and went to Philadelphia.

While in Philadelphia, Franklin caught the eye of William Keith, the governor of Pennsylvania, who paid his expenses to go to London in order to learn more about printing. There Benjamin worked as a journeyman printer for about a year, returning again to Philadelphia. After a short stint as an employee, he started his own business, and within ten years his was the most important printing shop in the American colonies. The *Pennsylvania Gazette*, which he purchased in 1729, became the largest newspaper in circulation at the time; aggressive advertising helped make it extremely profitable. But it was *Poor Richard's Almanack*, written in 1732, that developed the nucleus of Franklin's first fortune. Full of wise maxims and practical advice, many taken from Swift and Sterne, it was a best seller.

Whether or not Benjamin Franklin developed an interest in politics solely for the financial advantages it offered, the fact is that his political contacts were a great help to his printing business. In 1730 he became public printer for the colony of Pennsylvania, with a monopoly on all printed matter. In 1736, Franklin was chosen clerk of the Pennsylvania assembly, and in 1737 he became postmaster at Philadelphia.

Restless by nature, his income having risen to about £1,000 a year, Benjamin Franklin brought in a partner, David Hall, in 1748 and made an arrangement whereby the next year, at the young age of forty-three, he retired from daily business affairs. The partnership lasted until 1766; his 50 percent of the profits made him well off and independent. In effect, his partner handled the production while he took care of the advertising and political relations. It was at this time that he bought a farm of three hundred acres near Burlington, New Jersey, about which he wrote to a friend that his fortune was such that he could enjoy all the necessaries and many of the indulgences of life.

Though Benjamin Franklin is known as a notable eighteenth-century scientist, those activities took up only a small part of one decade of his long life.[1] He received a Leyden jar (an early form of electrical condenser, *i.e.,* for holding a greater charge) from England in 1745, made experiments, and wrote his last paper on electricity in 1754. Franklin's main contribution was the invention of the lightning rod, for which he is justly celebrated; and also the Franklin stove, which advanced the heating chamber in front of the chimney and thus saved much of the heat from escaping up the shaft.

About the time Franklin retired from business, he began his public political career. In 1748 he was elected as a member of the Philadelphia city council, and in 1750 he won a seat in the colonial assembly. The Quakers, who had great weight in the assembly, would not raise money for arms or soldiers, backed by many of the German immigrants out of respect for William Penn's memory. Benjamin Franklin was a leader in the fight for a colonial militia. In 1753 he was a member of the commission sent to confer with the Indians respecting a treaty in western Pennsylvania; this must have stimulated his interest in western lands. After Braddock's defeat in 1755, Franklin was in charge of organizing Pennsylvania's northwest frontier against Indian attacks.

By this time Benjamin Franklin was both rich and influential. His appointment by the British as deputy postmaster-general for America had helped him spread the sale of his *Pennsylvania Gazette* all over the colonies. He eagerly accepted the assembly's offer to go to England in 1757 to negotiate a compromise with the Penn proprietors respecting their freedom from taxes. These negotiations were completed in 1760. Having succeeded in getting the Penn family to accept some taxation, Franklin arrived back in Philadelphia in 1762. But John Penn, the new governor, repudiated the agreement, and Franklin, who now openly favored getting rid of the Penns, was sent again to England for that purpose in 1764.

The riots over the Stamp Act put Benjamin Franklin in a difficult position. He at first accepted the law and then, subject to sharp criticism, reversed his position. In his new role as champion of the colonies, Franklin became known as the leading American advocate in London. Already serving as colonial agent for the Anti-proprietary party in Pennsylvania, he was appointed the agent for Georgia, New Jersey, and Massachusetts as well, which brought him £1,500 annually (a great sum at the time). In effect, he was an American ambassador to England without portfolio.

Franklin's great ability to walk both sides of a fence caught up with him, however, in 1774, over the celebrated case of the Hutchinson letters. Through his official position, he had come to possess private letters from the governor of Massachusetts, Thomas Hutchinson, in which the Tory leader berated the colonials. Franklin sent the letters to friends in Massachusetts, where they were then used to petition the king to remove Hutchinson. These stolen letters were traced back to Franklin, who was called a thief by the king's attorney-general and dismissed as deputy postmaster-general. A loyal British subject was made a fervent American patriot, and the next year Franklin sailed for Philadelphia to join the forces of revolution. His later career as a member of Congress, postmaster-general of the colonies, and American commissioner in France during the Revolution is not relevant to this thumbnail sketch.

There are certain opinions about Benjamin Franklin that should be examined. The most common is that he was a fiery rebel. However, this is nowhere evident in his long career. Before all, Franklin was a very successful man of affairs who knew what the public wanted and gave it to them. With none of the background and family contacts of George Washington, by his late thirties Benjamin Franklin was well-off solely through his own efforts. The bourgeois traits of thrift, hard work, and persistence, which he illustrated and wrote about, are the reverse of the qualities making up a revolutionary.

Franklin also clearly understood the hinge upon which swung public

BENJAMIN FRANKLIN, AGE 20. Oil on canvas, by Sumner. Painted when Franklin was in London. From *The True Benjamin Franklin,* by Sydney G. Fisher, New York, J. B. Lippincott, 1899.

and private affairs and put that canny skill into practice to rise up in the political and financial worlds. His private printing career and his public political one in Pennsylvania went hand in glove, and the hand never moved without the glove. Every step in his early political life can be traced to some private advantage in business: this was well stated in the words of Daniel J. Boorstin: "Benjamin Franklin, Printer, with his sharp eye for the profitable marriage of public and private interests. . . ."[2]

Until his dismissal as deputy postmaster-general, Franklin was viewed with justice as a sound businessman and a loyal conservative. He insisted for many years that King George III was "the best king any nation was ever blessed with."[3] He thought that England's famous radical John Wilkes was an "outlaw," using the same kind of epithet hurled against himself by the Penn proprietors: but John Wilkes did not have an exclusive contract with the Pennsylvania assembly to sustain his rhetoric. As late as December 1773, on hearing the news of the Boston Tea Party, Franklin, without doubt in a tremble over his wobbling investment in the Walpole Company, said the leaders should be punished. It was only in 1774, as a result of being caught in the Hutchinson case and declared *persona non grata* in England, that Franklin came down firmly on the side of the Americans. In truth, there was little else to do; even if he wished, he could hardly join his son, Governor William Franklin, and his closest ally, Joseph Galloway, as a Tory.

The second common attitude to be disposed of is that of Benjamin Franklin the humanitarian. This has come about mainly because of some sympathy he expressed for Indians. In the early years of the French and Indian War, where he presumably picked up the idea from Henry Bouquet, commander at Fort Pitt, Franklin proposed to set on large English dogs against the Indians, a horrible method first used by the Spaniards in Hispaniola. Then in 1756, with Franklin as a leader, the Pennsylvania assembly put into effect the following bounties: "For the scalp of every male Indian enemy above the age of twelve years, produced as evidence of their being killed, the sum of one hundred and thirty pieces of eight. . . . For the scalp of every Indian woman produced as evidence of their being killed, the sum of fifty pieces of eight."[4] Most of the Quakers resigned from the assembly in protest after the passage of this law.

Benjamin Franklin looked down on most people who were not English, being a racist not only toward non-whites, but also within the white race. In the first edition of *Observations concerning the Increase of Mankind . . .,* Franklin wrote that only Englishmen should be allowed to come to the colonies, being especially resentful of the Pennsylvania Germans, whom he called "Palatine boors" and who—not incidentally—had the temerity to oppose him in the assembly. Franklin also wanted to exclude "all blacks and tawnys," the latter word referring to Orientals.[5] He likewise grouped in distaste "the Spaniards, Italians, French, Russians, and Swedes" as being of "swarthy complexion," though some of this anthropology puzzles. His attitudes of course were typical of the time and place; the point, however, is that his prejudices were no different than the common mass of colonials of English origin, except for the Quakers.

Benjamin Franklin's second fortune, after the one he amassed in printing, came about through land speculation. Here again he clearly saw, and used, the web of connections tying high public office to private profit. It is curious that almost nothing concerning this important phase of his life appears in much writing about Benjamin Franklin. In his own memoirs, later called the *Autobiography,* land speculation is completely absent. It is true that this work stops shortly after Franklin arrived in London in 1757, but he did write a preliminary outline that carried him through the time when he was sent to France during the Revolution. Though these notes refer to details such as "Stoves and Chimney plates" and "Glasses from Germany," there is only one reference to land: "Grant of Land in Nova Scotia." There is nothing about Thomas Walpole or Vandalia, surely the leading intrigue of his life.[6] Yet two top American historians, Thomas P. Abernethy and Charles A. Beard, label Franklin as one of the leading land speculators of the late eighteenth century.[7]

Perhaps Franklin did not mention this passion in his self-portrait because he was not altogether proud of the role; and other standard biographies have slighted this activity in favor of more patriotic goals. It was not for want of trying, but rather for want of great results, that prevented Franklin from being considered the equal of George Washington, Sir William Johnson, or Dr. Thomas Walker in this matter.

Benjamin Franklin first became interested in western lands when acting as a Pennsylvania commissioner to the Indians. In 1753 a group of Connecticut speculators had purchased from the Six Nations a large tract of land in the Susquehanna Valley, a claim on Pennsylvania territory that the Penn proprietors opposed. Franklin and his associate Joseph Galloway, both of whom were known for their opposition to the Penns, agreed to represent the Connecticut group. First they formed a "Friendly Association," which raised £4,000 to give presents to the Indians. Through this method they installed an ally as secretary to the chief of the Delawares, who claimed there was a cloud on the original Penn purchase. Then Franklin personally presented the British ministry with a demand to investigate the validity of the Penn claim. The clash of the two colonies over this claim went on even after the Revolution.

In 1763, Franklin became interested in the purchase of titles to lands south of Virginia; he persuaded Richard Jackson, later a Lord of the Admiralty, to search the title deeds in London. Nothing came of this, presumably because the titles were defective. The next year, however, Jackson suggested that Franklin might want a grant of land in Nova Scotia. Though the action was slow, in June 1766 the Board of Trade and the Privy Council approved and gave Franklin twenty thousand acres; he held this land all through the tumultuous years, eventually leaving this acreage to his son a quarter-century later.[8]

During the French and Indian War, though the fur trade was cut off, the Pennsylvania speculators kept busy. There was an active business in purchasing pre-war land claims in the hope of a sharp rise in prices after the French were driven out. Franklin bought the claim, belonging to Daniel Coxe, which had lapsed, but the 1763 Proclamation wiped out his investment. He then worked with the "Suffering Traders" in Pennsylvania and with Sir William Johnson in New York to form the Illinois Company, the first of the string of land speculative companies that blossomed into the Indiana Company and Vandalia.

Benjamin Franklin's relation to these companies has been studied in a previous chapter. Most historians in this special field agree that Franklin was the group's prime mover in England. In fact, Franklin was chosen as spokesman in the initial stages because he was very close to the Earl of Shelburne, then secretary of state for the colonies. When affirmative action on this patent was blocked by Lord Hillsborough, Shelburne's successor, Franklin had a major part in bringing down that intransigent minister. The slippery Philadelphian admitted as much when, on August 17, 1772, he wrote the following to his son: "The king too was tired of him [Hillsborough] and his administration, which had weakened the affection and respect of the colonies for a royal government of which (I may say to you) I had used proper means from time to time that His Majesty should have due information and convincing proofs."[9]

Like the leaders of the Virginia Colony, there was a symbiotic tie between Franklin's failure to put through land schemes for his pocketbook and his growing American patriotism. It may well be that the psychological moment at which the chain of Franklin's love for England snapped was not so much at the cross-examination involving the Hutchinson letters but rather with his disgust later in the same year at the blocked Walpole (Vandalia) patent. We know that, in a sweat over the Boston Tea Party, Thomas Wharton wrote from Philadelphia to his brother Samuel at London exclaiming with prophetic insight that it might kill their chances. After Franklin was dismissed from his official post because of the Hutchinson imbroglio, he had to give up his two shares in Vandalia. From that moment on his loyalties lay elsewhere.

In 1788, Benjamin Franklin's worth was estimated at $150,000: in comparative value his was a multi-million-dollar estate of today. Most of it was in land, which was confirmed by his will. He still held the 20,000 acres from the Nova Scotia patent, and he had acquired a large tract of land on the Ohio River. As colonial agent for Georgia, he received rights to 3,000 acres in that state in recompense for his unpaid salary while serving in France during the Revolution. He owned houses and lots in both Philadelphia and Boston. And as Franklin himself had noted in a personal letter in 1787, the value of his land by that date had more than tripled.

Toward the end of the Revolution, Benjamin Franklin presented, with Samuel Wharton, a joint plea to Congress in which it was argued that since the United States had obtained sovereignty over the territory formerly known as Vandalia, the contract should be respected and the terms of the grant renewed. This Congress, despite its great respect for the elderly gentleman, refused to do.

"Poor Richard" was not true to his own maxims. He agreed with fervor that "nothing but money is sweeter than honey," but he did not act as though "cunning proceeds from want of capacity." However, Benjamin Franklin did succeed in presenting to future generations a mythical picture of his own nature.[10]

Patrick Henry

> *"Don't believe those who so fervently preach liberty. Nearly all of them—probably every single one of them—had his own particular interests in mind."*
>
> Francesco Guicciardini, *Maxims and Reflections of a Renaissance Statesman,* No. 66

The general idea that most leaders of the American Revolution were born of modest background is as wrong for Patrick Henry as it is for George Washington. His father, John Henry, of Scotch birth, was surveyor of Hanover County in Virginia, colonel of the county regiment, and presiding judge of the county court. Patrick Henry's brother was rector of St. Paul's parish in Hanover, and his cousin David Henry was the editor of the much-esteemed *Gentleman's Magazine,* while another cousin William Robertson was principal of the University of Edinburgh and author of the *History of the Reign of the Emperor Charles V,* still read today. A cousin twice removed was Lord Brougham.

Patrick Henry's mother was also raised in a distinguished family: a Winston on her father's side and a Dabney on her mother's side. Widowed before her marriage to John Henry, she inherited a large estate, which she brought with her into the second marriage (always a factor in Virginia upper-class marriages). At the time of Patrick's birth, John Henry, a protégé of Sir William Gooch, the acting governor of Virginia, already owned over 25,000 acres independent of his wife's property.

Despite this background, young Patrick seemed destined to be a real disappointment to his family. He rejected education; married young to a woman who, before the age of thirty, went insane and had to be restrained in a strait-jacket; failed in various jobs in which he had been placed through family influence; and even lost a farm with a half-dozen slaves provided by his father-in-law. Then Patrick made that decision often seen in certain charming and smooth-tongued persons whose families have connections. He became a lawyer. Actually, he could not pass his examinations, which at that time in Virginia were simple enough; but with the influence of his father, who was a county judge and colonel, the matter was resolved.[11]

Patrick Henry rose to the public eye in "The Parson's Case" of 1763, involving a specific issue of damages but whose real issue was the refusal of Virginians to permit the Virginia Episcopal church to be dominated by its English mother church. Henry so mesmerized the jury that the plaintiff, a Reverend Mr. James Maury, was only awarded a symbolic one penny. The reverend, who had no reason to know at the time that he was standing on a high bench of history, later wrote in a confidential letter that Henry apologized after the trial and said to him that he engaged in the cause, and said what he had, solely "to render himself popular."[12] It was effective: for two years later, in 1765, Henry was elected to the Virginia assembly.

The rest is history. Short days after entering the legislature, he authored the "Virginia Resolutions," declaring the colony to be against the Stamp Act and asserting its right to legislate independently from the British Parliament. This was a cornerstone in the American independence movement and brought him to the attention of radicals throughout the colonies. In 1774 and 1775, Henry was a fiery delegate at the First and Second Continental Congresses. In 1775 he was a leader at the Virginia Revolutionary Convention. Viewing war with England as inevitable, he pressed resolutions, which were passed, to arm the Virginia militia as an autonomous body. It was there he gave his immortal, though possibly apocryphal "Give me liberty or give me death" speech, which is a part of the folklore of every American student.[13] The following year he was elected Virginia governor and returned to that post by the electorate for two more years. Prohibited from further immediate reelection by the new state constitution, he was elected governor after the Revolution, serving from 1784 to 1786.

Patrick Henry was a "states righter" and even opposed the Articles of Confederation as ceding too much to the central power. He most vigorously fought the proposed United States constitution, leading the unsuccesful opposition in Virginia. Patrick Henry was consistent; his opposition to federal power was so great that he refused a number of high offices: those of United States senator, secretary of state in Washington's cabinet, and chief justice of the U.S. Supreme Court. However, it should be noted that Henry's opposition to the national system was also, if not mainly, based on the fact that he considered it hostile to westward expansion on the part of Virginia and, as we will see, he was deeply involved in such speculation.[14]

Patrick Henry was one of the few well-known political figures whose avarice was greater than his lust for power. There were two passions in his life: independence for Virginia, and amassing a very large fortune. The two were kissing cousins. The way to such riches in the second half of the eighteenth century—each generation having its own technique—was to acquire great tracts of land through political influence.

Henry's first attempt at land speculation involved his own family. In 1765 he bought 1,700 acres on Roundabout Creek from his father for an unrecorded price. Shortly thereafter he obtained from his father-in-law 3,400 acres near the spot where Gate City in Virginia now stands. He did so by means of standing as collateral for loans. In 1767, his father-in-law having gotten himself into deep trouble, Henry bought from him a mortgage on six tracts, representing one share of a Walker speculation in western Kentucky near the junction of the Mississippi and Ohio rivers. His favorite sister, Anne, at this time married William Christian, the son of a prominent Staunton merchant and, like Henry and Walker, a Virginia burgess. Christian, later a colonel, also became a partner in land schemes. The many Henry girls married substantial settlers in the western region of Virginia, cementing on a personal level Patrick's growing political and economic power.

Patrick Henry and Dr. Thomas Walker, the Cardinal Richelieu of southern land speculation, came together as naturally and inevitably as the earth circles the sun. Their relation would blossom in many projects. Henry often acted as the popular mouthpiece for Walker in the Virginia burgess. For example, due to his efforts the legislative body went on record that the frontier be advanced southwest to include land Walker had acquired, thus validating the Loyal Company claim. In 1769, Henry and Walker drew up proposals for a speculative company that petitioned for fifty thousand acres on the Ohio River below the New River, promising

PORTRAIT OF PATRICK HENRY. Watercolor on ivory, by Lawrence Sully (1795), #1945.115. Courtesy of the Mead Art Museum, Amherst College, Amherst, Massachusetts, Bequest of Herbert L. Pratt, Class of 1895.

to buy the land from the Indians and settle five hundred families within seven years if the Crown would permit a purchase west of the 1763 Proclamation line. Besides Dr. Walker, Patrick's associates included his brother William Henry and his brother-in-law William Christian, as well as some of the old-guard aristocrats like the Thomas Nelsons, senior and junior. Thomas Jefferson also participated. It was obvious that Henry's political clout gave him entry into new realms. It was also obvious that if the English disappeared, taking with them their Proclamation Line, Patrick Henry would be much richer.

By 1771, Henry was earning £1,300 a year from his legal practice, in addition to income from his land speculations. In that year he acquired the great plantation of the grandee Charles Chiswell in upper Hanover County, including 960 acres and "Scotchtown," one of the largest houses in the entire colony.

In the period immediately preceding the Revolution, Patrick Henry concentrated his speculative efforts on the Illinois and Kentucky regions. He became the personal counsel of the Earl of Dunmore, then acting governor of Virginia, when Dunmore took a participation in the Illinois and Wabash land companies. Henry was also one of Washington's associates, with Andrew Lewis and William Byrd III, when the group received the two hundred thousand acres of western land provided as a settlement of veterans' claims from the French and Indian War. This meant, of course, that Henry had bought up these land bonuses on a discount basis. Henry, with Dr. Walker, then attempted to purchase from the Cherokees the Kentucky land that Judge Henderson had been quick to beat them to. Despite his disappointment, Henry made no attempt to block Henderson but in fact supported his position before the Virginia legislature. There is on record a strong letter of thanks written by Henderson on April 26, 1775,[15] which seems to indicate there must have been a secret understanding between the two as to the later allotment of this land.

Patrick Henry also become involved in Vandalia despite the fact that it was a rival Pennsylvania project. Though the proposed colony was bitterly opposed by the Virginian speculators, Henry wrote for the company a legal opinion that its claims against Virginia were valid. Benjamin Franklin, having returned to Philadelphia from England, and Samuel Wharton in London, tried to get the Continental Congress to validate the Vandalia claimants after the colony had been scuttled in England by the Privy Council. It is thus worthy to note that on August 7, 1775, Samuel Wharton wrote to his brother Thomas in Philadelphia that half shares in the company should be given to eight key members of the Continental Congress, "in addition to the share already aside for Patrick Henry."[16]

The Revolution offered new opportunities. The young and brash George Rogers Clark, whose land hunger was in the same ozone layer with that of Patrick Henry, mixed business with war in his famous conquest of the Northwest Territory. In late 1777, Clark set forth his plan of invasion to Governor Henry. Henry consulted the key Virginia politicians—Jefferson, Wythe, and Mason—"about future awards to the members of the expedition. As a result, Clark . . . got a private letter from these three gentlemen assuring him that if he and his associates were successful they might rely on the Assembly for grants from the conquered grounds." Dumas Malone, the great Jeffersonian historian, then continues: "Heartened by this extra-legal act, Lieutenant Colonal Clark proceeded to capture Kaskaskia."[17] As usual, Patrick Henry took a piece. "Indeed, Clark was so sure of success that he entered into a partnership with Henry for a tract of land in the Illinois country."[18] In fact, public knowledge of Henry's speculative activities in wartime became so embarrassing that the governor felt obliged to swear to a deposition on June 4, 1777, that he was not a party to purchase of Indian lands in Kentucky. Whether true or not, we do know that he took out patents for 10,000 acres of western land claimed by Virginia, paying forty pounds sterling to the newly organized Virginia land office set up despite the protest of the Continental Congress.[19]

Patrick Henry's political exploits, though not his political life, ended with his third term as governor of Virginia in 1778. Indeed, one might state that the true end of his exploits occurred on March 23, 1775, when he gave the "Give me liberty or give me death" address. Henry was one of those men, similar to Sam Adams, who was capable of stirring a revolution but then doing little constructive work thereafter.

One can without question use the end of this third gubernatorial term as a watershed in his life. It was then that he removed himself from the war, though the Revolution raged on for years, selling Scotchtown for £5,000 ("Negroes or money will be accepted in payment . . ." ran the original advertisement), and purchasd a ten thousand-acre plantation that he called Leatherwood. Jefferson, who despised Henry for his money greed, later remarked that he paid for the valuable property by installments "in depreciated paper not worth oak leaves." In legal terms it is no crime to take advantage by paying in depreciated currency: it is interesting, however, to point out that Henry fought against measures to curb the depreciation of the Virginia money.

The great private fief of Leatherwood was located in Henry County, named after him, to the extreme west along the North Carolina border. Henry's incompetent wife had died, leaving six children; the forty-one-year-old man remarried a much younger woman, Dolly Dandridge, kin to George

Washington's wife and of the highest society. Henry now started raising a new family. Residing on a remote Virginia frontier isolated in any immediate sense from the war, though he did serve in the assembly, surrounded by some fifty members of his family (the immediate family by two wives and married children with their families), the patriarchial figure of Patrick Henry becomes an enigma at this point. His claim to ill health was respected; but he lived on for many years and produced another half-dozen children, siring a round dozen in all.

The cable linking the two phases of Henry's life is his purchasing of land. In fact, his former activities were dwarfed by the later speculations. Although he did accept several additional terms as governor, he moved through them more as a living legend than an executive leader. And Henry's fight against the proposed U.S. Constitution, though it had laudable features, must be regarded from the historic point of view as a waste. His heart was not in politics anymore; it was consumed in making a large fortune. This he succeeded in doing. As Robert D. Meade, Henry's most well-known biographer, writes: "In 1788 Henry was one of the hundred largest land proprietors in Virginia. A decade later he ranked with Washington among the leading landed magnates of the state. . . ."[20] And this statement only referred to Virginia; his speculation covered other states as well.

It is difficult to follow Henry's finances because, like Washington, he often bought and sold quickly to turn over a profit. The records from the eighteenth century usually show only property held by the same individual or syndicate for some time. However, known activities can be listed. Henry acquired 4,000 acres on the Kentucky River, 500 acres on the Cumberland Trace, and 1,000 acres on Rolling Fork in Lincoln County. He owned, according to the 1788 Virginia tax rolls, 1,670 acres in Prince Edward County, 8,000 acres in Henry County, and nearly 14,000 acres in Princess Anne and Norfolk counties. Sixty-six slaves are listed as working on his properties. Though not individually listed because of defective records, Henry invested heavily in North Carolina land; we know, for example, that to wipe out a debt due him, he took an undivided fourth part of a tract containing over 25,000 acres. Some of his later dealings were made with General Henry Carter Lee—the father of Robert E. Lee—who went into land speculation after the Revolution, got caught short, and (though the details are not clear) borrowed from Henry, and was foreclosed. This caused much bitterness between the two.

Probably the most shady deal involving Patrick Henry was the Yazoo land speculation, the name being taken from the Yazoo River, a tributary of the Mississippi in the area west of Georgia. There is proof that almost all of the legislators of Georgia were bribed, either directly by money or through a speculative interest.[21] Henry and his associates, who took the name of the Virginia Yazoo Company, on December 21, 1789, received a grant of 11,400,000 acres in the northwestern part of what was then called the Georgia territory. Patrick Henry was so exultant that he wrote of settling in Georgia, "endeared" as he was by "the hope of being possessed of valuable property within her limits."[22]

This was one scheme that fell through. The land sale was ambiguous as to the question of Indian title and the company had to pay Georgia $93,750 within two years. Henry, thinking that Georgia would accept depreciated debt certificates in payment, his usual method of financing, had bought up a large amount of this paper at about ten percent of face value. But there was uneasiness throughout Georgia as evidence mounted of fraud. Payment in depreciated paper was rejected and the project collapsed.

The ubiquitous Henry was one of the two lawyers appointed to take action in this matter against the state of Georgia in the U.S. Supreme Court. But the suit was blocked by the Eleventh Amendment to the Constitution, which prohibited judicial suits by citizens of one state against another. It may be added that Alexander Hamilton's funding project, whereby the federal government took over state obligations, not only bailed Henry out but gave him a neat profit on the debt certificates he had bought. Thereafter, Hamilton became the political idol of Henry.

Perhaps the final statement on Patrick Henry's character was made by Thomas Abernethy in his definitive *Western Lands and the American Revolution*: "It is of no moment . . . just how many acres various individuals and companies acquired or tried to acquire during the era of exploitation of public lands. But it does matter that usually the most successful speculators and traders were those who betrayed public trust and used official position to bilk the people." Abernethy, a professor of history at the University of Virginia and dean of recent writers dealing with western lands, disposed of Virginia's first American governor with one devastating word: not "patriot" but "opportunist."[23]

George Washington

"George Washington throws off the Hero and takes up the chatty agreeable Companion—he can be down right impudent sometimes—such impudence, Fanny, as you and I like."

Letter of a Virginia woman, 1777

George Washington was born a Virginia aristocrat. The Washington line goes back to a great-grandfather, Colonel John Washington, who, as a supporter of the tyrannical Governor Berkeley, was elected to the Virginia House of Burgesses as a reward. Augustine, George's father, was a large landowner and master of six different plantations, among which was Hunting Creek, later called Mount Vernon. George's mother, Mary Ball, was the daughter of another aristocrat, Colonel Joseph Ball.

Augustine Washington died when George was eleven and Lawrence, George's his half brother, became his guardian. Lawrence had married the eldest daughter of Colonel William Fairfax, cousin of Thomas, Lord Fairfax, whose estate of some five million acres—the largest in Virginia—was run from Belvoir on the Potomac, the plantation adjoining Mount Vernon. Because of this Fairfax tie, George Washington at the age of seventeen was appointed surveyor at Culpeper County (Lord Fairfax's county), which made him—with Dr. Thomas Walker in Albemarle County and Patrick Henry's father in Hanover County[24]—one of the leaders in Virginia of this most important eighteenth-century profession. In a sense the surveyors in the South were like the lawyers in the North, for they established which land grants and purchases were legally marketable. It was "family pull," then, that brought young George this honor, as indeed family pull ran everything in Virginia at that time.

In 1752, Lawrence Washington died, followed by his daughter two months later. George, at the age of twenty, inherited his half-brother's estate. The legacy included much land as well as Mount Vernon, which stretched ten miles along the Potomac. Originally acquired by Colonel John Washington in 1674, the plantation had already belonged to the Washington family for almost eighty years.

The young George fit in well with the colonial aristocracy. His close neighbors and friends, besides the Fairfaxes, were the Masons, the Lees, the Fitzhughs, the Carters, and the Faunteloys. He was fond of riding, dancing, and the theater. At six-feet-two inches he was very tall compared to the men of his time. George had great body strength, reddish hair, and gray-blue eyes; he enjoyed flirting and wrote bad poetry for the ladies. The same year that young George inherited Mount Vernon he was made an adjutant of one of Virginia's four military districts, with the automatic rank of major. This, too, was secured through the Fairfax connection. Though bored by religion, George's civil responsibilities also included becoming a vestryman of the Episcopal church. In the words of Clifford Dowdey in *The Great Plantation,* a sympathetic account of plantation society in colonial Virginia, "First of all, George Washington was a product of the ruling class of Virginia's aristocratic republic."[25]

GEORGE WASHINGTON IN THE UNIFORM OF A COLONEL IN THE VIRGINIA MILITIA. Oil on canvas, by Charles Willson Peale (1772). This is the earliest known portrait of Washington. Courtesy of the Washington/Curtis/Lee Collection, Washington and Lee University, Lexington, Virginia.

How did this provincial figure become the richest man in Virginia, perhaps in all the colonies? All human beings are a medley, most particularly men who are as complex as Washington. Family connections, chance, character, and a will to power are important. Two factors do stand out: a wise and calculated marriage, and a passion for land speculation aided by the highest contacts. George Washington was a prime example of those gentry who were the colonial heirs of English aristocrats. One important reason for the American Revolution was the desire of such men to continue to enjoy the fruits of the mature oligarchic system that had been built by their families during the early years of colonial expansion, a system that was in much danger due to the shift in British imperial policy.

There exist many studies of George Washington's land activities and their relation to the social and political power structure of the colonies.[26] As noted, his brother's marriage into the powerful Fairfax family was the key to his early advancement. Young George was a favorite of Lord Fairfax, a bachelor who came at the age of fifty from London to live on his Virginia estates. While surveying for Fairfax, who paid him an above-market wage, George patented 550 acres in Frederick County, and then purchased another 456 acres as well. To this he added in his twentieth year 552 acres, thus owning some 1,500 acres in his own name by the time he inherited Mount Vernon from his half-brother, Lawrence.

The speculative land scheme known as the Ohio Company has already been discussed. An umbilical cord links this company to the Seven Years War and Washington's military activity, as well as to the large acreage he later received as a veteran's bonus. The Ohio Company, probably the largest colonial speculation at the time it was organized in 1747, was headed by Lawrence Washington from 1750 until his unexpected death in 1752. George Washington's position as executor of Lawrence's estate forced him to take an active role in the company business. It was because of his position as a leading Ohio Company stockholder, rather than for any known martial vigor, that the young major was picked by Virginia's Governor Dinwiddie, another stockholder, to warn the French off company property. As one authority acidly wrote:

Indeed, at the outset of this amateur provincial expedition against the French it is hard to shake off the conclusion that to George Washington himself —twenty-two in the year 1754—all of Dinwiddie's preliminary proceedings must have appeared in the light of an intimate family affair, in which patriotism, neighbors, and the family purse—a combination always dear to the Anglo-Saxon heart—had equal demands upon those involved. The lands in jeopardy on the Ohio were the gamble of his own brothers and neighbors;

the lands on the actual frontier were Lord Fairfax's; the governor was a company stockholder as well as the guardian of his king's cause and country."[27]

When young Washington's warning to the French was rebuffed, Governor Dinwiddie called for arms. But the Virginia burgesses refused money, correctly seeing this mainly as a war for private gain. The only way to entice volunteers was through a pledge of two hundred thousand acres of land from the Ohio Company grant, to be given after driving out the enemy. Major Washington was second in command on the advance guard, taking over on the death of his superior. And after the defeat of General Braddock and his regular troops, the governor appointed Washington to the chief command of the colony's militia. This was in fact a paper appointment because the French, in order better to defend Canada, withdrew their forces from the Ohio Valley. George, now Colonel Washington, and his local militia, therefore followed the rest of the war, fought in the North, through the gazettes.

It was in this period that Washington argued with the British high command over the appropriate westward route to send men and supplies in order to conquer Fort Duquesne. Brigadier General John Forbes, in charge of Britain's forces, was persuaded to run the new road through Pennsylvania as a shorter route. But Washington insisted that a more difficult road through the backcountry of Virginia, which would open up Ohio Company land, made more sense. According to historian Richard B. Morris, "Only an imputation of self-interest could explain how so knowledgeable an explorer as Washington could have persistently pressed for so wrongheaded a proposal."[28] And when the decision went against him, Washington reacted with great passion, writing to a friend, ". . . all is lost! All is lost by Heavens!"[29] Presumably he was not referring to the war.

In January 1759, while still a war hero in the public eye, George Washington married the wealthiest widow in Virginia, Martha Dandridge Custis, who had been married to the late Daniel Parke Custis and left by her former husband more than 17,000 acres of good land, 200 Negroes and £29,650 in cash and negotiable securities.[30] Under the law of colonial Virginia a wife's property belonged to her husband; overnight, then, Washington, at the age of twenty-seven, became one of the richest men in the colony. Equally important was Washington's move to the apex of Virginia's oligarchy. Its leading aristocrat was Benjamin Harrison V, whose wife's brother was married to the sister of Martha Dandridge, which put Washington into the charmed circle that controlled Virginia. As a result, Washington became a candidate for the house of burgesses and was elected in the same year as his marriage. He represented Frederick County until 1765 when he was elected to serve for Fairfax County and did so until his appointment as commander of the Revolutionary forces. Actually, Washington was not a very active burgess; a large part of his time was spent managing Mount Vernon or taking trips in order to speculate for land. In this period he was also handling the sale and leasing of Fairfax and Carter lands, which position gave him the first choice to acquire land at an inside price.

John Adams later declared that Washington rose on Martha Custis's money. But to condemn the future president for a rich marriage one would have to condemn the system itself rather than an individual. Washington did not marry solely for money; like all Virginia aristocrats, including Thomas Jefferson and Patrick Henry—indeed, like almost all eighteenth-century aristocrats everywhere—Washington picked Martha for a number of class reasons, of which money was only the most obvious.[31]

Before this felicitous union, Washington had already increased his land holdings to 5,000 acres of good land and 49 slaves. With Martha's money, George went on a buying spree: first 7,500 acres adjoining and near Mount Vernon, and then acreage in Frederick, King George, Hampshire, Loudon, and Fauquier counties. By 1771 he had acquired 13,000 additional acres in the Virginia counties.

The period following the defeat of the French and before the American Revolution was a great epoch for companies plunging in western land speculation. George Washington was active here as well. The Ohio Company claims having been blocked, the same interests organized the Mississippi Company in 1763, for which Washington wrote the incorporation papers. In this same year he became a leading promoter of the Great Dismal Swamp venture, involving land below Norfolk in Virginia. Organized by top southern magnates such as William and Thomas Nelson, Robert Burwell, John Robinson, Dr. Thomas Walker, and Fielding Lewis—the same names that appear over and over with almost monotonous regularity in land grants made by the Virginia oligarchy—the enterprise, which consisted of draining the swamp and building a waterway, was a great success. Washington, who was the managing director of the corporation from 1763 to 1768, sold his ten percent interest in the 40,000 acres to General Henry Lee in 1795.

After the victory over the French, Colonel Washington pushed with great zeal the claims to land of the 1754 Virginia regiment. At their validation, Washington received over 20,000 acres for his own services and purchased warrants from other veterans for an additional 25,000 acres. To hold a valid title the former soldiers had to have their land surveyed and staked, with the title recorded. Kentucky, where the land was awarded, seemed as far away from coastal Virginia at that time as would Mexico today. Many of these veterans sold their awards for next to nothing and Washington, with others like Patrick Henry, snapped them up. Washington wrote to his brother Charles, "As you are situated in a good place for seeing many of the officers at different times, I should be glad if you would (in a joking way rather than in earnest, at first) see what value they set on their lands."[32] This action, though rather shrewd, was perfectly legal.

The border between sharp trading and amoral conduct is at times hard to divine. A lopsided correspondence of thirty-seven letters between George Washington and his land agent, Colonel William Crawford, was published many years ago; the remainder of a larger group of letters was either lost or destroyed. Commencing September 21, 1767, and ending May 23, 1781, only four are from Washington to Crawford.[33] Perhaps for Washington's reputation this is a good thing. A few extracts bring this home.

On September 21, 1767, Washington wrote to Crawford from Mount Vernon:

> I am told that the land or surveyor's office is kept at Carlisle. If so, I am of opinion that Colonel Armstrong, an acquaintance of mine, has something to do in the direction of it, and I am persuaded he would readily serve me. I will write to him the first opportunity on that subject. . . . It is possible, but I do not know that it really is the case, that the custom in Pennsylvania will not admit so large a quantity of land as I require to be entered together; if so, this may perhaps be arranged by making several entries to the same amount, if the expense of doing it is not too heavy. This I only drop as a hint, leaving the whole to your discretion and good management.

Since certain land desired was beyond the Proclamation line, he ended the letter by suggesting that Crawford, to keep it a secret, should check out the best locations "under the guise of hunting game."

On April 20, 1771, Crawford responded to a letter now missing: "You may depend on my being as cautious as you could wish in every particular concerning the soldier lands." This is an obvious response to Washington's order to purchase at discount veterans' awards.

On September 25, 1773, Washington wrote that he had heard that salt springs were found in the area of what is now Louisville, Kentucky. He told Crawford to check the matter and if so, he should take up the land involved in the names of persons who had soldier warrants, but only if he could be sure of buying them out. Washington warned Crawford to do so with great circumspection.

In a separate letter of the same date in late September 1773, Washington advised Crawford to find out as soon as possible what surveys had already been made in order to avoid them, and to concentrate on purchasing the remaining best land before officers from other provinces would try to exercise their warrants.

George Washington was pulling so many strings in this period that it is difficult to follow his speculations, particularly since he sold quickly if he could make a proift. As was mentioned earlier, the records only indicate land held for some time. Several deals we know of are: 3,000 acres at Charters Creek, southwest of Pittsburgh (according to Abernethy, receiving this land from Lord Dunmore on July 5, 1775, that is, three weeks after being nominated to command the Congressional army); 1,200 acres on the Youghiogheny River near Pittsburgh; and an unrecorded number of acres, representing the claims of Captain John Posey and Reverend Dr. Thurston in West Florida.[34] In 1773 an advertisement appeared in the *Baltimore Journal* signed by Washington in which he offered 20,000 acres for sale on the Ohio and Great Kanawha rivers in what is now West Virginia.[35] Though he fought with all his power against the Vandalia Land Company—having written shortly before that it would be a fatal blow to Virginia—Washington wrote at this time to his friend Colonel George Mercer in London inquiring whether any shares in the new company were for sale. He also tried unsuccessfully to buy Colonel Croghan's two shares.

There is no question that Washington's disgust at British curbs on western land schemes, and especially the blocking of the Ohio Company and the Mississippi Company speculations, was a very important factor in his opting for revolution. Woodward amusingly writes, "A map of his political views in the pre-Revolutionary period would be simply a map of the Western Territory, with a few disappointing financial statements from his London agents tacked onto one corner."[36] The Quebec Act of 1774, which nullified all of his western patents aside from those for veterans, must have been the last straw. It is also evident that a major reason for the choice of Washington as commander of the Revolutionary troops had less to do with his previous military exploits, which had been mediocre, and more to do with the need of radical leaders of Massachusetts to promote unity with the South by choosing such an inviolate and monied Virginia aristocrat.

During the Revolution Washington had little time for land speculation but it never left his mind. Writing to his kinsman John Parke Custis from Valley Forge, in a very dark hour for the patriots, Washington stated, "Lands are permanent—rising fast in value—and will be very dear when our independency is established." And at the war's end, between the surrender of Cornwallis in October 1781 and the final peace negotiations, Washington rode by horseback with General George Clinton, then governor of New York, into that state's Mohawk Valley to buy land. There he purchased 6,050 acres in partnership with Clinton. He was also a partner with Clinton in foiled attempts to buy land at Saratoga and Fort Schuyler.

As an indication of Washington's brilliant sense of business, he refused to invest with Robert Morris, the leading financial figure in the North American Land Company speculation, organized after the Revolution to market six million acres of western land. Washington would not join because of the magnitude of the project, refusing to over-extend his credit. His judgment was correct and Morris ended up in debtor's prison when the scheme collapsed. Despite his shabby record in the matter of veterans' warrants after the Seven Years War, it is to Washington's honor that he declined his significant part of the land distribution made by Congress to veterans of the Revolutionary Army.

The last investment of George Washington was in the federal capital named after him, where he purchased four lots in 1793, three years after the district was created, and was one of the first to improve his property by building houses. His holdings had become so extensive that he seemed to have lost track of them. In early 1798, in a letter to his nephew Bushrod Washington, he questioned taxes on a tract which he "had almost forgot."[37]

Though he died unexpectedly in 1799 of quinsy from a chill, George Washington must have had some foreboding: for several months before writing his will the aging man sold off 28,400 acres.[38] Washington willed to individuals 9,227 acres appraised at $220,000; and left to be sold 50,975 acres appraised at $530,000.[39] The liquidation of the estate brought in a bit less, some $500,000, which is still an astronomical sum when one considers the inflation of the dollar since 1799. To give an example, three tracts, one in Pennsylvania, one on the Ohio River, and the third on the Great Kanawha (with great stores of coal in the subsoil) were appraised in the late 1920s at $40,000,000.[40] Indeed, in his charmed life Washington made one mistake and that was to have no children as heirs. Our first president was not only "first in war, first in peace, and first in the hearts of his countrymen," but also first in the annals of American land speculation.

16

Land Bounties Fueling the Revolution

"In 1821 Chief Justice John Jay said to his nephew William Heathcote De-
Lancey: 'Let me tell you, William: the true *history of the American Revolution*
can never be written.' Jay declined to give his reasons, saying, 'You must
be content to know that the fact is as I have said, and that a great many
people in those days were not at all what they seemed, nor what they are
generally believed to have been.' "

Edward Floyd DeLancey's introduction
to Thomas Jones's *History of New York*

The importance of western land as a factor leading to the American Revolution has been acknowledged by most historians. The use of this land as an incentive to recruit and re-enlist Revolutionary soldiers is less known.

The colonials went to war as a divided nation. John Adams, in later years, estimated that one-third of the people were rebels, one-third Loyalists, and the other third neutral. He was perhaps optimistic. The majority in Massachusetts, Connecticut, Maryland, and Virginia were indeed rebel. The evidence suggests, however, that in New York, New Jersey, and Georgia the Loyalists were a majority, while in Pennsylvania and Delaware, where Quaker influence was strong, and in the Carolinas, they were probably the larger element as well.[1] The New York delegation to the Second Continental Congress abstained from voting for Lee's independence resolution on July 2, 1776, over a year after the battle of Bunker Hill; and that state indeed furnished more soldiers to George III than to George Washington.[2]

Though no hard facts are available, this was probably true as well for Georgia and the Carolinas. Some thirty thousand men, more than Washington had in his army at any one time, volunteered to fight with the redcoats against their fellow countrymen.[3]

The British held all the major cities except Boston at various stages of the war and settled comfortably into New York, Philadelphia, Charleston, and Savannah with the assent of most of the citizens. Indeed, colonial society in those cities puffed up to make welcome the British officer class, being so hospitable that the top military brass hated having to go on campaign away from the allure of the urban centers. The farmers of New Jersey and Pennsylvania, as Washington bitterly noted, preferred selling their produce to the British in Philadelphia rather than to the American soldiers starving at Valley Forge. The most ardent patriotic appeals could not drum up a militia in New Jersey to fight; and as for the states south of Virginia, General Nathanael Greene, sent to liberate the Carolinas and Georgia, wrote that he seemed to be operating in enemy country. When the American troops entered Charleston after the British evacuation, they found the streets deserted, with the doors bolted and windows locked; it seemed as though the rebels were occupying rather than freeing the city. So many Loyalists fled the colonies that Shelburne, on the southeastern tip of Nova Scotia, an embarkment point to England, became for a short while the fourth largest city in North America.[4]

The state militias raised by the various provinces were very unreliable except when their home districts were in danger. At the crucial battle of Long Island, as Washington bitterly wrote, whole brigades "on the appearance of the enemy . . . ran away in the greatest confusion without firing a shot."[5] General Daniel Morgan said that the best way to deploy militia was to put them before picked troops who had orders to shoot them if they tried to run away.[6] General Greene shared this contempt. More charitable than Morgan, he would plant the raw recruits in the front line behind bushes and boulders, and ask them to fire two rounds before running back through the Continental Line. A smith and farmer from Rhode Island, General Greene pleaded for black soldiers. But the southern assemblies refused, being far more afraid of training their slaves to shoot guns than of losing the war to the enemy. Congress also got the cold shoulder. Christopher Gadsden of South Carolina, considered one of the most radical leaders of the Revolution, declared: "We are much disgusted here at Congress recommending us to arm our slaves."[7]

Anyone with the patience and the iron stomach to read details of the war years from the original chronicles must come to the objective conclusion that Americans did not win the Revolution so much as the British lost it. England, too, was divided about the war; its divisions were similar to those in the colonies. English records of the time reflect as much "treason" toward the home country as records in America reflect "loyalism." High officers in the British army and navy—including General Sir Jeffrey Amherst and Vice Admiral Augustus Keppel—refused to serve against the colonials. The top line of the navy, Whig by sentiment, was cleft. Sir William Howe, the British commander-in-chief, prior to the spring of 1778, had publicly declared himself in disagreement with royal policy and stated that he would not fight the Americans. He eventually yielded to the appeal of his king. The Duke of Gloucester, brother of George III, openly argued in favor of the colonial side even after the war broke out. Lord Chatham (William Pitt), the most popular political figure in England, was reported to have exclaimed, "I rejoice that America has resisted," when he heard the news of Lexington and Concord. The common people dissented with Crown policy simply by refusing to enlist for war service, thereby forcing the English high command to hire foreign mercenaries.

The American Revolution thus was as much a civil war as that waged on American soil less than a century later. In vying for incompetence, the laurels go to the English; in general it may be said that American generals were bad—except for Nathanael Greene—but that British generals were worse. After the first year of the war, the Americans fought poorly under bickering leaders while the British high officers preferred to lay abed with their American lady-friends hoping that not too many Hessian mercenaries would desert. As the English-oriented *Cambridge Modern History* delicately put it: "Whatever may be our view as to the influence of individuals on the events of history, one may safely say that the mother-country in the struggle with her colonies was singularly unfortunate alike in her military administrators and her commanders."[8]

The question has often been asked why the colonials, so bellicose in word and action up to 1775 and so great in spirit at Bunker Hill, lapsed into sloth in a rather short time. Fatigue and hardship are ready answers but only partly explain a loss of enthusiasm so obvious that the war would have almost surely been lost in a squalid series of soldier mutinies by the winter of 1780–81 if it had not been for French aid.

Simple statistics underscore this fact. Though there is no exact count, the colonial population at the outbreak of the revolt was somewhere between two and a half and three million persons. If one assumes that one-third of the total population was in active rebellion, close to one million persons were hostile to the British. On the usually accepted ratio that one-fifth of this number was composed of men of military age, there were some two hundred thousand soldiers available for service.[9] In the simple war

ENGLISH RECRUITS FOR AMERICA. Stipple engraving by Watson & Dickinson, after a drawing by W. H. Bunbury, London, 1780. The New York Public Library, Astor, Lenox and Tilden Foundations.

tactics of the eighteenth century, certainly half of this number, or one hundred thousand soldiers, could serve at the front. But the Continental Line at peak strength never reached thirty thousand men. When the struggle started, some ninety thousand men did indeed pick up guns and rush to join the various military forces. They then backtracked so quickly that in less than two years the army regulars shrank to five thousand.[10] By 1778 the utmost exertions of Congress brought the Continental Line up to twenty thousand men, from which point it slowly declined again to some six thousand soldiers at the end of the war. In 1777, and again in 1780–81, the British could easily have wiped out their American adversaries if they had been competently led. As the eminent historians Charles A. and Mary R. Beard comment: "When the struggle began a great crowd of patriotic volunteers rushed to the scene of excitement, but as soon as they got a thorough taste of bloodshed and death, masses of them showed a remarkable affection for their homes and safety."[11]

One asks why the colonials did not respond with steadfast bent to the War of Independence. There are of course no simple answers. Comparisons with the French Revolution, which broke out soon thereafter, are as erroneous as those made between peaches and plums. France was the world leader in culture and vied with England for industrial might. The revolutionary center of Paris, with a half million people, was the intellectual capital of the globe. Urban French citizens were already deeply influenced by radical ideas about the nature of society as distinct from a war of independence against a like people. But Americans were Englishmen revolting as Englishmen, with English ideas of law and social form, desiring to retain familiar modes of government even in their zeal as revolutionaries.

In colonial America, despite the oligarchic structure in certain provinces, there was no archaic feudal system or Versailles-type noble caste. There was no dug-in reactionary Church; indeed, all the churches of New England, even the Episcopal church, were for the revolution, while elsewhere Loyalist churches bowed low with prudence before the harsh winds. And the American colonies were stoutly rural, with over 95 percent of the people being farmers. It was no accident that progressive Massachusetts, with literate and cultural Boston as its hub, furnished almost one-third of the revolutionary troops. Even Sam Adams of Massachusetts, the sole indigenous American who in any European sense of the word could be called a radical (as distinguished from popular leaders like Patrick Henry, Christopher Gadsden, and John Hancock), was dominated by his more conservative relative John Adams.

The army—both the Continental Line and the state militias—was made up of these farmers who, once the immediate threat of British tyranny was removed (as they conceived it from the gazettes and pamphlets before the war), thought less of a "people's revolution" and more of the need to get home in spring to plant and in autumn to harvest. They were in truth "summer soldiers and sunshine patriots," in the words of Tom Paine, but they could hardly be otherwise. Their wives and children would starve if the fields were not seeded and reaped; that was the immediate reality, not the writings of Rousseau and Voltaire, nor even the more familiar phrases of Paine's *Common Sense*. From some available evidence, these simple folk (of which about one-third of the white population already was not English in origin) seemed to think that once the British saw that they no longer were wanted in America, George's troops would meekly pack up and go home.

The American soldiers were very poorly paid, and when they were it was in a currency that became almost valueless as the war went on. By November 1779, Congress had issued $241 million worth of Continental money with no specie backing. All the states likewise issued paper money; and together their total currency in circulation was nearly as much as that of the Continental Congress, and with the same lack of gold or silver backing. The pay of soldiers, $6.67 a month, had about $.16 in buying power by 1779. Faced with general discontent, Congress in 1780 issued new paper money, of different appearance, and exchanged it for the old currency on a ratio of forty to one, thus admitting that the Continental dollar had sunk to little more than $.02 in value. Still the inflation continued and "not worth a continental" became literally true, with pounds of paper money needed for the simplest purchase.

By late 1781, Continental currency became worthless while the state issues, guaranteed by Congress, were also unredeemable. The personal credit of Robert Morris, superintendent of finance, was of greater worth than that of the entire nation: during this crucial period he issued $20, $50, and $80 notes in his own name to pay for absolute wants. The army, the soldiers not paid for long periods in a coin of value, began to mutter of mutiny. Since Congress had no power to tax, and could not or would not enforce its requisitions from the states, loans from France[12] and seizure of Tory and British property were the only two real sources of income. Before the war was concluded, at least a third of all property in the colonies had been confiscated, but the benefit was never realized because of the wild inflation. As always, cunning speculators also began to reap their dirty harvest. William Tudor, an aide-de-camp to Washington, watched them at work. "At the end of a campaign," he wrote, "we find butchers, bakers, sutlers with a large army of contractors, with fortunes made at the public expense, whilst a young officer of merit on twenty-six dollars a month is a beggar."[13]

Many sullen soldiers refused to re-enlist, some became privateers, which was more profitable because the crews got a percentage of the haul. This profession, if it may be so deemed, counted in its ranks up to thirty thousand seamen, which is to say more men than served in the regular army. Privateering was almost exclusively a New England coastline monopoly. On the opposite side of the country, indifferent or hostile or disgusted with the war, families spilled west to take up land legally or otherwise. In 1778 alone, over eighteen thousand men, women, and children floated down the Ohio River, while Virginians and Carolinians poured through the passes into Kentucky and Tennessee. Colonel Daniel Brodhead at Fort Pitt bitterly complained that he could not recruit men west of the mountains and charged that the settlers migrated "chiefly to avoid militia duty and taxes," while Major William Croghan wrote, "The country beyond the Alleghenies talks of nothing but killing Indians and taking possession of their lands."[14]

The American Revolution thus cannot be compared to what happened in France. The War of Independence was a quagmire in which stubborn high-placed men sitting on opposed shores of the Atlantic Ocean, sharing a common language, religion, and set of values, waited to see which side would outlast the other. Finally, the military and economic strain of simultaneously fighting France, Spain, Holland, and the American colonies became too much for Britain. The French fleet was striking at the British West Indies, overseas trade was paralyzed with all enemy ports closed to their commerce, the public debt was piling up in a hurricane wall, and the English people were just plain fed up.

The major problem facing Congress (as well as the state assemblies) was how to pay its soldiers. Without the power to draft men for the Continental Line, the national government had in effect only the rudiments of a national army and was forced to cajole thirteen state governments controlling thirteen independent armies. Without the power to tax there were no funds available. In 1782, as the war neared its end, as examples, only South Carolina had paid its share of the costs (insisting the money be spent in the state); New York and Maryland complied with a mere five percent; New Hampshire less than one percent; while North Carolina, Delaware, and Georgia paid nothing at all.

In fact, the so-called national government was broke. It remained able to function only by French and Dutch loans. What it did have in abundance, however, was western land. The fact that this land did not belong to the colonials but rather to the Indians, the original native Americans, was an awkward but not insuperable problem. The further fact that the colonists were fighting a war to be masters of the land on which they were born, and at the same time hiring soldiers by giving away land belonging to others with the same claim, was a paradox that troubled few patriotic minds.

The two things that could be used to entice a soldier to enlist and re-enlist after the first enthusiasm for the war waned were land giveaways and slaves. Whiteskins were promised ever-larger warrants to land, which were based on killing or expelling redskins before the scrip could be used; and by pledging blackskins in yoke to work that land. General Thomas Sumter, operating in the South, even set a pay scale for his troops in slaves plundered from the Tories; a colonel would get three and a half slaves a year while a private would receive an adult slave, depending on the term of enlistment.[15]

From Patrick Henry, Thomas Jefferson, and the Lees in Virginia to John Hancock and the Adamses in Massachusetts it was agreed that rather than tax the rich patriots in order to support the war effort, it was better to pay soldiers by offering them western land and southern slaves. "We hold these truths to be self-evident," wrote Jefferson in the Declaration of Independence, "that all men are created equal," while at the same time he was binding in perpetual slavery men whose difference with him lay in their skin color. And this was equally true for Indians, who Washington described as "having nothing human except the shape."[16] John Adams, whose pithy views wear well the years, wrote to his friend Dr. Benjamin Rush that he had always considered the Declaration of Independence as theater and that Jefferson had run away with the stage effect.

Because the various states were anxious to enlist militiamen to protect their own citizens' property, Congress, without the power to tax, was outbid in offering land grants. Most Indian tribes, in fear of what did happen, supported the British: the Iroquois Confederation in New York, the Shawnees in Pennsylvania and that part of Virginia which later became Kentucky, and the greater part of the Creeks and Cherokees west of North Carolina and Georgia. This gave state assemblies the opportunity to endorse the legal fiction that since the Indians supported the British, their lands were spoils of war. In New York, privates were offered 600 acres of land, and officers far more, in the northwestern part of the state. Pennsylvania offered privates 200 acres in its northwest, and up to 2,000 acres for a major-general. Virginia bounties ranged from 100 to 15,000 acres for the top officers; North Carolina offered from 200 to 12,000 acres. As the war dragged on, the southerners began to offer package inducements. In 1780 and 1781, with Thomas Jefferson as governor, Virginia voted to award its soldiers with a bounty of 300 acres of land plus a slave. In the same period North Carolina increased its scrip offer to 640 acres and gave as well a bonus of $500 a year and a prime slave if a private would sign up for three years.[17]

The payoff to the top generals was also in land. General Nathanael Greene, who liberated the states of the far South, received from the South Carolina assembly an estate worth £10,000, from the North Carolina assembly 25,000 acres along the Cumberland River, and from Georgia the plantation that had formerly belonged to the loyalist state governor, a property long considered the most beautiful on the Savannah. General Anthony Wayne, transferred to the southern zone toward the end of the war, was likewise granted a baronial plantation by grateful Georgia, The two northern generals, both of whom had expressed dislike of slavery, moved south and promptly became large slaveholders. General George Rogers Clark was paid off in Kentucky land. "General" Ethan Allen of the Vermont militia became land rich by playing under the table with both warring sides. From privates to generals the American Revolution was fought by soldiers whose pay, at first in Continental paper that depreciated almost to no value, was then mainly shifted to land warrants (as well as slaves in the South) by both Congress and the state assemblies.

Before the ink was dry on the resolutions setting up these land bounties, a flourishing business sprang up buying the scrip at great discount for ready money. The state militiamen squandered their warrants because of desperate need. The warrants given to the Continental Line had an even more dismal history. It was not until June 1, 1796—over a decade after the end of the Revolution—that Congress set aside a large district in the Northwest Territory where the scrip would be honored. By that time the vast majority of the soldiers had sold their rights for a pittance to speculators. The system rewarded the old-guard, rich colonials who backed the Revolution and the newly rich created by war profiteering.[18] Philadelphia became the center for the discount acquisition of military warrants, and it was through mass purchase of this scrip that men such as Robert Morris, James Wilson, and John Nicholson rose to great fortune and then collapsed after overextending their speculations. A closer study of this scenario is necessary to understand how the nineteenth-century political structure spewed from these eighteenth-century bowels.

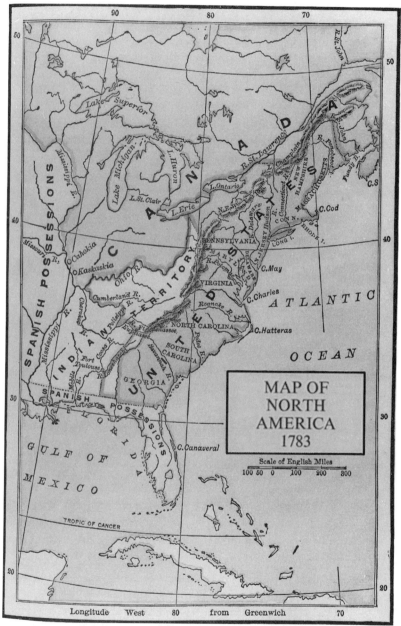

"MAP OF NORTH AMERICA, 1783." Boundaries of the United States, Canada, and Spanish possessions, according to the proposals of the Court of France in 1782. From *The Critical Period of American History (1787–1789),* by John Fiske, Boston, 1901.

17

The Articles of Confederation
and Western Land

*"The essential reason for the long delay in ratifying the Articles of Con-
federation was land-grabbing."*

Samuel Eliot Morison, *The Oxford History of the American People*

The American Revolution was not only a battlefield war between the thirteen
colonies and Great Britain, but an internal political war as well. The states
were often at loggerheads, as were the regions—New England, the Middle
States, and the South—to which they belonged. There was tension between
the planters and merchants, as well as between the rich seaboard and the
deprived back country, the hinterland to a large extent having been settled
by Protestant sects not English in origin. There was also the clash of creditors
and debtors. The slave question remained in dispute. Out from Pandora's
Box of revolution vented a dissident clang of tongues, most of which were
hastily slammed in again.

One conflict that could not be smothered was the struggle over western
land: who would own and who would use this land was to be crucial
for the future of the country. The various provinces had already been
squabbling over this issue by the middle of the eighteenth century. Freed
from British restraint, the squabbling worsened.

The land companies organized by men of these provinces, in particular
Virginia and Pennsylvania, took root during the twenty-five years before

the Revolution. The earliest was the Ohio Company, which was exclusively Virginian. Its rival in Virginia was the Loyal Company. The most powerful Pennsylvania company was that initiated by the "Suffering Traders," which changed its name and enlarged its ambitions to become the Indiana Company and then Vandalia. The Illinois and Wabash companies had Virginian shareholders but were dominated by the merchants of Philadelphia. The Transylvania Company, organized by Judge Richard Henderson of North Carolina, had powerful friends in Virginia. These were the land companies that still exercised influence at the outbreak of the Revolution. Since buying and selling of company shares continued throughout the war years, individuals from other states—especially Maryland and New Jersey—became shareholders as well. But the dominant interests remained the same.

Within the various state assemblies the conservative and popular factions jockeyed for power.[1] Many of the leading conservatives held shares in these companies and pressed to approve the legitimacy of the original Indian purchases or British grants on which company claims were based. The popular parties, especially those in the South where the states had enormous western land claims, pushed for state sovereignty with the declared aim that the poorer citizens could then join in the land rush. The conservatives based their argument on the sanctity of contracts. Their opponents retorted by quoting from the original state charters, whose land grants stretched westward. As the land companies saw the popular tide flowing against them, they then emphasized the need for a strong national policy. The popular parties rested their position on states' rights. This seemingly separate and unrelated issue was in fact intimately involved with the conflict, because the conservatives had control or great influence in many of the state assemblies in the middle and northern provinces, which could thus out-vote the southerners in Congress as to whether the claims of the land companies would be honored. It is therefore impossible to study the fight over confederation of the states—which was done by each state subscribing to the Articles of Confederation—without also dissecting the real purposes of the advocates of state control of western lands as against those pushing for national control of these lands.

The various states at the start of the Revolution can be divided into two groups with respect to this matter. The first group consisted of states with large land claims to the West, called the landed states. First and foremost was Virginia, which, on the basis of her original charter, insisted that the enormous territory due west and northwest belonged to her, including what would eventually become West Virginia, Kentucky, and the Northwest Territory—a block of land about as large as the original thirteen colonies put together. Georgia claimed the land west to the Mississippi.

North Carolina asserted a claim to the western land now making up Tennessee. New York, Massachusetts, and Connecticut all claimed specific parts of the Northwest Territory, though with less legal foundation: New York through Indian treaties, Massachusetts through its charter received from King James I, and Connecticut through the charter given by King Charles II.[2] The landless states, those with definite western boundaries, were Pennsylvania (aside from some disputes with Virginia in the Pittsburgh area), Maryland, New Jersey, Delaware, and Rhode Island. These, except for Pennsylvania, were also the smaller states.

The quarrel was soured by the fact that men with great power in the southern states had already patented or were set to patent vast areas west of the Alleghenies. The real fight, therefore, was not solely between southern radicals fighting to hold the land for small settlers, as claimed, but also between land speculators of the southern states against the shareholders of the land companies in the middle states. The shift to the battlefield of states' rights versus national primacy was in important ways a political charade behind which different power groups clashed.

Merrill Jensen, the historian whose writings have best illuminated this period, refers to the land company shareholders: "Before the Revolution it had been the British government to which they appealed for a share in 'the West' of the eighteenth century. Once the Revolution had begun, they turned from London to Philadelphia." And Jensen adds with justice, "The landed states may be pardoned their refusal to sacrifice their interests to the 'good of the whole' when it is recognized that they saw nothing in such phrases but the program of the speculators of the landless states."[3] This was the nub of the problem and explains why the Articles of Confederation were so long delayed in ratification, for the only way the men controlling the Indiana Company and the Illinois and Wabash companies—centered in Pennsylvania, New Jersey, and Maryland—could hope to block the southern states from their land to the west was to force a compromise by delaying formation of the new national government.[4]

The Articles of Confederation were a loose package, consisting in the main, like the Ten Commandments, of "shalt nots" rather than "shalts." Each state retained its sovereignty as well as those powers not expressly delegated to the central government. The states monopolized all revenue: Congress could ask for but could not enforce requisitions. The states still regulated their own commerce since Congress did not have the power to settle commercial disputes among the states or to enforce its will in any matter. In addition, the unanimous vote of all thirteen states was needed for amending the Articles.

Congress did have certain powers, a few of which vitally concerned

Virginia. Congress alone could deal with Indians outside of the states, including those living in the western lands to which Virginia laid claim. Congress had the sole right to declare peace or war, which meant Virginia had great interest in fending off a peace treaty that might involve compulsory settlement of unpaid debts owed to British merchants from before the Revolution.[5] Most important of all, Congress appointed generals and naval officers and directed the army. When the war in its later stages had moved to Virginia soil, and the state refused to compromise, she learned that this power alone—the Congressional power to redirect troops from one area to another—meant more to her than an intransigent position on the land question.

The ratification of the Articles of Confederation was delayed more than three years, from November of 1777 to February of 1781, due to the vicious squabbles among these land interests. Virginia was the leader of the landed states and Maryland, for reasons to be discussed, was the leader of those without western land claims.

If the fight had merely been between two groups of greedy men, it would have been compromised at an early date. But this land question was only part of a more complex background. Many southerners with no financial interest and who sincerely desired that these lands should be preempted for settlers or given to war veterans, felt that the power given Congress to decide company land claims was a direct infringement of the rights of a sovereign state. Thomas Jefferson and James Madison were among these advocates. Some supporters of the landless states, also with no personal interest, realized that only by ownership and sale of western land could cash be raised by Congress; and in fact the sale of such lands was the sole real source of federal income outside of foreign loans and Tory confiscations. For that reason those honest northerners supported the position of the smaller states. The land speculators were also aided by genuine concern on the part of certain middle states (mainly Delaware, Maryland, and New Jersey) that if the states farther south sold their western land cheaply to all comers, the smaller middle states would lose population while Virginia, North Carolina, and Georgia would grow rich at their expense.

The combatants were not unmindful of the stakes, and the Congressional records indicate astonishing frankness as well as mutual recriminations between the contenders. From these records we can follow the pattern of events.

The previous study of the land companies has already indicated the main personalities. The largest and most important company was that organized by the "Suffering Traders" from Pennsylvania who worked with

British interests through a series of changes that culminated in the Indiana Company, which was then called Vandalia, from the name given to their land grant. The principals were Samuel Wharton, his brother Thomas Wharton, (who took a less active role) and George Morgan, all of the Philadelphia firm of Baynton, Wharton, and Morgan. This firm went bankrupt and its successor in interest—though the original founders were still deeply involved—was David Franks and Company, the operating name for the Franks brothers. Tied in also were William Franklin, illegitimate son of Benjamin Franklin, who had been appointed British governor of New Jersey through his father's influence and was proxy for his father; Joseph Galloway, Benjamin Franklin's business associate and the richest merchant of Philadelphia; William Trent, a former Pennsylvanian who moved to New Jersey, where he became speaker of that state's assembly; and George Croghan, a founder of the Indiana Company and deputy superintendent of Indian affairs of the northern department under Sir William Johnson.

The Illinois and Wabash companies were separate until they merged their activities under the name of the United Illinois and Wabash Land Companies. The Illinois Company was dominated by the same Franks brothers who were involved in the Indiana Company, along with the Gratz brothers, who were likewise from Pennsylvania. The Wabash Company had as leading members Governor Thomas Johnson, ex-governor William Paca, Charles Carroll of Carrollton, and Samuel Chase, all of whom were from Maryland. William Paca was the brother-in-law of Robert Morris, the leading capitalistic plunger of eighteenth-century America, and the two worked very well together. These men, all but Johnson having been signers of the Declaration of Independence, dominated Maryland politics. James Wilson of Philadelphia, who became president of the combined Illinois-Wabash Companies, also had close business relations with Robert Morris, another shareholder.

Against these land companies were pitted most of the leaders of the southern states, each of whom had claims to enormous western lands. George Mason, one of the most powerful men in the Virginia assembly, was foremost in opposition to the Illinois-Wabash Companies, though he still hoped that the Ohio Company of Virginia, the earliest of the land companies whose shareholders were all from Virginia, could successfully reassert its claims once the northern land companies were eliminated. Fighting in Congress for Virginia were James Madison and Arthur Lee. In North Carolina, William Blount, Richard Caswell, and Alexander Martin, the trio of great land speculators with tentacles on their own west, stood behind Virginia at every turn.

The lineup was not cut and dried, for the Philadelphia merchants had many business associates and friends at the highest levels of the Virginia legislature. Patrick Henry's position was equivocal; as a shareholder of the Indiana Company, he initially endorsed the claims of that company and retreated into a passive position thereafter. Edmund Pendleton, president of the Virginia Committee of Safety under Patrick Henry, in 1776 gave his legal opinion that the claim of Indiana was invalid, only to reverse himself the next year, apparently for reasons unrelated to idealism.[6] Edmund Randolph, a prominent member of the Virginia legislature (and later the first attorney-general of the United States), still affirmed the validity of the land company Indian purchases as late as May 1779.[7] Robert Morris also did business with Benjamin Harrison and Carter Braxton, leaders of the conservative faction in the Virginia assembly, who were not hostile to the land company claims. James Mercer, though somewhat in limbo as former agent for Virginia under the Stamp Act, was known to favor Indiana.

Vandalia, as previously discussed, had been sunk by the British government, despite its many English investors, out of disgust with the colonial revolt. Thrashing about for a way to save their long investment of time and money, the American shareholders felt that the best approach would be to fall back upon the deed granted by the Six Nations at Fort Stanwix in 1768. Since the purchase from the Iroquois had been made by the Indiana Company, composed of Americans, this company was spun out from Vandalia, into which it had been dissolved, and reorganized in its original form.[8] The goal now would be to have the Fort Stanwix purchase approved by the Continental Congress. In a letter from Samuel Wharton to Benjamin Franklin dated April 17, 1775, Wharton urged Franklin to start a campaign to line up for support the most influential delegates to Congress then sitting at Philadelphia.[9]

In July of 1775, Franklin endorsed a formal written approval of the validity of the Indiana claim. To this Patrick Henry concurred, which on the surface was surprising for such a prominent Virginian. Henry took a fee from William Trent for this testimonial.[10] It has already been noted that Henry also received a share of company stock at this time. It should be added, however, that at this early point the leading principals of the Indiana Company, feeling that through influence they could adjust any problem with the Virginia legislature, had no objection to coming under the sovereignty of that state if they did not succeed in Congress.

Backed by the approval of Franklin and Henry, Samuel Wharton then suggested that the number of shares be increased by four and then split into half-shares in order to persuade eight key congressmen to aid in the passage of legislation validating company purchases from Indians or, in

Wharton's words, to "assiduously & faithfully unite" them with the land claimants.[11]

The outbreak of the actual fighting in the American Revolution created a curious analogy between the position of the Indiana Company and that of the Ohio Company of Virginia as a result of the Seven Years War. The Ohio Company shareholders were blocked by a change of attitude on the part of Great Britain after the war with France had started. Likewise, the sovereign state of Virginia, in whose western region (now called West Virginia) the Indiana Company lands were located, also changed tack after declaring independence. The Virginians, whose speculators were as aggressive as those from the middle provinces, saw no reason to let such a luscious plum fall into the hands of men from other states.

An Indiana Company advertisement in April 1776 to open a western sales office for land brought an immediate challenge by Virginia's members in Congress, who contested the Fort Stanwix cession and claimed the land in question had been purchased by Virginia at the Treaty of Lancaster in 1744 (then, as now, lawyers could always dig up a precedent to color their claims). Legal squabbling immediately started. At this crucial stage the Indiana Company partisans began to lose influence because of their Tory background. Governor William Franklin of New Jersey and Joseph Galloway, then president of the company, openly sided with the British. Franklin was imprisoned in Connecticut; Galloway fled to the safety of British forces in New Jersey. Thomas Wharton, vice-president of the company, along with seven other Pennsylvania Quakers who opposed war, was proscribed as a Loyalist. George Croghan also came under suspicion. Much of the leadership of the Indiana Company fell on George Morgan, who represented the "Suffering Traders," the original claimants.

Charges and countercharges, influences and counterinfluences, eddied around the issue for the next few years, both in Virginia and in Congress. The contest between Virginia, backed by the more southern states, and Pennsylvania, backed by the middle provinces as well as Maryland, became an open battle between competing groups of speculators cloaked in majestic phrases dealing with states' rights on the one hand and the necessity for national sovereignty on the other.

In Virginia the assembly took up the issue in the autumn of 1778. On November 4th all purchases from Indians were declared void within the bounds of the state charter. This invalidated the land company claims. However, a partial exception was made as to the Transylvania Company, organized by Judge Henderson of North Carolina. Henderson had powerful friends in Virginia, including Patrick Henry, and as a result a compromise was reached giving the company a large grant of land between the Green and Ohio rivers.

Still under pressure from the conservative faction, the assembly, anxious to settle the matter once and for all, called all representatives of the land companies to appear and defend their claims at the spring session of 1779. William Trent shrewdly sold some of his Indiana shares to William Grayson, thus assuring that the prominent Virginian would testify in support of the company. This was when Edmund Randolph also supported the company's position. Representatives of the Illinois-Wabash Companies and the Ohio Company presented their claims as well. Unfortunately for these companies, few of their shareholders came from Virginia (except the Ohio Company, which was still feuding in Virginia with its old rival, the Loyal Company).

George Mason, as always, led the opposition. He pointed out that the deeds of some of the companies had never been recorded in the general court of Virginia. Damaging testimony that William Crawford, land agent for George Washington, had earlier deposed before Virginia commissioners at Pittsburgh, was entered. Crawford stated that Indiana had not made a survey of the lands and thus did not even know its own boundaries. The point was stressed that the Pennsylvania "Suffering Traders," on whose claim Indiana was successor, should be granted compensation from that state's land rather than from Virginia. Mason concluded that Virginia was now a "nation" and accordingly the Indiana grant was void since it had been made to "foreigners."[12]

The case, as could have been foretold, was decided by Virginia against the "foreign" land companies. Several exceptions were again allowed. The Virginians stipulated that all previous land patents were valid. Included in this decision were those patents based upon Dinwiddie's grants made at the beginning of the war with the French, those made at the time of the 1763 Proclamation, grants from royal governors, and acreage settled by Virginia farmers before January 1, 1778. Thus the individual claims of men like George Washington and Dr. Thomas Walker were approved. The old Loyal Company likewise got two hundred thousand acres, while the Ohio Company was left out in the cold. Here again we see a reflection of the older Tidewater aristocrats, who were the leaders of the conservative faction of the Virginia assembly, being defeated by the newer aristocrats of the Piedmont, who dominated the popular faction in the assembly. In sum, the small settlers who had moved west were protected, as were the most influential native speculators of Virginia, while the claims of those from the other states operating through the land companies were thwarted.

Almost immediately, on June 22, 1779, a land office bill was passed and a land office opened for sales, "provided of course that the Virginia

GEORGE MASON OF VIRGINIA. Oil on canvas, by Dominic W. Boudet (1811), after a lost portrait by John Hesselius. Courtesy of the Virginia Museum of Fine Arts, Richmond, Virginia. Gift of David K. E. Bruce.

speculators had left any choice lots to be sold," as Merrill Jensen added sardonically.[13] Thomas P. Abernethy also points out that there was no limitation put on the amount of land that could be bought in the West. As a loyal Virginian, Abernethy prefers to call this a "colossal mistake, and then writes: "There is an element of historical irony in the fact that Jefferson, the father of democracy, should have helped to draft the act by which democracy was defeated in Virginia at the moment when it might have had its birth."[14] Given the nature of the men who controlled the legislature, this was a deliberate omission. We will shortly see what came about as a result.

After this defeat, the land company promoters went back to their initial position, namely, that the western lands belonged to the entire Confederation rather than the individual states and it was solely for Congress to decide the validity of the claims. The legal basis, so the lawyers argued, was that the area had been separated from Virginia by the British after the 1768 purchase from the Indians at Fort Stanwix and thus the Declaration of Independence had brought the land to the nation as a whole. The line of reasoning was the exact opposite to that used by these same lawyers shortly before when they asked Virginia, as the sovereign of the region, to confirm their land grants. But consistency was not the issue, for the companies "were, in fact, ready to uphold either national or state sovereignty if by either means they could get the land they wanted!"[15] The shareholders of the land companies had enough power in the middle and adjoining states to control the committees set up by Congress, all of which reported that the western lands belonged to the nation and it was the unique right of the nation as a whole, through Congress, to affirm the validity of land company grants. In response, Virginia, supported by North Carolina and Georgia,[16] haughtily stated that Congress had no right to interfere in the state's internal affairs. Back and forth the matter went, from committee to committee, for over a year.

So intense was this debate that foreign powers were actually sucked into the drama. The first two French ministers to the Confederation, Conrad Gerard and John Holker, bought shares in the Illinois-Wabash Companies, as did Silas Deane of Connecticut, who was involved in business relations with the French and, many years later, was exposed as a double agent. These men attempted to pressure Congress to invalidate the Virginia claim. Their smokescreen for this purpose was to assure Spain, as a new ally that France had succeeded in bringing into the war on the American side, that the new nation had no desire for a western empire. The Machiavellian dealings behind stage are still only partly known; bribery was widely suspected, and at one point Cyrus Griffin of Virginia charged that the Indiana

Company had offered Congress a present of £10,000 to confirm its grant. Samuel E. Morison wrote, "The Wabash Company engaged in tortuous negotiations with Congress, with Maryland and with France; an intrigue which, could it be unraveled, might prove more fascinating than the story of Arnold's treason or Burr's conspiracy."[17] On the other side, there is no question that the expedition of George Rogers Clark in 1778 was launched by Virginia as much to press its western land claims as to aid the Revolutionary struggle.[18] It should also be noted that both sides in the dispute mutually agreed on one point, that any rights of the Indians to the western land, so loudly debated in London before the war, did not exist. Independence was for white settlers, holding in subjugation black slaves, and western claims rested ultimately on the killing of the people living there.

Late in 1780 the news reached Virginia that the turncoat Benedict Arnold, in command of a large British army, was prepared to invade that state. The assembly frantically applied to Congress for Continental Line soldiers, who were far superior to the badly disciplined state militia. Nothing much happened. It did not take a long memory for the Virginia leaders to recall that when they had previously asked for Continental troops to support George Rogers Clark in his attempt to take Detroit, the congressmen from the landless states had turned them down. They were only too aware, with the constant friction in their own assembly between the conservative and popular factions, that victory or defeat can rest as much on a show of hands as on a volley of bullets.

The Virginia assembly, in its last act of January 2, 1781, before fleeing Richmond almost within earshot of British gunfire, agreed to compromise. The state accepted a cession to Congress of its land claims north of the Ohio River in the Northwest Territory, subject to certain conditions: the land reserved to pay military bounties was to be respected, the expense of Clark's expedition would be reimbursed, Virginia's land claims south of the Ohio River were to be recognized, the last states not yet ratifying the Articles of Confederation must do so, and all private purchases of Indian land were to be voided. Even at a time when one could almost hear a death rattle, with Governor Thomas Jefferson preparing to flee as though a fugitive, the Virginia land speculators were powerful enough to insert that last clause, which meant the elimination of their northern rivals in West Virginia and Kentucky. Yet this was a compromise that let in the first sharp light of hope for a united Confederation of States. Abernethy, with great restraint, concludes: "The gloomy outlook by that event [Benedict's invasion] may have had some connection with the new stand taken."[19]

Congress itself was also facing serious problems. A mutiny of unpaid soldiers which forced the congressmen to flee Philadelphia, brought into stark relief the need to satisfy the soldier's land warrants through assuming ownership of the West. By the terms of the Virginia cession the Northwest Territory could become federal property only if the land company claims were somehow bypassed. A new committee was set up to review the matter again and this time its membership was not dominated by the landless states, which is to say, the land company speculators. This committee moved toward the Virginia position. Congress approved the report and accepted Virginia's cession of the area north of the Ohio River without guarantees to the land companies.[20] The French ministers with shares in the Illinois-Wabash Companies were instructed by their home government, staggering under a tremendous debt due to aid for the Revolution, to push Maryland, the final holdout, to ratify the Articles of Confederation in order to create a specific body of authority, the Confederation, to negotiate a peace. The Maryland assembly became tired of its obstructionist role, influenced as well by the fear of invasion from the British troops moving north through Virginia. On March 1, 1781, Maryland ratified the Articles and the American child at last poked its head out from the inflamed womb of real estate.

To compress a most complex series of events, the land speculators of Virginia, backed by those of North Carolina and Georgia, defeated those of Pennsylvania, Maryland, and New Jersey. The alarming state of the public credit and the need to back soldier warrants by actual land forced Congress to accept Virginia's modified position. Maryland's refusal to sign the Articles of Confederation, which had been instigated by the shareholders in the private land companies, had made Virginia relinquish its claims to the vast land mass of the Northwest Territory; but Virginia received the area southwest of the Ohio River as compensation and also was reimbursed for the cost of the George Rogers Clark expedition.

When the peace treaty was signed with Great Britain in 1783, the Confederation acquired a land mass greater than any nation in all Europe, save Russia. The lower part went to the speculators from the southern states operating in what became West Virginia, Kentucky, Tennessee, Alabama, and Mississippi. The northern part belonged to the federal government. A tremendous block of land, later known as the states of Ohio, Indiana, Illinois, Michigan, and Wisconsin, now shimmered before the covetous eyes of the men from New England and the middle states, who regarded this territory as their bailiwick. We shall see what both groups of speculators did.

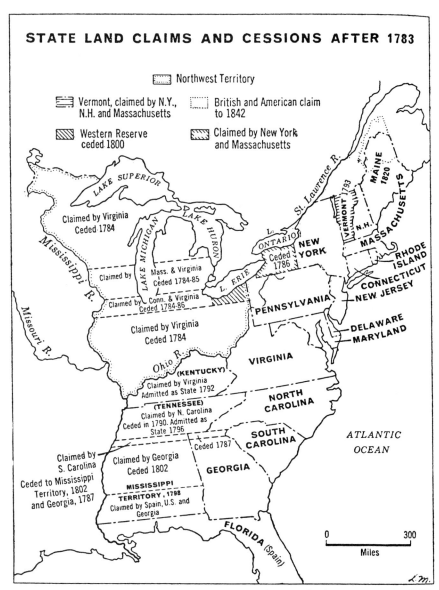

From *The Rise of the West: 1754–1830,* by Francis S. Philbrick, New York, 1965.
Reproduced by permission of HarperCollins Publishers.

Part Three

Land Speculation
in the Southern States

18

George Rogers Clark

"Land is the only thing in the world that amounts to anything, for 'tis the only thing in this world that lasts, and don't you be forgetting it!"

Gerald O'Hara to his daughter Scarlett in
Gone With the Wind, by Margaret Mitchell

George Rogers Clark is one of the most interesting medical cases in the history of the United States. The well-known Spanish doctor Gregorio Marañon wrote a fascinating biography of the Roman Emperor Tiberius, subtitling the study "History of a Resentment." Some psychologist with a gift for writing could probably trace with similar depth the sickness of George Rogers Clark.

The future general came from the planter cast eof Virginia. His parents had their estate on the tract next to the Jeffersons in Albemarle County and the two men knew each other from youth. Another neighbor was Dr. Thomas Walker. As has been pointed out earlier, these new aristocrats from the Piedmont in Virginia were more aggressive than their rivals, the older aristocrats from the Tidewater, though the two cliques often made common cause when it came to speculation farther west. Young Clark therefore naturally assumed a commanding role when he was appointed a captain of militia in Lord Dunmore's War. Because of family contacts, he was then chosen deputy to Colonel Hancock Lee, George Washington's successor as chief surveyor for the Ohio Company. Sent to what would be central Kentucky, part of the Ohio Company claims, the surveyors laid out a town near present-day Frankfort, where Clark decided to settle. The basis on which he had joined the surveying party was a small salary with the right to take for himself at no cost a percentage of the land. In a letter to his brother at this time he wrote, "I am engrossing all ye land I possibly can."[1] Possessing only incomplete records, we do not know the precise extent of young Clark's claims, but various sources list two different stakes: a tract of 1,400 acres containing a rare and valuable salt "lick," from which salt was boiled from water to preserve meat for winter use; and a claim from 1773 at the mouth of Fishing Creek on the Ohio River. It should be emphasized that all this activity was illegal since the area was west of the Proclamation line; in a technical sense, like Richard Henderson of the Transylvania Company, George Rogers Clark was an outlaw under British law.

At the outbreak of the Revolution, the advance frontiersmen in what is now Kentucky were in a desperately exposed position and it seemed that they would be forced to retreat east to Virginia, as many had done, or stand and fight. A third approach was to counterattack the Illinois country and relieve pressure on the isolated Kentucky settlements. The advantages of such a surprise move were many. Indians were very impressed by such tactics and this would neutralize certain tribes who were yet unsure as to whom to support in the war. If the scattered white settlers left Kentucky, any claims to the region in the future peace negotiations would be endangered; on the other hand, new territory seized would be the basis for enlarged claims. Most of all, the conquerors, taking unsettled lands, would have first rights to the soil. The mixture of the desire for military glory in creating a greater Virginia and personal lust for land pushed audacious souls to take the chance. Many powerful interests, as we will soon discover, silently backed such a decision.

A young popular man with military experience, knowledge of the country to be crossed, and unquestioned loyalty to Virginia was needed to head such an expedition. The choice was George Rogers Clark, a man of good Virginia stock, a former militia captain familiar with the western terrain, and hungry both for land and glory. The comparison of Clark to young Washington before the Seven Years War is irresistible, and for the next few years, before certain strains in his nature showed, it seemed that Clark might become a new Washington.

Under the Quebec Act of 1774 the enormous area that included the Illinois country was made part of the province of Quebec. Though administered from New York, a lieutenant-governor as well as one of the four district courts were established at Kaskaskia, the link in the main trade route that ran from Philadelphia through Pittsburgh and down river to New Orleans. The brilliant conquest of Kaskaskia by George Rogers Clark is an epic often told. The background to this feat and the puzzling lack of all resistance at Kaskaskia is another matter. The Virginia historian Thomas P. Abernethy does some interesting detective work in relating the 1778 Clark expedition to the interest of the land companies operating in the area.[2]

Abernethy points out that William Murray, kinsman of the Earl of Dunmore, had worked at Kaskaskia for several years as agent for the Franks brothers, who organized the Illinois and Wabash companies in which Murray was an important shareholder. William Murray's brother, Daniel Murray, who was also located at Kaskaskia, and John Campbell, agent for the Franks and Gratz interests and holder of the position of county lieutenant of Yohogania (one of the most westerly Virginia counties), also were shareholders. These men had close ties with the French inhabitants of the Illinois country who had become part of the English booty in the Seven Years War and would not be disappointed to see Britain beaten. They also had close trading connections with the Indians of the region.

The British, to avoid unnecessary expense, had withdrawn their regular troops from Kaskaskia in the spring of 1776. It was evident to the Illinois-Wabash shareholders that the Illinois country could be easily seized if Virginia would send troops, a decision that would naturally aid Virginia's claims to the territory and strengthen the claims of the various land companies.[3] Gunpowder was needed, of which Virginia was in very short supply, but this could be obtained through the Spanish at New Orleans.

In May 1776, Colonel George Gibson, brother of the commander of one of the Virginia regiments on the Pittsburgh frontier and a member of the Indiana Company, travelled to Williamsburg and secured official letters from Oliver Pollock, New Orleans representative of the American cause and a close friend of the Spanish governor. At this time William Murray was also at New Orleans on business. Gibson set out on the long river voyage down the Mississippi to New Orleans, where he bought twelve thousand pounds of powder paid for by Virginia. The round trip took much time and it was spring of 1777 before the precious cargo arrived at the mouth of the Ohio River. Letters were also brought from William Murray to his brother Daniel at Kaskaskia as well as another American merchant there, informing them that the Kaskaskia merchants should be prepared to receive any Americans who might arrive. On April 20, George Rogers Clark sent his agents to contact the key merchants. It was a remarkably coordinated effort. On June 22, Clark's agents returned with the news that an American invasion would be welcomed.

GEORGE ROGERS CLARK. From a portrait painted
by John Wesley Jarvis.

It was at this point that Clark set out for Williamsburg and asked permission to conquer the Illinois country. The House of Delegates and the Virginia council approved and on January 2, 1778, Governor Patrick Henry gave Clark instructions to take Kaskaskia, the expedition to be kept as secret as possible because Virginia did not have the approval of Congress. Arrangements were made with Clark to pay each volunteer three hundred acres out of the conquered land if the expedition were successful. "So confident was he of the outcome that he entered into partnership with the Governor for securing possession of a tract of land."[4] As Abernethy writes, "It is obvious that the Illinois land company interests, through the Kaskaskia merchants and apparently through General Hand (American commander at Pittsburgh) who had bought thousands of acres from Croghan[5] and was otherwise connected with them, were cooperating with Henry in the conquest of the Northwest."[6] On the night of July 4, 1778, Clark captured Kaskaskia without a struggle.

This is not to say that the forced marches through hostile Indian country by a small force under George Rogers Clark was an event of no importance for the Revolutionary cause. Indeed, the taking of Kaskaskia and then Vincennes (another of the district administrative centers for the Northwest Territory) on February 25, 1779, laid one of the groundworks at the Paris peace negotiations for American claims to the land between the Alleghenies and the Mississippi River.[7] It should be evident, however, that it is easier to conquer an enemy that has already agreed to surrender than one that stoutly resists. In fact, the subsequent failure of Clark to take Detroit in a series of campaigns over several years was precisely because that fort was occupied by English soldiers determined to fight back rather than by Frenchmen who took pleasure, as at Kaskaskia, in seeing their ancient British enemy humbled by buckskin frontiersmen.

The western campaigns of Clark were neither authorized nor approved by Congress. During the Revolution George Rogers Clark was acting as a military officer for Virginia, not for the confederated states. It may be noted that as long as events were favorable, this relation was preferred by Clark and the leaders of his native state. Behind this attitude was the all-engrossing question being fought out in Congress as to whether the western lands belonged to the entire nation or to the separate states having specific claims. Virginia sent Clark as a native son to conquer territory for Virginia and had no intention of ceding the conquered territory to the nation as a whole. Clark, as an individual, passionately supported by Governor Patrick Henry and the land speculators so influential in the Virginia government, wanted to hold Kentucky and conquer the Illinois country in order to patent the land.[8] At first the organized land companies backed

Virginia under the assumption that their claims would be recognized by the state's legislature.

The young hero's troubles began when the Virginia speculators, swollen with delight on seeing the whole Northwest about to fall into their laps, made an about-face and refused to "cut in" the shareholders from the middle provinces who controlled the land companies with previous claims to the Illinois country. Exerting pressure through Congress, these powerful interests then began to isolate Virginia by withholding Congressional money and military aid. Clark's last failed campaign to take Detroit was impelled indeed by the need of Virginia to solidify its claim to all the western territory while the dominant faction of Congress watched passively, not willing to raise a finger until Virginia would share with the other states, and their speculators, the land she considered private booty.

The American Revolution had been won, Kentucky was secured for Virginia, and the Northwest Territory conceded at the peace treaty to be American territory in part due to his conquests; George Rogers Clark— just thirty years old—was at the height of fortune. He had no way of knowing that the rest of his life would be all downhill, but there were already vague disquieting reports that friends passed off as envy. The hostility to Clark's impressment of soldiers in Kentucky, an illegal action which he had done under extreme desperation, was forgotten in the exultation of triumph. It was already known that he was a very heavy drinker, but this was common enough on the frontier—indeed, everywhere in eighteenth-century America. The charges of general corruption and swindling of merchants in the Illinois country, mainly unfounded as we now know, were casually investigated and just as casually dropped. Other than a brief and probably apocryphal romance, Clark showed no interest in women; but frontier Kentucky was not a lair for the sensual. Even his hot rages and arrogance were natural enough in a conqueror of such relative youth.

In 1784, through the influence of Jefferson, Clark was appointed one of the national commissioners for Indian affairs, the sole representative from the West, as well as president of the board whose members were to distribute the one hundred and fifty thousand acres awarded to veterans of his campaign. A town called Clarksville—the site chosen being across from Louisville—was founded and surveys were authorized. This was the period when Kentuckians—now of mixed population, with loyal Virginians in the minority—started to push for independent statehood. Clark, in loyalty to his native state, opposed all such separatist movements. The charming villain James Wilkinson, of whom more will be heard later, had settled in Kentucky. Subtle and understanding the gregarious ways of the frontier, he was soon a more popular figure. Clark began to retreat into the bottle.

Furthermore, he received no pay during the war and, having personally assumed the debts incurred for supplies, he found that the land certificates received as commander of the western forces of Virginia had little value in the post-war depression. The Commonwealth of Virginia considered his constant requests for compensation more and more vexing, and when the rumors of his drunken bouts began to circulate, now deliberately exaggerated by the conniving of Wilkinson, even Clark's friends started to have second thoughts about his competence. The first setback was his dismissal as one of the commissioners for Indian affairs.

George Rogers Clark was a bad businessman and, as the son of a southern plantation owner, he had contempt for the type of ordered avidity and pragmatic conduct necessary to such a way of life. In 1788 he settled, with several dozen black slaves to serve him, on a mile-square tract called Mulberry Hill, overlooking the town of Louisville. There he devoted himself to hunting and exploring prehistoric Indian remains.[9] It was in this period that both his physical and mental powers began to decline. His dreams still focused on becoming a great military hero and, revealingly, the one request for a book among his few remaining letters was for a volume on the life of King Frederick the Great of Prussia.

Feeling neglected by his own country, George Rogers Clark became susceptible to the blandishments of foreign intrigue in the border country. Barely middle aged, muddled by drink, subject to hypochondria and self-pity, he first turned to the Spanish. Writing to Don Diego de Gardoqui, the first Spanish envoy to the United States, he proposed to found a colony of Americans on the west bank of the Mississippi under the flag of Spain. The colony was to be one hundred miles square of territory, with freedom of religion and six councillors elected to serve under a governor appointed by the Spanish king. The governor of course was to be Clark. Some five years after the treaty settling the Revolution, the general who conquered the Illinois country for America was proposing to become a Spanish subject and induce other Americans to follow him. As that ultrapatriot Theodore Roosevelt put it, Clark was "quite willing to do his fighting in behalf of Spain instead of against her!"[10] The offer came to nothing because of Spain's irresolute policy.

The wars with the Indians in the Northwest Territory gave Clark new hope for military glory. Two American armies had been smashed and he wrote to his old friend Thomas Jefferson, pleading for the chance to lead an avenging force. The plea went unanswered. Jefferson touched on the reason in a sympathetic letter written in March 1791 to a mutual friend: "I knew the greatness of his mind, and am mortified at the cause which obscured it. Had this not unhappily taken place there was nothing he might not have hoped. . . ."[11] The cause, of course, was John Barleycorn, who now had Clark firmly in his toxic grip.

The clang of the French Revolution on the frontier awakened Clark from his apathy. The settlers in Kentucky and Tennessee were violent partisans of the French for a mixed bag of reasons. Many had fled the control of the aristocrats back East and felt an undoubted sympathy. A more important reason was the shrewd French promise to free the Mississippi River from trade restrictions if the Spanish, now enemies of France, were defeated.

Letters in the files of the French government,[12] as well as correspondence of Thomas Paine, make it abundantly clear that George Rogers Clark approached French officials on his own initiative and offered to attack Louisiana, resigning his American citizenship to become a French citizen. Barely forty years of age, ambitious, passed over for those he considered his military inferiors, it was evident that Clark's patriotism had rotted to the point of stink. His friend Tom Paine's acceptance of French citizenship at this time may have been an added factor.

The French government accepted Clark's offer and bestowed on him the rank of major-general in their army and commander-in-chief of the French Revolutionary Legion on the Mississippi River. Citizen Edmond Genêt, the minister to the United States of the new French republic and the go-between, received a letter from Clark requesting £3,000 sterling to raise an army to invade Spanish Louisiana. Before going ahead, Genêt contacted his friend and sympathizer Thomas Jefferson, "not as Secretary of State, but as Mr. Jefferson,"[13] and told him the plan.

Jefferson was no George Rogers Clark, who could in one decade be an American or a Spaniard or a Frenchman. Against profound personal feelings, since his heart was for the cause of the French Revolution, Jefferson made his decision. "I told him" Jefferson said, "that his enticing officers and souldiers from Kentucky to go against Spain, was really putting a halter about their necks, for they would assuredly be hung, if they commd. [commenced] hostilities agt. [against] a nation at peace with the U.S. . . ."[14]

Not knowing of this rebuff, Clark continued to plan the invasion. He made an open appeal for volunteers, offering one dollar a day or one thousand acres of conquered land if the expedition were a success. This offer clearly shows that Genêt was authorized to grant an unknown but obviously huge land grant to Clark as part of the overall agreement.

Blocked by Jefferson, Genêt never advanced the money requested. He was soon commanded to return to France.[15] The new French minister issued a statement in March 1794 forbidding any action that violated the neutrality of the United States, reinforced by a proclamation from Washington making it unlawful for American citizens to enlist for such purposes. Clark was undone.

Several times thereafter Clark tried to connive with both Spanish and French authorities. He became involved with Dr. James O'Fallon (who married Frances, Clark's youngest sister) in the promotion of the South Carolina Yazoo Company, whose grant of land from Georgia was in territory claimed by the Spanish. O'Fallon, a rogue and adventurer, conceived the scheme with Clark of setting up an independent state and offered to make an offensive and defensive alliance with Spain if that country would recognize their land claims. The project fizzled when Washington, fearful of a conflict caused by such speculative companies, confirmed the rights of the Indians to their land. And in 1798, when Clark took refuge at St. Louis during the epoch of the Alien and Sedition laws (a warrant for his arrest having been issued in Kentucky because of his refusal to resign his commission in the French army), he again tried to incite the French to launch an expedition under his direction against Spanish Louisiana. By this time, however, the teeth of the aging lion were too loose to frighten anyone.

Clark returned to Kentucky when the Alien and Sedition Laws were repealed after Thomas Jefferson became president. In 1803 he settled in Clarksville. Contrary to the impression given by certain biographers, Clark was not a poor man. Owner of what was a frontier mansion on a large tract of land, with dozens of slaves, the records indicate that in 1803 he cleared an indebtedness to his brother William by a transfer of 73,962 acres; and the following year he made an additional transfer of 15,000 acres. These 89,000 acres were part of the original treasury warrants granted by Virginia to Clark after the conquest of Kaskaskia and Vincennes.[16] But he was becoming increasingly frail and helpless though his body, early inured to hardships, refused to crumble as soon as the mind. In 1811, when his brother Jonathan died unexpectedly, Clark said something that revealed his tortured soul: "It was hard that he, who wanted to live, should die, while I, who wanted to die, should live."[17] Further horrors came: paralysis, leg amputation, a series of strokes, and then, finally, he went to merciful release in 1818.

One feels sympathy for George Rogers Clark but historical judgment must take in all the facts. He tried to model himself on the image of the young George Washington but was made of inferior clay. In the heat of youth, he cut a glamorous figure as the hero of the West, but by the age of thirty his weak character was already apparent. Unlike Washington, he never grew out of parochial loyalty for his "country"—namely, Virginia— to become an American with a larger view, and thus could easily slip into treason after being rejected by his beloved Virginia. There is no question that George Rogers Clark had many sound reasons for feeling he was treated unfairly, as did Benedict Arnold; but it does not follow that humiliation justifies treason, for in that case there would be few cases of loyalty in any great career, which, when lived long enough, has many ups and downs. In a little more than ten years General Clark was America's idol on the western frontier in the war against Great Britain, a volunteer to become governor of an American colony in Spanish territory as a Spanish citizen, coauthor of an attempt to form an independent state based upon Spanish good will, and a recruiter to take Spanish Louisiana for the French as a French citizen. The leitmotif was personal ambition and a desire for land riches. The harsh conclusion of Bernard DeVoto is still valid: "Of the plots to settle the issue [who would own the territory east of the Mississippi] by force some used, and more tried to use, George Rogers Clark. The hero's hour had passed; bankrupt, his just claims unpaid, all his land speculations unsound, he slipped into gaudy imperial fantasies, drunkenness and sedition."[18]

19

The American Settlement of Kentucky

"The people who own the country ought to govern it."

John Jay, First Chief Justice

The territory of Kentucky, which Virginia won in the final showdown with Congress, was an enormous land mass. Over forty thousand square miles in size, with almost twenty-six million acres, it was much larger than eight of the thirteen original colonies. Kentucky was larger than Vermont, which preceded it the year before into statehood, and almost precisely the same size as its mother state of Virginia. The land was fertile and well watered, the climate benign.

When George Rogers Clark took the southern half of the Illinois country, he "secured" Kentucky, the word used in standard histories to mean that the Shawnee Indians were killed or driven from their hunting grounds. An avalanche of white men poured in, some with their slaves. Before 1775 not a single white man in all of Kentucky had yet made his home permanent. It has been estimated that two years after the opening of the Virginia land office in the spring of 1779 some twenty thousand people entered Kentucky. In another two years, the population had risen to thirty thousand, and by 1788 it was about sixty-six thousand.[1]

We have an interesting picture of this land rush. When the British launched a counterattack to retake the Illinois country, Clark went to Harrodsburg, the largest settlement in Kentucky, to get recruits. He found that the Virginia land office had just opened, contrary to the request of Congress, with over 1.6 million acres of choice tracts entered on the first day. Clark asked for volunteers but the crowd, solely concerned with land, showed no interest. Clark then asked the register of the office to close, which he refused to do. Usurping his authority, Clark ordered the office closed. The disappointed claimants started to pack to go back home, but Clark seized their horses and ammunition. Only then would some volunteer. Such was American patriotism in the West.[2]

As will be seen, insiders patented most of the good land almost immediately. Tension on the part of thwarted ordinary people grew to the point of explosion over the next few years, culminating in a secession movement from Virginia. In 1783 the bitter settlers petitioned the Virginia assembly for relief, describing how they were being frozen out by those with political contacts: "In the late act of the Assembly in opening and establishing a land office many of the petitioners are not able to get as much as one hundred acres. Unless there is some redress, this must be the unhappy event that we must lie under the disagreeable necessity of going down the Mississippi to the Spanish protection or becoming tenants to private gentlemen who have men employed at this juncture in this country at one hundred pounds per thousand for running round the lands."[3] Five years after the Kentucky country was opened, the lands had been so engrossed by absentee speculators that the settlers pleaded for Virginia to take corrective action or they would have to cross over to Spanish territory or become tenant farmers.

When General Clark conquered Kaskaskia and Vincennes and the authority of Virginia extended over the region stretching from the Ohio River to the Illinois River as well as some 140 miles up the Wabash, the same process started. The Indians, who would sell thousands of acres for a jug of rum, soon gave away most of the territory. Adventurers from all the states flocked in to grab what they could. Nor were the Virginia politicians shy in this new scramble. In a report later made to Congress, it was affirmed that members of the court established by Virginia at Vincennes had, before dissolution of their authority, divided among themselves the entire region to which the Indian title had been extinguished, "each member absenting himself from the court on the day that the order was to be made in his favor, so that it might appear to be the act of his fellows only."[4]

The speculative scandal seeped back to Congress, which in September 1783 issued a proclamation forbidding "all persons from making settlements on land inhabited or claimed by Indians" beyond the limits of the states. The next year, Washington reinforced this proclamation with one of his own and emphasized that great tension with the Indian tribes was building up to a war on the western frontier.

The commander-in-chief was right, and the war did come. But there is an ironic twist, for with the responsibility of power George Washington was repeating the same complaint of Lord Hillsborough before the Revolution, when facing the same problem. It all depends on which foot the shoe fits. In fact, Washington's own officers were deeply involved. On news of the projected opening of a land office in Kentucky, the Virginia gentry serving with Washington in New York sent Colonel William Wood with a petition to their home assembly, resulting in the act previously noted whereby a tract of land alongside that granted to Judge Henderson of Transylvania was reserved for them. The Ohio Company, where Washington was an important shareholder, also became active again, its role now enhanced because George Rogers Clark had been assistant surveyor in command of its Kentucky claim. When Clark crossed north of the Ohio River and Virginia set up a new county in the Illinois country, the Ohio Company immediately petitioned that it should receive patents based on the earlier surveys of Hancock, Lee, and Clark himself.

Speculation on lands north of the Ohio River will be dealt with in detail elsewhere. But within Kentucky, we are very fortunate in having a precise written record of all land grants. *The Kentucky Land Grants*, a massive tome by Willard Rouse Jillson, lists them by name, size, and location. The earliest group, known as "the Virginia grants," deals with those issued from 1782 to 1792, including warrants for military service in the French and Indian War and later in the Revolution. The second category, "Old Kentucky land grants," relates to those from 1793 on, after Kentucky attained statehood. Some of these, however, were based on warrants and surveys made by Virginians prior to this period. For the sake of convenience this study will be limited to the 1780s and 1790s, for by 1800 the greatest part of the land was engrossed.

It is evident that the appeal presented by the actual settlers to Virginia's assembly was correct: all the best land was being taken by absentee speculators, thus leaving them with little. The size of many of the grants are so unbelievably large that the only real comparison is with the period when King Charles II gave enormous chunks of Virginia and North Carolina to his noble cronies. Since the Virginia speculators controlled the land offices, they were more rapacious than their Philadelphia rivals, though the two groups often worked through the same key officials and their interests could only be separated with considerable difficulty.

The internal organization of Kentucky by Virginia should first be noted. John Harvie, a friend and neighbor of Jefferson from Albemarle County, was put in administrative charge of the land office for the new western territory of Virginia. George May, from a very prominent and politically active family, opened the surveyor's office for Kentucky County at Harrodsburg on May 1, 1779. This, as previously noted, was the office George Rogers Clark shut down in order to force volunteers into his army. Kentucky filled up with settlers so rapidly that in May 1780, only one year later, the Virginia assembly divided Kentucky County into three new counties, Jefferson, Lincoln, and Fayette. George May was appointed head of the surveyor's office of Jefferson County. Thomas Marshall, a business associate of the Clark family, was made head of the same office in Fayette County. James Thompson, through the influence of Colonel (later General) William Thompson—an early surveyor and speculator in Kentucky land—headed the surveyor's office in Lincoln County. These were the key men who dictated the patenting of all land. We may now proceed to the records shown in the *Kentucky Land Grants*.

The May family (John, George, William, and Leo) received almost a million acres of Kentucky in blocks running from over 157,000 acres, or almost 247 square miles, down to 100 acres.[5] John May had been clerk to Governor Botetourt before the Revolution and enjoyed great influence at Williamsburg. He was a colleague in land speculation with both Dr. Thomas Walker and Patrick Henry. To round out his influence, John May became clerk to the sole district court established for all of Kentucky. With a brother as head of a county surveyor's office, we can see how the May family members picked up total land patents equalling the size of Delaware.

John Craig, a Virginian who had business connections with the Gratz brothers of Philadelphia, acquired for himself some 270,000 acres; other members of the Craig family picked up additional acreage. John Craig, who worked with James Wilkinson, signed the document in which that perfidious Spanish agent, addressing Virginia's governor, falsely accused George Rogers Clark of corruption.

A group of huge land grants to unknown persons requires a separate explanation. The land books of Kentucky just tell part of the true story because they only show immediate assignments; we can rarely trace the real names behind dummies who make later transfers. There were many of these because popular politicians, knowing the discontent brewing in Kentucky among the landless settlers, did not want to be seen for what they were—namely, very greedy. For example, there is a letter of complaint sent to Clark about all the choice land being gobbled up by absentee owners, of which follows an extract: "And when I was with you I thought my acquaintance Mr. Randolph was likewise attached to the Interest of the Kentucky settlements but I am sorry to inform you that I have reason to believe the contrary for on looking over the books in the Land office I found a certain Mr. Bealls had taken out warrants to the amount of one hundred and forty thousand Acres of Land at least, part of which was enterd, [sic] assigned to Mr. N. Randolph. . . ." The "N." might be a misread "E." for Edmund Randolph; but regardless, this was obviously a member of the prominent Virginia Randolph family.[6]

Those unknown men, conduits to funnel patents to prominent individuals who wanted to remain anonymous, were: Thomas Shore, who received 463,000 acres; Kennon Jones, 413,000 acres; Christopher McConnico, over 400,000 acres; Henry Banks, 310,000 acres; and Richard Graham, over 340,000 acres. Most of these grants were made in block allotments of 157,722 acres.

Grantees of from 200,000 to 300,000 acres include one dubious figure. He was the notorious James Reynolds of New York, who, through contacts in the U.S. Treasury Department, had picked up a list of Virginia veterans holding military warrants and bought out their paper at three shillings on the pound. Jailed for corrupting an official in 1791, it came out that Maria Reynolds, his wife, had been having an affair with Alexander Hamilton, secretary of the treasury: the evidence seems to indicate that James Reynolds encouraged the liaison, though it should be stated that the amorous relation seemed to have occurred after the purchase of the discounted paper.[7]

Other speculators in the range of 300,000 acres included John Banister, David Ross, Thomas Franklin, Charles Morgan, Benjamin Wyncoop, and Philip Barbour. Banister was a powerful political figure in Virginia, a business associate of Robert Morris, and a U.S. congressman. Ross was a founding partner, with Patrick Henry, of the Virginia Yazoo Company. The others are unknown, which leads one to suspect they also acted as dummies for later transfers.

Many more prominent Virginia families pulled strings in Kentucky. George Lewis picked up 151,000 acres, while other Lewis family members received less. They were cousins to the Jeffersons (and for that reason Jefferson chose Captain Meriwether Lewis to command the Lewis and Clark Expedition, the Clark part being a younger brother to George Rogers). The Marshall family was deeply involved. Thomas and Humphrey Marshall, as well as other family members, acquired some 280,000 acres—almost half the size of the land mass of Rhode Island. As previously noted, Thomas Marshall was head of the surveyor's office of Fayette County. Later commissioned Colonel Marshall, he was taken in as a partner of the Gratz brothers' firm in Philadelphia to locate and make legal warrants for the Gratzes, and for himself. Thomas, the father of John Marshall (who was to become the future chief justice of the U.S. Supreme Court) patented almost 10,000 acres in his own name. Still more grants were obtained by George Keith Taylor, who married Thomas Marshall's daughter. Humphrey

Marshall, a fiery Federalist as befits one of the business associates of Robert Morris, became a U.S. senator from Kentucky and wrote a book on early Kentucky history. The surveyor's office of Fayette County thus was a launching pad for the Marshall family.

The Tidewater aristocrats were also well represented. George Mason, lifelong friend and partner of George Washington in the Ohio Company, consoled himself with 45,000 acres; since he left in his will 60,000 acres in Kentucky to his family, he obviously acquired more through others. Mason, as has been repeatedly noted, was for decades one of the political bosses of Virginia. "His Excellency Washington, Geo.," got a mere $4,717\frac{2}{3}$ acres, all military warrants, probably deriving from claims from the French and Indian War. Washington had opposed opening Virginia's western land office because, as Clark was also aware, the lure would draw away desperately needed soldiers. Given his stiff integrity during the war years, Washington could not, therefore, take advantage of his prestige to speculate in Kentucky. Benjamin Harrison, Jr., picked up about 23,000 acres. The Harrisons were top Virginia aristocrats. Benjamin, Sr., was governor of Virginia in the early 1780s and leader of the conservative wing of the Virginia assembly, and, as already discussed, he was closely involved with Robert Morris and the Pennsylvania land companies. Beniamin, Jr., thanks to papa, was paymaster of the military forces in Virginia during the Revolution. The Mercers received some 50,000 acres; Hugh with his father, John, and his more prominent brother George, were early members of the Ohio Company. The Lees, the Fitzhughs, the Campbells, and the Randolphs are all registered for varying thousands of acres.

The Piedmont-Shenandoah axis was equally represented. Isaac Hite, grandson of Yost Hite, who had received one of the largest grants in 1730 from Governor Gooch, acquired with his son 57,157 acres. Other Hite family members took lesser amounts. In this case, the patents were deserved. Isaac Hite, one of the first white men to penetrate Kentucky, was a settler and not an absentee speculator. The Meriwether family, a part of the Albemarle County clique, vaulting to money and fame through their connection with Thomas Jefferson, took over 73,000 acres. Dr. Thomas Walker's son, John, one of Jefferson's closest boyhood friends and later a U.S. senator, was also involved. The list could continue, but the point is that the Virginia aristocracy—which by now more closely fitted the definition of an oligarchy—simply expanded into Kentucky under the same biased system they had used when they were British subjects. Not even a change of names was involved.

Patrick Henry took out patents for 10,000 acres of Virginia's western land, though only 2,500 acres are recorded in Kentucky.[8] His brother-in-law and close associate William Christian shows up owning 9,000 acres. Since Henry, as governor in 1777, was forced to swear a deposition that he was not a party to the purchase of Indian lands in Kentucky, either Henry and Christian did not plunge to a greater extent for fear of public censure or, possibly, they worked through some of the unknown names above listed who took such enormous acreage. George Rogers Clark received 86,662 acres, including military warrants; his brothers Jonathan and Daniel, his cousin William, and other family members picked up an additional 132,000 acres, also including military warrants. William Croghan, who married a sister of Clark, showed up owing some 75,000 acres. He was a nephew of George Croghan: where there were western lands, there was always a Croghan. Isaac Shelby acquired 9,591 acres; his father, Evan Shelby, and other Shelbys took possession of almost the same amount. Evan Shelby had been one of the original "Suffering Traders" and a member of the Indiana Company; he had moved to southwest Virginia and become an early political leader there. The son Isaac later became the first governor of Kentucky and one of the military heroes of the War of 1812.[10]

Though outmaneuvered by Virginia, the land company speculators of Pennsylvania were not asleep at the switch. They were "foreigners," in the words of George Mason, and could not pull strings to the same extent, but they did very well through various deals and infiltrations. The Gratz brothers, as noted, brought in as a partner Thomas Marshall, head of the Fayette County land surveyor's office. They also worked closely with Charles Willing, partner to Robert Morris, and with another Morris associate, Dorsey Pentecost, originally from Virginia and well-connected politically. The Gratzes and Willing bought land warrants on a discount basis using depreciated currency; Marshall and Pentecost saw to it that they were made legal by physical location and survey. Robert Morris himself, James Wilson, and Levi Holl ngsworth then joined the syndicate, taking a partner, John Harvie, then in charge of all Kentucky land office business. Harvie's long personal friendship with Thomas Jefferson made him the ideal contact man.

Michael Gratz acquired 32,000 acres.[11] Charles Willing took 58,000 acres. Robert Morris, in this early period, only patented 25,022 acres. Dorsey Pentecost took 53,000 acres, amusingly in neat bunches of fifty-three claims of 1,000 acres each, and all were located in Fayette County. Levi Hollingsworth acquired 81,966 acres, also in Fayette County. Though John Harvie is only listed for 10,850 acres, a "John Harvey" in the same period patented 66,295 acres. Being in charge of the land office, such a little error might be overlooked.

Some interesting new names now appear in the records. James Robertson and Anthony Bledsoe, the principal leaders of the Cumberland (pre-Tennessee) settlers, took fliers for several thousand acres each. James Wilkinson, the *éminence grise* of the post-Revolutionary West, acquired some 38,000 acres. James Madison timidly dipped his toes into land speculation for 2,900 acres,[12] while James Monroe was more forthright with 63,884 acres. The very young Henry Clay took 8,439 acres. Miscellaneous political figures like the U.S. congressman from Virginia, Abraham Venable, show up as well; Venable, like David Ross, was a founder of the Virginia Yazoo Company.

About 6.5 million acres were patented by the people involved in this brief survey, more than 25 percent of the entire land mass of all Kentucky and, we may be sure, the most fertile and well-located parts. This is double the size of Connecticut, greater than that of the state of New Jersey, and slightly more acres than in all of Massachusetts and Delaware combined. Most of this land was acquired by absentee speculators, living in Virginia proper or in Pennsylvania, who had purchased military warrants on a discount basis or connived for them through political savvy. At the same time many thousands of settlers streamed into Kentucky but, without the know-how and contacts, were unable to buy for themselves homesteads on which to live and raise families.

It is also apparent from studying Jillson's *Kentucky Land Grants* that the entire political structure of the United States, from the lower levels of state legislators and governors to the U.S. legislature and then the Supreme Court and presidency, was fueled for many decades thereafter by money made in this land speculation. As the Kentucky limestone bluffs fertilized the soil, so the purchase of discounted military warrants from impoverished veterans, as well as great tracts swindled by cliques dominating the land offices, enriched the men (or their heirs) who then went on to run the political and economic structure of the United States.

The great American historian Frederick Jackson Turner has illuminated a less obvious facet of speculation in Kentucky lands, namely, its impetus to the fixing of slavery as a permanent southern institution in the spread westward. Turner comments:

> While the Indian fighters on the upper waters of the Ohio, and on the tributaries of the Tennessee, had been striving for independent statehood, the Kentucky riflemen in their turn had been seeking the same object. The lands for which they had risked their lives in conflict with the savages, were being seized by speculative purchasers from Virginia, who took advantage of the imperfect titles of the pioneers. One of the most important features of the economic history of the West in the eighteenth century, is the way in which preparations

for a later aristocracy were being made, by the amassing of vast estates of wilderness through grant or purchase. For the time being these estates did not materially affect social conditions, for they were but wilderness; but they served as nuclei for the movement of assimilation of the frontier to the Southern type when the slave population began its westward march.[13]

The 1800 census already indicated that almost one in every five persons settling in Kentucky was a black slave. Soon the most revered politician from the South would be a John C. Calhoun rather than a George Washington.

20

The Land Claims of Spain
Southwest of the Alleghenies

*"**BOUNDARY,** n. In political geography, an imaginary line between two nations, separating the imaginary rights of one from the imaginary rights of the other."*

Ambrose Bierce, *The Devil's Dictionary*

One fact delaying the peace between the Confederated States and Great Britain was the question of who was to control the West. Though fishing rights and free navigation on the Mississippi were issues, the boundary with Canada and the dispute over West Florida were also problems; the destiny of the land southwest of the Alleghenies and along the Mississippi River was also a root issue. Spain, which had been thrust into the war by pressure from France, had two main goals. The first was to regain control of Gibraltar. The second was to push her American territory east from the Mississippi in order to make the Gulf of Mexico a closed Spanish sea. Only by breaking a promise not to negotiate separately with Great Britain did the Americans receive this crucial western land mass, in a word deceiving their wartime allies, France and Spain. It was brilliant strategy on the part of John Adams and John Jay; it might be called Machiavellian by an outside observer, considering the tremendous aid in both military force and money that France had given the fledgling nation. Spain could not forget this affront and would be an enemy in the West as a result.

JOHN JAY. Miniature on wood panel, by John Trumbull (1793). Courtesy of the Yale University Art Gallery.

The Spaniards were on the horns of a dilemma. On the one hand, England was Spain's bitter eternal foe, and to humble Britain was excellent politics. England held Gibraltar, the Spanish island of Minorca in the Balearic group (given up at the Paris treaties), and by its historic alliance with Portugal, Britain stopped Spain from taking the rest of the Iberian peninsula. On the other hand, the success of a colonial revolt could infect the Spanish colonies. As well put by the Count of Floridablanca, there was "a sort of equality of enmity which makes it difficult to prefer either of them."[1] Reluctantly, Spain had joined the conflict but only by agreement with France that no peace would be made without the return of Gibraltar, Minorca, West Florida and, it was hoped, the area between the east bank of the Mississippi River and south of the Alleghenies. Spanish indignation on hearing of the separate treaty signed between the Americans and the British was certainly understandable.

Another point poisoning the Spanish attitude was also easy to understand. The Paris treaty of peace ceded East and West Florida to Spain. West Florida by definition included the southern parts of what are now the states of Alabama and Mississippi, with a bit of Louisiana. The treaty between the American states and Great Britain set the northern boundary of West Florida at the 31st parallel latitude. Spain, on the other hand, stoutly insisted that this line was too low and that the boundary should be placed a hundred miles farther north, near the present site of Vicksburg.

However a secret article in this peace treaty provided that if England could manage to hold on to West Florida rather than yield it to Spain, then the Americans would recognize the boundary at the point farther south. Put at its most simple, Great Britain and the Confederated States, enemies in the War of Independence, privately agreed to a boundary line with each other that both refused to accede to Spain, America's ally. The Spanish learned of this secret article and were properly indignant, though an expert on this period claims that "contrary to the common assumption of American historians," Floridablanca was never aware of this clause.[2] Yet, the suspicions in Madrid were well-founded. Both Count Aranda, the Spanish ambassador in Paris, and Martin Navarro, the intendant of Louisiana, warned their government to be on guard against the "turbulent, ambitious Americans."[3] Count Aranda also went on to prophesy that the Americans would first take Florida and then attack Mexico in the near future.

One must understand the influence of western speculators on the hardness of the American position regarding the disputed West. Certain prominent political figures in Congress from the northern and middle states would not have been unwilling to give up navigation on the Mississippi River

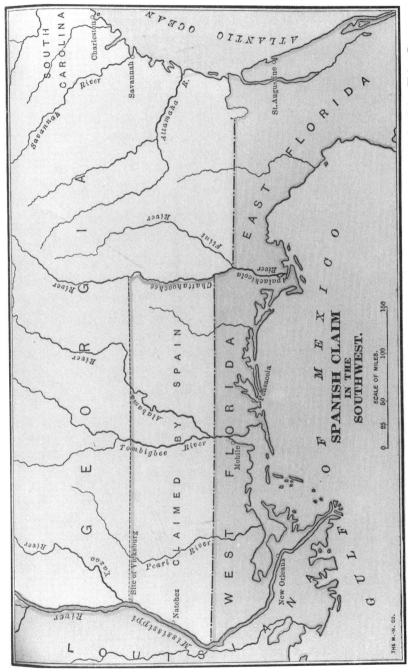

SPANISH CLAIM IN THE SOUTHWEST. From *The Critical Period of American History (1787-1789)*, by John Fiske, Boston, 1901.

and, to a lesser degree, acceding to Spain's land claims southwest of the Alleghenies. But Sam Adams and John Adams of Massachusetts were closely allied with the Lees, particularly Richard Henry Lee of Virginia. These men, called "The Junto," were also head and shoulders above the average American politicians. They knew that Virginia and North Carolina—with their stakes already deep in what later became Kentucky and Tennessee—would never agree to abandon this territory. It is important to remember that in the southern states there was no real difference between the interests of the governments and the land speculators, because in a profound sense the governments were the speculators. Men like George Mason and Patrick Henry in Virginia, with their expedition leader, George Rogers Clark, in Kentucky, and men like William Blount, Richard Caswell, and Alexander Martin in North Carolina, dominated the state legislatures and congressional elections. It was staggering to them that the Revolution should be won and the West lost, for, as has been detailed above, the lands of the West were what had brought the most influential part of the southern planters to support the rebellion.

It should also be noted that the mercantile interests separated the question of free navigation on the Mississippi from that of who would own the land southwest of the Alleghenies. Those of the middle provinces in particular would not give Spain land but were willing to close American navigation on the great river. Their shipping interests, they felt, would be threatened if western trade flowed down the Mississippi instead of east across the mountains; and this in turn might lead to their loss of political and economic control of the burgeoning new country. The sharp division in Congress therefore was more over Mississippi river rights than over land.

Fomenting discord in the American Southwest was about the only option left to the Spanish after these rebuffs, for they were too weak in numbers to be aggressive. In 1786 the total colonial population of Spanish-held East Florida was less than 1,500 persons, including slaves. That of West Florida was only slightly greater. All of Louisiana contained perhaps 10,000 white colonists, the majority being French and not Spanish. On the other hand, by 1785 the four American frontier communities of Georgia, Holston, Cumberland, and Kentucky had an estimated population of around 75,000 persons, many times greater than all the neighboring Spanish provinces put together.[4]

As the antagonists knew, the Indians were a far more effective deterrent to American expansion. The Creeks, the most formidable tribe, had some 6,000 warriors; the Choctaws about 5,000; the Cherokees 2,000; and the Chickasaws, who were friendly to Americans, had perhaps 500.[5] The Creeks were led by Alexander McGillivry, three-quarters white with a Scottish

Loyalist father, who was belligerently anti-American despite the blandishments of U.S. political leaders. Thirteen thousand Indian warriors could be marshalled if united, a much more effective force than any army the Spanish could put in the field. But the Indians, because of age-old tribal conflicts, never could properly cooperate. Alert Americans saw that time was on their side and they delayed while breeding and immigration increased their numbers. The sole Spanish hope was intrigue in Kentucky and Tennessee, splitting the transmontane region from the coast. And this could only be successful, the Spaniards realized, by buying prominent American frontier leaders through special trading privileges and large land grants.

From this point in history one may wonder why the Spaniards thought they might split the Americans west of the mountains from those east. But the passage of time buried their many real opportunities, for what we think today has no relation to the reality at that time. It will be recalled that one of the most effective arguments of George Mason of Virginia against the land companies with shareholders from Pennsylvania, Maryland, and New Jersey was to attack them as "foreigners." This was no hyperbole, for the thirteen states in actual fact were thirteen separate bodies. The early history of America is usually treated from a rational point of view, with a rare side glance at "parochial" factors as though they were of little import. The reverse is closer to the truth, as has been touched on in the study relating to the Articles of Confederation. Indeed, one might state that imposing a national view was an invention of the Federalists so subtle and yet teflonic that, though largely a myth, it became the accepted historical reality.[6] Citizens of different states in the eighteenth century never viewed America or the Confederated States or the United States as their homeland. The country of a Virginian was Virginia; the country of a Pennsylvanian was Pennsylvania. Thomas Jefferson always called Virginia "my country" when writing and, indeed, such was his pride in this, his country, that an undoubted force in his assault against Aaron Burr, who came from New York, was Jefferson's desire to set up a dynasty of Virginian presidents. Among his friends, John Adams likewise referred to Massachusetts as "our country" and the letters he sent home from Congress at Philadelphia were welcomed as news from a "far country."[7] If a greater loyalty was felt beyond one's state, it was to the region. The New England states supported the secession of Vermont from New York as New Englanders, the Allens having come from Connecticut. The Carolinas stood behind Virginia in all congressional clashes as fellow southerners.

Relevant to the factional fights on the western frontier, which aided the agents of Spanish intrigue, is the sad truth that masses of men are often more swayed by dislike of others than like of their own kind. Suspicion and hate among citizens of the various provinces persisted before and after the Revolution. Carter Braxton, a leading southern conservative, spoke of the people of New England in the Virginia convention: "I abhor their manners—I abhor their laws—I abhor their governments—I abhor their religion."[8] George Washington wrote privately to Lund Washington during the Revolution that New Englanders "are an exceedingly dirty and nasty people."[9] The expression "damn'd Yankees" was coined at this time and not during the Civil War.[10] Great tension also existed between the middle and northern provinces; a brigadier-general wrote that "the Pennsylvania and New England troops would as soon fight each other as the British."[11] Even a man as broad in his outlook as James Madison wrote that past history and public sentiment made it obvious "that the first and most natural attachment of the people" would always "be to the governments of their respective States."[12]

Furthermore, the spirit of local autonomy violently rejected outside authority. In some of his youthful thinking, Thomas Jefferson insisted that any group of Americans might associate, secede, change government, and promote revolution as they desired. Dr. Thomas Burke of North Carolina stated in Congress that any attempt to infringe on states' rights and home rule was "an arbitrary discrition [sic]"[13] and, with this view supported by New Hampshire, Maryland, Virginia, and South Carolina, the conservatives gave up hope of majority rule. Indeed, it is an interesting aspect of this same fervid local patriotism that many of the top men with a vision of the national idea were not born in the colonies and in fact had just come over. Tom Paine, who invented the phrase "The United States of America," arrived on this shore in November 1774, after the First Continental Congress had assembled. Alexander Hamilton, born in the British West Indies, came in late 1772 and was doubly an outsider: his mother, married to a Danish Jew, conceived her brilliant son from a Scottish merchant in circumstances that are still not crystal clear.[14] Oliver Pollack, the financier of the West, was a recent Irish immigrant. Albert Gallatin, the political pilot of Jefferson, arrived in 1780. It would seem that the idea of a united American commonwealth with loyalties above the local and state level was possible in many cases only when one had the mentality of a newcomer.

If the greatest native-born Americans first showed attachment to their home state, it can easily be seen how loosely lay national loyalty on the common folk. This was even more true of those men with few roots and little introspection who left the settled communities to move into dangerous and primitive Indian territory. The proclamations of George Washington and Congress, flowing from Philadelphia, had as much force to them as had the same edicts flowing from London on the pre-war colonials. Brute geography made this analogy even more true. The distance separating a seacoast American city dweller from the English coast was less than that separating him from a settler in what is now Kentucky or Tennessee. In the last decade of the eighteenth century it took stagecoach travellers from eight to ten days to go from New York to Washington or to Boston. The stage fare was $25 (a very large sum at that time), which did not include food and lodging. One can barely guess at the great time and expense to transport human beings, let alone massive amounts of goods,[15] over the mountains to the eastern seaboard. Distance and the cost of travel scraped loyalties to a frazzle.

The common bond among these tough frontiersmen was the desire to get rich, a goal that could be accomplished in two ways, land or trade. The land had already been largely patented by the speculators with great political power or wealth, as has been seen in the case of Kentucky. But trade—in tobacco, tallow, flour, ham, and beef—had not yet been preempted. The key to wealth in trade was the river traffic on the Mississippi. The Spaniards still controlled a considerable amount of the land southeast of the Mississippi as well as all traffic across the river, while at the same time they had a monopoly on who could use the great river since they controlled its terminus at New Orleans. The combination of turbulent anarchy and lust for money, which dominated the western frontier, made it an ideal place for Spanish penetration. We have already seen these factors operating on George Rogers Clark. They were even more pronounced in the case of John Sevier, whose career will be discussed shortly. Arthur P. Whitaker, after praising the energy of Sevier, thumbs his character: "He bought, sold and used slaves without compunction, winked at if he did not openly permit the cold-blooded murder of unoffending Indians, intrigued with Spain, and while governor of Tennessee [1796] openly condoned the violation of a federal proclamation." Then, adding that Sevier was industrious, a churchgoer, and a good father, Whitaker concludes, "His were the virtues of a frontier community."[16] Though in exaggerated form, this sums up the western frontier.

Yet the Spanish effort to subvert the development of the United States failed. A weighty factor in this failure was the hatred—ingrained by over two centuries of almost continual war—that Protestant settlers felt for the Spaniards. The religion, the customs, and the stifling grip of Spain were offensive to Americans to a degree voiding the mighty economic and geographic assets. It tells volumes that General James Wilkinson, their agent, was of Irish parentage and spoke hardly any Spanish at all. Dr. James White, Jesuit-trained, was more fluent in French than Spanish. James O'Fallon, an Irish Catholic, was ignorant both of Spanish ways and the

Spanish tongue. Yet these were the men who were for the main pro-Spanish. One could hardly imagine two more antagonistic cultures. Coming to the aid of American loyalty was the appointment by Washington of Thomas Jefferson as secretary of state. Jefferson, who had taken the lead in opposing Jay's recommendation to give up American rights to ship on the Mississippi, confirmed many wavering frontiersmen in their belief that a more sympathetic hand would now grasp the helm.

A cynic might also refer to the fact that land speculation was opposed by the Spanish government. Land grants were only made to genuine settlers and varied in size according to the settler's family. Land grants that were not passed through the family by inheritance reverted to the Crown. This was repugnant to the most aggressive frontiersmen despite private deals offered to the privileged few. As A. P. Whitaker remarks with delicious humor, ". . . one can hardly conceive of an American frontier community, even under the Spanish government, without its political conventions and its land speculators."[17]

A good part of the failure of Spanish intrigue may also be attributed to that government's own bungling. Don Diego de Gardoqui, a timid man, was afraid of Governor Esteban Miró of Louisiana and would take no initiative; Miró in turn was contemptuous of Don Diego, and the two men thus worked at cross purposes. Frontier mad-caps and Spanish sloths could not press a common policy. But most of all, there was one great gulf between the two groups that nothing could bridge: the Indians were the chief bastion of Spanish power in the Southwest, and the aim of the American settlers was to crush the Indians. This was particularly true in the crucial hub of the Tennessee River, whose possession was the base for John Sevier's sedition. Georgia was flanked by the Creeks, and what became Tennessee by the Cherokees. The Cumberland plateau and the area due west became very important as hunting grounds for both these tribes as they were pushed back from their traditional lands by white settlers. It was Indian carcasses that Sevier demanded as the price of his allegiance to Spain; while Indian strength was the key to Spanish policy. The two positions were completely incompatible.[18]

Spain was the sick man of Europe at the time. A flare of creative activity went on under King Charles III, who died in 1788. Don Manuel de Godoy, who had already started his amour with Maria Luisa, wife of the man who became King Charles IV, then took over the destiny of that country. The *ménage à trois* involving Charles IV; his wife, Maria Luisa; and Godoy is one of the more curious in European history. Don Manuel, childish and sensual, had a nature untethered by brains, and strained in this matter with some success to equal those of the king and queen. Though the position of Spain was most difficult, torn as it was between its age-old enemy England and revolutionary France, Godoy picked the worst of alternatives on almost every occasion: his appointment of Hector, Baron de Carondelet, as successor to Esteban Miró for the Louisiana provinces and his general neglect of the Spanish-American colonies are glaring examples.

By the early 1790s Don Manuel, frightened by the sweep of the a   ies of revolutionary France, decided it was time to come to terms with his American neighbor and scotch the threat of war on two fronts. Spanish leaders were also ill at ease conspiring with men such as Wilkinson, Sevier, and Clark. As was natural, Spanish royalty felt more at home with the legitimate and conservative forces embodied in President Washington himself. Furthermore, Spanish policy east of the Missisippi had been a complete failure and the Floridas and Louisiana were governed at a net loss of about half a million dollars each year. The strain of deficit financing, part of which involved Indian subsidies, began to take its toll and feelers were sent out to see what could be salvaged.

In 1795 the Treaty of San Lorenzo was concluded, in which Thomas Pinckney of South Carolina acted for the United States. Spain consented to the 31st parallel as the southern American border and agreed to allow American river transport on the Mississippi. The powerful Creek tribe, cut off from its supplies, sullenly agreed to an uneasy but sustained peace, The whole eastern basin of the Mississippi River now became a gigantic plum for speculation and settlement in the next forward leap of American empire. A detailed study of the intrigue involved in this period is essential, for the internal structure of much of the country over the next century was to be forged in the process.

21

¡Viva el General Jaime Wilkinson!

"Evil has its heroes as well as good."

La Rochefoucauld, Maxim 185

James Wilkinson is unique in the history of the United States. A mixture of Alcibiades, the amoral Athenian general, and Talleyrand, the wily French statesman, he cut an extraordinary path across the late eighteenth-century American landscape. James R. Jacobs, his leading biographer, compliments Wilkinson by titling his study *The Tarnished Warrior*. Frederick J. Turner called Wilkinson our most consummate artist in treason, while a contemporary of Wilkinson, John Randolph of Roanoke, described him as "a rogue, peculator, and would-be murderer."[1] To Bodley Temple, who studied with care Wilkinson's axing of George Rogers Clark, he was a monster incarnate. Yet almost all who knew Wilkinson at the time agreed that he had enormous charm. Humphrey Marshall, a U.S. senator from Kentucky and Wilkinson's bitter enemy, tells of his astounding success in manipulating people:

> A person not quite tall enough to be perfectly elegant, compensated by symmetry and appearance of health and strength; a countenance open, mild, capacious, and beaming with intelligence; a gait firm, manly, and facile; manners bland, accommodating and popular; and address easy, polite and gracious, invited approach, gave access, assured attention, cordiality and ease. By these fair terms, he conciliated; by these he captivated.[2]

232

James Wilkinson, born in 1757 the son of a wealthy Maryland planter, entered the Revolutionary Army while still an adolescent. First attached to Colonel Benedict Arnold, from whose career he absorbed much, Wilkinson was his companion in the march against Quebec. When conflict arose between Arnold and General Horatio Gates, Wilkinson left Arnold and became an aide to Gates. After General Burgoyne's surrender to Gates at Saratoga, one of the few great American victories during the Revolution, Gates sent Wilkinson to inform Congress. That body appointed him a brigadier-general in the flush of triumph. Top commands in the Revolutionary Army were more easily given when the person involved was a foreign nobleman or from the colonial aristocracy.

General Gates was appointed president of the Board of War and his charming young aide went along as secretary. This was the seat from which the "Conway Cabal" operated to dismiss George Washington and make Gates commander-in-chief. Wilkinson was obviously involved. In line with his character, when Wilkinson saw that the plot would fail, he implicated Gates. Learning this, Gates challenged the youthful Machiavelli to a duel, which Wilkinson avoided by claiming what he said was only "in a convivial hour," that is, while drunk. However, anticipating trouble, he resigned his commission.

After Benedict Arnold was appointed military commander of Philadelphia and, seduced by the Tories of that city, began to plot treason, his former confidant Wilkinson secretly charged him with corruption. Then Wilkinson was appointed clothier-general of the American forces, but finding himself suspected of venality, he offered to resign, which offer Congress immediately accepted. A letter from Washington indicates that he agreed with the charges. Wilkinson was never happy in the position for, aside from its need for detailed work which the young man found irksome, he had purchased with depreciated currency the attainted estate of Joseph Galloway outside Philadelphia, some 444 acres of good land improved with houses, and wanted to set himself up as a gentleman farmer.

James Wilkinson was no better a farmer than he was a businessman, and his debts started to rise. After the war, claiming to be the chief agent of a large Philadelphia commercial house—the firm had merely given him some goods to sell—he put up his estate for sale and set out for Kentucky. Arriving at Louisville in January 1784, he immediately started to speculate in land. As one could prophesy, he became friendly with Thomas Marshall, head of the surveyor's office of Fayette County. Jillson's *The Kentucky Land Grants* tells us that Wilkinson bought claims for some 38,000 acres. As part of a company made up of friends from Pennsylvania, he then took an option on nearly two million acres north of the Ohio

GENERAL JAMES WILKINSON. From a portrait by Charles Balthazar
Julien Fevret de Saint-Mémin. From *The Saint-Mémin Collection of
Portraits,* East Dexter, New York, 1862.

River, an illegal operation since this land was off limits to settlement. The purpose was to mark out the choice tracts in order to have first claim when the country was opened.[3] This must have been the time when the thought came to him that rather than waiting for Congress to authorize new western land grants, it would be easier to get them from the Spanish if one had the right contacts.

Double-dealing was Wilkinson's real forte. The high positions he had held in the army and his personal charm propelled him to the front ranks of Kentucky frontier society. Furthermore, coming from a landed Maryland family and married to a Biddle from Philadelphia,[4] Wilkinson was soon courted by the local political leaders.

The first opportunity this afforded had as its foundation that great division which later erupted into the Civil War, namely, the tension between the northern and southern states. Kentucky, where mass immigration had diluted the original Virginia population, was demanding separate statehood. Virginia, tired from the expense of carrying its distant counties, was willing to give Kentucky independence but insisted first that Congress should accept the new state into the Confederation. The northern states, however, did not want to impair their slender majority in Congress. Eventually, after seven years, a compromise was worked out whereby Vermont was admitted to offset Kentucky and thus maintain the fragile balance of power. It was during these seven years that Wilkinson weaved his fine threads of intrigue.

The core of Kentucky discontent lay in the fact that commerce was much cheaper by water transport via the Ohio and Mississippi rivers and then through New Orleans than it was by sending goods back by mule-pack across the Allegheny Mountains to western Virginia. But the Spanish refused to permit this traffic. The people of Kentucky were in an uproar over this problem. Wilkinson saw that by wheedling his way into the confidence of the Spanish he could represent the Kentuckians and gain great personal advantage not only through large land grants but by control of this trade as well.

In May 1787, Wilkinson sent a boatload of Kentucky goods to New Orleans, boldly following himself. Through a resident agent, who later became his partner, Wilkinson warned Governor Miró that if he were arrested it might precipitate a war. Then Wilkinson asked for an interview with Miró, which was granted. He told Miró that General Clark was planning an invasion of Louisiana, which he alone could thwart by making use of his great influence in Kentucky. Wilkinson demanded trade privileges on the Kentucky route to New Orleans in return for his cooperation. "Thereupon Wilkinson took a secret oath of allegiance to the Spanish King, and undertook, as his Majesty's emissary, to detach Kentucky from the United States and make it Spain's ally."[5] as Bodley phrased it, his words backed up by the secret correspondence now available at the General Archives of the Indies in Seville, Spain. There is some evidence that Miró also became a silent partner in the Kentucky-New Orleans trade syndicate created as a result. At the same time, Wilkinson urged the Spanish governor not to allow American navigation on the Mississippi except that which he controlled, for this would appease western resentment against Congress. He likewise wrote to his friend Arthur St. Clair, then president of Congress, recommending that the treaty should be signed with Spain forbidding such navigation. His aim was to encourage revolt in Kentucky and become head of a trans-Appalachian state allied with Spain.

Governor Miró seems to have been completely duped by the threat of Clark's invasion. Wilkinson had forged papers showing that a great army was being gathered to invade Louisiana and, through testimonials signed by prominent Kentucky leaders, proved his undoubted influence in that territory.

Wilkinson then turned his attention to destroying General Clark, which was made easier by Clark's unpopularity in Kentucky. Wilkinson sent to Governor Randolph of Virginia various forged and anonymous papers stating that Clark was a sot; that he had plundered Spanish goods; and that, contrary to orders, he was assembling an army to invade Louisiana. The job was done so cleverly that Randolph, fearing a Spanish war, condemned Clark without sufficient inquiry and suggested to Congress that he be replaced by Wilkinson as commissioner of Indian affairs. Copies of these resolutions were promptly sent by Wilkinson to Miró, reinforcing his position with the Spanish. It should also be mentioned that Governor Randolph was a partner with Wilkinson in Kentucky land speculation at this time.

Congress, alarmed by the inventions of Wilkinson and by the seething discontent in the West, feared to push the commercial treaty that would have sealed off trade along the Mississippi. Historian Temple Bodley concludes: "The resolutions of the Virginia Council and Congress, condemning General Clark, had accomplished Wilkinson's first object in his scheme to fool Miró and get the trade privilege. . . . He led the Spaniards to look to him as their friend; he outwitted the experienced and wily Miró; he killed Jay's commercial treaty, and thus perhaps saved both the Mississippi and the Confederation; he balked the adroit Gardoqui (Miró's superior) and rendered abortive Spain's whole diplomatic policy in America; and, for all this, he received the coveted privilege of trade with New Orleans and a yearly pension from the Spanish King!"[6] The benefits to his homeland were not of course part of Wilkinson's plan.

In 1789, Wilkinson made a second trip to New Orleans. He pressed for large money subsidies to subvert key Kentuckians to agitate for a separate state, which would act as a bumper between the United States and Spanish possessions, most particularly the Mexican silver mines, about which the Spanish authorities were obsessively worried. He also tried to push a petition for a personal land grant of six hundred thousand acres "to which he and his followers might repair in case their programs were defeated in Kentucky."[7] After accepting a loan from Miró some years earlier, in 1792 Wilkinson was formally put on the Spanish payroll, which was backdated to January 1, 1789, to wipe out the loan.[8] It was during these years that plans were made by Wilkinson to separate Kentucky and tie it to Spain. His main accomplice in the scheme was Judge Harry Inness of Kentucky, who, according to some evidence, also was on the payroll of the Spanish. The project received great impetus when Hector, Baron de Carondelet (called "Cochon de lait" or "milk pig" by the French Creoles in Louisiana) took over Miró's position in very late 1791.

The turmoil surrounding the French Revolution aided Wilkinson. This revolt was enthusiastically backed by the frontiersmen. Their belief in the freedom to rebel against authority, which was directed as much against Washington's policy of restraint and neutrality as it was against Spanish autocracy, meant the right to overrun Spain's American colonies, establish elections and Protestant churches, and seize Spanish land and ore mines— an intoxicating alloy of ideology and self-interest. As Wilkinson's friend General John Adair wrote him later on the same subject: "The Kentuckians are full of enterprise and although not poor [are] as greedy after plunder as ever the old Romans were. Mexico glitters in our Eyes—the word is all we wait for."[9] The hour of Wilkinson seemed at hand. If Miró had been duped by the American fox, Carondelet was even more so. As part of Edmund Genêt's revolutionary war against Iberian tyranny, George Rogers Clark started to raise his voluntary army; and Wilkinson, pulling the strings backstage, urgently sent messages to his Spanish master that all would be lost if large sums of money were not sent to subvert Kentucky. The people there, he reiterated, were losing patience with the federal government and had vowed to crack open the Mississippi; and, in Wilkinson's words, it depended upon Spain whether by secession from the Union or conquest of Louisiana.

Goaded on by Wilkinson, from April to July 1794 Carondelet wrote Manuel de Godoy (who controlled King Charles IV) in Madrid, that either Spain must send over a large army and stir up the Indians or pay great sums to subvert Kentucky. This correspondence was received in Madrid just after the Council of State had approved Godoy's proposal to make

DON FRANCISCO LOUIS HECTOR, Baron de Carondelet Noyelles. From an illustration in *A History of Louisiana*, by Alcée Fortier, New York, 1904.

DON ESTEBAN MIRÓ. Courtesy of the Louisiana State Museum.

fresh overtures to the United States over the problems separating the two nations. The matter was now brought to sharp focus. Should Spain, at the cost of territorial concessions and opening the Mississippi to navigation, placate the Americans and remove them from among her enemies in this war-torn and revolutionary period? Or should Spain take advantage of frontier discontent, pouring money into Kentucky in the hope of creating a split in the United States?

The Council of State met with Manuel de Godoy on July 25, 1794, and came to a decision. The utmost attempt must be made to come to terms with the Americans, and the Kentucky intrigue had to be put aside until accord with the United States was deemed impossible.

James Wilkinson had lost his last great hope of being the president of a separate western republic. Money was the real reason behind Godoy's decision: the Louisiana and Florida provinces were operating at deficits and the additional cost of this intrigue, as the Spanish minister of finance had pointed out to the council at the July meeting, would be crushing. Furthermore, success in Kentucky could lead to war with the United States— the last thing Spain wanted. Suspicion that Wilkinson might be a double agent was a factor as well. But George Washington was known throughout the world as a rich conservative and no friend of the French Revolution. Spanish royalty could do business with such a man. Feelers were put out and the Treaty of San Lorenzo, settling the problems between the two countries, followed in 1795. The borders claimed by the United States at the end of the Revolution, with more rhetoric than reason were now established.[10]

Though the historic importance of James Wilkinson ends with this treaty, it is of great interest to follow the later career of this wily chameleon. In 1791, Wilkinson re-entered military service, strapped for money because of his extravagant way of life. With Indian troubles brewing in the Northwest, Wilkinson accepted a commission as lieutenant-colonel of the Second U.S. Infantry, serving directly under his old friend General Arthur St. Clair. As an aside it may be added that Wilkinson, who seemed to flourish by the reverse of Abraham Lincoln's famous adage—acting with charity toward none and with malice for all—made an exception in the case of St. Clair. The reason probably is that they were associates in a land speculation. Wilkinson, St. Clair, Jonathan Dayton (speaker of the U.S. House of Representatives) and Israel Ludlow (a top land surveyor in the Ohio country) had formed a syndicate and purchased a large tract between the Miami and Mad rivers.[11]

Not tainted by St. Clair's Indian debacle in 1792, Wilkinson was raised to the rank of brigadier-general. Nine months after this promotion, in

December 1792, he wrote to Carondelet, his Spanish superior, calling Washington "an ignorant commander in chief" and referring to his homeland as "contemptible."[12] The Spanish, however, did not seem to give him enough money to support his high lifestyle and in November 1792 he sold Louisville property, while in the following January he had to turn over to creditors an interest in about 150,000 acres of Kentucky land.

General Anthony Wayne succeeded St. Clair after the latter's defeat and dismissal. Wilkinson was second in command and, maddened by not receiving top authority, he trumpeted vile charges against Wayne to Henry Knox, secretary of war. Wayne's great victory at Fallen Timbers, crushing the northwest Indians forever, prevented Wilkinson from doing the same hatchet job on him as had been done on George Rogers Clark. But in 1796, after Wayne's death, Wilkinson became general-in-chief of the American Army while at the same time secretly a Spanish subject and pensioner of the king of Spain. This may be the only such case in all of military history.

After the Louisiana Purchase in 1803, General Wilkinson was appointed governor of the northern part of the newly formed territory, with headquarters at St. Louis. The sly chameleon used this post to scheme with Aaron Burr and then, in his usual pattern, turned against him when things went sour. Wilkinson escaped censure by the skin of his teeth, with a much-clouded reputation; if it had not been for President Jefferson's nearly pathological hatred of Burr, which prompted him to support Wilkinson's role in ruining Burr, Wilkinson probably would have been dismissed from the service.

As a Louisiana governor, Wilkinson, consistent with his nature, used this official position for personal advantage. Through one of his fellow officers, Captain John McClellan, he shipped goods at government expense and then sold them at a profit in St. Louis. He also bought some five hundred acres adjacent to the military post at Belle Fontaine as well as Dauphin Island at the mouth of Mobile Bay.[13] Then in 1809 he was transferred to New Orleans, where he promptly worked out a deal to get a kickback from James Morrison, with whom he had contracted to supply food for the army. The flour was full of worms and bugs, the pork rancid, the beef rotten. Disease broke out among the troops, but as Morrison wrote Wilkinson on July 28, 1809: "You know whether the contract is profitable depends on the commander-in-chief. . . . Should a part [of the flour] become unfit for use, I have directed them [his agents] to purchase and mix with sweet flour so as to make it palatable. Don't I pray you order an examination unless in the last resort."[14] It is rather interesting that James R. Jacobs's biographical study does not specially condemn

Wilkinson for this corruption, because it would seem to have been a universal practice at the time.

Transferred to the North in the War of 1812, Wilkinson twice performed badly while in direct command of offensive troops: first before Montreal and then along the New York-Canadian border above Plattsburg. In April 1814 he was relieved of his command. Surviving several courts-martial, both as to suspicion of his Spanish intrigues and for military incompetence, he then became involved in plots to conquer Texas. This was the period when Mexico had begun its war of independence against Spain and in 1822 Wilkinson sailed for Veracruz, hoping to finagle both land grants and trade concessions in the midst of the chaos surrounding the pangs of independence. Pliant and charming as ever even when aged, and a high priest in the litany of corruption, Wilkinson almost succeeded.[15] Governor Trespalacios of Texas, for whom Wilkinson had done favors while he rose to power, in early 1825 gave the old sick general a grant of one hundred thousand acres. But it was too late to benefit the declining schemer. That summer Wilkinson fell deathly ill with chronic diarrhea— a Mexican savior against northern aggression—and in December 1825, at the age of sixty-eight, death stole his last sanguine hope. Though a Protestant, Wilkinson was buried with Catholic rites; a few years later his bones were thrown into a common vault.

Supporters of James Wilkinson insisted for many decades that he was innocent of the charges of treason. It was only when the Spanish opened their secret files that the depth of his duplicity was exposed in all its sordid reality.[16]

22

Colonel George Morgan's New Madrid

"Grimly they [the western settlers] drove the Indians out before them, and exploited natural resources, slaves and public office, trampling down with pitiless determination every obstacle to prosperity. In these same men we perceive an equally intense devotion to the republican faith, a mystic sense of union with the deity of republicanism, and a conviction that their god would let none but the faithful prosper. They had their rainbow, and at its end was a pot of gold."

Arthur Preston Whitaker, *The Spanish-American Frontier: 1783-1795*

George Morgan, like most of the Revolutionary leaders, came from a top colonial family. His grandfather, who had emigrated from Wales to Pennsylvania at the beginning of the eighteenth century, was proud of his good birth. Morgan's father invested in real estate and was also a prominent merchant; though he had nine children, each inherited a comfortable living. George's brother John was the founder of the medical school of the college of Philadelphia, now the University of Pennsylvania. On their mother's side the Morgans descended from seventeenth-century immigrants of even more distinguished stock, including colleagues of William Penn.

George Morgan, in accordance with the custom of the time, was apprenticed to the Philadelphia firm of Baynton and Wharton at the age of thirteen and rose to be the bookkeeper in four years. At the age of twenty-one he married Mary Baynton, daughter of John Baynton, the senior partner. Morgan added his capital to the firm, which in 1763 became known as Baynton, Wharton, and Morgan, a partnership we have met previously in its involvement with the "Suffering Traders," the Indiana Company, and Vandalia. It may be added that Mary Baynton was herself a colonial aristocrat. John Baynton, at various times a member of the Pennsylvania assembly and a provincial commissioner, was the son of prominent Philadelphians on both sides. The Morgans and Bayntons thus stood high in the social and economic life of Philadelphia, and the marriage cemented an alliance between two distinguished families.

The firm of Baynton, Wharton, and Morgan was deeply involved in western trade. Shortly after his marriage, George Morgan set out to handle the business in the Illinois country, where he spent several years. There he became familiar both with the potential of western land and the ways of the Indians. Because of this, when the Revolution started, Morgan was appointed agent for Indian affairs in the middle department, that is, the country to the west of the middle states. Gaining national attention for his ability to pacify the Indians, he received the rank of colonel. Indeed, Morgan was one of the few Americans of the period who had respect for Indian ways and an understanding of their psychology.

After the Revolution, Morgan became the guiding spirit of the resurrected Indiana Company, whose claims, as we have learned, were struck down by Virginia after a long fight. Morgan, who had moved from Pennsylvania to New Jersey in 1779, made powerful friends in his new home state and fought desperately to validate Indiana's claims to the very end. Under Article IX of the Confederation, Congress could act to settle disputes between states, and Morgan, arranging his appointment as agent of New Jersey, was commissioned to prepare a memorial to Congress setting forth the complaints of New Jersey against the treatment of the Indiana Company by Virginia. This action continued after the adoption of the Constitution and led to the passage of the Eleventh Amendment, which put an end to all suits brought against a state by citizens of another state.

Bitterly disappointed over the voiding of the Indiana Company claims, Morgan then attempted to emulate the success of the New England syndicate headed by General Putnam and Manasseh Cutler, which, as will be analyzed, succeeded in obtaining a grant of 1.5 million acres in the newly formed Northwest Territory. He set up the New Jersey Land Society, including in its membership persons prominent in that state's politics and high society. The society offered to buy from Congress what is now the southwestern part of the state of Illinois for thirty-three cents an acre. Congress accepted the offer, subject, however, to the purchase price being doubled. Morgan backed off, claiming the price was too high. He probably could have negotiated a compromise and acquired the grant, as did John

Cleves Symmes and his syndicate from New Jersey in this same period, but Morgan dropped the matter. The real reason was his involvement in another and more promising scheme.

As we learned earlier, Spain's policy after the Revolution centered on blocking the Americans from further westward expansion by sealing off navigation on the lower Mississippi River and attempting to create a buffer province or dependent states southwest of the Alleghenies. Diego de Gardoqui was also empowered to encourage the foundation of colonies of Americans in Spanish Louisiana through the tantalizing offer of trade concessions and land grants, conditioned, however, upon the settlers becoming Spanish subjects.

News of George Morgan's attempt to obtain a large land grant in the Northwest Territory reached Gardoqui. He was aware of the colonel's high social standing and influence, and probably also of his resentment over the failure of the Indiana Company to validate its claims against Virginia. Furthermore, Morgan's well-known respect for Indian ways, and his ability to reside in peace with them, was a factor in the Spanish desire to bring him over to their side. Gardoqui thought that Morgan might be susceptible to an offer of land in Spanish Louisiana. Max Savelle, the leading biographer of George Morgan, conveys the situation as follows: "But the proposal must come from Morgan, for it would hardly be diplomatic for the minister openly to propose the alienation of so prominent an American subject. So by an indirect channel, probably through Thomas Hutchins[1], intimate friend of both Gardoqui and Morgan, the minister conveyed to the colonel the suggestion that he would receive favorably a proposal for a grant of land on the west side of the Mississippi."[2]

Diego de Gardoqui's delicacy was unnecessary, for Morgan jumped at the chance. He wrote to Gardoqui that, provided religious tolerance was granted, he would take the oath of allegiance to the Spanish king and lead a group of Americans to Spanish Louisiana as commander of a new colony. The concession desired was opposite the mouth of the Ohio River and had to be at least equal in size to the grant that the New Jersey Land Society had requested of Congress. Morgan significantly noted his bitterness with the treatment accorded him in his own country, and assured the Spanish minister he would be loyal to Spain.[3]

The negotiations were intense: in return for command of the colony and a large personal land grant, as well as a salary and the same rank in the Spanish service that he held in the American army, Morgan agreed that all laws of the settlement would be subject to the veto of the representative of the king; that he would create two companies of militia, to be paid by Spain; and that he would send his two little girls to a religious school in New Orleans, this last being a subtle touch showing his good faith by giving his children as hostages.

In autumn 1788, Gardoqui authorized the colonel to survey the land for the colony, and advanced the required money. Morgan advertised the project and, selecting some seventy men, gathered them at Fort Pitt, from where they went downriver, a spectacular adventure that greatly disturbed Congress and caused mighty rumbles in Kentucky. Indeed, it was an important factor in the more sympathetic attention given by Congress to the problems of the western frontier. We have on record Madison's plea to George Washington that the government should change its policy on the matter of navigation on the Mississippi.[4]

Morgan's grant was an enormous tract containing some 15 million acres, extending both north and south of the Ohio River in what is now Missouri and Arkansas. The party arrived in February 1789 and proceeded to survey the grant. Called New Madrid, the capital was located near the mouth of the Ohio, where the Chepoussa joins the Mississippi. Once set in motion, Colonel Morgan proceeded downriver to New Orleans in May in order to discuss the project with Esteban Miró, the Spanish governor of Louisiana.

From this point in time we know that the failure of the undertaking —which could have changed the course of United States history—was due to the influence of James Wilkinson on the Spanish governor. Wilkinson seems to have enthralled Miró, which was helped substantially by the suspicion and dislike that existed between Miró and Gardoqui, so that the agent of one would often become the enemy of the other.

Wilkinson, whose collusion with Miró was already established, regarded with hate the prospective colony of New Madrid. It was in direct conflict with his own grandiose scheme not only to obtain for himself such a land grant but also politically to dominate a vassal or quasi-independent territory stretching from the southwestern slopes of the Allegheny Mountains to the Mississippi River. Wilkinson set himself to destroy George Morgan as he had already destroyed George Rogers Clark. And he succeeded. Several points aided him. Morgan's demand for complete religious freedom for settlers allowed Wilkinson to take advantage of Miró's bigotry by stating that this would create a nest of heretics on Spanish soil.[5] Morgan desired to establish friendly relations with the Kentuckians by creating a port of entry for their goods at New Madrid, but Wilkinson stated that this would calm Kentucky and thwart his plan to separate the territory from the other American states and annex it to Spain. The basic difference of course was that Morgan hoped to promote good relations between the two countries by creating a common culture on both sides of the mighty river, while

Wilkinson's future was tied to stirring muddy waters.[6] One must add that, given the closed nature of the Spanish mind during the eighteenth century, Wilkinson's plan made sense. Had Americans been permitted to cross the Mississippi but keep their religion, language, and historic roots, they would most likely have opted for the United States in a time of crisis.

Miró, impressed by Wilkinson's arguments, became worried. He reported on the project unfavorably to the secretary for the Indies, Don Antonio Valdez, emphasizing the danger to Louisiana and Mexico of a Spanish colony being granted religious freedom. Although personally impressed by George Morgan after their meeting in New Orleans, he continued to oppose the plan.

Colonel Morgan was thunderstruck when he learned of Miró's opposition. It is true that Gardoqui's offer had been provisional, but Morgan was under the impression that this was merely a matter of caution before receiving the king's edict. Miró stuck two darts into the heart of the project: public worship by non-Catholics would not be granted and Morgan's authority to sell land in New Madrid was withdrawn. In fact, Miró objected to selling the acreage and proposed to give small grants of land freely. Finally, Miró rebuked Morgan for telling the proposed settlers that he had received the large grant when Diego de Gardoqui had only authorized him to examine the country. As Max Savelle states, "The hand of Wilkinson is seen in all Miró's objections. . . ." The Spanish governor was not only a dupe of Wilkinson but a man of dull wit as well; he wrote his report of the meeting with Morgan to Valdez in a mood of self-congratulation, explaining how he had turned a bad business into a good one. In reality, Miró had put the kiss of death on New Madrid. When he found that his religion would be oppressed and that he would neither receive land nor control its sale, Morgan lost interest. Max Savelle also points out that just at this time Dr. John Morgan died, leaving his brother George the bulk of his large estate. Now independently wealthy, the colonel decided that the drawbacks of a Spanish settlement were greater than the rewards.

New Madrid had the greatest potential of any Spanish scheme on the North American continent. In the generation before, some 140,000 settlers had poured over the Alleghenies into Kentucky and the same process was beginning to repeat itself in Tennessee. The American birthrate was high and emigrants from Europe had started the western trek as well. The land involved in the project was rich, with the added advantage of free trade down the Mississippi. Discontented settlers in Kentucky and Tennessee would have flowed into New Madrid; in fact, surveys for a thousand farms had already been completed. But with the withdrawal of the colonel the entire project fell through.

Why? Part of the answer lies in the spirit of the age as much as in the foxy tactics of Wilkinson. Men like George Morgan, John Sevier, and George Rogers Clark, to mention only the most prominent persons—putting Wilkinson aside in a special filthy bracket—displayed an amazing indifference whether to be American or Spanish. But Morgan did owe allegiance to other values and these, admirably expressed in a letter he wrote to Gardoqui, sum up what many Americans felt at that time:

> Our love of Liberty Civil and religious is our ruling Passion: Give us these & all Princes or Rulers & all Countries are alike to Us: but they must be given as our Right & not as an Indulgence which we may be deprived of at Pleasure by any man or Sett of Men whatever. If Spain does not adopt this Idea in regard to farming her Settlements on the Mississippi She will have no Settlements there six Months after the first Dispute between her and the U.S.[8]

Nothing better can describe the attitude of certain Americans at the time, liberated from national prejudice by the winds sweeping out from the French Revolution. This paragraph from Morgan's letter nearly single-handedly explains why the United States waxed and Spain waned in the New World.

However, one must intrude with a sardonic note. Such rhetoric often seemed to be related to the promise of large land grants offered by Spain. In the same year that George Morgan wrote these uplifting words to Gardoqui, he also appealed again to the Virginia assembly for reconsideration of the Indiana Company claim. George Mason of Virginia retorted: "Mr. Morgan is entitled to as much *justice* as any other man, but surely no man who has endeavored to depopulate the United States by reducing their citizens to quit their own country and settle in the Spanish territory has little pretensions to *favor* from us."[9]

23

William Blount, John Sevier, and Tennessee

"The striking and peculiar characteristic of American society is that it is not so much a democracy as a huge commercial company for the discovery, cultivation, and capitalization of its enormous territory."

Professor Émile Gaston Boutmy

The weave of the state of Tennessee was braided by two very different personalities, William Blount and John Sevier. The order of priority goes to the first of these two men.

William Blount, born in 1749 in the tidewater section of North Carolina, was of Cavalier descent, his great-grandfather, Sir William Blount, having been imprisoned by Cromwell as a royalist baronet and supporter of Charles I. Named after this aristocratic ancestor, young William, with his father, had fought on the side of the British governor Tryon in 1771 against the Regulators, the backwoods libertarian revolt in North Carolina. Despite this royalist background, Blount opted for independence and during the Revolution filled important state offices as well as serving as a delegate to the Continental Congress in 1782. His close political colleagues were Richard Caswell and Alexander Martin, both of whom gained fame during the Revolution. These men were neither radical nor conservative. As Thomas P. Abernethy has put it so well, in politics "they cared less for principles than for power and in many cases they were able to straddle issues and draw strength from both sides because of their reputation and influence.

Their alignment was always dictated by their interests."[1] That is to say, they were in the mainstream of most successful American politicians.

The great land holdings of these men, most of all William Blount, arose from the opportunities that opened up after the Revolution when huge land grants could be bought with depreciated currency. The first North Carolina legislative session in 1783, after the restoration of peace, reopened the land offices with the intention of discharging the public debt by selling western tracts in what is now Tennessee. Most of the area beyond the Appalachians was still in Indian hands but the native rights (except for a small district reserved for the Cherokees) were ignored because, it was claimed, they had largely supported the British during the war. The transmontane country was now thrown on the market. William Blount, who had returned from Philadelphia for this legislative session, proposed a new issue of paper money for the purchase of the western domain. At this same session Blount met James Robertson, one of the first settlers beyond the mountains, and the two made an agreement whereby Blount would buy at discount military scrip given to Revolutionary soldiers while Robertson surveyed the land, a process needed in order to obtain clear title. For this surveying Robertson would receive a one-quarter interest.

It should not be assumed that the Blount-Robertson arrangement was unique. Blount, with his half-brother Willie and his brother John Gray, employed some half-dozen agents.[2] Another example is the agreement Blount had with an explorer named James White,[3] who marked out the site where Knoxville was founded in 1791. It was therefore no accident that Blount, when he later became governor of the Southwest Territory, chose this town as the capital even before the streets were laid down.

William Blount was the leading but by no means the only land syndicator. A similar group was put together by Richard Castrell and James Glasgow; the latter's position as secretary of state for North Carolina smoothed, so to speak, the paper on which titles were recorded. Caswell and Glasgow engaged Stockley Donelson, surveyor of Sullivan County in the western part of the state, whose sister married Andrew Jackson. Colonel John Donelson, their father, applied for the position as surveyor for the newly formed Greene County, west of the mountains. Patrick Henry also sent an agent, Joseph Martin, into the Holston Valley to select plots; Martin had already acted as an agent for Dr. Walker and Henderson in previous schemes. The backwoods were swarming with adventurers. The eastern men bought up military claims with depreciated currency and the western men staked the claims. According to Abernethy, only one North Carolina soldier from the Revolution actually settled on the land given him by way of military scrip; all the other grants were bought up by speculators.

Nearly four million acres were entered under the provisions of the 1783 act.[4] Though there has been no printed study of this first deep thrust into Tennessee land, as in the case of Jillson's analysis of Kentucky grants, the warrant books give some background. The surveyors appointed by the North Carolina legislature were William Terrell Lewis for the western district, William Polk for the central district, and Stockley Donelson for the eastern district. We can follow to some extent how they feathered their own nests. Thanks to Mr. Ken Fieth, senior archivist, I received a microfilm of Record Group No. 50, "Early Land Records," from the Tennessee State Library Archives at Nashville. Despite problems with the handwriting and poor organization of the headings and columns, much of the tape can still be read.

In the period from 1784 to 1786, and then again in 1807, the Lewis family had a land banquet. It would seem that William Terrell Lewis sat his whole family at the table. In the first two years the land office had been open, he patented 10,000 acres for himself. Sarah T. Lewis, apparently a sister, received 1,500 acres. James Lewis received 12,000 acres; and a James M. Lewis, probably the same person, took another 2,500 acres. Tipton Lewis is down for 3,000 acres, and Thomas Lewis appears for 7,000 acres. These were multiple grants of between 1,000 and 5,000 acres each.

The Lewis family does not appear on the warrant books for some time after; perhaps their overt grabbing led to a rebuke. Then, over twenty years later, in 1807, a flareup of new activity shows. In this year, William T. Lewis took for himself 23,000 acres, James Lewis 8,000 acres, Tipton Lewis 3,000 acres, and Sarah T. Lewis 1,500 acres. Shortly thereafter, though without date, another patent to William T. Lewis appears for 3,000 more acres. Again these patents were for between 1,000 and 5,000 acres each. Thus, putting aside assignments and only noting those entries clearly showing the family name (a portion of the writing is illegible), the Lewis family acquired through William Terrell's official post as surveyor 74,500 acres.

Stockley Donelson was head of the eastern district. In 1794 he patented for himself 5,000 acres. Far more important, the following year he acquired 20,000 acres in the area of the present city of Chattanooga: he sensed the commercial importance of that site. His father, Colonel John Donelson, took eight small grants when the land office first opened, amounting to over 3,000 acres; other Donelson family members show up as well for various small grants.

Colonel William Polk, surveyor for the central district, dwarfed the activities of his two fellow district surveyors. He does not appear on the records in the early years. But in 1807 he entered with a great dive. Directly for himself in that year he took 13,000 acres in six separate patents. But his great acquisitions came from original assignments made by a Geo. Doherty of Hillsborough. It hardly seems possible, but in less than two weeks, from late July to early August 1807, Colonel William Polk received 100,000 acres in large blocks of multiple entries that cover almost two pages of the warrant records. The Polk descendants fattened on this land for generations thereafter.

It may be added, relevant to all three surveyors, that there was a legal stop under the act of 1783 limiting patents to no more than 5,000 acres total for any one man. But the foxes were guards at the chicken coop. And of course the warrant records tell us neither of later assignments nor of dummies.

The process at bottom was quite simple. The leading western land speculators controlled North Carolina politics, with the surveyors being servants who got their cut. Alexander Martin, from the western part of the state, ran against Richard Caswell for governor in 1783. Martin was elected and the defeated Caswell was chosen speaker of the senate. In 1784, Caswell was elected governor and held the position for the legal limit of three terms. In the 1784 assembly William Blount was elected speaker of the house. Thus the same men dictated the issue of depreciated currency, set the value of western land, bought military scrip from the veterans, appointed the surveyors to the western counties and had them mark off and clear title, often through dummies or forgeries. It is for that reason the names of these men rarely appear on the official warrant lists. An excellent example is the Blount brothers: "By 1798, upwards of 100,000 acres of forged duplicate warrants were discovered in their account."[5] The movement of North Carolina into Tennessee, like that of Virginia into Kentucky, was a change from colonial to patriotic aristocracy, and not a change of system. This is the other side of the folklore of American pioneers. Men like Daniel Boone and David Crockett became mythical heroes but it was the Richard Hendersons and William Blounts who got the land.[6]

This land-rich elite split over the question of whether North Carolina should cede its western counties to Congress. The schism was deep and bitter. Blount supported cession, while Martin opposed it. The eastern tidewater districts favored giving up the land, for the Indian wars were expensive and the cost was mainly borne by the wealthier East. The backcountry settlements, whose families had moved farther west, felt their kinship and opposed separation. Blount, free of state jingoism, preferred killing Indians with out-of-state troops at Congressional expense to validate his land claims rather than have the state legislature raise the money.[7] There would, however, never be a question as to who owned the land. Though the cession by North Carolina to Congress for what is now Tennessee had been passed, repealed, and finally re-passed, the terms always included a provision that all land grants previously issued by the state should be validated. Thus, whether North Carolina or Tennessee, the speculators were sure they would hold their land. And, as will be seen shortly, they even extended this protective mechanism to the question of whether the United States or Spain might ultimately own the territory.

William Blount was a persuasive man. Francis S. Philbrick, remarkable in his charity toward James Wilkinson, stated in a thumbnail sketch, "Blount was a man of predatory instincts. Perjury, fraud, forgery, misuse of public office, subornation, and corruption of public officials—all were counseled or practiced by him with brazen audacity."[8] What Philbrick does not write, and what is equally valid, is that neither a whore ascends to a lady nor a politician to great fortune without favorable spore. And Blount's success led him to venture farther west. The area chosen, at Muscle Shoals (also called the "Bend" or "Bent," referring to a turn of the Tennessee River) was near what is now Decatur, Alabama, to the extreme north of that state. Many felt that the "Bend" might become the center point of western commerce because it was an easy link to the Tennessee settlements of Holston and Cumberland—and then north to Kentucky and Illinois—as well as several portages south to connecting waterways and then to the Tombigbee River down to the Gulf of Mexico at what is now Mobile.[9]

Blount brought his usual cronies into this speculation: Richard Caswell, then speaker of the North Carolina senate and governor a year later; Griffith Rutherford, a Revolutionary general; Colonel John Donelson, former associate of Richard Henderson and county surveyor for North Carolina on the Holston; Joseph Martin, land agent for Patrick Henry; and also John Sevier, soon to be the governor of Franklin, a short-lived independent state set up by disgruntled settlers in what is now Tennessee. John Sevier, an emigrant from the Shenandoah Valley of Virginia, was among the first settlers to penetrate the transmontane region and had been a Revolutionary war hero at the famous battle of King's Mountain. Blount, Caswell, and Rutherford, the three easterners, were to supply the capital; Donelson, Martin, and Sevier were to come to agreement with the Indians and make the necessary surveys.

The character of John Sevier has already been touched on through a quotation from the writing of A. P. Whitaker. Descriptions of historic figures often tell as much about the historians as they do about their subjects. This is how Archibald Henderson saw Sevier: "In this daring and impetuous young man, fair-haired, blue-eyed, magnetic, debonair—of powerful build, splendid proportions, and athletic skill—we behold the gallant exemplar of the truly heroic life of the frontier."[10] We will see shortly the hero in action.

JOHN SEVIER. Miniature attributed to Charles Willson Peale.

The first step of the Blount syndicate was to buy the Cherokee claim to the Muscle Shoals region, undoubtedly using as a prototype Henderson's earlier purchase from the Cherokees of the region to the east. The fact that the area was also Creek and Shawnee hunting grounds did not seem to matter. The purchase was made by Donelson and Martin in November 1783, while officially employed by Virginia to conclude a trade treaty with the nearby friendly Chickasaws. We do not know the price that was paid, but Blount, the head of the company, wrote thanking them for a "cheap enough" purchase.[11]

Muscle Shoals was west of North Carolina and claimed by Georgia. William Blount resigned his seat in Congress and went to Georgia the next year, where he petitioned the legislature for a grant of these western lands. The Georgia legislature, well shown by the later Yazoo land company grants as among the most venal of all state bodies, graciously agreed and created a new county, later called Houston County, which embraced the tract lying between the Tennessee River and the southern border of North Carolina. Seven commissioners were appointed to survey the region, three by Blount himself (Donelson, Martin, and Sevier); while the other four were Georgians about whom Blount—an expert in such matters—remarked, "they all appear to have a great Thirst for Tenese Lands."[12]

In July 1784 a majority of the commission met at Muscle Shoals, where they appointed as militia officers of the new county John Sevier, John Donelson, and Valentine Sevier, John Sevier's son. A land office for the new county was projected for early the next year and Colonel John Donelson was appointed county surveyor. With the preliminaries worked out, now all that was needed were settlers to buy the land. Blount, concerned that Georgia might revoke its grant if the land were not quickly settled, wrote Donelson to "keep up a Report of as many settlers being about to remove as you possibly can *whether true or not.*"[13]

Though the new county was officially a part of Georgia, Blount's company controlled all the public offices and land sales. It was provided, according to Blount's interpretation of some ambiguous wording, that the company should also receive a grant of land in compensation for the services of the commissioners. As an example of the approach, we know of a warrant of the state of Georgia instructing John Donelson to survey for John Sevier a thousand acres. The warrant was signed by Donelson and Sevier![14] Also on record is correspondence between Blount and the commissioners appointed by him in which it was suggested that fictitious names be supplied to take up thousand-acre plots at the most valuable part of the "Bend."[15]

The Muscle Shoals speculation, so brilliantly conceived, was to fail as a result of unexpected events. In December 1784 the settlers of Holston and Watauga, at the northwest corner of what is now Tennessee, between Virginia and North Carolina, became so disgusted with North Carolina because of the lack of protection afforded them against Indian attacks that they called into being the new "state" of Franklin.[16] For four years (1784–1788) the turmoil surrounding the brief life of this state brought to a stop speculation farther west and the Muscle Shoals land office never opened. As a result the project was aborted.

The aftermath of such a failure, however, can teach much about the settling of the West. John Sevier, who initially opposed the separatist movement because of its threat to his investment at Muscle Shoals, then turned a somersault and seized control of the dissidents, becoming governor of the new state of Franklin. Stokeley Donelson, Colonel John Donelson's son, was made surveyor. In a letter dated December 20, 1786, from a gentleman living in the area declared independent, the writer describes the setting up "last week" of the new state, and adds: "If I was to venture a conjecture, the good of the commonwealth is not at the bottom, but the views of a few crafty landjobbers, whom you know, who are aiming at purchasing the great bent of Tenasee [Muscle Shoals] from the Indians. . . ."[17] It was evident that Sevier and his colleagues felt that political control of Franklin would aid them in their Muscle Shoals venture.

The land speculators who dominated the South only controlled a small part of the thirteen states, and even within their own states there were opposing factions. Congress was trying desperately to maintain peace with Spain, a position backed by mercantile interests seeking the right to trade with the Spanish colonies. The last thing the northern and middle states wanted was a series of Indian wars on top of all their other problems. The result was the Treaty of Hopewell, negotiated in 1785 between the natives and commissioners of Congress, which fixed the Cherokee boundary line far up the Tennessee River above Muscle Shoals and guaranteed this territory to the Indians. Franklin was not admitted into the Confederation and frontier expansion was temporarily restrained.

During the brief life of Franklin, William Blount with his partner Richard Caswell, the governor of the state of North Carolina, had most amiable relations with John Sevier, their business partner, despite the fact that he was then governor of a state illegally carved out of Carolina territory. As Merrill Jensen stated simply, "Franklin was run by the land speculators who had staked out much of the state before it was created. While Sevier was governor of the 'rebel' state, he was, unknown to the people of Franklin, actually working closely with Richard Caswell, Governor of North Carolina."[18] Profit from their joint enterprises was more important than the

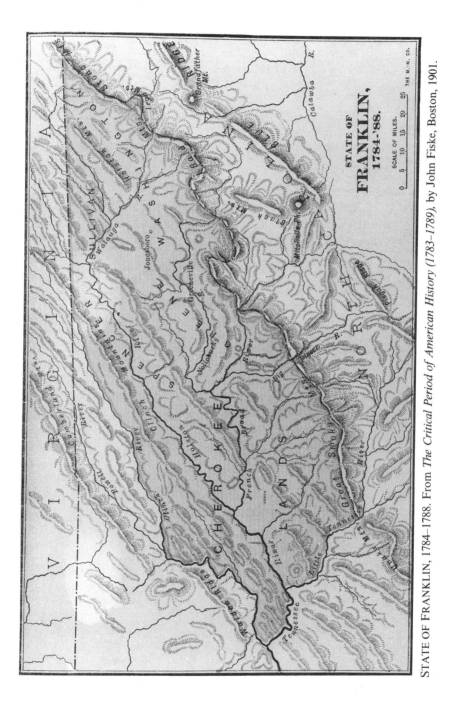

STATE OF FRANKLIN, 1784–1788. From *The Critical Period of American History (1783–1789)*, by John Fiske, Boston, 1901.

question of political control. In fact, Caswell, as governor, wrote to Sevier when a renegade, wasting no time on politics but rather asking how land grants could be adjusted to the new situation: "The Bent of Tenesee [Muscle Shoals] is still an Object with me of an Interesting Nature. . . . I will attend to the Grant you wish to Caveat, in Bumper's Cove; pray will it not be necessary for you to have returns made of our lands on the French Broad so that Grants issue from this State?"[19]

Blount and Caswell were realists above all and they soon saw that the wind was blowing against Franklin. In 1786, Georgia and the Creek Indians went to war over westward expansion, against the expressed opposition of Congress. One of the reasons for the war was Creek resentment over "the Attempt of Settling the Bent of Tennessee."[20] The bellicose Georgians soon learned that Indian wars without national troops were expensive.[21] At the end of 1787, Georgia accepted the federal Constitution, thus submitting to the national policy of a more gradual extension of the frontier. This meant abandoning of the Muscle Shoals speculation and delivering a death-blow to the isolated "state" of Franklin.

John Sevier's political career seemed to have reached its end. Trying desperately to retrieve his reputation, he fell back on doing what he knew best, butchering Indians. Sevier retreated to the southern counties of what had been Franklin, where his influence was greatest, and started the most savage Indian war Americans had known since the Revolution. During these 1788 campaigns, troops under his command massacred some of the most prominent Indian chiefs while under the protection of a white flag of truce. This only increased the admiration of his followers.[22] In the meantime, Samuel Johnston, who opposed the libertarian movement in the western provinces, succeeded Caswell as governor of North Carolina and ordered the arrest of John Sevier. However, he was unable to enforce the warrant against the rabid anti-Indian leader in the sympathetic frontier settlements.

It was precisely at this desperate juncture that Sevier started his intrigue with Spain, paralleling the activities of General Wilkinson and George Rogers Clark to the north in Kentucky. Their stories have already been told. In what is now Tennessee, the main tool of Spain was Dr. James White, superintendent of Indian affairs for the southern department under Congress from 1786 to 1788. Dr. White, a Catholic from Pennsylvania, studied medicine in Philadelphia. He took his money and his orders from Diego de Gardoqui, also stationed in Philadelphia. At the same time, White was involved in land speculation as a business associate of William Blount, of whom he was also a political protégé.

In July 1788, only two months after resigning his federal post, Dr.

White went to Tennessee, visiting both the Cumberland settlement and the separatist state of Franklin. His intention was to entice for the Spanish cause John Sevier at Franklin and General Daniel Smith and Colonel James Robertson, the leaders of Cumberland. The evidence shows that White succeeded.

The timing was perfect at Franklin for it was precisely then that Sevier was in disgrace. Dr. White won him over with little resistance, for Sevier wrote two letters to Don Diego in September 1788, delivered by his son, in one of which he stated that the inhabitants of Franklin were "unanimous in their vehement desire to form an alliance and treaty of commerce with Spain, and put themselves under her protection."[23] Sevier requested money, munitions, and commercial concessions from Spain; he also specifically spoke of the settlement planned at Muscle Shoals.[24] We know from Dr. White's talks in Havana, where he was laid over in December 1788 for several weeks while waiting for a boat to take him to report to Governor Miró at New Orleans, that the key issue for the pro-Spanish group in Franklin was to get possession of a belt of land extending from Franklin down the Tennessee on both sides of the river well below Muscle Shoals; if this land were granted them, they would swear allegiance to the king of Spain.[25]

Dr. White was equally successful at Cumberland, where both Smith and Robertson quickly assented to become vassals of Spain if Indian attacks were eased and trade opened on the Mississippi. In fact, the Cumberland settlers changed the name of the district to "Mero," misspelling it in the process, in honor of the Spanish governor. General Smith wrote directly to the governor in Louisiana on March 4, 1789, that the inhabitants would send delegates to North Carolina the following September in order to solicit an act of separation and, as soon as that could be obtained, agents from Cumberland would go to New Orleans in order to place the territory under the dominion of the Spanish king.[26]

It is of value to relate these political actions to the individual careers of the gentlemen in question. The backgrounds of Sevier and Robertson have been touched on, and their business relations with Blount. Smith, the other Cumberland leader involved, was a prominent western speculator in Virginia and a colleague of Dr. Thomas Walker, in whose Loyal Company he had invested. Smith had moved west in order to handle his speculations personally; he felt them much endangered by Indian attacks. The correspondence shows that these Tennessee settlers were not only aware of the intrigues in their own area and in those to the north in Kentucky, but they also kept in contact with the top political figures in North Carolina. Again much could be traced back to William Blount, Robertson's boss in land speculation. It seems impossible that Robertson would agree to a Spanish alliance without the approval, express or implied, of Blount. As has been pointed out, despite their political differences, Sevier and Blount also continued to do business together. Abernethy, who goes into the matter in detail in his massive studies of this period, came to the conclusion that Blount, Caswell, and their friends in North Carolina rode both horses, being far more concerned with the value of their land than with whether the United States or Spain held the transmontane region. If White, Robertson, Sevier, and their allies succeeded in breaking away under the Spanish flag, Muscle Shoals would be linked up to the Gulf of Mobile Bay and their land would rise in value; if the land were ceded to the federal government (and all these men were Federalist in politics), their great tracts to the west of North Carolina would also rise in value under protection by government troops from Indian attack.[27]

In December 1789 the North Carolina legislature ceded its western territory to the United States, the cession being accepted by Congress in April 1790. The southern representatives in Congress had succeeded in blocking any move by treaty with Spain to restrict navigation on the Mississippi. George Washington, who had just been elected president, chose Thomas Jefferson as his secretary of state. Both men were from Virginia and Jefferson in particular was known for his strong pro-western views. Diego de Gardoqui had been called back to Spain, Governor Miró was preparing to leave, and the web of intimate contacts these Spaniards had with the American conspirators was sundered. Spanish wobbling and American pragmatism broke the threat, and the separatist movements in Tennessee and Kentucky faded away.

There was a happy ending for all concerned. When Blount was appointed governor of the Southwest Territory—an area which included Kentucky, Tennessee, and the region down to the 31st parallel claimed by Georgia— as well as superintendent of Indian affairs in the South by George Washington in 1790, Blount made his old friend John Sevier brigadier general for the district of Washington, and with their mutual interest in land warrants (which office Blount now directly controlled as governor), Sevier rose again like a cork. The two men were deep into the Yazoo frauds (which will be discussed in the next chapter). Colonel James Robertson was appointed by Blount as brigadier general for the district of Mero. General Daniel Smith, also of Cumberland, was appointed secretary as well as surveyor for the Southwest Territory: we already know the uses of that office. And even Dr. James White, probably the only dyed-in-the-wool adherent of Spain, returned to his Cumberland estate as an honored citizen and was elected to Congress.[28] Thus was divided loyalty at best, treason

at worst, rewarded by a federal government eager to placate the turbulent western frontiersmen.[29]

The Southwest Territory filled with settlers and in 1795 a census revealed the requisite sixty thousand inhabitants. In 1796, Tennessee became
the sixteenth state admitted into the Union. William Blount, who by 1794
owned at least a million acres,[30] was elected to the United States Senate.
The man who spent a long and successful life dancing his own manikins
made one fatal slip at the end of his career. Overextended in land speculation, as was Robert Morris in this same period, and in need of specie,
he sold his services to the British. In 1796, Spain had allied itself with
France against Great Britain and Blount aided in organizing an illegal
filibustering expedition against Spanish West Florida and Louisiana. A
letter was intercepted and for "high misdemeanor inconsistent with public
trust and duty" William Blount was expelled from the U.S. Senate. He
died shortly thereafter, in 1800, and lies buried in Knoxville.

John Sevier's luck held out to the very end. The Indian butcher was
revered as a heroic figure from the misty days of the forest primeval and
the Cherokee tomahawk. Sevier, after Blount's elevation as U.S. senator,
was elected governor of the new state. A tremendous land fraud scandal
involving the governor and a clique of his own cronies, wherein forgeries
would have turned over about one-sixth of the public domain of Tennessee
to the inside group, was uncovered in his administration,[31] but the charmer
slithered away from public censure. Sevier was sent to Congress on his
retirement and, after screaming for war with Great Britain as a leader of
the War Hawks, he died in 1815. His remains are at Knoxville, topped
by a high marble spire. A medal was issued in the bicentennial year to
celebrate his contribution to American history.

It must be added for the sake of balance that about one-third of the
early pioneers who went to Tennessee between 1776 and 1796 were killed
by Indians, and John Sevier made his reputation as the most intransigent
of Indian fighters. The eighteenth-century frontier was a time of race war
pure and simple, with the land-hungry whites of the Southwest intent on
wiping out the Shawnee, the Cherokee, and the Creek. If the mark of
civilization at that time was the excision of reds for whites, with their black
slaves trod below, then John Sevier is the very model of the hero.[32]

24

The Yazoo Land Frauds of Georgia

"And thus in politics, there is the government of the many and the government of the few; or a democracy and an oligarchy. . . ."

Aristotle, *The Politics*

After the Revolution, the territory west of Georgia now comprising the states of Alabama and Mississippi, was the subject of conflicting claims. Both South Carolina and Georgia considered it part of their original charters. The federal government claimed the land had been ceded to the nation by the treaty of peace, while Spain denied England's right to cede the area at all. Far more important, Indian tribes occupied the vast territory; the Creeks and Cherokees alone were strong enough to make a farce of any land grants without their approval. Thus, no matter how good Georgia's title was—and it was eventually validated—the ultimate value of the land depended on the power to oust the Indians. This was the background for Georgia's readiness to dispose of the lands on any kind of favorable condition.

The history of speculation in these western lands, called the Yazoo land grants, is complicated because there were two separate and distinct time periods, involving different companies. A chronological study is the easiest approach.

The Yazoo River flows north and south in the central part of what is now the state of Mississippi, toward the western border; the nearest city of size (though a Yazoo City exists) is the state capital of Jackson. The importance of the Yazoo River was that it met the Tallahatchie River in the north while to the south it emptied into the Mississippi at Walnut Hills (now Vicksburg), thus serving as a liquid belt for goods from a very large region. The land speculations were not limited to this area; they covered the entire west beyond Georgia's colonial line to the Mississippi River. In summary, the Georgia grants were given in territory that Spain felt belonged to her, while the land was used as hunting grounds by two of the most powerful Indian tribes on the North American continent.

In late 1789 the Georgia legislature was petitioned for three huge land grants by companies whose stated aim was to create settlements in the West. The original public records dealing with the petitions have been lost, or more likely destroyed, but in December of that year an omnibus bill was passed without trouble and soon after received the governor's signature. Almost all the western lands of Georgia were bestowed in this single act. The South Carolina Yazoo Company received over 10 million acres of what is now southern Mississippi and Alabama, centering on Walnut Hills. The Virginia Yazoo Company received 11.4 million acres, including most of the northern part of these future states. The Tennessee Company took 4 million acres in the region of the Tennessee River that included Muscle Shoals.[1] The companies were to pay within two years $66,964, $93,741, and $46,875 respectively. Significantly, the act only referred to the number of dollars in each case, not whether the sums were to be paid in specie or paper.[2] Furthermore, Georgia specifically exempted itself from liability on previous claims or for protecting the grantees from Indian attacks.

The South Carolina Yazoo Company, the initial sponsor, had an interesting background. In the late 1780s a Georgian adventurer by the name of Major Thomas Washington (whose real name was Walsh) set about organizing a company to create a settlement near the mouth of the Yazoo River. The flavor of the company can be tasted from the fact that this promoter was hanged at Charleston in 1791 for counterfeiting South Carolina debt certificates. Washington brought into his scheme several prominent men from South Carolina, including Alexander Moultrie who, as half-brother to General William Moultrie, elected governor of South Carolina in 1785 and again in 1794, provided a prime political contact. Moultrie's share, one of twenty, covered a tract of half a million acres.

Following these land grants by Georgia, the South Carolina Yazoo Company was the most active. It picked as its agent Dr. James O'Fallon, an unscrupulous liar cut from the same cloth as his boss, Washington. Dr. O'Fallon set out northward early in 1790 for Lexington, Kentucky, where he was to see John Holder who, several years earlier, attempted to make a settlement at Walnut Hills on the basis of a deed for several million acres obtained from the Choctaw Indians. Passing through what is now Tennessee, O'Fallon secured the services of John Sevier as a sub-agent by promising him a share in the company. In Kentucky he contacted General Wilkinson and requested his cooperation in calming the Spanish. A rare set of vipers were suckling.

Wilkinson, a consummate artist in all intrigues, immediately contacted Governor Esteban Miró of Louisiana, stating that he was taking an active interest in the project since the settlement would become a Spanish colony: "I am persuaded that I shall experience no difficulty in adding their establishment to the domains of his Majesty, and this they will soon discover to be their interest. . . . I will keep you well informed of every movement which I shall observe. . . ."[3] However, Miró replied that the territory belonged to the Indians under the protection of Spain and that the colony would not be allowed. After his troubles in Kentucky and Tennessee, Miró had apparently lost confidence in American adventurers.[4]

Assessing this setback directly to Miró, O'Fallon tried to out-Wilkinson Wilkinson. In a fawning letter written directly to Miró, O'Fallon stated that his real purpose was to make the settlement a Spanish bulwark and that, with full powers conceded to him by the company, he had enlisted stockholder approval and "insensibly prevailed upon them to acquiesce in [his] political views, and led them to consent to be the slaves of Spain, under the appearance of a free and independent colony. . . ."[5] The only concessions he desired were liberty of conscience and autonomous civil government. In all his contacts with the Spanish, O'Fallon emphasized his Irish Catholic background.

According to available evidence, this petty schemer was backed, if not anticipated, by the company directors. Even before O'Fallon arrived in Kentucky, they had written a letter to John Holder recommending full cooperation with the Spanish.[6] Similar phrasing indicates that O'Fallon was probably repeating the contents of a letter already known to him.

In August of 1790, Miró sent to Madrid the correspondence together with his comments. Skeptical after his recent frontier setbacks, he doubted the advantages of "taking a foreign state to board"[7] and recommended rather that the home country should people the territory directly with Spaniards: in which position he was without question correct. Miró added that he had promised to supply the Indians with powder and ball for their defense.

The activities of the South Carolina Yazoo Company were brought to the attention of the federal government, and in the same month that Miró sent the correspondence to Madrid, George Washington issued a proclamation reviewing the Treaty of Hopewell of 1785, which guaranteed the land involved to the Indians, and ordered its observance. O'Fallon forwarded a soothing letter to the president and then proceeded as though the proclamation had not been issued. Operating from the home of George Rogers Clark, whose sister he married the following year, O'Fallon described Clark in his letters to Miró as his expedition leader and set about organizing a battalion with a troop of cavalry, a company of artillery, and eight companies of riflemen. General Scott was to take five hundred families to the settlement while Wilkinson and Sevier were to follow, each with a thousand fighting men and their families.

When this news reached the federal capital, it caused an uproar, for it meant a possible widespread Indian war as well as a crisis with Spain. George Washington issued a new and sharper proclamation mentioning O'Fallon and his associates and warning that the United States district attorney would issue a writ against any company settlement.[9] The president also invited to New York City McGillivry of the Creeks, the renowned head of the most powerful southern tribe. There a treaty of friendship was signed and the United States discreetly tripled the subsidy that McGillivry had been receiving from Spain. This assured peace in the area of the land grant and blocked the speculators.

That was the end of the South Carolina Yazoo Company. Wilkinson, with his usual finger to the breeze, deserted, calling O'Fallon a vain blockhead. George Rogers Clark slid down again into his bottle, while O'Fallon's war caricature melted into the air. It was one thing to hazard an expedition against the Indians and quite another to take on the military forces of the United States. The shareholders, led by the well-placed Alexander Moultrie, refused to concede defeat, however, and brought up claims for lost money before the Supreme Court. Then, after Georgia ceded its western lands to the federal government, the same shareholders brought their claims before Congress. Since payment for the grant had been tendered in discounted paper rather than specie, the real question was whether the original bill had defined the medium of payment. The Georgia state authorities held that the act implied payment in coin only and this position was validated on all appeals. For some odd reason no one raised the point as to why shareholders who were planning a settlement independent of the United States and vassal to Spain should be granted financial relief through federal tax revenue.

The Virginia Yazoo Company had a less speckled and more successful history. It was dominated by Patrick Henry, who brought with him as partners old Virginia friends like Abraham Venable and David Ross, whom we met in the insider Kentucky land grants. Henry, cautious in middle age, forbade settlement on company lands until the Indian claims could be quieted in accordance with the federal treaty. Failing in this, depreciated public certificates purchased at an average of about ten per-cent of face value were offered in payment but refused by the Georgia authorities. The Henry syndicate was not only bailed out, however, but made a very great profit as a result of Alexander Hamilton's funding sys-tem by which these depreciated certificates were redeemed at par by the federal government.[10] As Jefferson wrote to Washington on April 24, 1791, regarding Henry and his fellow investors in the Virginia Yazoo Company, "Since the rise in value of the public paper, they have gained as much on that as they would have done by investing it in the Yazoo lands: perhaps more, as it puts a large sum of specie at their command, which they can turn to better account."[11] Jefferson's claim that Patrick Henry shifted to the Federalist party in gratitude for Hamilton's action is well known.

The Tennessee Company, the third of the speculative companies in-volved in the original Georgia bill, was the brainchild of Zachariah Cox, another adventurer in this spawning shoal of plungers. Cox had been associated with John Sevier at Muscle Shoals and the two men, with other prominent Tennessee settlers, put in their stake for this far corner of Geor-gia's western land. In early 1791, despite warnings from President Wash-ington, eighteen men erected a blockhouse at "the Bend" of the Tennes-see, but beat a hasty retreat on the arrival of a war band of Cherokees. Just as in the case of the two larger companies, payment to Georgia was tendered in depreciated script and refused by that state. The company went into hibernation.

The lack of success involved in the 1789 first group of Yazoo land grants only whetted the taste buds of speculators. The Georgia legislature began to be bombarded again. The initial new proposal came in November 1794 from an agent by the name of John Wereat, who represented a trio of prominent financiers offering to pick up the South Carolina Yazoo Company grant for the same price at which the company had defaulted a few years before. They were Albert Gallatin, a Pennsylvania banker and prominent political backer of Thomas Jefferson, who in the decade fol-lowing would be secretary of the treasury in Jefferson's cabinet; A. J. Dal-las, a Pennsylvania lawyer who also backed Jefferson's political ambitions; and Jared Ingersoll, likewise a lawyer from Pennsylvania, whose politics were Federalist and who was attorney and personal advisor to the great mercantile prince Stephen Girard. Thus northern money was involved but the contacts ate at both political tables.

Immediately after this offer, four southern companies, with some Penn-sylvania backing, entered the picture and made higher bids. Petitions from these companies were referred to a sympathetic legislative committee. John Wereat raised his offer but the proposal was rejected. The bill was then revised to meet certain objections on the part of the governor. Again Wereat outbid the other companies but his higher offer was refused by the legislature, which hurried through a bill, signed by the governor in January 1795, granting the greater part of what is now Alabama and Mississippi —over 30 million acres—to four syndicates whose members paid on average a cent and half an acre. The lion's share of the land went to the Georgia Company, which received some 17 million acres for $250,000. The area purchased was greater than the combined states of Massachusetts, Rhode Island, Connecticut, New Jersey, and Delaware. The Georgia Mississippi Company received about 7 million acres at the southwest corner of Georgia's western territory for $155,000. The Tennessee Company, which was simply a resurrection of the same company from five years earlier, received the 4 million acres it had been granted before for $60,000; Zachariah Cox reappeared as a leading shareholder allied with William Blount and John Sevier. A strip of 3 million acres to the extreme northwest went to the Upper Mississippi Company for $35,000.

The Georgia Company, which dominated the other land grants, was led by General James Gunn, one of Georgia's two U.S. senators. Among those involved in this and the other syndicates were Matthew McAllister, U.S. attorney for the district of Georgia; Robert Goodloe Harper[12] and Thomas P. Carnes, Georgia congressman; General Wade Hampton, one of the richest of southern planters, who would shortly become a Georgia congressman; Nathaniel Pendleton, a federal judge from Georgia; and William Stith, a Georgia Supreme Court judge. This was the cream of Georgia's high society. Working with them from the more northern states were the ubiquitous Robert Morris, U.S. Supreme Court judge James Wilson, the great speculator James Greenleaf, and Oliver Phelps, who in this same period had contracted to buy about one-sixth of New York State. The Georgia Company issued ten shares, three of which went to General Wade Hampton and two to Senator James Gunn. The other companies spread their shares to a larger group; Judge James Wilson was the third largest holder of total shares.

The insiders from Georgia put up token payments needed before passage of the act approving the land grants. They used their influence to get the grant through the legislation, while their northern partners advanced the larger sums required to take title. As Francis Watkins, a partner in the earlier Virginia Yazoo Company, wrote to Patrick Henry: "Gunn, Pendleton & Cox, (all with money of their own) with a few associates, have done the business, Judge Wilson & others, the money."[13] What came

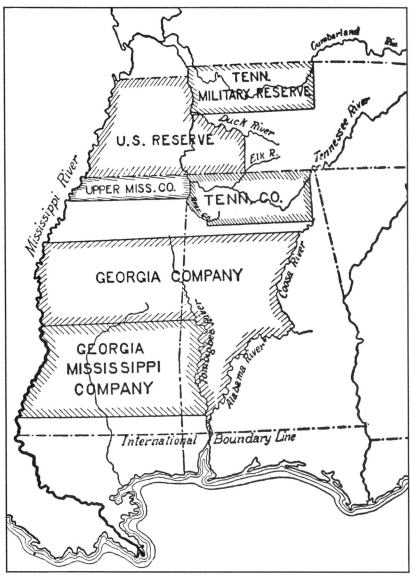

YAZOO LAND CLAIMS, TENNESSEE AND MISSISSIPPI TERRITORY. From *The National Land System, 1785–1820,* by Payson J. Treat, New York, 1910.

out later was that, with but a single exception, every member of the Georgia legislature who voted for the act had received part shares in one or more of the four companies. It is a mystery why this one peculiar individual gave his vote without selling it.[14] The symmetry in corruption was rare even for eighteenth-century America; in the nineteenth century, a simple corrupt majority would most often suffice.

Like a dead rat under the floor boards, this fraud was too rank to pass by. John Randolph of Virginia demonstrated an especial distaste for the deal and started a public fracas, stating with perhaps a bit too much rhetoric for a man some of whose ancestors had acquired much power through dubious methods, "A more flagrant case of wholesale legislative corruption had never been known."[15] Great indignation swept Georgia, with public meetings, newspaper attacks, and numerous protest petitions. James Jackson, the other U.S. senator from Georgia besides Gunn, resigned his seat and went home to head an "Anti-Yazoo" party, which elected a majority to the next legislature. A committee headed by Jackson then examined the validity of the grants and issued proofs of corruption. In February 1797 the sale was declared null and void, the public records relating to it were ordered burned, and the return of the purchase money mandated.

This was not a happy ending where virtue triumphed over vice. Instead, it was just the start of the Yazoo drama. Far too many rich and powerful men had their fingers in the pie to give up the eating.

It was obvious to the Georgians who had set up the fraudulent grants that their paper house was shaking. Many promptly set about to sell before the grants would be voided. The Georgia Mississippi Company, for example, immediately sold a large part of its grant to James Greenleaf, who promptly resold a block of a million acres to Judge James Wilson, another block of a million acres to Zachariah Cox, and a large part of the remainder to Boston and New York buyers. Hampton and Gunn of the Georgia Company sold their five of the ten shares to Hugh Ross of Philadelphia, who resold a half-interest in them in England. Offices were also organized throughout the middle and northern states to market the land, with an extensive program of advertising through newspapers and pamphlets.

These activities, centered at Boston, were particularly aggressive in New England. A violent speculative spirit swept lower New England, with purchases and sales following daily, usually in the form of notes turned over quickly on discount. By the time news reached Boston of a possible repeal of the sale by the new Georgia legislature a good part of the land had been sold: in fact, 11 million acres of land were conveyed the very day of the rescinding act, which indicated early information received by private courier. The investment in Boston alone amounted to over two million dollars, an enormous sum of money at that time. A contemporary report described the fury of the speculation, "Every class of men, even watch-makers, hair-dressers and mechanics of all descriptions, eagerly ran after this deception."[16] Prominent men were deeply involved as well: James Sullivan, attorney general of Massachusetts from 1790 to 1807 and later governor; Harrison Gray Otis, nephew of James Otis and a leader of the Massachusetts legislature before going to the U.S. Senate; and Gideon Granger, postmaster general in the cabinet of President Jefferson. In addition, there were top capitalists like Nathaniel Prime, promoter of the first American banking house, Leonard Bleecker, a founder of the New York Stock Exchange; and James Strawbridge of Philadelphia.

The interests of such powerful men as well as a multitude of small investors were now so mixed that the position of the original defrauders was greatly aided. A group of the new purchasers under the name of the New England Mississippi Company entered the battle in order to validate their claims. There were two avenues of approach. The first was to apply directly to Congress for compensation as a result of Georgia having ceded its western lands to the federal government shortly after the land grants. The second was to press in the courts to have the rescinding act of the later Georgia legislature declared void.

When the question of compensating Yazoo shareholders came before Congress, John Randolph led the opposition. He undoubtedly thought it wrong that individuals should profit from their corrupt acts. As a strict adherent of states' rights, he also felt that a denial of the rescinding act struck a blow against republican principles. Mixed with these laudable views, however, was the practical politics of a political struggle for leadership taking place within the Jeffersonian party between Randolph and Madison, the stake being the party's next candidate for president. James Madison was then called the least Virginian of all the prominent Virginians because of support from northern Jeffersonians, which Randolph lacked. Madison, to appease his New England backers, many of whom had a financial interest in the Yazoo question, pushed for compromise. Thus Yazoo became a political football within the ruling Jeffersonian party. The issue before Congress dragged on for years and was an important factor in John Randolph's fall from power; indeed it created the first split between northern and southern Democrats (as they later came to be known), a harbinger of events to come.

The invective during this fight is almost impossible to believe compared to present debates in Congress. Postmaster General Granger, a party to the speculation, appeared as an agent for the New England Mississippi

Company. This called forth from Randolph a mountain of purple oratory: "His gigantic grasp embraces with one hand the shores of Lake Erie,[17] and stretches with the other to the Bay of Mobile. Millions of acres are easily digested by such stomachs. . . . They buy and sell corruption in the gross, and a few millions, more or less, is hardly felt in the account." Then turning to Madison's partisans, he said: "What is the spirit against which we now struggle, and which we have vainly endeavored to stifle? A monster generated by fraud, nursed in corruption, that in grim silence awaits its prey. . . ."[18]

Matthew Lyon of Kentucky, who held several mail contracts from Granger and thus felt himself impugned, then rose and called Randolph a jackal and a madman with the face of a monkey. As Henry Adams wrote, the dispute had passed rational argument and was the key to the struggle between Madison and Randolph.[19] John Randolph did succeed in blocking the Yazoo speculators' claims but, also due to his quarrelsome and arrogant nature, destroyed his own political chances and paved the way for Madison's election as fourth president of the United States.

Parallel with the attempt to gain compensation directly from Congress, the claimants also requested judicial review. In March of 1809 the case was argued before the Supreme Court of the United States, one of the three lawyers for the Yazoo shareholders being Robert Goodloe Harper, brother-in-law of Alexander Hamilton and a leading shareholder in the Georgia Company, which in 1795 had promulgated the swindle. A defect in the pleading threw the case over to the next session and on March 16, 1810, Chief Justice John Marshall rendered his famous decision in *Fletcher* v. *Peck,* affirming the position taken in 1795 by Alexander Hamilton in a similar matter, namely, that the rescinding act of Georgia impaired the obligation of contracts and was therefore contrary to the Constitution of the United States. The reasoning was that an act, whether public or private, is an executed contract and a court cannot investigate the question of possible fraud when the forms of law were used by a legislature acting within its rights.

Now the way was clear for all claims, though it took several years to set up the proper mechanism. A congressional act of March 31, 1814, put aside $5,000,000 to be paid to the shareholders of the four original companies. The holders of shares in the Upper Mississippi Company, who had paid $35,000 for the original grant, received $350,000; those of the Tennessee Company, who had paid $60,000, were awarded $600,000; those of the Georgia Mississippi Company, who had paid $155,000, were given $1,550,000; and those of the largest of the original companies, the Georgia Company, who had paid $250,000, were handed a windfall of $2,250,000.

The sum of $250,000 was held from the last claim to settle certain shares that had accrued to the United States. The judicial decision thus called for a payment of ten times the cost to the original shareholders, who in many cases were the legislators or judges receiving stock in these companies to vote for or to exert pressure for the fraud. The later speculators fared even better. Charles H. Haskins, who wrote the most detailed study of Yazoo, concluded: "Owing to the delay of Congress in providing for a settlement of the claims, much of this amount went, not to the defrauded claimants,[20] but to those who had purchased from them at a discount."[21] The money was pocketed by the speculators; the Creeks and the Cherokees would soon know the other face of indemnification.

Part Four

Land Speculation
in the Northern States

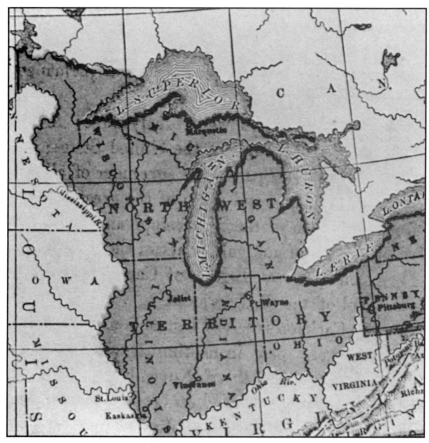

THE NORTHWEST TERRITORY. Western lands ceded by Virginia, Massachusetts, and Connecticut. Courtesy of The New York Public Library, Astor, Lenox and Tilden Foundations.

25

The Northwest Territory

"The best investment is land, because they ain't making any more of it."

Will Rogers

The Virginia assembly on January 2, 1781, ceded to the U.S. Congress its land claim northwest of the Ohio River. Because of political fighting over restrictive clauses in the cession, the actual deed to the Northwest Territory was not conveyed to Congress until March 1, 1784.

Taking over this enormous land mass, some 220,000 square miles of rich soil with its great water system (which eventually formed the five states of Ohio, Indiana, Illinois, Michigan, and Wisconsin),[1] brought Congress a new challenge. All agreed that part of the land should be reserved to satisfy the Continental Line military warrants that had been the main pay of soldiers during the Revolution. But opinions parted thereafter. At bottom, there were two schools of thought. The first believed in giving the rest of the land to other settlers on the most liberal of terms. The second insisted that the land should be sold to raise cash for the floundering new republic.

Thomas Jefferson, who wrote the original 1784 ordinance dealing with the problem, felt initially that the land should be handed out in a general distribution. The British had still not given up their western posts despite the terms of the Paris peace treaty,[2] and it was generally agreed that the quicker the northwest lands were settled the more effective would be the barrier to future British aggression. Virginians were particularly anxious in this matter in order to protect their land in Kentucky. Jefferson's position was supported by a groundswell of opinion that it was the natural right of landless men to settle at no cost this enormous tract and farm it in small parcels.[3]

Alexander Hamilton favored selling the land. At that time there were no general taxes, for Congress did not dare impose taxes nor did it have any way to enforce them even if they were to be enacted. Federal monies came in only from special import fees on luxury items, a general duty on other imports, and contributions from the states. Hamilton insisted that the one great national asset, the western land, should be sold to raise money to pay for the functions of government as well as discharging the national debt.

George Washington was of two minds. In 1784 he made a tour west of the Alleghenies. On his return he wrote: "Such is the rage for speculation in and forestalling of lands on the northwest of the Ohio that scarcely a valuable spot, within a tolerable distance of it, is left without a claimant. Men in these times talk with as much facility of fifty, a hundred, and even five hundred thousand acres, as a gentleman would formerly do of one thousand."[4] Washington favored control over absentee speculation because it would slow settlement, but he sided with Hamilton in the desperate need for revenue. After much debate it was Hamilton who prevailed. The 1784 ordinance was revised in 1785 and then finalized in 1787, establishing a method of land sale and a structure of political authority.

These ordinances provided that after the land was purchased from the Indians and properly surveyed, the government would sell it at public auction in fee simple to the highest bidder. The minimum price was set at one dollar an acre, paid one-third cash with the rest in three months. Certain specified U.S. certificates were also accepted in payment, as well as one-seventh of the total in military warrants. When the population increased, three to five new states might be created, of not less than sixty thousand persons each. A Bill of Rights was provided, with slavery prohibited throughout the Northwest.

On paper these ordinances seemed just and reasonable. The problem is that they had nothing to do with reality. A main reason was the price of one dollar per acre later increased to two dollars in 1796, with one-third cash and the rest due in three months. Also the smallest unit that could be sold was 640 acres. The states were selling their land much cheaper and in smaller lots. New York was charging between twenty cents and a dollar an acre for its western lands, with credit advanced to the purchaser; Massachusetts was selling at fifty cents an acre in what became the state of Maine; while the poorer lands remaining in Kentucky and Tennessee were available for even less.[5] Pennsylvania opened its western lands for sale in 1784 and the average of all auction sales was thirty-four cents an acre.[6] Virginia's system even encouraged squatting, for in 1779 it provided that a soldier's bounty warrant was void on lands actually occupied, with a charge of twenty-five cents an acre to the preemptors.[7]

Indeed, many settlers simply paid no attention to the law, located wherever they pleased, and fought eviction. Most of the western courts were sympathetic; even George Washington lost an eviction case on his frontier land. Congressman Thomas Scott from the western part of Pennsylvania, one of the few legislators familiar with the frontier, stated in 1789 that there were already 7,000 people settled on unsurveyed public land.[8] Amusingly, the government census of 1790 reported the entire population northwest of the Ohio as 4,280.[9] These figures alone show the lack of realism of the rules set up under the ordinances.

Thomas Hutchins (the close friend of both George Morgan and Don Diego de Gardoqui, who had probably acted as midwife for New Madrid), was appointed to supervise the Ohio land survey. He fell ill during the first three years with little more than half the surveying completed. Hostile Indians, who clearly saw their doom in this work, attacked the crews. It was only after the battle of Fallen Timbers and the subsequent Treaty of Greenville in 1795 that the Ohio country was really opened. Bureaucratic delays and a lack of money to establish land offices took more time, and it was not until 1800 before valid deeds were given to settlers. By that time the speculators had bought up at discount the greater part of the war bonuses. The war was over by 1783, but the final ordinance was not adopted until 1787. The Virginia Reserve (for its own troops) was only approved by Congress in 1791 and the U.S. Military Reserve (for general Continental Line warrants) was approved in 1796. "The long delay had induced many of the veterans—soldiers and officers alike—to sell not only their certificates for half pay and arrearages but also their bounty warrants."[10] The soldiers, excepting a restless few, had long since returned home to their families and, without interest in wilderness land far away, they sold their warrants for a nominal sum to men with ready cash. Despite the initial intent of the ordinances, it was the speculators in Philadelphia, New York, and Boston who reaped the harvest. One statistic tells all. "A total of 2,095,220 acres were patented in the U.S. Military district, 70 percent of it by approximately one hundred men."[11] The sales to the general public were even less: before the year 1800, only 50,000 acres had been sold under the rules set up by the ordinances.[12]

For this reason Tom Paine, whose logical but suspicious mind presumed a plot, wrote that Washington and the Federalists deliberately dragged their feet in order to cheat veterans and bona fide settlers of their land. The simpler truth could be found in inertia, confusion, and disorder. The finances of the Confederation were chaotic. Shays's Rebellion had just been put down, leaving much bitter feeling. In 1787 the Federal Convention assembled to try and revise the hodgepodge under the Articles of Confederation. This is the background for the tremendous grants to private companies, the Ohio Company and the Miami Purchase, both of which will be discussed.

However, it was not the entire Northwest Territory that initially had been opened for sale under the ordinances, but rather Ohio, the most westerly area. Here a large amount of land was reserved for other purposes, in each of which speculation was rampant. As mentioned, the U.S. Military District was set aside for Continental Line soldiers while Virginia also had claims to be honored for its own veterans under the original cession. Connecticut demanded the satisfaction of its western land claim, and there were patents to original French settlers in the Illinois country, west of Ohio, which became entangled in speculative schemes. These separate grants call for a brief review.

The earliest problem involved the territory settled by the French in the first part of the eighteenth century. This was along the Kaskaskia River, which flowed southwest into the Mississippi from central Illinois, the area George Rogers Clark had seized during the Revolution. After the Northwest Territory was ceded to the Confederation in the Paris peace treaty, Congress recognized and accepted the legitimacy of the land titles of these French settlers.

When the Ordinance of 1787 was issued, a rumor spread—whether by accident or on purpose—that the Americans would force the French to convert to the Protestant faith. Many French Catholics fled across the Mississippi to Spanish territory, selling their land for a pittance. A market sprang up dealing with these titles. William Henry Harrison, the first secretary of the Northwest Territory (who publicly attacked land speculators), was among those who bought some of these French lands. Governor Arthur St. Clair made no purchases for himself but confirmed large transfers to his son John Murray and his partner and associate, John Edgar, who acquired 49,200 acres as a result. Edgar became the largest landholder amongst those speculating in the French titles. Governor St. Clair was rebuked by Washington and then, in 1802, removed from office by President Jefferson for, among other reasons, these dubious transactions.[13] So much forgery and corruption was involved that almost half the deeds were voided and it took until 1820 for Congress and the land officials to clear up old land titles in the Kaskaskia district.[14]

The Virginia claim sprang from a different background. Holding such enormous tracts of land under its colonial charter, Virginia was far more

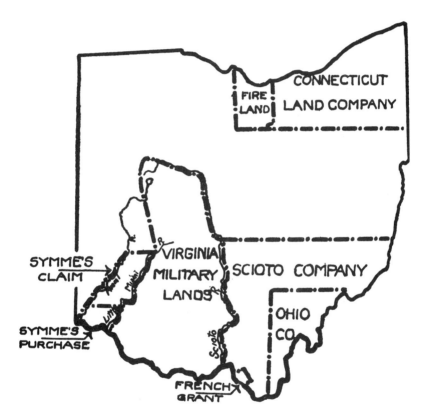

THE OHIO LAND GRANTS. From *The Great American Land Bubble,* by Aaron M. Sakolski, New York, 1932. Reproduced by permission of HarperCollins Publishers.

liberal than Congress in granting bounties to its Revolutionary troops. By October 1779 all its officers had been given ten times as much land as did Congress for the general Continental Line; noncommissioned officers four times, and privates two times. A year later, all military bounties were increased by one third, and in 1782 further increases were granted for three-year enlistments. As a result, when Virginia ceded her land northwest of the Ohio River, she insisted that if the total bounty claims of her Revolutionary soldiers exceeded the land set aside for that purpose due west of the state, then the deficiency was to be met by land in the ceded area. These claims amounted to 3,770,000 acres.[15]

Congress was hesitant to take out such a large block from the proposed sale of land in the Northwest Territory but finally agreed to set up what was called the Virginia Military Reserve. The area, stretching northwest of the Ohio River between the Scioto and Little Miami rivers, was excluded from the ordinances passed by Congress and subject only to Virginia laws.[16] The speculators from that state, who had bought up the greater part of the military warrants at sharp discount, used the same approach here as they did in Kentucky. Interest focused only on the best land, especially the river bottoms; as a result, the Virginia Reserve was filled with widely scattered and remote settlements soon after titles began to be conveyed in 1791.

Two of the three persons chosen by Virginia to distribute state militia bounty land were Thomas and Humphrey Marshall, while claims of the Continental State Line were handled by William Croghan. We have met these men before, their pockets stuffed with Kentucky soil. The head surveyor appointed for the Virginia Reserve was Colonel Richard C. Anderson, a brother-in-law of George Rogers Clark, who retained the post for many years. Anderson chose as deputy surveyors Nathaniel Massie, James Lytle, James Taylor, Duncan McArthur, and Lucas Sullivant. "These men together with Anderson himself, were soon among the largest of the land speculators of the Virginia Military District."[17] *The Virginia Military Lands Patentee Index*[18] indicates that twenty-two men patented over one million acres, a quarter of the entire tract that, in theory, was created for the thousands of Virginia soldiers who had fought to win the Revolution. Colonel Anderson, oddly enough, is only set down for 23,421 acres; however, Allen Latham, his son-in-law, received 30,370 acres. Nathaniel Massie, who had moved north from Kentucky where he speculated with James Wilkinson, patented 124,150 acres. James Taylor is listed for 118,601 acres. Duncan McArthur, a chain man under Massie and then in his own right a speculator, took 90,947 acres. He later became governor of Ohio. Lucas Sullivant patented 49,271 acres, and Lytle (though listed as W. rather than J.) is listed as having received 39,625 acres. Unknown names with patents for land running between 40,000 and 920,000 acres indicate almost surely that the top appointees, like Patrick Henry had done in Kentucky, operated through dummies to protect their political careers.

Though massive, these patents cannot compare with the fantastic breadth of the earlier Kentucky grants. The Virginia Military Reserve was only one-sixth the size of Kentucky. But there was a more basic reason. The Northwest Territory ordinances forbade slavery and, despite the efforts of William Henry Harrison and other powerful southerners, the prohibition stayed. Not being able to apply the plantation system to this southwest corner of Ohio, the Virginia speculators were more interested in a quick profit by selling to settlers rather than holding the land for cultivation. This was equally true in southern Indiana and Illinois. In an important sense the Civil War was fought and won in the Northwest Territory seventy years before it erupted.

Connecticut, like Virginia, was one of the states that had claims to a huge western territory under its original charter. The Connecticut assembly could hardly maintain that southern New York and the bulk of northern Pennsylvania, both heavily settled, belonged to that state. Connecticut still held claim, however, to the western area of Pennsylvania as well as the enormous stretch due west in the Northwest Territory. As part of previous compromises, Connecticut settled all of its claims except that to the land south of Lake Erie. It was a tract extending one hundred twenty miles west of Pennsylvania and, in round terms, lying between the 41st and 42nd degrees parallel north, being about 3.5 million acres in total. The area became known as the Western Reserve of Connecticut in Ohio and was indeed larger than the home state. Consisting of a half-million acres, that part farthest west was reserved as a pool of indemnity for Connecticut citizens who had suffered destruction of their property by fire from British raids during the Revolution. This block was called the Fire Land or the Firelands. The rest of the Western Reserve was thrown on the market by Connecticut in May 1795 at a price not less than a third of a dollar an acre.

Two syndicates appeared and fought to buy the three million acres. One was led by John Livingston of New York City, a major speculator in his home state. The other, made up of influential New Englanders, was headed by Oliver Phelps of Hartford, a very great speculator in New York western lands. The Phelps syndicate included nine shareholders in the Ohio Company, another Ohio speculative group that we will analyze. Rather than drive up the price by competing with one another, Phelps suggested that if the Livingston group dropped out of the bidding, then his syndicate would give it all land in excess of three million acres after final survey.

Livingston accepted and then sold this agreement to General William Hull (the incompetent officer who surrendered Detroit to the British in the War of 1812) for fifty thousand dollars. As an aside, it may be added that the final survey indicated no excess acreage but to avoid trouble Phelps cut Hull in for a small position.[19]

In September 1795 Connecticut sold its Western Reserve minus the Fire Land to the Phelps syndicate for $1.2 million or forty cents an acre, with payment in specie to be made in September 1800 and interest, after a grace period of two years, at six percent. Of the total monies, Oliver Phelps subscribed $168,185 on his own and another $80,000 jointly with Gideon Granger, the two men, as already noted, being speculative partners in the Yazoo frauds.

The purchasers organized themselves into the Connecticut Land Company. Sales went slowly at first because of confusion as to whether Connecticut or the U.S. Congress had jurisdiction. This was settled in 1800 when, for a political surrender by Connecticut of her western territory, Congress acknowledged the state's right to own and sell the soil—a situation which in certain respects repeated the position for these Connecticut speculators that William Blount and his group took in respect to the western lands of North Carolina.

With jurisdiction settled, sales zoomed. A rage to move West threatened to depopulate Connecticut. The Connecticut Land Company sold its lots at such favorable prices that by 1809 the shareholders divided the little land that was left and dissolved the company. The censuses in 1800 and 1810 showed Connecticut towns at no increase in population over twenty years; many had declined.[20] At the height of the frenzy to move to Ohio, the Connecticut legislature was even urged to void the company charter in order to slow the exodus. Indeed, within the short space of ten years 150,000 white inhabitants settled in and around Cleveland in what became the northern part of Ohio.[21]

As noted, a section of the Western Reserve was put aside to indemnify Connecticut residents whose property had been ravaged by fire. Between 1777 and 1781 the British unleashed four major raids on nine Connecticut waterfront towns, burning homes, wharfs, churches, and public property. The last attack was directed at New London where the redcoats were led by the traitor Benedict Arnold who had been born only fourteen miles away.

In a memorial to Hartford in 1787, the nine towns united to petition for relief. There was no action. Another petition was presented in 1790, to which was appended a list of sufferers with their losses classified by the various towns. Finally, in 1792, the Connecticut legislature voted to assign 500,000 acres of the extreme western part of the Western Reserve to the "fire sufferers."

The process of indemnification moved like a slug. In 1796 the claimants or their assigns were granted proportionate shares to the land. Facts about who got what and for what reason are nonexistent. "Records of the company thus created, if extant, are unavailable. Occasional newspaper notices, some old tax deeds, and a single entry in the accounts of the company which succeeded it comprise the only sources upon the activities. . . ."[22] It was not until 1805 that surveys were authorized; they were started in 1806 and concluded two years later. Thus, more than thirty years had gone by since the first British troops set fire to Connecticut homes in 1777 and actual compensation was offered in the Firelands. With what may be unintended irony Helen M. Carpenter, who made the only close study of this grant, concluded: "To trace through the location of the original settlers, their heirs or assignees in the townships and sections allotted in the partition [of the lands] is beyond the province of this work."[23] Indeed, if one out of ten of the original sufferers or their heirs received land, it would be a surprise; probably almost all the claims were sold at discount several times over during these three decades until they reached the final haven of the last speculator.

26

The Ohio Company
and the Scioto Associates

"Throughout the history of the public domain, fraud has been prevalent. It has been for the most part almost transparent fraud."

Benjamin Horace Hibbard, *A History of the Public Land Policies*

Rufus Putnam of Massachusetts was a man who turned to land speculation as a heliotrope veers to the sun. A veteran of the French and Indian War, he wrangled a seat on a committee sent to Florida in 1773 to check Crown lands for officers of provincial regiments who had enlisted against the French. This was the group dominated by General Phineas Lyman's Company of Military Adventurers (Lyman himself being in England at this time pushing for the land grant), whereby officers in the war were to receive nineteen townships of about 23,000 acres each in West Florida, A surveyor by profession, Putnam was made deputy-surveyor of Florida by the British governor in charge of the land distribution. Putnam accompanied the exploratory expedition up the Mississippi River to the Yazoo country.

The Revolution broke out soon after the expedition started, and Putnam, taking an active part, rose to the rank of brigadier general. As chairman of the officers' organization, he framed the Newburgh Petition—which took its name from the winter quarters of the Revolutionary army in 1783 before the disbandment—asking Congress to allot army bounty lands in a colony north of the Ohio River. The officers had a special interest in such a project because military warrants of the Continental Line, good for land in the public domain, were on the order of eleven hundred acres to a major general, five hundred to a colonel, while only one hundred were awarded to a private. Nearly all these men were members of the Cincinnati Society, considered by some a military organization whose aim was to subvert the new republic.

George Washington, Putnam's good friend, accepted the petition. Congress at this date, however, had not yet formally approved the Virginia cession of the land that became known as the Northwest Territory. When it did in 1784, General Putnam again appealed to his former commander-in-chief, claiming that many officer veterans were unemployed. Toward the end of 1785 Putnam found a vigorous colleague in Samuel Holden Parsons of Connecticut, also a brigadier general in the Revolution, who had descended the Ohio and fallen in love with the country. Parsons was at that time one of the three U.S. commissioners (George Rogers Clark and Colonel Richard Butler being the other two) who had concluded a treaty with the Shawnees whereby the Indians renounced all claims to any land east of the main branch of the Great Miami River. This opened to settlement a good part of what is now the state of Ohio.

Parsons may have sent advance word of the coming treaty by private courier, for six days before the actual signing Rufus Putnam and a colleague, Benjamin Tupper (himself a general during the Revolution, who had surveyed the Ohio and knew its rich potential), published in the newspapers of Massachusetts an invitation to form the Ohio Company of Associates[1] in order to purchase and colonize a large land tract between the Ohio River and Lake Erie. Representatives from eight counties of Massachusetts met in Boston in early 1786. Rufus Putnam was elected chairman of the meeting and Major Winthrop Sargent, of high social standing, was chosen secretary. An early enthusiast to join was the versatile Manasseh Cutler, former botanist, lawyer, and merchant, more recently a chaplain in the Revolutionary army and then a practicing doctor as well as Congregational pastor.

Looking ahead, it may be noted that this meeting changed the lives of all concerned. Sargent became acting governor of the Northwest Territory under General St. Clair and then first governor of the Mississippi Territory. Putnam was appointed a federal court judge and then surveyor-general of the United States. Parsons became first judge of the Northwest Territory but drowned in 1788 when his canoe overturned in the rapids of the Big Beaver River. Cutler refused an appointment in the Territory but later served two terms (1801-1805) as a congressman from Massachusetts.

It was decided at the Boston meeting to issue one thousand Ohio Company shares to subscribers, each share valued at one thousand dollars in continental certificates, which then had a real value of one hundred and twenty-five dollars in specie. A year was allowed for subscription.[2] At the end of that time the subscribers chose Parsons, Putnam, and Cutler as directors to ask Congress for a purchase of Ohio land.

It is of great interest to watch the progress of this petition from start to finish. The reason is twofold. First, the Ohio Company, though speculative by nature, was backed by people with patriotic records who had given years of their lives, at great personal sacrifice in many cases, to fight for American independence. Second, the only way the company could succeed was by acquiescing to fraud. The Ohio Company is thus a prototype of a certain type of American enterprise when dependent on political contacts.

On May 9, 1787, the same day on which the act setting up a government for the newly created Northwest Territory was ordered to a third reading, General Parsons, as agent for the Ohio Company, presented his petition to Congress. It was immediately referred to a committee consisting of Edward Carrington, Rufus King, Nathan Dane, James Madison, and Egbert Benson. Though Madison was on the committee, the group was dominated by those of Federalist politics. In fact, Rufus King was later Federalist candidate for vice president in 1804 and 1808 and for president in 1816. The top echelon of the Ohio Company, coming from Massachusetts and Connecticut, was likewise composed of powerful Federalist figures.

There was no quorum of Congress between May 11 and July 3 of 1787. On July 5, Manasseh Cutler arrived to continue the negotiations. On July 10, Carrington, representing the committee, read to Congress a report supporting the Ohio Company's petition. The grant, apart from land set aside for education and religious purposes, was to be paid for in U.S. debt certificates or specie. For bad land, expenses of surveying, and incidentals, an allowance up to one-third of a dollar an acre was permitted. The price, therefore, was about sixty-seven cents for each acre, but since certificates of indebtedness were then worth some twelve cents on the dollar, the real price was only eight to nine cents an acre. Military bounty rights could be offered, up to one seventh of the whole amount.[3]

At this point opposition rose. The whole point of selling western land was to pay off the federal debt caused by the War of Independence. How was the country to benefit by such a cheap deal? Congressmen rose and demanded a higher price from the Ohio Company, payable three months after closing rather than over an extended period. Cutler refused, and the prospects dimmed.

Then Manasseh Cutler was approached by Colonel William Duer, one of the three members of the Board of the Treasury and its operating secretary.[4] Duer, a compulsive speculator, suggested that the Federalists could drum up enough votes to approve the Ohio Company petition if it were enlarged to include another three and a half million acres, which would be assigned, after approval, to the "Scioto project," a new group hastily organized, but this aspect of the deal must be kept "in profound secret" for it involved a "a number of the principal characters of the City."[5] As added bait Duer also agreed to advance $100,000 to Cutler toward the first payment of $500,000 required under the terms of the Ohio Company land grant.[6]

It is not known whether Reverend Manasseh Cutler wrestled with his New England conscience over this unexpected turn of events. As Walter Havighurst writes, "Over an oyster dinner in Brooklyn, with a procession of fine wines, Cutler agreed to Duer's plan."[7] Then the federal treasury official went out and won over reluctant congressmen: how we may suspect, but we have no specific report. We do know, however, that General St. Clair, at first reluctant, changed ground and supported the petition after getting shares in the company plus the offer of the salaried post as governor in the Northwest Territory.[8] General Knox, secretary of war, also became one of the organizers of the Ohio Company.[9]

On July 13, 1787, the compromise was passed forbidding slavery in the Northwest Territory but forcing the return of fugitive slaves to those states where the practice was accepted.[10] The ordinance establishing the Territory was then approved. Immediately thereafter, the terms of a sale between the United States on one hand and Manasseh Cutler and Winthrop Sargent as agents of the Ohio Company on the other were likewise approved in their enlarged form but substantially on the basis of the report of Carrington.

The act giving some 1.5 million rich acres to a private group of New Englanders for the equivalent of less than nine cents an acre in specie was hustled through Congress in little more than two months, the greater part of which time Congress was not in session. Rolled into this bill was a grant for some 3.5 million acres, the fraudulent Scioto Associates assignment. Honorable men assented to this corruption in order to get what they wanted. As Manasseh Cutler wrote on July 27, 1787:

At half past three I was informed Congress had passed an ordinance on the terms stated in our letter without the least variation and that the Board of Treasury was directed to close the contract. . . . By this ordinance, we obtained the grant of near five million acres of land, amounting to three million and a half of dollars, one million and a half of acres for the Ohio Company and the remainder for a private speculation, in which many of the most prominent characters in America are concerned; without connecting this speculation, similar terms and advantages could not have been obtained for the Ohio Company.[11]

The Scioto Associates, the alter ego of the Ohio Company, may actually be viewed as a double fraud. It was dubious, if not illicit, in origin, being in the nature of a rider to the Ohio Company bill, which only passed because members of Congress and the executive branch took a pecuniary interest. And it was not even a grant, but rather an option to pick up these millions of acres when the money—funneled through the Ohio Company—would be paid to Congress.[12] Thus, the Duer syndicate members received an option, without legal title, and would only pay for the land after selling it, a practice then called "dodging." As we know now from the reconstruction of events, Duer and his partners intended to sell the land in Europe even before the specified installment payments came due.

The story of Scioto, depending on one's view of history, is among the most pathetic or comic in all of real estate. Now that Duer had made good his swindle, where and how would he market the land? He turned to the Reverend Cutler, who came up with an ideal person to send to France in order to sell the enormous acreage. This was Joel Barlow of Connecticut, agent for the Ohio Company in that state and a young man of remarkable abilities. In 1789, Barlow arrived in Paris with a sheaf of blank contracts for the sale of western land that he did not own, and a personal contract for 50,000 acres if he could do so.

Joel Barlow—minister, poet, political writer, financier, and diplomat— was among the more curious figures spawned by the American Revolution. A graduate of Yale, he became a chaplain during the Revolution, which was his initial contact with Manasseh Cutler, also from Yale. Like that gentleman, he was rapt with the possibilities of western land, which he saw as the great expanding frontier of American democracy: again like Cutler, and indeed Jefferson, he somehow blotted out the obtrusive fact that the people living on the land had to be wiped out before the benefits of democracy could be applied. That the pursuit of such a high ideal would be immensely profitable for him as well was not a tether.

After dashing off *The Vision of Columbus,* a 1787 epic poem of democratic delirium, Barlow took up the more rewarding job of land huckster in 1788 and went to Paris for Duer. There he first did poorly. Then Barlow met an Englishman, William Playfair (oddly named for his role),[13] who knew better how to deal with the monied elite. The two formed a company, the Compagnie du Scioto. They brought in as shareholders a delegate of the French National Assembly, the comptroller of the king's pay office, and several prominent merchants. Eight thousand shares were floated, valued at one thousand francs each. Maps and pamphlets were issued. Scioto was described as a land flowing with milk and honey—in the French version, it flowed with vineyards and ore mines. The soil was fertile, the climate

SALE OF THE SCIOTO DESERTS BY THE ANGLO-AMERICANS. Engraving published in Paris (1790). Courtesy of the American Antiquarian Society, Worcester, Massachusetts.

AN AMERICAN LOG-HOUSE, 1796. Engraving after a drawing by Victor Collot. Illustration from *Voyage dans L'Amérique Septentrionale*, by Collot. Rare Books and Manuscripts Division, The New York Public Library, Astor, Lenox and Tilden Foundations.

benign; the river banks were already settled, the region "the garden of the universe, the center of wealth, a place destined to be the heart of a great Empire."[14] Framed in Barlow's office was a certificate from Thomas Jefferson, then American minister to France, testifying to Barlow's character and to Duer's wealth.[15]

The propaganda was cunning; more important, the time was ripe. This was 1789, the Bastille had been stormed and King Louis had been brought back to Paris from Versailles and clapped in jail. The French nobles and the new rich were cringing in their castles and palaces. Where could they put their capital beyond the reach of the revolution? What investment beyond France would stand up in the storm?

Before the end of 1789, some one hundred thousand acres had been sold in the nonexistent Paradise that the sellers did not own. Over a series of months, in 1790, several hundred French families assembled and embarked on five vessels bound for the New World.

One can imagine what tremors this stirred in the breasts of the Scioto Associates who, having made no payments to Congress, did not own an inch of land on which to settle the voyagers. After an emergency meeting called by Duer, the directors of the Ohio Company agreed by financial juggling to provide room on their land for the exotic strangers. General Rufus Putnam as agent for the Scioto Associates sent fifty farmers from Massachusetts to a site a short distance from the mouth of the Great Kanawha. Christened Gallipolis or "City of the Gauls," the site was cleared of trees from which log cabins were erected. Here, four thousand miles from France, was the end of the journey for the bewildered immigrants.

Unlike the pamphlets issued by Barlow and Playfair, the climate was not benign and the Ohio River froze solid to the Kentucky shore that first winter. The following summer malaria struck. Between cold and disease one-third of the French settlers died. Some then drifted back to France or to the eastern cities, some to their countrymen at New Orleans; the poorer settlers with no other resources stayed on. In 1795 a repentant Congress made these Frenchmen a grant of twenty-four thousand acres on the Ohio River forty miles west of Gallipolis. It was called the French Grant, and a few relocated there. A French remnant remained while American settlers took the place of those who had gone. Not more than sixteen French families were left by 1800. In just a few years Gallipolis was no different from any other Ohio river town.

Joel Barlow remained in France. Making enough money from the Scioto fraud to live like a gentleman, with Tom Paine he became a French citizen and tried to stand for election to represent Savoy during the French Revolution. Shrewdly he invested in French bonds, which rose greatly in value with the victories of Napoleon. Barlow continued to write with undiminished enthusiasm of liberty, equality, and fraternity. Coming back to the United States after seventeen years, he was then appointed American minister to France and sent by President Madison to meet Napoleon in Russia. There Joel Barlow became another victim of "General Winter," dying of pneumonia during the disastrous retreat of the French army.[16] His epic poem, the stilted *Columbiad,* an enlarged version of the earlier *Vision of Columbus,* appeared in 1807; immense both in size and boredom, it is still inflicted on some college students of American literature.

As to William Duer, he, with his partner Alexander Macomb, over-extended his land and bond speculations and went bankrupt. Duer ended his life in a New York debtors' prison.[17]

27

John Cleves Symmes and
the Miami Purchase

"Were I to characterize the United States, it would be by the appellation of the land of speculations."

William Priest, 1796

John Cleves Symmes was of distinguished early colonial stock on both sides of his family. A surveyor as a young man, he became an officer during the Revolution, a judge of the Supreme Court of New Jersey, and then a member of Congress from that state. Noting the technique used to create the Ohio Company, Symmes decided to float a similar syndicate. In November 1787, only four months after that company's grant, he put together a group whose shareholders were Jerseyites. These included John Witherspoon, who had signed the Declaration of Independence and was then president of Princeton College; Elias Boudinot, a New Jersey congressman who had at one time been president of the Continental Congress; and Jonathan Dayton,[1] also a congressman and later to become speaker of the U.S. House of Representatives.

This influential group asked Congress for two million acres in the newly created Northwest Territory between the Great and Little Miami rivers, in the southwest corner of what is now the state of Ohio. Following the precedent of the Ohio Company, Congress approved the Miami Purchase on the same financial basis, that is to say, about sixty-seven cents for each

JOHN CLEVES SYMMES. Reproduced by permission from The Collections of The Cincinnati Historical Society.

acre but whose real cost was between eight and nine cents because U.S. debt certificates, allowed as payment, could be acquired at such a deep discount. The site of the grant was reduced to one million acres, however, which included land fronting twenty miles on the Ohio River. The contract was signed on October 15, 1788, and a down payment of $82,198, one seventh in military warrants and the rest in debt certificates, was given.[2] According to Forrest McDonald, "Dayton's task in the venture was to buy and manipulate securities for the syndicate. In this he was eminently successful; he managed to acquire about $190,000 in public securities with an investment of probably no more than $75,000 cash, and military warrants of an equal face value."[3]

A publicity campaign was set afoot describing the area in gilded words. Cheap prices for land were touted for early subscribers. Symmes and Boudinot (the latter's great political influence being mainly responsible for the approval of the grant) put aside over forty thousand acres for themselves directly on the Ohio River, including the location of present-day Cincinnati,[4] a natural site because of the confluence of so many nearby rivers. This was the most valuable acreage and Symmes and Boudinot sold off part of this personal holding to other speculators even before signing the purchase contract.[5]

In August 1788, also before the contract was signed, Symmes—who had already been appointed a judge for the new territory—started west with sixty settlers. Arthur St. Clair, the newly named governor for the territory, came down the following year and made the rude outpost of Losantiville his capital, which he renamed Cincinnati after the society of Revolutionary officers. In a few years Cincinnati became the American key to western frontier advance.

The Miami Purchase should have been a fabulous success since the land grant was the center of the political and economic growth of the Northwest Territory. Aggressive promotion did indeed bring in many settlers from New Jersey as well as closer regions. In fact, Symmes extended his holdings, investing a total of about $50,000 to own a third of a million acres. In 1795 he remarried, his new wife being Susanna Livingston of New York City, an alliance which tied him to one of America's grandest families.

But Symmes's efforts ultimately failed. The reason was greed. Not only did the hungry judge extend himself too far in borrowing to buy more land—a common disease of the time—but more seriously, he indulged a bad habit of selling land not belonging to him.[6] Symmes became known in the Miami Valley as "the greatest landjobber on the face of the earth"[7]— the expression then used to describe the least attractive type of speculator

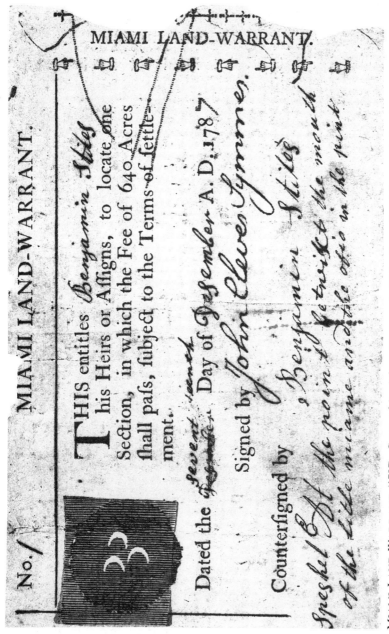

—and was involved for years in litigation over claims, which frittered away his fortunes. Falling behind in payments to Congress, he went through the shame of being declared a squatter himself—the biggest squatter of them all—on land he considered his own. In 1802 he was arrested on several counts, the most venal being that as a judge he had decided land disputes to his own personal advantage.

Unable to give clear title to his settlers, Symmes became the most hated man on the western frontier. In 1811 a band set fire to his house, burning all his records. Thereafter land payments to him stopped altogether. In what a modern doctor might call a psychosomatic syndrome, Symmes sickened, got worse and—a minor shoot from the great speculative sequoias such as James Wilson and Robert Morris—died in early 1814, a poor, lonely, and bitter man. His sole consolation was that his daughter in early and better years had married William Henry Harrison, who trod the eighteenth-century tradition of loving more easily an heiress; and Symmes lived long enough to see his son-in-law acclaimed after the War of 1812 as "the Washington of the West." William Henry Harrison became the ninth president and Symmes's great-grandson, Benjamin Harrison, was elected the twenty-third president of the United States.

28

Tecumseh: The View from the Other Side

*"The most ultimately righteous of all wars is a war with savages . . . it is
a silly morality which would forbid a course of conquest that has turned
whole continents into seats of mighty and flourishing nations . . . [that]
whether the whites won the land by treaty, by armed conquest, or, as was
actually the case by a mixture of both, mattered comparatively little so long
as the land was won."*

Theodore Roosevelt, *Winning of the West*, IV, 52-56

To the victor belongs the spoils, and the cheerleader of victory is the national historian. Livy, despite the brilliance of his pen portrait, did not
root for Hannibal. Heinrich von Treitschke was as lean in praise of Napoleon as Jules Michelet was of Bismarck. Edward Gibbon spent decades
penning the decline of classic Rome, but as an English member of Parliament during the American Revolution he uttered not a croak against the
pig-headed George III. It is a rare event indeed when a few great recent
historians—such Americans as Charles M. Andrews, Thomas P. Abernethy,
Merrill Jensen, and Francis Jennings—publish a body of work based on
balanced facts rather than high-class ethnic and folk reflexes. The more
popular historian, to give an excellent example from rather recent times,
is Claude G. Bowers, the Parson Weems of Jefferson, who plastered a
Byzantine icon over the bones of that shrewd and canting sage of Monti-

cello. When to the tale of rivalry is added the mischief of race, then the white man's conceit distorts history even more.

The tragedy of the North American Indian can best be sized by a striking phrase from Francis Jennings: "Heedless of theories, Americans began their building of empire with an inheritance of ethnocentric semantics that made logic valid to themselves out of the strange proposition that invasion, conquest and dispossession of other peoples support the principle that all men are created equal."[1] Even in better history books Indians are still defined as "savages" and their way of life as "primitive." In contrast the white man, and most of all when from British stock, is "civilized." Among such "civilized" men Governor William Henry Harrison of the Indiana Territory admitted "a great many of the Inhabitants of the Fronteers [sic] consider the murdering of the Indians in the highest degree meritorious"; while men like Tom Quick of Pennsylvania and John Sevier of Tennessee would have made excellent Nazi SS commanders.

Perverse logic is part of most histories. The Indian defense against the American colonists who took their land is known as Pontiac's Rebellion or Pontiac's Conspiracy, which makes even less sense than calling the American Revolution Washington's Rebellion or Washington's Conspiracy. Simon Girty is loathed as a "renegade" because he was a Loyalist during the Revolution—as were many other colonials—and as effectively ambushed Americans as they did Indians. Probably the best-known American hero of the French and Indian War was Robert Rogers, head of the frontier rangers and later commander at Mackinac in the Northwest Territory. No lover of Indians, he sided with the British in the Revolution and was bumped from U.S. history. And so it has been with Indian society. Demonized and despised, sometimes both together, the North American Indian only recently has come to be viewed as human; a few scholars see them as living in a different, as distinct from inferior, culture.

The greatest Indian in North America was Tecumseh. To quote William Henry Harrison again, whose victory at Tippecanoe many years later won him the presidency: "If it were not for the vicinity of the United States, he would perhaps be the founder of an Empire that would rival in glory that of Mexico or Peru."[2] Let us try to put ourselves in the mind of this great Indian leader who watched with horror the ravage of his people for their land.

Tecumseh was born in 1768 in an Indian village near present-day Dayton, Ohio. His rather unusual ancestry gives a hint as to how he became one of the few American Indians to reach beyond tribal limits to a pan-Indian philosophy. His father was a Shawnee war chief in Florida, his mother a Creek from Alabama. Thus, Tecumseh's background represented two

INDIAN HOLDINGS EAST OF THE MISSISSIPPI, 1800. From *Disinherited: The Lost Birthright of the American Indian,* by Dale Van Every, New York, 1966. Reproduced by permission of William Morrow and Company, Inc./Publishers.

of the most powerful Indian tribes east of the Mississippi River. The Shawnee were Indians of the Appalachian Mountains. Probably originating in the Ohio Valley, by the seventeenth century they had spread to the Cumberland in Tennessee and Kentucky, from where groups migrated to South Carolina and were called Savannah. Then, moving in separate bands, they migrated west to settle among the Creeks in Georgia and Alabama, while others went north into the Delaware country of western Pennsylvania.

The Shawnee, because of their large numbers and the location of their hunting grounds, were hated by frontiersmen above all the other tribes. They were the first tribe to receive the brunt of westward settlement, and they fought back fiercely. In the French and Indian War, the Shawnee sided with the French. During the Pontiac War, they took the field against the English. After Pontiac's defeat, they still fought on against the waves of settlers, especially in the hills of Kentucky and Tennessee. In 1774, when Tecumseh was six years old, Lord Dunmore, the British governor of Virginia, concocted his private war to take Indian land for himself. The Shawnee leader Cornstalk, after his defeat at Point Pleasant, was forced to cede the Indian claim to Kentucky and retreat north across the Ohio River. Tecumseh's father and oldest brother campaigned with Cornstalk.

Lord Dunmore agreed to the Shawnee rights north of the Ohio as part of the treaty following the battle at Point Pleasant. Despite this treaty white settlers continued to enter Indian territory. A band of frontiersmen met Tecumseh's father in the woods and shot him.[3] Shortly after Cornstalk visited an American fort in friendship under the terms of the Dunmore Treaty, a soldier killed him in cold blood. Tecumseh's memories had taught him the value of the white man's word and pact on the American frontier. Tecumseh later said that he resolved to be a warrior, "a fire spreading over the hill and valley, consuming the race of dark souls."[4]

The Shawnee sided with the British during the American Revolution, and, as a youth, Tecumseh was witness to the frontier war that raged through Kentucky and the Ohio Valley. In 1780, when Tecumseh was twelve, George Rogers Clark burned his birthplace. Two years later, now a very young Indian fighter, he joined a British and Indian force that defeated a Kentucky army on the Licking River. He must have exulted that the Americans could be turned back.

After the defeat of the English, the Shawnee gave up all hope for Kentucky and moved north of the Ohio; in fact, a large group migrated west of the Mississippi River, settling in what is now Missouri. The teenage Tecumseh refused to leave; instead, he joined a band attacking Ohio river traffic in hopes of slowing down the invasion of the dwindling Indian homeland. In these raids another of his brothers was killed.[5]

TECUMSEH. Courtesy of the Field Museum of Natural History (Neg #A93851.1), Chicago, Illinois.

As he grew into his late teens, Tecumseh became a leader of his own band of warriors, all of whom vowed to fight without rest against the torrent of white settlers. In 1790 he was in the thick of the battle with the troops of General Josiah Harmar, forcing American withdrawal from the Ohio country. The next year he led a raiding party in the great Indian victory over General Arthur St. Clair, governor of the Northwest Territory, when six hundred American soldiers were killed in one of the worst defeats ever inflicted on an official U.S. army. Then, in 1792, Tecumseh responded to an appeal from an older brother fighting in Tennessee and marched south with a band of warriors, joining his Shawnee with Cherokee and Creek to attack Tennessee settlements. Upon his brother's death in battle, Tecumseh was chosen as head of all the Shawnee warriors in the area. During the campaign he bivouacked from Tennessee to Florida making friends with many tribal leaders. These friendships would be a big factor in later events. But in 1793 he hurried north to join the fight against the army of Major General Anthony Wayne, who had come to the Northwest Territory to avenge the defeat of Arthur St. Clair.

The success of these Indian counterattacks can be shown by the fact that from 1790 to 1796 almost five-sixths of the general expenses of the federal government were devoted to the wars in the West. The Indians were so dreaded that in 1794 subscriptions were made to a common fund at Cincinnati, the administrative center of the Northwest, which offered from $95 to $136 for Indian scalps.[6] Eventually the uneven weight of money and numbers was too great and the American army at Fallen Timbers, both well-trained and triple the size of its foe, broke Indian power north of the Ohio River. When during the next spring General Wayne invited the chiefs of twelve different Northwest tribes to meet with him and forced them to cede to the United States an enormous tract of land at the Treaty of Greenville, Tecumseh—who had fought with courage at Fallen Timbers— refused to attend. Withdrawing into unsettled Indiana, he vowed resistance. He attracted Indian warriors who opposed their chiefs for giving up. Gradually Tecumseh was recognized as the leader of the intransigents.

Liquor, with small pox, were more formidable in the white man's campaign to destroy the Indians than the Kentucky rifle. The defeated chiefs, with their braves, took the monies General Wayne paid them for their land and drank to forget. Within a few years the abuse of liquor turned most of the proud tribesmen into abject alcoholics.[7] The Miami tribe, the most powerful contingent in the Indian forces and the tribe that had broken Arthur St. Clair's army, was almost extinct in less than two decades. The Piankashaw and Wea were "the most depraved wretches on earth" and the Chippewa were "frightful drunkards."[8] The Shawnee also began to fall under the influence of the whiskey traders. Lauleswasika, the last brother of Tecumseh, was one of the most notorious drunks when in 1805, probably influenced by the shaker preachers who then jerked and moaned and danced, he fell into a deep trance and met the Master of Life, the supreme Indian god, who told him to abstain from liquor and seek a new path. Changing his name to Tenskwatawa or "the open door" (a name probably taken from the saying of Jesus, "I am the door"), he preached abstinence. Tecumseh's influence made him broaden his doctrine to a rejection of all the ways of the white man.

An Indian revival took place. Tenskwatawa, now revered as the Prophet, urged the Indians to return to the purity of their former life. The new prophecy, spoken through the mouth of Tenskwatawa by Tecumseh,[9] was that all Indians were one people, that their tribal divisions false and ruinous, and that they must band together to repel the white man. This startling new idea[10] was what raised Tecumseh over other leaders of Indian revolts and made him, to quote Harrison again, "one of those uncommon geniuses, which spring up occasionally to produce revolutions and overturn the established order of things":[11] the established order being of course the murder or excretion of all Indians.

In May 1808, Tecumseh and the Prophet set out on a long journey in a desperate attempt to unite the tribes. They had mixed success, for many of the Indians were already too sunk in sloth, resigned to fate, or would not unite with ancient enemies. In what is now Wisconsin, most of the Winnebago and Menominee backed them, while the more important Sauk and Fox held aloof. In Indiana and Illinois, the Kickapoo, the Ottawa, the Wyandot, and the Potawatomi pledged support, while the remnants of the Miami and Mississinewa refused. In the South, the Cherokee and Creek, hating each other, would not work together, while the Seminoles in Florida and the Osage across the river in Missouri showed sympathy. At the end of 1808, Tecumseh, with a small band of warriors, swung north to New York and tried without success to rouse the Iroquois.[12] Despite many setbacks, the Shawnee war chief and his brother had seeded the only pan-Indian confederation in the history of the native tribes belting the Great Lakes to the Gulf of Mexico.

To understand Tecumseh's raging hate of white men it is necessary not only to know his personal experience but also briefly to review American land policy in the Northwest Territory after the Indian defeat at Fallen Timbers and the subsequent treaty signed at Greenville. Thomas Jefferson wrote in 1786 that not a foot of land would ever be taken from the Indians without their consent. History records what Thomas Jefferson did as president of the United States after 1801. His willing tool was young William

Henry Harrison. The two Virginia aristocrats and slave owners, both sons of land speculators, did their job well; when Harrison slacked, Jefferson egged him on.[13]

At Greenville most of Ohio plus a strip of southeastern Indiana was ceded to the Americans. The annuities were $2,500, with up to $1,500 a year extra "to civilize the Indians."[14] Since the treaty line around Vincennes was imprecise, Harrison's first step was to interpret the cession to the white man's great advantage. In 1803 he then forced on the Kaskaskia an agreement by which the Americans received a big chunk of Illinois for an annuity of $400, a house for the chief, a log church, and fifteen fenced acres. In 1804, Harrison secured two cessions: the first was for most of southern Indiana, while the second ate into Missouri. The first cession, with the Delaware and Piankashaw, was for annuities of $300 plus some trade goods; the second, with the Osage, Sac, and Fox tribes, included annuities of about $1,000. In 1805 there were more cessions through pressure, mainly from the debauched remnants of the Piankashaw. Harrison, who got six million acres, was unusually generous that year, giving $4,000 worth of merchandise plus annuities of $1,600 for ten years. The 1805 treaties swallowed the last Indian lands in Ohio plus a part of Wisconsin. After only five years as governor of the Indiana Territory, Harrison had squeezed out of the Indians the rest of Ohio, southern Indiana, some of Illinois, and southern Wisconsin.

For a time the threats of Tecumseh and his brother the Prophet stopped more forced cessions, but Jefferson was urging that additional lands should be opened and, in the face of strong Indian opposition, Harrison pushed through the Treaty of Fort Wayne in 1809, which ceded three million more acres of northern Indiana as well as another piece of Illinois. In sum, between 1795 and 1809 debauched Indian chiefs of the Northwest were rounded up by government officials and plied with bribes and whiskey until they had signed away their rights to forty-eight million acres of land.

One need not wonder what Tecumseh thought of this farce. But the Fort Wayne treaty, contrived when he had been in upper New York, was the final catalyst. Cowed chiefs gave away much land not owned by their own tribes. They also included Shawnee hunting grounds without the consent of Tecumseh. Thunderstruck, he sent word that the sale was illegal. Angry tribesmen flocked to his side and by the spring of 1810 a thousand warriors vowed to repel any attempt on the part of white settlers to enter the newly ceded land. Governor Harrison, disturbed on hearing this news, asked Tecumseh and the Prophet to see him at his headquarters in Vincennes.

The council took place in August 1810, and an account still exists. The Shawnee chief first reminded Harrison of the many wrongs committed

INDIAN LAND TREATIES, 1802–1809. The map shows present state lines. From *Old Tippecanoe,* by Francis Cleaves, Charles Scribner's Sons, New York, 1939. Reproduced by permission of Macmillan Publishing Company.

against the Indians in the Ohio Valley. Then he stated, "No tribe has a right to sell, even to each other, much less to strangers, who demand all, and will take no less. . . . Sell a country! Why not sell the air, the clouds and the great sea, as well as the earth?" Then Tecumseh made a shrewd thrust. He spoke of the United States: "The states have set the example of forming a union among all the fires [states]—why should they censure the Indians for following it?"[15]

Governor Harrison's reply stated that Tecumseh, as a Shawnee, had no right to dispute the sale of land in Indiana because the Shawnee had come from farther south. Tecumseh refused to budge, stating that the cession was void. Harrison was equally insistent that it was valid. Tecumseh walked out of the meeting. Six weeks later, the governor, addressing the Indiana legislature, stated: "Is one of the fairest portions of the globe to remain in a state of nature, the haunt of a few wretched savages, when it seems destined, by the Creator, to give support to a large population, and to be the seat of civilization, of science, and true religion?"[16]

Tecumseh and the Prophet, seeing that a clash was inevitable, made a rapid tour through the remaining Northwest Territory still held by Indians and pleaded for a united stand. In late 1810, Tecumseh crossed the border and asked aid of the Canadian Indians.[17] The Prophet went back to his home at the point where Tippecanoe Creek flows into the Wabash. Soon thereafter, Tecumseh set off for a second tour to gain support in the South.

Governor Harrison did not wait for Tecumseh to return. He decided to strike. Marching at the head of almost a thousand regulars, he moved to the center of Indian strength on the Tippecanoe. There he camped on the night of November 6, 1811.

Tenskwatawa, the Prophet, was unsure what to do without his brother's guidance. Urged to attack, he finally agreed. In the early hours of the following day, a force somewhat less than half the size of the American army swooped down on Harrison's camp but was beaten off. Then Harrison moved into the Indian village and burned the buildings and the stored harvest of five thousand bushels of corn, which struck an even more severe blow. Though the final casualty figures were 61 Americans dead and 127 wounded, while the Indian losses were estimated between 25 and 40 killed, the governor wrote the secretary of war that "the Indians have never sustained so severe a defeat since their acquaintance with the white people."[18] This myth caught on and Harrison became the hero of the West.

When Tecumseh returned several months later, in his anger he grasped his brother by the hair, threatened to kill him, and drove him from Shawnee soil. The disowned Prophet moved across the Mississippi River, where he lived in obscurity for the rest of his life.[19] Tecumseh redoubled his efforts to forge an iron Indian chain to bar the flood of American settlers. The "War Hawks" under Henry Clay of Tennessee, with John Sevier breathing fire by his side, clamored for what the twentieth century has called "a final solution," falsely believing that Tecumseh was a British agent. The party in Congress that was urging immediate conquest of Canada gained strength, and the end result was the War of 1812.

Though not of his doing, this war was Tecumseh's last golden hope. American envoys sent to Fort Wayne were rebuffed. Twice Tecumseh broke peace pipes. Addressing the war chiefs, an American translator took down his words:

> Here is a chance, yes, a chance such as will never occur again—for us Indians of North America to form ourselves into one great combination and cast our lot with the British in this war. And should they conquer and again get the mastery of all North America, our rights to at least a portion of the land of our Fathers would be respected by the King. If they should not win and the whole country should pass into the hands of the Long Knives—we see this plainly—it will not be many years before our last place of abode and our last hunting ground will be taken from us. . . .[20]

The Americans did win and this indeed was the final solution. But history records that Tecumseh fought with more tenacity and greater courage than his British ally; indeed, he was the chief of a confederated force of Shawnee, Delaware, Kickapoo, and Potawatomi, amounting to three thousand warriors, while associated chieftains like Black Hawk, the Sauk, Fox, Winnebago, Chippewa, and Sioux tribes. This is not the place to recount the details of the War of 1812, which at first was headed by incompetent generals on both sides but finally produced superior American leadership. On October 5, 1813, at the Thames River in southwestern Ontario a U.S. army under General Harrison[21] caught up with a British force half its size, which was partly led by Tecumseh. The confederated Indians were stationed on the flanks, the white troops between them. Harrison struck at the center with his cavalry and the English soldiers gave way, surrendering in a body. Tecumseh, who commanded the right flank, drove back the Americans until support infantry came up. The Indian leader was hit several times, with blood pouring from his mouth. Darkness came and the battle subsided; the Shawnee claimed later to have buried their chief secretly that night.

The battle of the Thames was the end of serious Indian resistance to American advance in the Northwest. As Walter Havighurst concludes, "What Indians were left east of the Mississippi were enclosed on reservations.

WILLIAM HENRY HARRISON. *Obv.* Bust of the President. *Rev.* Within a pearled ring, a laurel wreath. Inaugurated President of the United States, March 4, 1841. Died April 4, 1841. Engraving by George T. Morgan.

GOVERNOR ISAAC SHELBY. *Obv.* Bust of Governor Shelby in a General's Uniform, facing the right. *Rev.* Battle of the Thames. October 5, 1813. The battle of the Thames; in the background, a forest; in the foreground, the mounted riflemen are charging the enemy. Exergue: Resolution of Congress, April 4, 1818. Engraving by Moritz Furst.

Even these were to be taken from them when the tribes were herded forever out of their traditional country."[22]

Looking back, it is hard to understand why President Thomas Jefferson, the man who so graced the ideals of the American Revolution and the hopes of ordinary men everywhere, should not have set aside a terrain for the original holders of the land as Indiana, an Indian state. There was precedent for such an action. In 1778 the Delaware signed a treaty of friendship with the American revolutionaries. It included a suggestion that an Indian fourteenth state be created in the Northwest. This idea was buried. As late as 1804, the act of Congress setting up the Territory of Orleans after the purchase of Louisiana empowered President Jefferson to reserve land for Indian removal from east of the Mississippi; indeed, a condition stipulated was that the assigned land could not be alienated. Jefferson was verbally sympathetic but did nothing.[23] We can only surmise that Jefferson would not stand against the bitter partisan emotions of his fellow citizens, behind which peered greed for the Indian land and race prejudice. Alexander Hamilton, who worked intimately with Jefferson for years and knew him well, wrote a letter to James A. Bayard on January 16, 1801, explaining why he supported Jefferson against Aaron Burr in the tied vote as to which man would succeed John Adams as president.[24] For Hamilton, Jefferson was the lesser of two evils because he "had some pretensions to character," which were totally lacking in Burr. Besides, Hamilton continued, Jefferson was not "zealot enough to do any thing in pursuance of his principles which will contravene his popularity or his interest. He is as likely as any man I know to temporize—to calculate what will be likely to promote his own reputation and advantage."

29

The Allen Clan and Vermont

"The great and chief end, therefore, of men uniting into commonwealths and putting themselves under government, is the preservation of their property."

John Locke, *Second Treatise on Civil Government,* Chapter IX

The great land speculations after the Revolution focused on the tremendous area west of the Alleghenies. The older eastern states, though centers for local land jobbing, had already knotted by the time of the Revolution. There is one curious case, however, where a fight between speculators actually gave rise to a new separate state. The history of Vermont is the story of greed marching with flags aloft in the name of local patriotism.

What is now Vermont was part of the land grant given by the Duke of York to create the royal colony of New York, whose northeast boundary extended to the Connecticut River. Vermont came into being by two accidents: the avidity of Benning Wentworth, the British royal governor of New Hampshire, and the collision of the vested interests, created as a result, between land speculators from the provinces of New York and New Hampshire.

It will be recalled that Benning Wentworth ran out of soil to grant in New Hampshire and started to patent land west of the Connecticut River. This was an area under the jurisdiction of Albany County in New York, but the insatiable New Hampshire governor ignored this fact and,

311

indeed, founded the town of Bennington, named after himself, thirty-five miles west of the legal boundary.

When Lieutenant Governor Cadwallader Colden of New York protested, Wentworth made an agreement with him in 1751 that neither should grant land in this disputed region until His Majesty reviewed the dispute. Colden, knowing the strength of his case, turned to other matters; while Wentworth ignored the accord and went on to patent 130 town grants each about six miles square, amounting to some three million acres or almost half the state of Vermont as it is now known. As usual, Benning Wentworth reserved 500 acres for himself in each grant in butting corners so as to acquire contiguous areas, finally putting together some 65,000 acres in his own name. He also exacted heavy money fees for the grants. To strengthen his position, the wily governor reserved land in each grant for the Church of England and its subsidiary, the Society for the Propagation of the Gospel, thus creating a powerful ally in the future conflict between the two colonies.

In 1764, young King George III confirmed the old line of the Connecticut River, disallowing the grants made by New Hampshire. Before this, however, the purchasers and their assignees, who felt the titles were legal, had started to develop their property.

On receiving the decision in favor of New York, Cadwallader Colden began to grant the same land in the areas already settled, ignoring the claims of the settlers from New England. Though Colden and his successors kept some of the acreage themselves, it was small compared to the grants and purchases made by and for top New York speculators. The recipients were influential men as always. William Smith, a leading lawyer in New York City and married to Janet of the Livingston clan, owned thousands of acres upstate and property in the city as well. James DeLancey, whose father had been lieutenant governor and chief justice of New York province, was heir-apparent to the most powerful Loyalist family in the province, with vast property holdings in the Mohawk Valley. John Tabor Kempe was New York's attorney general. Isaac Low was a merchant prince of New York City. John Jay is a name, of course, of great historic importance. Egbert Benson was a member of the Congressional committee, which, after the Revolution, approved the Ohio Company's grant in the Northwest Territory subject to a spinoff of the Scioto Company for the inside clique. James Duane, who acted as legal advisor for New York in the dispute, was married to a daughter of Colonel Robert Livingston, lord of Livingston Manor. Among the most aggressive of those benefiting from high connections, he acquired more than 65,000 acres in the disputed area.[1]

The New York speculators were "the most powerful politicians in New York state . . . practically sufficient to control state politics by themselves."[2] It was thus a typical closely held deal where the well-born and the well-connected used their political influence to extend their land holdings; and these aristocratic Yorkers had much to gain—or lose—depending on the validity of their claims. However, in their avarice and confidence they made two serious mistakes. They refused to discuss compensation for the New England settlers, and they also rejected an attempt to adjust the difference in quitrents, which in New York were more than double those called for in New Hampshire.

A frontier war ensued. New York surveyors were beaten by the Yankee farmers. New York sheriffs who attempted to evict settlers were met with a hanging rope. New York land agents were whipped to the bone. Houses and mills of new deedholders were burned down. Men garbed as Indians branded the flesh of newcomers from New York with the "birch seal," the emblem of the original settlers. Gradually the name of Green Mountain Boys ("Vermont" meaning "Green Mountain" from the original French of the earliest settlers who pushed south from Canada) was attached to these guerrilla-type farmers.[3] The New Hampshire grantees, with the aid of the Society for the Propagation of the Gospel, also sent an agent to London in 1767 to obtain a stay on new grants.

A court decision in 1770 went against New Hampshire.[4] Three New York counties were set up: Cumberland, Gloucester, and then Charlotte, all of which sent representatives to the New York assembly during the 1770s. Most of the eastern population of the disputed area along the Connecticut River, including that of Brattleboro, agreed to the decision. In time the tumult would have quieted, but for a family named Allen.

Ethan, Heman, Heber, Levi, Zimri, and Ira Allen were six brothers. They had four cousins of the same Allen name: Caleb, Ebenezer, Elihu, and Joseph. In addition, there were two other cousins with the names of Remember Baker and Seth Warner.[5] These twelve Puritans, with several associates, formed a clan which, both in Hebraic names and zealotry, may be compared to the Maccabees of the Old Testament in their revolt against the Greeks. Though Ira Allen is considered the first statesman of Vermont, possibly because he was a member of that key eighteenth-century profession, surveyor, Ethan Allen was the inspiration of this mountain resistance to what the New England settlers saw as New York imperialism.[6]

The first reaction of Governor Tryon of New York was to outlaw the Allens, putting a price of £20 on each of their heads. Then in 1774 New York passed a riot act threatening death to the leaders. Ethan Allen sarcastically issued a counter-broadside inviting "Yorker jobbers" to come into the mountains in order to give the "outlaws" some target practice.

It must be said, just to balance the scale, that the Allens were as much land speculators as the men they opposed. Land greed was so scrambled with their rhetoric, as with Patrick Henry, that one could not tell from the omelet what had been the white and what the yellow. A top historian summarized: "Although the Allen brothers used the language of patriotism, they were primarily interested in land."[7] Like most clan chieftains, native cunning played a large part in Ethan Allen's leadership. In 1770, for example, James Duane noted in his diary, "Paid Ethan Allen for going among the people to quiet them."[8] Allen of course took the cash and then used it to stir up more revolt.

Ethan Allen, his brothers, and their associates were no band of Robin Hoods. Their specialty was to buy up the land claims of discouraged settlers at tremendous discount. Their initial activity involved property on what is now the Winooski River. The initial purchase was made with Thomas Chittenden, who became the first governor of the independent republic of Vermont. In fact, the officers of the Onion River Company (the vehicle of purchase they used), namely, Chittenden and Ira and Ethan Allen, were most of the time the same men who ran the politics and occupied the top executive offices of Vermont. The Onion River Company was speculative and not directed toward settlement. During three years 77,622 acres were bought and 16,793 were sold; the remaining acreage was valued at $297,408.50 in 1776.[9] Several historians have suggested that Ethan Allen's eagerness to conquer Fort Ticonderoga, the exploit that brought him national esteem, arose at least in part from its nearness to their land and the desire to assert control before New York troops could move in.[10] Ira Allen bought out Ethan's position in 1787 and, continuing his activities, was by 1793 the largest owner of Vermont land, one of the largest land owners in New England, and among the wealthiest men in the United States.[11] To protect their dubious legal position, the Allens and Chittenden were forced to continue resistance to the legal confirmation of the New York claims. Even a sympathetic historian of Ethan Allen noted, "The determination of Vermont to remain Vermont was aided and abetted by the fact that the Governor of Vermont and most of its leading men owned doubtful titles to enormous tracts of Vermont land."[12]

It is quite clear that patriotism to the Allens meant not much more than Vermont independence for reasons allied to their purses. Like Richard Henderson, who had been proscribed by the British as a pirate in his Kentucky schemes, the American Revolution saved Ethan Allen and his brothers from at worst, hanging, or at best, a prison sentence. They were less concerned with the thirteen colonies, and certainly not with New York; independence meant legal title to Allen land and political sovereignty for the Green Mountain Boys. One can imagine the astonishment of New York's aristocratic leaders when a man they considered a common outlaw abruptly became a national hero by his capture of Fort Ticonderoga "in the name of the great Jehovah and the Continental Congress,"[13] though neither God nor Congress were held in great esteem by Ethan. But the Allen change of status did not mean that harmony was to prevail in the Green Mountains, for both parties to the conflict were avid speculators and no quarter was expected or given.

When Congress during the Revolution became deadlocked over the question as to whether Vermont should become a separate state, Ethan Allen, who had been in secret contact with Sir Henry Clinton, British commander in New York, as well as Governor Frederick Haldimand of Canada, threatened to leave the conflict unless his demands were recognized. In late 1778 he travelled to Philadelphia to present his case to Congress. The evidence indicates that he brought with him blank deeds to land claims in order to distribute them among the delegates for a favorable decision.[14] As chairman of the Vermont land committee from 1779 to 1781, Ethan also arranged for land grants to high officers in the Continental army. On hearing that two generals, Gates and Glover, had accepted Vermont land, Washington was so disturbed that he inquired as to whether the intention was to corrupt the army.[15] Allen knew the gauge of his fellow countrymen, but was blocked by a combination of New York hostility and a rising fear in New Hampshire because certain towns on its side of the Connecticut River had begun to show interest in the Vermont secession.

In this same year of 1778, Governor George Clinton of New York, repealing the acts of outlawry against the Allens, offered to confirm New Hampshire land titles, The reason behind this move was that several of the more important New York speculators having sided with the British, the land conflict now was of less significance.[16] The taste of power for the Allens by this time had become too savory for them to accept lesser roles; indeed, turning the table, Ethan Allen in 1781 extended Vermont's claims westward to the Hudson River and then in 1782 arrested New York sympathizers, declaring he would make their homes "as desolate as Sodom and Gomorrah." It was apparent that the leaders of Vermont were now doubting the advantage of entering the Confederation.[17]

There are two schools of thought as to what may politely be called the dubious patriotism of Ethan Allen. The evidence is massive that both during and after the Revolution he negotiated with the British. The first school feels that after 1778 he definitely decided to bring Vermont into an alliance with Canada but could not make other Vermonters go along. The second school contends that Ethan Allen used his negotiations with the enemy as a ramrod to force Congress to give Vermont statehood. It is hard to swallow the latter surmise, for as late as June of 1782, when Lord Shelburne had already come to power and England was making every effort to conclude peace, Ethan Allen in a letter to Haldimand made the flat statement, "I shall do anything in my power to render this State a British Province."[18] Furthermore, despite the many British campaigns in northern New York, an area that suffered terribly during the Revolution, British forces moving south from Canada never engaged the Green Mountain Boys' militia, by what seemed mutual agreement. The most charitable view of Ethan Allen's conduct, given our most recent information from the British archives, is that he feared domination by New York, the loss of his land titles, and the reduction of his personal power more than he did playing second fiddle in the British Empire.

After the American victory, the Vermont leaders cooled off even more toward confederation. The postwar depression and depreciation of the Continental currency were major reasons. Levi Allen went to London to discuss joining with Canada, an effort that failed more because of British dawdling than Allen double-talk: in fact Levi Allen received a pension from the British government as a self-declared Loyalist during the Revolution. Ethan, in communication with Governor Haldimand of Canada during this same period, bluntly rejected union with the other colonies: "for this is a territory that is not in confederacy with the revolted colonies, but are willing not only to trade, but to be a British Colony, as soon as the pleasure of his Majesty and the present troubles will admit."[19] The hero of Ticonderoga had indeed moved a long way in less than ten years from his high rhetoric of liberty and independence.

With the war behind him and real estate booming, "General Allen," as he was now called by grace of the Vermont militia, entered new realms. His wife having died, Ethan at the age of forty-five married a twenty-four-year-old heiress, Fanny Montresor, daughter of a French officer serving in the British army; she brought to the marriage twenty thousand acres of Vermont land. Fanny, who was only a bit older than Ethan's daughters (a situation again parallel with Patrick Henry), soon bore Ethan a son, who, as one might guess, was named Hannibal.

Then Ethan Allen got involved in a new imbroglio. The restless man accepted a top role in a revolt organized by Connecticut proprietors of what was then known as the Wyoming Valley in western Pennsylvania. This was a very similar situation to that which had created Vermont, for the Connecticut settlers considered the isolated territory, near Scranton and separated from their mother state by the bulk of New York, a part of Connecticut. Again as in Vermont, there were double land grants and bloody clashes. The Susquehanna Company, proprietary owner of the land in question, whose original association had as its purpose "to spread Christianity as also to promote their own Temporal Interest," gave Ethan Allen a financial interest for his services. In 1786 the general, in gold-braided costume and cocked hat, twice rode into the Wyoming Valley, creating a sensation but, contrary to the hopes of the proprietors, without the Green Mountain Boys. The grandiose gesture was futile, for both Congress and the United States courts supported the position of Pennsylvania. It was during this same period that Ethan published a deist book—anticipating Thomas Paine's *The Age of Reason* by a decade—which derided both the Old and New Testaments and suggested that all Christian priests and ministers be fired and and their salaries used to buy "good wine or old spirits to make the heart glad." This quite naturally infuriated the pulpit and alienated many of his sympathizers.[20]

In 1787, Shays's Rebellion exploded in Massachusetts. When the revolt was sinking, Daniel Shays sent a message to Ethan Allen inviting him to command the remnants of his army "and be king of Massachusetts when they had conquered it."[21] Allen turned down the offer, though he was thought to be in sympathy with the revolting farmers: excessive drinking had undermined his health and he took a personal dislike to Day and Parsons, Shays's main lieutenants. In a rather shameful episode, if one considers his own history of revolt, Allen personally took part in the capture of two of Shays's soldiers when they passed in flight near his home.

Early in February 1789 a group of the founders of the Green Mountain Boys got together to talk over the good old days at the home of cousin Ebenezer Allen.[22] Though there are disputed versions, the story goes that the punch, as always, passed generously and it was close to dawn when the general was poured into the back of the ox-driven cart. During the return home he fell backward, struggled, became still, and lapsed into a coma from which he never woke. He was fifty years old but worn out from coxcombry.

In 1790 New York gave up its last land claims, and the next year Vermont entered the Union as the fourteenth state, in part a result of the practical compromise to keep a balance between free and slave states, Vermont being set off against the coming admission of Kentucky. The local supporters of New York in the conflict were granted as compensation a tract of sixty-four square miles in that state's Chenango County while a small fiscal settlement was given to the New York speculators. The only similar story in the history of the United States to this odd secession is that of West Virginia, which as a result of the Civil War was allowed to secede in the same fashion from its mother state of Virginia.

The fate of the other main actors is instructive. Ira Allen, the favorite brother and companion of Ethan in every adventure, had gathered to himself some 300,000 acres in Vermont.[23] While on a mission to purchase arms in France for the Vermont militia,[24] he was captured by the British and charged with selling weapons to the Irish insurrection. Detained first in England and then put in prison in France, his land, which had been heavily pledged for loans, was foreclosed to satisfy tax liens. Ira Allen was forced to flee Vermont on his return home in order to evade jail for unpaid debts, and ended his life as a fugitive in Philadelphia. Levi Allen got into the same trouble and died in 1801 in a Burlington prison. Speculation first made and then broke the Allen clan. Their final legacy was not a land empire but the state of Vermont.

Part Five

Federalism at the Helm

30

The United States Constitution
and Land Speculation

"Speculation in lands was the most absorbing American enterprise during the later Colonial, the Revolutionary, and the early Republican periods. . . . The insatiable desire for territory manifested by young and land-poor America cannot be fully comprehended unless it is understood that, in those days, the country was run largely by speculators in real estate."

Thomas P. Abernethy, *From Frontier to Plantation in Tennessee*

From May 25 to September 17 of 1787, the U.S. Constitution was drafted by a convention of twelve states in Philadelphia. Fifty-five delegates attended out of seventy-three chosen: Rhode Island as a bloc, as well as many individuals from other states refused to come. The cream of America's landowners and speculators were there. Among the delegates from Virginia were George Washington, chosen president of the convention, along with John Blair, George Mason, and Edmund Randolph; from Pennsylvania, Benjamin Franklin, Robert Morris, Gouverneur Morris, Thomas Fitzsimons, James Wilson, and Thomas Mifflin; from Massachusetts, Nathaniel Gorham and Elbridge Gerry; from New Jersey, Jonathan Dayton, William Paterson, and William Livingston; from New York, John Lansing, Jr.; from North Carolina, William Blount, Hugh Williamson, Alexander Martin, William R. Davie, and Richard D. Spaight; from South Carolina, John Rutledge, Pierce Butler, and the two Pinckneys; from Delaware, John Dickinson and Richard Bassett; from Maryland, Daniel Carroll, Luther Martin, Daniel Jenifer, and John F. Mercer; and from Georgia, William Few and William Houstoun. Thus, thirty-three of the fifty-five delegates—60 percent of the entire group—made their primary living through farming plantations that they or their fathers had acquired by means of speculating in land and improved property or, as was common, by a combination of these methods. One might state that the Constitutional Convention was in large part a national real estate convention.[1]

Top luminaries were not at the convention. John Adams as minister to England and Thomas Jefferson as minister to France were out of the country, as was Secretary of Foreign Affairs John Jay. Patrick Henry[2] and Richard Henry Lee, of Virginia, as well as Willie Jones, "the Jefferson of North Carolina," declined to come. So did Sam Adams and John Hancock of Massachusetts. Christopher Gadsden, the firebrand of South Carolina, was not a delegate. Tom Paine was England-bound to raise trouble for George III. Governor George Clinton of New York violently opposed the whole idea of a convention.[3]

On September 17, thirty-nine delegates, little more than half of those originally chosen, signed the Constitution. Alexander Hamilton had left in a huff because his royal bias was made light of, but came back at the end. Edmund Randolph, then governor of Virginia, and George Mason, author of Virginia's constitution and bill of rights, refused to sign for fear of a strong national government. Luther Martin of Maryland had already stormed out over that same issue. Elbridge Gerry of Massachusetts, repelled by both democracy and tyranny, would not sign; John Lansing, Jr., from New York, had left for much the same reason. All these men, except Randolph (who was persuaded by Washington), later fought ratification. Two of the twelve states present would not go on record as being officially in favor: South Carolina was divided and New York did not vote. Thus was made pregnant the Constitution.

In the age of innocence before World War I, Americans saw the birth of the Constitution, which is to say its ratification by nine of the thirteen states, as a phoenix sprung from ashes. The Founding Fathers were demigods, with various theories put forward by patriotic historians as to why: they were in the blood line of their Teutonic forebears who trekked from Turkistan to Tennessee; they were agents of God's providence; they were midwives to one or another semi-cabalistic egg hatch. The views of Charles A. Beard, whose book *An Economic Interpretation of the Constitution* appeared in 1913, were a bomb blast in these holy precincts.

Charles Beard put his pen on three groups that Alexander Hamilton organized to support the Constitutional Convention. They were: the creditors, that is, the financiers, bankers, and money lenders; the merchants and manufacturers who wanted protective tariffs; and the land speculators. Without the consolidation of these three groups into one interest, the new government could neither have been founded nor have continued. As Beard summed up, the Constitution had two main purposes. It created a government committed to breaking the force of majority rule and to preventing the invasion of property rights; and one that would restrict the state legislatures, then in the hands of the debtors.

It is curious, looking back more than three-quarters of a century, how many intelligent Americans howled that Beard had profaned true history or was a closet communist. After all, Aristotle almost two thousand five hundred years ago wrote that the distribution of wealth is the chief factor in fixing the form of the state and that history is made by the clash of class interests in society. This view was in large part endorsed by John Locke, Alexander Hamilton, John Adams, and James Madison long before Karl Marx petrified the idea into an iron corpse.

A few typical quotes may fix this point. On June 18, 1787, Alexander Hamilton said in the Constitutional Convention: "All communities divide themselves into the few and the many. The first are the rich and well born, the other the mass of the people. . . . The people are turbulent and changing; they seldom judge or determine right." Hamilton, who wrote the largest number of essays making up *The Federalist*, the articles written to support ratification, stated in the thirtieth essay, "Money is, with propriety, considered as the vital principle of the body politic." He then added, "The new Constitution has in favor of its success these circumstances . . . the good will of most men of property in the several states who wish a government of the union able to protect them against domestic violence and the depradations which the democratic spirit is apt to make on property."

James Madison agreed. Considered the father of the Constitution, he wrote in his famous tenth essay, "The most common and durable source of factions has been the various and unequal distribution of property. Those who hold and those who are without property have ever formed distinct interests in society. . . . The diversities in the faculties of men, from which the rights of property originate, is not less an insuperable obstacle to a uniformity of interests. The protection of these faculties is the first object of government." John Adams was in accord and even more specific when writing later. "The Federal Convention was the work of the commercial people in the seaport towns, of the slave-holding states, of the officers of the revolutionary army, and the property holders everywhere." Indeed, Niccolò Machiavelli summed things up centuries earlier in a pithy sentence. In *The Prince,* he counseled an aspirant to that office: "But, above all, he must abstain from the property of others. For men will sooner forget the death of their father than the loss of their patrimony."

The Constitution was dictated in great part by men of wealth and buoyed by subtle techniques over a squirming majority. Edward M. Earle, the authority on the subject, wrote, "It would have been a counsel of perfection to consign the new Constitution to the tender mercies of the legislatures . . . ratification then would have had the same chance as the Scriptural camel passing through the eye of a needle."[4] Indeed, in the first essay of *Letters from the Federal Farmer*, the Antifederalist response ascribed to Richard Henry Lee of Virginia, the point is made that if people had known the true reason for the Constitutional Convention, called merely to amend the Articles of Confederation, probably no state would have appointed delegates; and further, the results would have been very different if the states-rights advocates, such as Patrick Henry, Willie Jones, and Lee himself, had not declined to come.[5]

The convention strategy used thus was not only to declare that the Constitution should go into effect when nine of the thirteen states ratified, but also to bypass the state legislatures and elect separate conventions in each state that would be more amenable. A further advantage of this method was that judges, ministers, and others ineligible for election to state legislatures would now constitute a more dependable pool of conservative delegates.[6]

It does not follow that because a class interest is explicit in the Constitution, every conservative was for ratification or that individuals voted merely out of personal interest like Pavlov's famous dogs trained to a conditioned response. People are complex, with mixed and often contradictory traits, and certainly not mere salivating canines. Men such as George Mason, Patrick Henry, and Elbridge Gerry, who fought against ratification, were among the richest Americans. Speculators like Robert Morris, Nathaniel Gorham, and John Cleves Symmes had bought land on the installment plan, expecting to pay in depreciated scrip. With Hamilton's funding plan, they suffered severe losses. Yet they supported the Constitution.

Nor does it follow that voting a class interest is automatically a low and despicable activity. There can be little question that the men who created the Constitution identified their class interest with the country's interest. The failure of collectivist societies in the twentieth century clearly shows that self-interest, within a responsible social framework, can be a major force to advance the general welfare. The writers Robert E. Brown and Forrest McDonald have refuted the validity of certain categories of analysis, as well as individual facts, presented by Charles A. Beard. Beard was a pioneer whose views were tilted by a preconceived position flowing from his sympathy with the Progressive movement of the first decade of this century. But despite mistakes, the foundation of his economic theory still has not crumpled.[7]

As noted, one of the tripods of the Constitution was a group of major land speculators. Beard, in dividing the delegates into classes, states that fourteen of the fifty-five delegates fit in this category, the most important of them being Washington and Franklin—the two titans—as well as Blount, Dayton, Gorham, Robert Morris, and Wilson.[8] If plantation owners who speculated in western land are also included, the number is much greater. Amid the swirl of dispute surrounding the origins of the Constitution, this point is without dispute.

The Constitution itself has few direct references to land matters, nor indeed do the essays of *The Federalist*. In the third essay, John Jay states that a prudent national government will less likely involve the country in war than would individual states bordering on Spanish and British territories; and such a government will also be more cautious in avoiding Indian hostilities. Always the realist, Hamilton, in the twenty-fifth essay, notes the same points and states that "common councils" and "a common treasury" are the best guards of a strong national government, implying that this would be equally true in aggression as well as defense.[9]

Political reality and parchment printing are very different things. The Constitution shifted to the central government the power to deal with the Indians, which in fact meant taking Indian land with a national army rather than weak state militias. As Charles Beard stated:

> Speculation in western lands was one of the leading activities of capitalists in those days. . . . The chief obstacle in the way of the rapid appreciation of these lands was the weakness of the national government which prevented the complete subjugation of the Indians, the destruction of old Indian claims, and the orderly settlement of the frontier. Every leading capitalist of the time thoroughly understood the relation of a new constitution to the rise in land values beyond the Alleghenies.[10]

To underscore the influence of this factor it is necessary to look at the positions taken by the various delegates of the state conventions in the subsequent fight to ratify the Constitution. Despite what modern parlance would call rigging, the battle was intense in certain states. Indeed, North Carolina and New York resisted to the very end while Rhode Island did not join the union until Providence and Newport threatened to secede from that state. For some time the issue was in doubt. Since nine of the thirteen states had to ratify the Constitution before it could go into effect, with Rhode Island always recognized as set not to assent, a shift of only a few states one way or the other would decide the issue. Thus, those states in the South that voted yea in order to protect and enlarge their western frontiers and thus assure an increase in land value for their speculators (who very often were the lawmakers), were in effect the margin of difference between ratification and defeat.

Ironically, it is Forrest McDonald, the sharpest critic of Charles A. Beard, who supplies us with this information. In *We the People,* a book written to refute the Beardian interpretation of the Constitution, one of the few points of accord between the two men is the importance of western land. McDonald almost quotes Beard verbatim: "Lands located in areas where the Indians were a threat quickly appreciated in value in the face of the promised strength of the new general government."[11] State by state McDonald analyzes what happened in the local conventions and proves clearly that in Georgia, South Carolina, and Virginia it was the impact of western lands that decided the vote in favor of ratification. Indeed, if Virginia had not ratified, New York and North Carolina never would have; and without these three states the Constitution was only an empty fuel tank.

For Georgia, McDonald writes, "From start to finish the ratification movement in Georgia was dominated by the proximity and hostility of the Indians. . . . The Constitution, promising national help against the Indians, was locally thought of simply as one of several measures that would provide for the defense of the state. . . ."[12]

For South Carolina, McDonald discusses three reasons ratification won. The first, and presumably the most important, "was the military lesson the war had taught. The state had learned that its geographical position made it vulnerable to attacks by Indians on the frontier . . . only a strong general government could furnish the military and naval strength needed for security."[13]

For the keystone of Virginia: The western posts of the British, which had not been evacuated, "were inimical to the interests of the [Shenandoah] Valley and Trans-Allegheny regions, and to those of the land speculators who held titles to vast tracts in the [Northwest] Territory. . . . These areas sent twenty-eight delegates to the convention, twenty-seven of whom voted for ratification."[14] Since the final vote was 89 for and 79 against, these votes were far and away the margin of difference.

Although a consensus supported by all historians would not be possible, it is apparent that the Constitution did not spring full-blown from the minds of patriots who thought only of lofty abstract principles. The writings of the most gifted of these men, some of whom have been quoted, indicate they were aware of the economic interests both of individuals and of classes that lay behind much of the conflict to create and then ratify the Constitution. Regardless of the criteria used to describe property holders—and the five categories set up by Beard were without doubt organized to support a view the historian already had previous to the facts—it is certain that the elite of the former colonial society, which supported the Revolution, viewed with dread the control of state legislatures by farmers who issued runs of paper money in order to lighten their mortgage debts. It is equally certain that western land values were static due to the lack of a national army capable of destroying the Indians.

Since the main objective of northern manufacturers was tariff protection to aid their budding industry, which would work against the agrarian interests of the South, it is curious that many of the large plantation owners supported the Constitution. One reason was fear of slave revolts, which could be put down with the help of federal troops if necessary. But a determining argument was the need to stabilize the situation in western lands. As Hugh Williamson, a member of the convention from North Carolina, put it: "For myself, I conceive that my opinions are not biassed by private Interests, but having claims to a considerable quantity of land in the Western Country, I am fully persuaded that the Value of those lands must be increased by an efficient federal government."[15]

In summarizing, then, almost all the richer Americans were concerned with the radical trend of state legislatures. National power meant protective tariffs for northern manufacturers, federal rather than state regulation of trade for importing merchants, security against slave insurrections for southern planters, and profit for speculators everywhere on public securities and land scrip bought at discount. Many of the southern plantation owners and the northern merchants had a stake in western land, for which a national army was necessary to eliminate the Indians. It should be stressed that in practice these various categories of property holders are often abstractions. The planter might as readily invest in depreciated public securities as a merchant would buy land scrip at a discount. Even the division of capital holders into merchants and planters is somewhat artificial, especially in the South, for the planters often had mercantile connections. The essential point is that the wealthy came together and compromised their differences in order to create a more effective national system. It cannot be said that the Constitution was a vehicle of the landlords, and certainly not of the large majority of small farmers of that time, since it served most clearly the merchants and the holders of public securities; but it can be affirmed that without the support of key political figures deeply involved in land speculation, the Constitution would not have been adopted.

31

Federalism and the Final Frenzy
of Land Plunging

"We have one material which actually constitutes an aristocracy that governs the nation. That material is wealth. Talents, birth, virtues, services, sacrifices, are of little consideration with us."

John Adams, 1808

From 1789 to 1801, during two administrations of George Washington and one of John Adams, the United States was governed by the Federalists. Through much of this time they did not stand for a political party but rather a total philosophy of government. In many important ways Federalism was a modified form of the earlier New England Puritan faith of God's elected, made secular to embrace top elements of the southern plantation and commercial classes. The Jeffersonian sweep at the turn of the century, which drove the Federalists from power, in most respects changed the rhetoric and not the substance. Indeed, Jefferson's purchase of the Louisiana Territory, doubling the national domain, was an act of imperialism eclipsing the most delicious dreams of Alexander Hamilton.

In its initial form, Federalist philosophy rose out of the shambles created by thirteen states with different interests during the Revolution. Superintendent of Finance Robert Morris found by hard experience that the states would not contribute money to the Confederation and that Congress had no power to compel them to do so. Nor was there any way to repay

328

the French and Dutch loans, which had been the lifeblood of the war effort. In frustration, Morris exclaimed, "The duty to pay is absolute, but the means can only be derived from the states. If the states refuse, have Congress a right to compel? The answer to this question decides whether we be one or thirteen."[1]

The palsy of the Confederation after the war forced thinking men to impose the Constitution on a public still in love with cheap money and absolute freedom. Samuel E. Morison summed up the situation neatly. "Federalists believed that the slogans of 1776 were outmoded; that America needed more national power, that the immediate peril was not tyranny but dissolution; that certain political powers such as foreign affairs, war and commerce were national by nature, that the right to tax was essential to any government, and that power wrested from king and parliament should not be divided among thirteen states."[2] Related to these issues were the sanctity of private property and of contract obligation. After independence, the practical work was to keep a peaceful social order, which meant payment of debts, a sound financial system, and conditions favorable to develop the natural resources. Men of this mind were neither philosophers like Thomas Jefferson and George Mason, whose slaves worked the plantation while they wrote about civil rights or practiced diplomacy, nor agitated more by ideas than material goods like Tom Paine and Sam Adams. They were men of property, intent on getting more. The fact that interest had not been paid on the national and state debts between 1783 and 1789 was of far more concern to them than whether man was entitled by natural or acquired right to free speech and press.

Since the bulk of farmers throughout the thirteen states had borrowed to buy their land, and the cheaper the money the easier it was to pay off loans in paper whose face value steadily went down, the Federalist view of sound currency was opposed by a majority. Also, with inflation, farm products rose in value relative to paper money and securities. In reaction to this stance, Federalism more and more took on an anti-democratic bias even among those who had been the popular leaders of the Revolution, recruiting men such as Patrick Henry, Christopher Gadsden, and Richard Henry Lee. Though the right to vote was very limited under the British, the Federalists in some states attempted to curtail it more. And as the only pool of voters, namely, the majority of free white Protestant men with some property, saw the system unfold, they often lost interest in the electoral process even when they could vote. In some elections concerning national issues (for example those in the early 1790s), only about three percent of the population voted.[3]

Though Robert Morris was the warhorse, the brains of the Federal party belonged to Alexander Hamilton, a case that many psychiatrists would crave to have on the couch. Hamilton was technically the West Indian bastard that John Adams called him: even more abasing for Hamilton was that he could not deny the fact, because the alternative was worse; if indeed legitimate, he would then be Alexander Levine, the son of a Jew with property at St. Croix. Fathered by an itinerant Scotsman, at times called a "merchant" and at times a "peddler," who later abandoned his ersatz family, Hamilton's mother was Rachel Faucette, of French Huguenot descent. This was the man who English diplomats found so pro-British in all dealings, and who indeed had been inclined toward the royalist side before becoming a protégé of the Livingstons in 1774. "We think in English," Hamilton was reported to tell a top British emissary, though without a drop of English blood in his veins. Poor as the proverbial church mouse in origins, charm, good looks, and brilliance helped Hamilton move into top circles during the Revolution. He then married the daughter of New York's society leader. Envying Washington for the family and character he himself lacked, Hamilton would slight his commander-in-chief. Washington was either unaware of these remarks or ignored them. But Hamilton's worst fury was reserved for Aaron Burr, who was not only everything Hamilton wished for himself but also took the side of the popular party. Burr's father, of the same name, was an eminent descendant of New Englanders who had come to Massachusetts Bay Colony with Winthrop in 1630, Aaron Burr, Sr., was also president of the College of New Jersey, later to be known as Princeton. Burr's mother, also of most eminent background, wa Esther Edwards, daughter of the famous theologian Jonathan Edwards. Like Hamilton, Aaron Burr, Jr., was a brilliant student, graduating New Jersey College at sixteen and then rising to be a colonel through personal distinction in the Revolution. To understand these facts gives some insight into Alexander Hamilton's malevolent hate of Aaron Burr and its classic Greek-tragedy end.

This dazzling Scotch-French illegitimate child of an adventurer was the showman of cynical aristocracy. A few typical phrases illustrate. The most notorious is the snort: "The people!—the people is a great beast." A few comments taken down when he addressed the Constitutional Convention or wrote to friends are combined here: "Nothing but a permanent body can check the imprudence of democracy. Their turbulent and uncontrolling disposition requires checks. . . . Our real disease, which is democracy, the position of which will only be the more concentrated in each part and consequently the more virulent. . . . Take mankind in general, they are vicious. . . . Experience is a continual comment on the worthlessness of the human race." And perhaps most revealing, for it tells more about

Hamilton than of what he writes: "Till the millennium comes, in spite of all our boasted light and purification, hypocrisy and treachery will continue to be the most successful commodities in the political market."[4]

Such a philosophy could not long dominate the politics of the United States. Less than being wrong—for belief in the wisdom of the people is as much an article of faith as the catechism of any religion—it was out of step with the times. The Federalists, as exemplified by Hamilton, meant what they said and said what they meant. Possibly the most sincere politicians in this country's history, they made no pretense of being other than upper-class Americans who had a natural right to rule their inferiors in the social and economic realm. As the best-known historian of that era wrote: "Being men of wealth and high social position, the Federalist leaders fell easily into the assumption that there was a close connection between the ownership of property and the possession of the talents necessary to the efficient administration of government."[5] Most were not, however, barely disguised monarchists as was Hamilton; their ideal was rather an oligarchic republic.[6] Furthermore, unlike more recent politicians who share their view, they had not yet learned that to say a thing and do another is the high art of political advance. A Ronald Reagan was inconceivable in the American eighteenth-century republic. The Federalist party thus was by its nature self-destructive in a bubbling young America. The top leaders indeed were a minority within a minority. For despite the contradictions, the citizens of the new land also needed some dream of spiritual generosity, some flaming star to rise toward. The tension between the words of Jefferson and Hamilton ring down through our history; and a descendant of John Adams, the historian James Truslow Adams, put it this way: "As America grew she tried to serve, so to say, God and Mammon—that is, she insisted upon clinging to the ideal of Jeffersonianism while gathering in the money profits of Hamiltonianism."[7]

The financial and political links among the Federalists were anchored to a plinth of kith and kin. The southern wing centered on the close relation between George Washington and Robert Morris. Washington and his wife, Martha, stayed at the Morris mansion during the time the president lived in Philadelphia. The affection between the two couples was so deep that at all presidential receptions Morris sat to the right of the president while his wife, Mollie, was to the right of Martha. Benjamin Harrison, Jr., the leader of Virginia's aristocracy, was Morris's business partner; John Banister, John Harvie, and Carter Braxton, top commercial figures from Virginia, were also his associates in business—all these men were deep in Kentucky land. Hetty, Robert Morris's oldest daughter, married James Marshall of Virginia, a younger brother of John Marshall who became chief justice of the U.S. Supreme Court after serving as secretary of state in the last years of President Adams's cabinet. Former Governor William Paca of Maryland, so deeply involved in the struggle of the land speculators over adopting the Articles of Confederation, was a brother-in-law to Robert Morris. Robert Goodloe Harper of the Yazoo frauds, congressman from South Carolina and brother-in-law to Alexander Hamilton, was another business associate of Morris.

The northern wing of the Federalists was led by Alexander Hamilton. When Morris turned down the post of secretary of the treasury under Washington, being anxious to return to business, he suggested Hamilton in his stead. Hamilton chose as assistant secretary Colonel William Duer. The wives of Hamilton and Duer were cousins; Duer, who organized the Scioto Company, was also a protégé of Morris. General Philip Schuyler, head of the New York aristocracy, was Hamilton's father-in-law; William Duer's partner, Alexander Macomb, was also a business associate of General Schuyler. Another daughter of General Schuyler was married to John B, Church, a wealthy New Yorker who in turn was partnered with Jeremiah Wadsworth of Hartford, probably the most active land speculator from Connecticut. Church and Wadsworth were likewise holders of the two largest blocks of shares in the Bank of North America. Alexander Hamilton was Church's attorney and agent.

Colonel Robert R. Livingston of the powerful New York State family, had been secretary of foreign affairs during the Revolution while Robert Morris was superintendent of finance. Colonel Livingston's daughter Mary married James Duane, who speculated heavily in Vermont land and was first mayor of New York City. Livingston's other daughter Kitty, who lived with the Morris family several seasons in Philadelphia, married Matthew Ridley, one of Morris's closest friends. William Livingston, a cousin of Colonel Robert (both men were grandchildren of Robert Livingston, Sr., first lord of Livingston Manor), and governor of New Jersey during the Revolution, had two daughters who made illustrious marriages. Sarah (Sally) married John Jay.[8] Susanna married John Cleves Symmes of the Miami Purchase.

Gouverneur Morris (no relation to Robert), proprietor of New York's Morrisiania manor, was Robert Morris's assistant when the latter became superintendent of finance. The two Morrises joined William Constable, the top securities trader in New York City, to create the firm of William Constable and Company, specialists in the manipulation of depreciated paper. Constable partnered in land speculations with Alexander Macomb. Macomb's other associates, the Ogdens, were related to Gouverneur Morris by marriage. The famous Ogden Purchase in the Adirondack region of upper New York was a syndicate of these friends and kinsmen including as well General Henry Knox, Washington's secretary of war.

In Philadelphia, the leading commercial center, Thomas Willing, Robert Morris's partner in the shipping firm of Willing, Morris & Co., was perennial president of the Bank of North America and also father-in-law to the merchant prince William Bingham. Bingham had been Morris's agent in the West Indies during the Revolution, and with General Knox bought two million acres in Maine. James Wilson, the greatest land speculator after Robert Morris, was the latter's attorney and ofttimes partner. Somewhat on the fringe, General James Wilkinson married Anne Biddle, whose cousin Nicholas Biddle later became president of the Second Bank of the United States.

As may be noted, we have met almost all these persons while they pushed high chips in land roulette. It was as though the leaders of the Federalist party were one happy family busy gorging champagne and caviar at the Robert Morris smorgasbord. If the Jefferson forces in late 1800 had not won the election, replacing this clique with their own, the political structure of fledgling America might have become in another generation a closed blood line aristocracy like those that largely ran Virginia and New York.

It has often been asked why most of these men, with great credit lines and the highest political contacts, went broke in the period between 1792 and 1800. Indeed, it would seem a basic refutation of the thesis that a type of modified oligarchy ruled the United States if its leaders ended bankrupt, often landing in debtor's jail. There were sound reasons, but to understand this seeming paradox it is necessary to see the changes going on during the Federalist era in the United States' economic structure.

The fact that land speculation was the prime investment in America through most of the eighteenth century had a valid base. To begin with, native families were large; like Mexico and Brazil at the present time, the internal population doubled each generation. And immigration was enormous. It was generally thought that most of Europe would move to the new country, where society was mobile and in relative terms without sharp class lines. In 1783, the Revolution having been won, Silas Deane wrote to James Wilson: "There is at this time a general spirit for emigration from Europe to America. . . ."[9] The Indians, no longer protected by the British, were being reduced as a block in the West. For the same reason, the Mohawk Valley was opened. Maine and New Hampshire, with Vermont, were almost empty. A great quantity of Tory property had been thrown on the market. The speculators were justified in their optimism.

Furthermore, risk capital was willing and ready to invest. The English had long experience with profits from American land speculation. Commercial relations between the old and new country were never completely severed during the Revolution, which in some cases had been treated as a trivial sideshow by friends with longtime business contacts. Dutch capitalists were fascinated by American land investment; indeed, they had made fortunes speculating in national and state government paper due to Hamilton's funding. Besides, large tracts of land at less than a dollar an acre seemed an incredible bargain to bankers in Holland, where land cost one hundred times more.[10] It may be added that much of this capital was war profits, for the English merchants and the neutral Dutch thrived mightily on the almost continual eighteenth-century wars. This interest in American land speculation was even greater than normal as the tremors of the French Revolution sent much loose capital in search of a safe haven.

Another important factor was the ratification of the U.S. Constitution and the compact union it created, which not only set up a fertile environment for investment but provided a new national land market as well. Before these events, speculation was still largely local, intrastate, or regional. Virginians viewed their West—the Shenandoah Valley and then Kentucky— as a natural arena. In the same way, when Carolinians speculated, they turned to Tennessee. If a southern speculator, such as Patrick Henry, thought in grandiose terms, he would survey adjoining areas like Georgia's Yazoo region or southern Ohio. This was also true in the North, where the speculators of New York fought with those of Vermont while those of Connecticut and Massachusetts looked to western New York and Pennsylvania as well as land claimed by Connecticut and Pennsylvania in northern Ohio. These various schemes have already been analyzed.

The central government brought to the fore a new type of speculator who thought in national terms and regarded state borders as mere artificial lines. Much as European capital today is overflowing the various state borders and investing with an eye to the coming economic unification of the Continent, so the same movement went on in the United States after integration of the thirteen states. Robert Morris and James Wilson, to take the two leading examples (their activities will be reviewed momentarily), were both from Pennsylvania but they did not consider the home state as their "country" as did Americans before the war. The entire nation was now a field for speculation. The opportunities and risks grew in measure, as did the capital required. Land was no longer a symbol of status to these men, as it was to southern plantation owners. Nor was it pride of inheritance and local attachment, as in New England. Land was simply a saleable commodity like bonds and stocks. It could be located anywhere. No sentiment was attached to ownership. If the land sold at a profit, fine;

if not, then if it were bought with almost no equity, it would be dropped on tax forfeiture with barely a thought. Land thus became unrelated to its function as a source of crops or human habitation; little consideration was given to building improvements or community infrastructure. It was simply a "throw-away" consumer product not much different from old clothes or used tissue. Abstracting land from its function aided its fluidity as a capital speculation. It was a market item with which plungers—putting the smallest amount of money possible into the deals—could make big profits on a quick turn.

The approach of the top land speculators was correct in pure economic terms, but life has a mysterious way of straying from logic. Several unexpected events sickened the golden geese. To begin with, the law of supply and demand did not work out the way it was thought to. Too much land coming on the market after the Revolution made it very cheap. The federal and state governments competed to sell their surplus, leading to a price war not only between the national government and the states but among the states themselves. With the Indian population and threat reduced, many settlers simply thumbed their noses and squatted; in several states, like Virginia and Pennsylvania, their influence on western state legislators was so great that ultimately squatters rights were legalized.

At the same time that the supply was great the demand weakened. The outbreak of the French Revolution followed by the Napoleonic wars and the invasion of other countries by mighty French armies, destroyed the hope for a great migration to America. All available males were sucked into the maelstrom. Mutual slaughter reduced their numbers. The British fleet blockaded the Continent, making it almost impossible for emigrants to slip through. The whole pattern of supply and demand, so apparent to hard-headed businessmen, turned out to be a mirage.

The last straw was the loss of European credit. The Bank of England in early 1792 suspended specie payments. This led to a panic in the New York securities market, which caused men like Colonel William Duer and his partner Alexander Macomb to go bankrupt. Robert Morris lost £124,000 when his London bank failed in 1793.[11] He suffered similar but smaller losses from a bank failure in Dublin.[12] The revolutionary armies of France occupied the Netherlands in 1795, thus cutting off Dutch capital. This was the final blow. By 1795, specie was so scarce that interest had risen up from two and one-half percent to four percent a month.[13] The credit lines that the great land speculators had cultivated, which in normal times would have held up, fizzled overnight. Not only did Robert Morris, John Nicholson, and James Greenleaf, the powerful trio of land plungers, end up in jail for unpaid debts, but other top financiers joined them as well. Eminent men such as Ira Allen of Vermont and James Wilson of the U.S. Supreme Court became fugitives from justice.

Aside from George Washington, who had foreseen the storm and reined in his appetite, there were two noted survivors of the tidal wave choking the over-extended land speculators during the long panic running from 1795 to 1800. The first was William Bingham, Philadelphia magnate and U.S. senator, whose daughter married Alexander Baring, the English banker. Loans from his son-in-law kept Bingham afloat. He was able to hold on to a two-million-acre tract in Maine, which he had bought from General Henry Knox and Colonel William Duer. The second survivor was John Marshall (with his brother James, who married Robert Morris's daughter), the future chief justice of the U.S. Supreme Court. President Washington, stepping in to save old family friends, chose John Marshall to negotiate a treaty with France, for which eleven months' service he received almost $20,000, a very large sum in that period. This money gave the Marshall brothers time to hang on to their 160,000 acres in Virginia. It always helps to know the right people, and early America was no exception to the rule.

A major change in capital investment patterns was the development of the West. By 1800 a million Americans had settled beyond the mountains. Before commercial use of the steamboat, the two-way passage between Pittsburgh and New Orleans on the Mississippi River took over four months. With the steamboat, up-river passage became easy and regular. In 1801 the gulf port's trade was valued at $3,649,000; in fifteen years it almost tripled.[14] Because of the expense of shipping downriver or over the mountains, Pittsburgh, and Lexington to a lesser extent, started to create their own industrial markets. In Pittsburgh, iron was the key and the city was soon dubbed "Iron City." Factories turned out nails, metal bars, and cast parts for machinery. The first rolling mill was established in 1811; in 1819 the refining technique known as puddling was introduced. The glass industry followed and "Pittsburgh Glass" became well-known throughout the country. What was even more remarkable, most of the capital invested in trans-montane industry came from local sources.[15]

Along the eastern seaboard, the capital shortage of the late eighteenth century did not affect agriculture, shipping, and manufacturing to the same extent as it did land speculation. With low tariffs and discriminatory tonnage duties, the ship owners and merchants of New England were making new fortunes. Jay's treaty, negotiated in 1794, adjusted the trade problems the Americans had with Great Britain and led to a three hundred percent increase in the value of American exports to the British Empire from 1795 to 1800.[16] Eli Whitney's invention of the cotton gin in 1793 permitted southern money to flow into cotton plantations as it had a century before into tobacco.

Exports of cotton jumped from six million pounds in 1796 to twenty million pounds in 1801.[17]

Yankee sailing ships began to appear in ports all over the world. From around 1794, trade with China and India developed. Ginseng and then furs were bought in the Pacific Northwest and sold at high prices in the Far East; then tea, silk, spices, and chinaware came back on the same ships. Consuls were designated in nineteen foreign ports.

Not only raw cotton but finished cotton goods began to be shipped overseas. In 1790, Samuel Slater left England after memorizing the details of the Arkwright power loom, and built cotton-spinning machinery for two Providence merchants. Cotton factories began to appear in southern New England, This led Rhode Island merchants to invest in textile-related activities like machine tools. In New Haven, Eli Whitney, whose cotton gin was pirated everywhere, turned out precisely tooled firearms whose parts were interchangeable. Hamilton's policy of protective tariffs—*i.e.,* protection to encourage domestic production while at the same time raising revenue for the new central government—proved successful. Powerful New England families like the Cabots, the Derbys, the Crowninshields, owned fleets of vessels that carried American grain, salt fish and beef, tobacco and cotton, iron and leather, and rum distilled from the West Indies to European ports and returned laden with manufactured goods from England and wines from France and Portugal. Up to five hundred sails at a time could be seen tied up at Boston's Long Wharf or anchored in the bay.[18]

The careers of Robert Morris and James Wilson are symbolic of the final frenzy of large-scale land speculation. In an important way the financial collapse of these men was the end of an epoch. Land plunging would, of course, thrive throughout American history. With the purchase of the Louisiana Territory, it would move west of the Mississippi River; and in the 1830s and 1840s the influence of these speculators would be a big factor in stirring up the Mexican secessions and wars, which ate almost one half of Mexico and absorbed it into the American digestive body. Also in the nineteenth century, speculators would turn in force to urban property, changing the basis of land sales from miles to acres to lots to square feet. But despite this activity, land speculation never again dominated American economic or political history to the same extent after the eighteenth century. With the growing industrialization of the country, plus the related mining, construction, and service trades, land speculation still remained a prince but it was no longer king.

32

The Strange Case of Robert Morris

"Mr. Morris . . . asked me if back lands could still be taken up. I told him, yes. He immediately proposed to me to join him in a speculation in lands, which, he thought that he, from his connections in Europe, could sell at one dollar per acre. I paused a minute. Said as our waste lands were totally unproductive, such a thing ought to be beneficial to the public as well as ourselves. . . ."

Journals of William Maclay, March 16, 1790
U.S. Senator from Pennsylvania

The father of Robert Morris was an English merchant sent to Maryland as the factor for a Liverpool firm. His son, born in England, was brought to America at the age of thirteen and placed with the mercantile house of the Willings at Philadelphia. In 1754 he and young Thomas Willing were taken into the firm as partners. Fifteen years later, Robert Morris married Mary White, daughter of Colonel Thomas White, whose brother was the first bishop of the Episcopal Church in Pennsylvania. This was an upper-class marriage on both sides. Morris's father had been killed at forty in a shipboard accident, leaving his son nearly $7,000 in cash plus real estate (minus some bequests to two sisters and his father's mistress). Morris's wife had inherited property, which her husband sold for $15,860. Robert Morris thus had an early start, for the sums involved were great at that time.

Morris was forty-one when the Revolution began. The house of Willing,

ROBERT MORRIS. Oil on canvas, by Charles Willson Peale (1782). Courtesy of the Independence National Historical Park Collection, Philadelphia, Pennsylvania.

Morris & Co., had varying fortunes before this event, prospering greatly during the French and Indian War but being troubled shortly before the outbreak of the Revolution.[1]

Morris was one of the four Pennsylvania delegates so opposed to American independence that he would not yield. Pennsylvania only voted to break with the British because he, with John Dickinson, agreed not to sit at the final ballot, thus permitting the other two opposing votes to be outvoted by the three in favor. War brought with it a boom in business. From 1775 to 1777 nearly a fourth of all foreign procurements were contracted through his firm.[2] By 1779, Morris was considered a very rich man, possibly the richest man in America. He later wrote that he had owned more ships than any other shipper. When in the spring of 1781 Morris was appointed superintendent of finance under Congress, in total charge of the war effort, all biographers agree that he made still more money. In fact, his personal credit was considered better than that of the government he represented.

There is no question that Robert Morris made a huge fortune during the Revolution by mixing public and private interest in ways considered immoral even for his own time. Yet, in the end, his financial genius was as indispensable on the economic front as was that of Washington's rock-solid character on the military front. Despite legitimate proofs of his conniving, the fact that George Washington, Benjamin Franklin, John Jay, Alexander Hamilton, Gouverneur Morris (no relation), John Hancock, John Paul Jones, General Nathanael Greene, and even James Madison (who sharply opposed his politics) expressed such deep admiration for Morris's efforts is evidence that he performed his duties brilliantly.

Morris's political influence was enormous after the war. He was one of the four delegates who nominated George Washington as the presiding officer of the Federal Convention, which created the U.S. Constitution. The Pennsylvania assembly in 1788 promptly chose Morris as one of the two U.S. senators to represent the state. Washington offered him the post of secretary of the treasury but Morris, anxious to enlarge his private fortune, declined and recommended that Alexander Hamilton be appointed instead.

Morris reached the peak of his influence when the seat of national power was moved from New York City to Philadelphia before the Capitol was built at Washington, D.C. Known as the "Great Man" both by friends and enemies, Forrest McDonald states, "The power he [Morris] held in the 1780's may be compared to that of the House of Morgan in the early twentieth century, which means that no one knows exactly how great it was. Probably J. P. Morgan would have had to add the secretaryship of

THE TWO MORRIS HOUSES IN HIGH, NOW MARKET, STREET, PHILADELPHIA. The house on the left was placed at the disposal of President Washington, while Mr. Morris and his family removed to the other mansion at the corner of Sixth Street. Originally in the Collections of the Historical Society of Pennsylvania. This illustration is from *Robert Morris, Patriot and Financier*, by Ellis P. Oberholtzer, New York, 1903.

the treasury and the control of Tammany Hall to match Morris' power."[3] It was at this time that Edmond Genêt, the agent of the French Convention who had been sent to bring America into an alliance with revolutionary France, was told by his advisers that he must place all financial contracts in the hands of Morris if he desired his mission to succeed.

In 1795 both houses of the Pennsylvania legislature assured Robert Morris that he would receive a unanimous vote for a second term as U.S. senator, but he announced his determination to retire. For Morris knew, even if his fellow citizens did not, how deeply he was mired in financial reverses. At that time he was three years from debtor's prison, from which the most brilliant political contacts could not save him. It was his megalomania, the refusal to recognize limits, that brought him down. His activities in land speculation, not unlike those of Washington, are often difficult to follow in precise detail because of quick turnover for a profit. They are also complex due to the many financial tricks used to move property through various shells.

The relation of Robert Morris to the founding of the national capital at Washington, D.C., is another episode in moral juggling. Morris had acquired 2,500 acres on the Delaware River opposite Trenton at a low price during the Revolution and tried to convince Congress to put the national capital nearby in order to enhance the value of his property. Ellis P. Oberholtzer, for whom Morris could do no wrong, writes: "He made an attempt to persuade Congress to fix the Federal capital upon these lands, but never pressed his suggestion. . . ."[4] The facts seem different. Earlier thoughts had focused on the cities of Trenton and Philadelphia, and it would seem that a site on the Delaware between Pennsylvania and New Jersey might be the favored location. In 1785, Morris was elected one of three commissioners under the resolution for building a Federal city on the Delaware River. In 1789 he proposed a location near his land and worked hard to defeat a motion to put it on the Susquehanna instead; when the motion was carried, Morris was chagrined and Senator Maclay, Morris's colleague, wrote in a private letter at the time: "He [Morris] mentions with apparent regret some rich lands in the Conestoga Manor which he had exchanged with John Musser for lands on the Delaware."[5]

Morris fought for his site but was defeated by an influence even greater than his own, that of the person for whom the capital city was named. After much logrolling, the southern Congressional delegation accepted federal assumption of state war debts and in return the northern delegates, many of whom speculated in this scrip, agreed to place the national capital near Georgetown on the Potomac River. Morris did not oppose this deal, which his friend Alexander Hamilton hammered out with Thomas Jefferson whereby northern speculators made fortunes in the depreciated scrip.[6] Since among the top security brokers in this business of scrip speculation was the firm of William Constable and Company, whose partners were Constable and Morris, joined by Gouverneur Morris after 1787,[7] we can surmise that the right hand made far more money than what the left hand lost.

At the start Robert Morris, whose main interest had been shipping, only dabbled in the various land companies set up by others. He had a small position in the Illinois and Wabash Company, and took a share in the Virginia Yazoo Company, the Patrick Henry speculation. Morris was also involved in the Tennessee Company, another of the Yazoo schemes. To get the site on which he was building his mansion in Philadelphia, Morris swapped 74,000 acres at the mouth of the Tennessee River.

These land deals, even including Washington, D.C., were in comparative terms small when measured against Morris's plunge into western New York land. On August 10, 1790, he bought 952,000 acres from Oliver Phelps and Nathaniel Gorham in the name of the New York Genesee Land Company, payment for which was to be made over two years, His partners, or creditors to be more precise, were Samuel Ogden, with an interest in 300,000 acres, Gouverneur Morris with 250,000 acres, Richard Soderstrom[8] with 100,000 acres, and William Constable with 50,000 acres.[9] All these men, except Soderstrom, were among the top land plungers of the time. Morris also gave Alexander Hamilton an interest in 100,000 acres to secure Hamilton's borrowing of more than $80,000 from a third party.

Morris had appointed as his London agent Benjamin Franklin's grandson, William Temple Franklin, who approached Sir William Pulteney, England's most prominent speculator. Pulteney set up an association which in February 1791 bought the entire acreage at a price that netted Morris a profit of $216,128, reduced somewhat by the fact that, already deeply in debt, he accepted less money to accelerate the payment schedule.

In December 1790, Morris, with Phelps and Gorham as his partners, bought a tract of about four million acres of land in northwest New York. Sensing that the other two men were getting cold feet, Morris arranged an assignment of the total acreage to himself, paying approximately $366,333 for the massive block, which was in five separate tracts.

Holland and England were at that time the leading centers for speculative capital. When Morris approached Dutch bankers, several showed interest, and in December of 1792 he sold two of the five tracts, together about a million acres, on a complicated formula whose major payment was $330,000. Morris had given his son Robert Morris, Jr., who was working for him in Amsterdam as well, an assignment of two of the remaining tracts. Young Morris sold these two in a very complex transaction which amounted to a sale of another 1.8 million acres for $500,000.[10] The Dutch bankers in 1796 put together their various purchases—including another 500,000 acres from James Wilson—and formed the Holland Land Company ("Hollandshe Land") whose speckled history later added bizarre touches to life in upper New York during the first half of the nineteenth century.[11]

To summarize, Morris in his Dutch dealings sold four out of his five tracts for more than $830,000, bought for $366,333, thus netting him $463,667 or more than double his money: "his money" being understood as a very small sum because the greatest part was borrowed from others. Since Morris had purchased 4 million acres and sold 2.8 million, he still retained, 1.2 million acres or over twenty-five percent of the land. And to cap his joy, the wheeler-dealer succeeded in unloading this last large chunk of land to other Dutch bankers shortly thereafter. In less than five years Robert Morris had bought and sold all of New York west of Seneca Lake, one-sixth of the entire state.[12]

The great success of this vast project was perhaps the worst thing for Morris because, as is often the case when a gambler hits big early, it left him convinced he was omniscient. Indeed, when bankrupt later, he regretted not holding on to part of this land and marketing it retail over the years rather than leaping into new projects.

In 1793, Robert Morris began to operate with two partners in most of his speculative schemes. One was John Nicholson, a younger clone. The two became inseparable and stayed fast friends up to and including debtor's prison, where Nicholson died in the year 1800 at the age of forty. Out of nowhere the young Nicholson was appointed comptroller-general of Pennsylvania in 1782 and occupied the post for years. He was impeached in 1789 on charges of dishonesty but not convicted. Responsible for the state's disposal of military land warrants, he became familiar with the best sites and bought them for himself.[13] Speculating to the hilt, he was to become in a decade the largest landowner in Pennsylvania, acquiring title to almost four million acres. Overextended, he turned to Robert Morris for help.

The other partner who became at the end a bitter enemy of both Morris and Nicholson, was James Greenleaf, from a top New England family and related to the poet John Greenleaf Whittier. During the Revolution, Greenleaf made a great deal of money in shipping and, more important for Morris, was on intimate business terms with Dutch bankers. As noted before, it was Greenleaf who in 1795 would foist the sale in the northern commercial centers of the largest block of Georgia Mississippi Company (Yazoo) stock. Greenleaf was a picaresque charmer who married a baroness in Europe and left her with two children; his second marriage, to Ann Penn Allen of the Penn family, put him in the highest American society. His father-in-law was William Allen, former chief justice of Pennsylvania; one brother-in-law was William Tilghman, a Washington aide during the Revolution and then chief justice after William Allen; while another brother-in-law was Henry W. Livingston of the Livingston dynasty. Greenleaf was also a financial partner with Tobias Lear, the personal secretary of George Washington.

The three men participated jointly in land deals as Morris, Nicholson, and Greenleaf. It was Greenleaf who turned Morris's interest toward speculation in the new federal district. Fresh from his success in selling off the vast acreage of the New York Genesee Land Company, Morris was itching for new worlds to conquer. One year after George Washington laid the cornerstone for the Capitol, in 1793, Morris and Greenleaf, joined shortly after by Nicholson, bought six thousand lots in what is now Washington, D.C., averaging over 5,000 square feet each. The partners then sold half of these lots almost immediately to other speculators at some three hundred percent profit.[14] It may be noted that the entire original package was bought from the government, such sales being assigned only as President Washington, Morris's good friend and house guest in Philadelphia, should approve.

Fired by their initial success, the three partners continued to buy, from private owners as well as the government. Within a short time, each holding equal shares, Greenleaf, Nicholson, and Morris owned 7,234 lots. Then, in 1795, Morris and Nicholson bought out Greenleaf.[15]

At this point the financial juggling began to overwhelm the three men. The original purchase contract stated that twenty brick houses, two stories high and covering 1,200 square feet each, should be built each year. But the partners were only interested in turning over the lots at a profit, relying on their political contacts to protect them from any loss. They forgot that Robert Morris in his curt march up had not only made great Federalist friends but also powerful enemies in the Jefferson camp. The associates were forced to fulfill their contract and build the houses, most of which did not sell and some of which were left incomplete.[16] At the same time, the European wars began and the Dutch bankers stopped all loans. President Washington tried to rescue his friends, as well as protect his own investment in federal district real estate. He was unsuccessful at raising money in London through his personal secretary, Tobias Lear, himself enmeshed with Greenleaf.[17]

The recourse taken by the partners was to assign and reassign the properties. In 1797, Morris and Nicholson were forced to convey their interest to the trustees of Greenleaf[18] to secure an obligation amounting to over

$700,000. Greenleaf also conveyed to the same trustees other property whose worth was estimated at around $500,000. This property in turn was to be conveyed to Morris and Nicholson upon the settlement of their obligation. Thereupon Morris and Nicholson formed a new company having 300,000 shares, being held in equal parts. Out of his half Morris transferred to various persons over 50,000 shares as security for other debts. Though rumor had it that Morris, Nicholson, and Greenleaf had ten million dollars worth of land among them, their notes began to circulate at fifteen cents on the dollar. The pack of greasy cards was slipping through their fingers.

This was only part of the paper castle that Robert Morris had built, for in this same period he was working on other grandiose land deals, most often with the same partners. In 1794, Morris and Nicholson organized the Asylum Company, the name coming from the fact that it was created to sell land to rich aristocrats fleeing the French Revolution. The so-called assets were a million acres in Pennsylvania, western wilderness land already mortgaged to the limit and which Nicholson could not move. The two men failed to sell the shares and the few subscribers were forced to buy in the other shares snd reorganize. It took more than twenty years (until 1819) before a secure footing permitted the normal sale of land.

In 1795, Morris, Nicholson, and Greenleaf formed the North American Land Company, called the largest land trust ever put together in America outside of railroad grants following the Civil War.[19] The three men deeded to the company some six million acres, including 647,046 acres in Pennsylvania (of which 250,000 were mainly situated near the present site of Pittsburgh, underlaid by heavy undiscovered coal deposits); 932,621 acres in Virginia; 717,249 acres in North Carolina; 957,238 acres in South Carolina; 431,043 acres in Kentucky; and 2,314,796 acres in Georgia (the "Pine Barrens"), the last enormous parcel coming in part from the fraudulent Georgia Company of Yazoo fame.[20]

The North America Land Company was a shaky device to get rid of all the vast tracts picked up on notes endorsed or acquired through depreciated scrip. "The only purpose served by this enterprise in which Morris reposed so much faith was the creation of a new class of certificates with an appearance of value, which he could send to insistent creditors, and thus postpone his inevitable collapse."[21] Robert Goodloe Harper, so prominent in Yazoo affairs, was involved and prepared the prospectus for the company, stuffing it with glowing descriptions of his native southland. The secretary was James Marshall, a younger brother of Chief Justice Marshall, who had recently married Morris's eldest daughter. The company was capitalized at three million dollars (fifty cents an acre) and the title was vested in trustees to evade personal liability. The next step was to publish a book that, including Harper's eulogies, not only lauded the venture but claimed that land in America had doubled in value during the previous six years.

This was a speculation in which George Washington refused to invest, correctly saying it was too ambitious. In fact, he urged his old friend Robert Morris not to embark on the project.[22] Even earlier, Gouverneur Morris wrote that he was "sick at heart" at Morris's excessive speculations and urged him "to wind up some concerns *even with a loss.*"[23] And Joseph Fauchet, France's minister to the United States, who had replaced the incredible Edmond Genêt, sent letters to Paris warning Frenchmen not to invest. Morris's feeble financial state was public knowledge.

In May of 1796, Morris and Nicholson, at loggerheads with Greenleaf, bought out the latter's one-third share in the North America Land Company for $1,150,000,[24] payable in drafts that were almost worthless in a very short time. Some were used as collateral at ten cents on the dollar, and a court judgment allowed their delivery at less than four cents on the dollar in 1797. The complicated sleights-of-hand involved in the floating of this company, and the juggling among the partners, were so intricate that legal action in matters concerning the North America Land Company went on until 1871, with the final auditor's report being issued in 1880, almost a century after the original company had been set up.

By late 1797 the walls started to crumble. It was now apparent even to the most patient creditor that the Morris barrel was dry. His partner Thomas Willing, along with Alexander Hamilton, Benjamin Harrison, Bishop White (his wife's brother), Gouverneur Morris, and John Jay were among the distinguished list of those owed large sums. Thomas Fitzsimons, a director of the Bank of North America, claimed to be ruined.[25] By supreme irony the legal action was begun by three banks for all of which Robert Morris had been a co-founder. The man who had owned more ships and more land than any other American,[26] who had steered the finances of the Revolution and dictated the policies of the Federalist party, was cornered like a fox by hounds. Holed up in his house for over a year with sheriffs tenting on the grounds, Morris tried to evade jail by assigning his property—furniture, rugs, tapestries, landscape shrubbery and at the end his silver dinner service—to the baying creditors. In February 1798, his health affected by the bitter cold, Robert Morris's spirit finally cracked and he let enter a bailiff. He spent the next three and a half years in prison. A broken old man, Morris died in his seventy-third year, owing the United States almost $100,000 and sighing like King Solomon in Ecclesiastes that all is vanity. More to the point is the fable of the Greedy Dog who in his anxiety to attend two wedding breakfasts on the same day missed both.

33

James Wilson: A Morality Tale

"Whilst that for which all virtue now is sold,
And almost every vice—almighty gold."

Ben Jonson, *Epistle to Elizabeth, Countess of Rutland*

James Wilson, a poor Scotsman, came to the colonies in 1765 at the age of twenty-three and learned the uses of land during his very first year. Unable to pay to study his chosen field of law under John Dickinson in Philadelphia, the answer to his problem came through a generous cousin named Reverend Mr. Annan. This cleric's spiritual duties had not prevented amassing the goods of this world by speculation in land on the side. The reverend sold Wilson a farm for £500, taking a note in return. Wilson then sold the farm to Dickinson to pay his fee, with enough left over to live on for the duration of his studies.

After his year with Dickinson, the ambitious young man settled in Reading, some fifty miles northwest of Philadelphia. Still a frontier town, Reading's thousand people were buttressed by thirty-one taverns. Wilson became a protégé of Nicholas Wain, one of the three lawyers who controlled most of the Reading practice. Of quick intelligence and with a sprouting legal career, Wilson's next leap forward occurred in 1771 through the time-honored method of a rich marriage. Rachel Bird, sister of Mark Bird and step-daughter of Colonel John Patton, belonged to the high Pennsylvania burgher class. William Bird, her deceased father, had been the great iron-

348

JAMES WILSON, 1742–1798, REVOLUTIONARY STATESMAN. Sepia watercolor on artist board, by James Barton Longacre (1825). Courtesy of the National Portrait Gallery, Smithsonian Institution.

master of Birdsboro, on the Schuykill River. Colonel Patton, who had married Bird's widow, shared with the family members other business interests also started by Rachel's father. Allied to the Bird family was George Ross of Lancaster, whose sister Mary was married to Mark Bird.

Upon marrying Rachel Bird, the energetic James Wilson immediately moved into the top echelon of western Pennsylvania society. In his biography of Wilson, Page Smith makes an interesting observation about such lawyers: "In every frontier community, the most essential task was to impose form on the chaotic elements that swirled around and through it. The land problem—who owned what acres—was simply another manifestation, if perhaps the most dramatic, of the problem of order. Law was form and in the several decades preceding the American Revolution, the founders and first citizens of frontier communities almost invariably became lawyers, because by so doing they were able to bring the whole awesome weight of English law to bear on the intractable and anarchical forces of the frontier. . . . The frontier lawyer, often a farmer himself, was the principal instrument of a ruling class, charged with superintending the orderly digesting of hundreds of thousands of new acres in the west."[1] Put more bluntly, the lawyer made legal the expropriated Indian lands.

Wilson was as capable as he was now well connected. In just the first year of his marriage, Robert Morris and Thomas Willing of Philadelphia chose him as their attorney in an important land case: this was the first contact between Morris and Wilson, one that would flourish. In 1773, Wilson became involved in the Pennsylvania-Virginia dispute over western lands, the training ground of many of the colonial speculators, Westmoreland County was created by Pennsylvania to counter Virginia's West Augusta County in the disputed area beyond Maryland's western boundary. Wilson acted as counsel for the officials of the new Pennsylvania county.

Wilson's rise was in rhythm with the growing pace of independence. In the commercial colonies the fight against the British was dominated by upper-class lawyers whose economic opinions were conservative. This was perhaps even more true in Pennsylvania than elsewhere because the hatred of the Penn proprietors added fuel to the fire; or more properly, the lawyers wanted to eat the fruits of power rather than merely crate them for overlords. Wilson was elected a delegate from Carlisle to attend a convention at Philadelphia to protest British measures. All but one of the Carlisle representatives, to which town he had moved, were lawyers and members of the town elite. Delegates from his former town of Reading included Mark Bird and Colonel Patton. The revolutionary Pennsylvania delegates at this early stage were in some respects a family club of rich colonial burghers opposed to a family club of rich British aristocrats.

Gifted in the baroque use of words passing as oratory at that time, James Wilson was elected a Pennsylvania delegate to the 1775 Second Continental Congress. He immediately gravitated to western affairs, the smell of land being a powerful magnet, and was appointed to the Committee on Indian Affairs. The tone of this committee may be judged by his fellow members, which included Philip Schuyler and Philip Livingston, both holding great fiefs in New York, and Patrick Henry of Virginia, then replaced by Dr. Thomas Walker. In 1775 and 1776, Wilson was the most active delegate in tying relations between Congress and the border tribes. It is at this time that he began speculating in shares of the land companies.

Pennsylvania, more than most other states, turned left during the early years of the Revolution. James Wilson, viewed as too moderate, was not reelected to Congress in 1777. This marked a turning point for him. Political office seemed closed because of the hostility of the radicals, but while in Congress, he made friends with many of the most wealthy and influential men in the colonies. Wilson then turned to business ventures and land speculation. Many of these involved his friend Robert Morris, shortly to be made superintendent of finance. He also built up a large practice at the bar, becoming known for his defense of Tories and Quakers accused of pro-British or neutral views. His clients included the ranking merchants and conservatives, including the Penns. His stance was so obvious that in October 1779 a faction of the Philadelphia militia tried without success to burn down his house with him in it.[2]

Reference has already been made to the United Illinois and Wabash land companies, in which Robert Morris, Silas Deane, and James Wilson had purchased shares during the war. George Ross, Wilson's kinsman by marriage, was made president after the two pre-revolutionary land ventures had merged. When Ross died in 1780, Wilson took over the post.

The United Illinois and Wabash claim was to 60 million acres. There were eighty-four shares in the reorganized company; thus each share represented more than 700,000 acres of land. Ten of these shares were set aside "for purposes most conducive to general interest,"[3] as Wilson wrote in a private letter; that is, for corruption of congressmen. This was standard practice, and it will be recalled that the Indiana Company did exactly the same thing. Wilson had bought one share and received a half share for his services as the company lawyer, thus having a claim to over one million acres of fertile Illinois land, if validated by Congress. In his legal capacity, Wilson also voted proxies covering a share held by Maryland interests and another share from the estate of George Ross. These three and a half shares, aside from the Franks and Gratz brothers, were the single largest block controlled by one individual. It becomes obvious, therefore, why

Wilson campaigned so hard while in Congress against Virginia taking the western lands.

The United Illinois and Wabash speculation was one among many. With William Bingham (who had made a fortune in the West Indies while acting both as an agent for Robert Morris and for Congress during the Revolution), his brother-in-law Mark Bird, and a wealthy New Jersey speculator by the name of Robert Hooper, James Wilson started the Canaan Company in 1783. Some 100,000 acres were purchased on New York's Susquehanna River, the sole memory of this deal being the city of Binghamton, named for William Bingham.

Wilson and Hooper also plunged into Pennsylvania military warrants. The two men together, sometimes Wilson alone, bought claims for several hundred thousand acres. A small down payment was the first step. This authorized the holder to make a survey. After the survey, the remainder of the payment was deposited in the land office and a clear title was issued. Such a system was open both to corruption and excessive speculation, as has already been shown in the case of John Nicholson, for the surveyors and the land personnel were bought and sold like the land. Wilson's buoyant optimism and the steady rise in land values induced him to buy more and more warrants and begin surveys on larger tracts of land than he could afford.

The same warrant system was used in other states and Wilson, again on the model of Robert Morris, began to speculate in many areas. He bought warrants for 56,000 acres in Virginia. In a syndicate with Michael and Bernard Gratz, Robert Morris, Levi Hollingsworth, Charles Willing, and Dorsey Pentecost, he purchased 321,000 acres south of the Ohio River, a matter already pointed out in our discussion of the land deals in Kentucky. Since the interests of Pennsylvania and Virginia speculators clashed violently during this period, both in and out of Congress, the warrants obtained in Virginia's western lands by Pennsylvanians seem difficult to understand, but "The cooperation of John Harvie, who was in charge of the Virginia land office, was of material aid to the partners in securing these choice western acres."[4] We already are aware of the form of this cooperation. Dorsey Pentecost was also of great help. An official in Virginia's West Augusta County during the clash between the two states, Pentecost knew the right people on the other side and was thus brought into the Pennsylvania combine.

The years from 1781 to 1783 saw a reaction against the radicals in Pennsylvania, and Wilson was reelected to Congress on January 2, 1783. During this same period, George Washington asked Wilson to take his nephew Bushrod Washington into his office as a law clerk. The Federalist net of family and friendships was beginning to take hold. On December 30, 1786, Wilson was selected by Pennsylvania as one of the state delegates to frame a new instrument of government, which became the Constitution.

Immediately after the peace treaty with England in 1783, James Wilson requested that a committee be set up in Congress to report on measures to be taken with respect to the western lands ceded to the Americans. It was apparent that the first real order of business for him was to ensure his title to the land of the United Illinois and Wabash Companies. Other congressmen pointed out that there was more important work at hand. Wilson persisted to the point that he was severely called to order and the delegates turned to more pressing matters.

A week before Washington's inaugural, Wilson, never a blushing violet, asked for the position of chief justice of the newly formed Supreme Court. He was appointed an associate judge, the main post going to John Jay. General opinion already linked him too closely to land speculation with an over-heavy debt structure and Washington may have felt that giving him the top position would not be wise.

It is astounding that Wilson did not go bankrupt earlier. There is no careful record of his inexorable down-spin as there was in the case of Robert Morris, but there are hints. In 1791, pinched for funds, Wilson approached the Bank of North America for a new loan to cover the purchase of 133,000 acres. Though the directors were personal friends and political allies, his mountain of debt led to refusal. Somehow Wilson found the money. It may be that William Bingham lent it to him on the security of their joint holdings. Then in March 1792, William Duer of Scioto Company fame, overextended in land and stock speculation, defaulted on the stupendous sum (for that time) of over two million dollars. Panic hit Philadelphia and New York, and in the widespread collapse Walter Livingston of the Livingston clan went bankrupt. Real estate in Pennsylvania dropped to one-third its former value. Wilson found some relief by selling a half million acres of western Pennsylvania lands to the Holland Land Company, which the Dutch bankers picked up at about the same time they bought the enormous New York tract from Robert Morris. Since Wilson was Morris's lawyer and occasional partner, we can presume a joint participation.[5] Creditors also hesitated to foreclose dormant mortgages or bring action against a U.S. Supreme Court judge whose position was so high in the dominant Federalist party.

In 1793 a second crisis shook the financial markets and again his friend and associate William Bingham stepped in with a loan to forestall the loss of 60,000 acres. When John Jay resigned as chief justice after being elected governor of New York State, Washington again passed over Wilson. As

Page Smith writes, "The mere fact of speculations could not have alarmed the President, who was himself a speculator, but the colossal scale of Wilson's undertakings, his precarious financial position, his constant borrowings, the kind of desperate recklessness which marked his ventures—all these must have been known to Washington."[6]

The odd part is that James Wilson, almost daily on the edge of ruin, still expanded his paper empire. The popular impression that he had vast wealth helped to get him money when there was any to be had, though often at usurious rates of interest. He bought from "Light Horse" Harry Lee and William Pierce a package of southern lands, borrowing $80,000 from a wealthy Baltimore merchant. He became involved with Patrick Henry in several ventures and in a letter dated July 29, 1795, Henry offered Wilson "the greatest part of the Carolina land with all that I sold you in Virginia," adding that in a few weeks "I shall be ready with the residue in Carolina."[7] Less than a month later he bought a million acres of Georgia Company (Yazoo) land from James Greenleaf, and in this case sold the acreage in a very short time. Indeed, Wilson was the third largest holder of stock in all the Yazoo companies; and as has been discussed in chapter 24 on these land frauds, Wilson with Robert Morris, James Greenleaf, and Oliver Phelps were the northern hand of the Georgia Company, which had received the biggest block of Yazoo land. In the same period, Wilson agreed to buy several large tracts near the Dismal Swamp in Virginia, where Washington had done so well. Hoping that European investors would solve his many problems, Wilson wrote at this time to England, having been turned down already in Holland, listing 450,000 acres in eight counties of Pennsylvania for sale.[8] As though in a delirium of land lust, it would seem that Wilson was acting out the sombre lines of the Greek tragedian Euripedes: "Those whom the gods wish to destroy they first drive mad."

The bumpy last plunge of the financial collapse, which started in 1792, was triggered by a credit call on the part of the Bank of England in 1796. American banks and investors in turn called their loans. Wilson was frantic for cash. The money crisis grew during the summer of that year: America's first great depression, in part created by wild land speculation, had begun.

James Wilson attended the opening of the Supreme Court in August, sick for the first time in his life. Blessed with a stout constitution, his mind began to give way before his body. When the Court adjourned, he took to the Southern Circuit, where he ran the risk of arrest by creditors while sitting court. Returning to Philadelphia, he found that Morris, Nicholson, and Greenleaf were sinking into the same morass. After the 1797 spring circuit he skipped to Bethlehem, Pennsylvania, and then to Burlington, New Jersey, where a creditor finally served him. A friend put up three hundred dollars to satisfy the judgment and Wilson fled south, where he hid in a small town in North Carolina. Despite pleas from his friends, Wilson, steadfastly hoping for a miracle, refused to dismember his vast land holdings. Addle-brained under the crushing weight of his debts, he even disdained conveying his property to trustees in order to escape personal judgment. He wrote in a letter of May 24, 1798, "the season is approaching when such exertions [discharging his debt] may be crowned with the most abundant success.[9]

Unkempt, listless, soaked in alcohol, James Wilson—considered by many the second most astute financier in the United States as well as the most important man (after Madison), in framing the U.S. Constitution— was forced to lodge in dreary rooms above a tavern when he was struck by malaria early in June 1798. Then came a stroke, during which he raved of bad debts and bankruptcy, clinging to life as he had clung to his lands, moaning in delirious fear of jail. On August 21, 1798, at the age of fifty-six, James Wilson left his flesh, a fugitive from creditors and absent over a year as associate judge of the Supreme Court of the United States. The man who but for his mania of land speculation would have been chief justice of the highest tribunal of our land, got a curt obituary from an eminent though unsympathetic historian: "James Wilson died . . . an insolvent debtor, a victim of alcohol, disease and unwise investments in real estate."[10]

The auction of the personal belongings of the dead man, held to cover the cost of closing the estate, brought a grand total of less than five hundred dollars.

34

Summary

"The real test of the teachers and writers of history . . . is when they contend against no human antagonist, but the errors that creep in through gradually unnoted changes in language, in manners, in circumstances, in habits of thought, errors that are assisted by man's enormous capacity to believe whatever he finds it pleasant or convenient to believe."

Gerald W. Johnson, *American Heroes and Hero-Worship*

The bedrock on which rests early American history is the use of land to gain wealth and reach high political office. This thesis has been developed in separate chapters and can be summarized.

The Revolution could never have been won without incentive payments given to the soldiers in military scrip for claims on western land. As war weariness grew, especially after 1779, the use of such scrip was a main reason soldiers reenlisted. This was even more true for officers, for whom the acreage received was much greater. One result of this device to prop up lagging patriotism was the need to kill off the Indians on the land in order to make valid the scrip. Only through a national army could the Indians be crushed, and the end result was a powerful push toward creating the U.S. Constitution.

As the soldiers received land bonuses in the hundreds of acres and the officers in the thousands, so the conquering heroes like Generals Greene, Wayne, and Clark received from the grateful South western land and plantations in the tens of thousands of acres. The British had released a large number of slaves during the war and others had taken the opportunity to flee to Spanish and Indian country. These generals, some of whom were from the North and had been foes of slavery, now needed forced labor to work their plantations. Their influence was added to the voice of southern planters not only to continue the slave system that many southerners already thought archaic, but also to insist on the continued import of new slaves from overseas, at least (as finally decided in the Constitution) until 1808. The "peculiar institution" then moved west with the southern speculators and a problem that might have been solved in the eighteenth century became the Pandora's box of the nineteenth century with the rise of a cotton economy.

Related to these developments was the booming discount market in military scrip. Most soldiers, anxious to return home and pick up the pieces of their former lives, were willing to sell their warrants at a great discount when hard times replaced the artificial boom during the war period. The Duke La Rochefoucauld-Liancourt, a French nobleman who travelled in the United States shortly after the Revolution, quotes examples where soldiers sold their military warrants to get any cash they could. The same scrip was resold by speculators between three and five years later for prices from four to twenty-five times the original purchase price. The great market was Philadelphia, where the merchant leaders of what became the Federalist party bought large blocks of this scrip at discount. They also reactivated the dormant land companies from the colonial period and pressed claims for similar great tracts of land.

The old colonial plantation and patroon elite that backed the Revolution did not lag behind. Their specialty was to use cheap state paper money (which was mandated legal by the same leaders who used it for speculation) to buy up the enormous Loyalist properties that had been confiscated and thrown on the market. Estates such as those of Sir John Wentworth, royal governor of New Hampshire, the Philipse and DeLancey families of New York, Sir John Johnson (heir to Sir William Johnson, Bart) in the Mohawk Valley of the same state, as well as Sir James Wright of Georgia, were not so much parcelled out as gobbled up in large pieces by their erstwhile friends and neighbors who had picked the winning side in the conflict.[1] During the last years of the Revolution and the decade following, these same men and their allies controlled the state land office sales, especially in the areas west of Virginia and North Carolina, which became the states of Kentucky and Tennessee. Working directly with the land office personnel and the county surveyors, they preempted the best western lands. Indeed, one can state that in Virginia and North Carolina there was almost no difference between the legislative and executive state leaders and the western land speculators. The struggle between the revived pre-Revolutionary land companies that were dominated by the more northern merchants and the speculators of the southern states ended in a temporary victory for the southerners, dignified in history by the adoption of the Articles of Confederation. But when hard times after the War of Independence brought the overextended speculative planter class to the point of bankruptcy, syndicates of northern merchants stepped in to join with or replace the grandees of the South. In the Northwest Territory, joint stock companies set up by men from New England and the middle states bought from Congress great tracts on which payment was made mainly in discounted military warrants and public securities. In some cases, through influence of key congressmen who also were shareholders, the small percentage of cash to discounted paper was reduced even further when payments were due.

The universal greed to acquire western land more strongly motivated many men, including those in very high places, than did the question of whether the territory between the Alleghenies and the Mississippi would be American or Spanish. The historical evidence clearly proves that Generals Wilkinson and Clark, as well as John Sevier of Tennessee, actively schemed with the Spanish to subvert the United States for personal gain. Stained with the same activity but to a lesser degree are Colonel George Morgan and William Blount. In Vermont the Allen clan walked the narrow line between neutrality and treason for years, playing the British against the leaders of Congress in order to make legal their land claims.

The load of discounted paper in the form of military warrants and public securities was a lead weight on an impotent Confederation, deprived of the right to tax and levy duties, with each of the states moving in separate directions to further its own special interests. The long western frontier was also in constant tension due to Indian discontent and the schemes of the Spanish and the British. Hardheaded leaders then realized that the old rivalries between Virginia planters and Pennsylvania merchants, between southern agrarian interests and northern shippers and manufacturers, were blocking the growth of a nationwide capital market. This national outlook led to the calling of a convention to create a new Constitution in order to replace the toothless Articles of Confederation. The creation and ratification of this Constitution has been fully discussed. Among the first effective acts of the new national government was the funding at full value of the public securities bought by speculators at discounts, an act that not only put fortunes into the pockets of the most prominent speculators but also made wealthy men of congressmen who already owned or acquired the discounted paper in forethought of their own vote. Somewhat later came the famous Supreme Court decision by which a contract was declared valid despite its fraudulent basis, thus assuring the Yazoo land speculators profits equalling in percentage if not in total dollar value those gained by the holders of discounted public paper. The confidence gained by the speculating class was so pronounced that the military scrip bought at great discount then started to rise toward par.

An objective observer might conclude that the new American system was to a large extent propped up by political devices that had been organized by the rich and well-connected to control the different branches of government so that what seemed like checks and balances was in effect a narrow corset of monied privilege at times trussed by corruption. That most of the great land speculators overextended themselves and went broke in the long panic that set in at the end of the eighteenth century is of less importance than the fact that the pre-Revolutionary colonial system, which openly operated for the benefit of the British aristocracy and its hirelings, had been recast to a significant extent, though in modified form, for the benefit of the post-colonial American upper class.[2] The structure set up in this crucial period—from the Revolution to the election of Thomas Jefferson as president—became a prototype for government in the emergent republic, whose techniques still remain with us in one distorted shape or another. Furthermore, the seeds sown by the Declaration of Independence, which originally had printed in invisible ink on the top "For Male Protestant Whites" and on the bottom "For Property Holders," were long inert.

It would take a good many decades before the real meaning of the French Revolution, as distinct from mouthed slogans, would swim the Atlantic Ocean and perk in the wits of Americans. Tom Paine may have written *The Rights of Man,* but the American Revolution was probably better summed up for many southern aristocrats in a single indignant sentence written by George Mason to Patrick Henry on May 6, 1783: "If we are to pay the debts due the British merchants, what have we been fighting for all this while."[3] The shrewd Swiss-American Albert Gallatin, the financial brains of the Jefferson administration and a western land speculator himself, knew his adopted country and its people very well when, during the 1796 debates on public land, he declared: "If the cause of the happiness of this country was examined into, it would be found to arise as much from the great plenty of land in proportion to the inhabitants, which their citizens enjoyed, as from the wisdom of their political institutions."[4]

Notes

(Except where otherwise indicated by full citation, all notes refer to works listed in the Selected Bibliography.)

PART ONE: THE FORMATION OF THE COLONIES

Chapter 1. The Period of Exploration

1. In the twentieth century a new school of thought claims that inclosure has been exaggerated as a factor in English history. This is best exemplified by Mildred Campbell's study *The English Yeoman Under Elizabeth and the Early Stuarts.* However, Campbell admits that the most conservative estimate held an acre of inclosed land was worth one and a half acres uninclosed; and "This being true and the tenor of the age what it was, it was inevitable that inclosing would continue" (pp. 86 and 87). The author even quotes a ballad from the time of James I: "There be many rich men, Both Yeoman and Gentry, who for theire owne private gaine, Hurt a whole country."

2. King, 52.

3. Rogers, 57.

4. The writer does not deny the religious and political convulsions woven into these economic factors. This study, however, is concerned with the influence of land on shaping the colonial period in the settlement of the North American continent.

5. "John Cabot's Discovery of North America," *American Historical Documents, 1000–1904,* The Harvard Classics, Vol. 43, New York, 1910, 48–50.

6. Hayes, *Voyages and Travels, Ancient and Modern.* The Harvard Classics, Vol. 33, New York, 1910, pp. 271 and 276.

7. "First Charter of Virginia (1606)," The Harvard Classics, Vol. 43, New York, 1910, pp. 52 and 60. This relic of the feudal period was a legal phrase meaning that the "tenant"

had to perform certain services for the "lord." At this period the services were nominal, such as giving a beaver skin.

8. Drake, The Harvard Classics, Vol. 33, New York, 1910, 143.

9. Raleigh, The Harvard Classics, Vol. 33, New York, 1910, 39 and 393.

10. Christopher Columbus is an excellent example: in the fifteen years from 1492 to 1507, he reduced the Indians of Hispaniola from over a million to some sixty thousand persons, through a policy of forced labor and depredation (as well as white man's diseases). This is the minimum figure for the original population: Coe (p. 21) and Morgan ([1975], p. 7), place the original population figure much higher.

11. Except, of course, for such groups as the Albigenses and Hussites, against whom the Church launched successful crusades.

Chapter 2: Sacking Indian Lands

1. The examples quoted below are from Axtell (1985), 219–20; Jennings (1975), 23–31; Lamar, 190–91; and Sheehan (1980), 180. For Puritan apologetics denying both of these figures and the views expressed, see Vaughan.

2. Jennings (1975), 24, 28–31.

3. Axtell (1985), 220.

4. Leon-Portilla, 92–93. The Maya of Guatemala from the year 1520 have a similar record. See The Annals of the Cakchiquels, Norman, Okla., 1953, 115–16.

5. This was involuntary bacterial genocide. It was Venice that invented germ warfare. In 1649 she sent a physician with a flask containing buboes to spread bubonic plague in the Turkish army at Crete.

6. Axtell (1985), 135.

7. Ibid., 133.

8. Washburn (1971), 36. Also see Driver (p. 480) for a similar attitude held by the Puritans.

9. Morgan (1975), 100; Washburn, (1971), 37.

10. Morgan (1975), 130.

11. Billington and Ridge, 147. Bouquet sent along Amherst's request to Captain Ecuyer, who summoned Delaware chiefs to a parley and presented to them, as "tokens of his personal esteem," infected blankets from Fort Pitt's hospital. An epidemic broke out among the Delawares after this event. See Jennimgs (1988), 447. The original proposal to use dogs came from the Reverend Solomon Stoddard of Northampton, Massachusetts, in 1703, for the Indians "act like wolves and are to be dealt with as wolves." See Turner (1962), 45.

12. In Johnson v. M'Intosh, Chief Justice Marshall, speaking for the court, reiterated an Old World belief that "the bestowing of civilization and Christianity upon the imhabitants of the New World itself constituted ample compensation for the denial of sovereignty to its original inhabitants" (Sutton, 72). This case occurred in 1823.

13. Driver, 278. Also Sutton, 6; Van Every, 10.

14. Axtell (1985), 137.

15. Ibid., 155.

16. Egleston, 8. Thereafter, the General Court controlled the granting of townships. This occurred in Massachusetts Bay Colony in 1637, in 1639 in Connecticut, and in 1644 in Rhode Island. See Barck and Lefler, 325.

17. Egleston, 10.

18. Harris, 176–77.

Chapter 3: America as a Land Speculation

1. It is difficult, for lack of exact records and certain corruption involved, to form a clear direct chain between the London and Plymouth financial groups, or of the successive changes occurring whereby the group called the Plymouth Company reorganized, with new elements, to become the New England Company and then, in 1629, the Massachusetts Bay Company. The territory desired for settlement had already been granted to the Council of New England, itself a corporate successor to the Plymouth Company, and it would seem that the Earl of Warwick, a Puritan sympathizer, operated with other powerful friends "with great cost, favor of personages of note, and much labor"—i.e., bribing where necessary — to receive the requisite charter in order to settle Massachusetts Bay. The personal enmity between the Earl of Warwick and Sir Ferdinand Gorges, strongly of the Anglican persuasion, also led to much infighting on the highest levels. Apparently the wealthy investors originally forming the Plymouth Company split into factions, partly caused by strife between Puritans and the Church of England, and went different corporate ways.

2. That is, separated from the Church of England. They were considered the communists of their time.

3. Woodward (1937), 43.

Chapter 4: The Southern Colonies

1. Standard figures quoted. Robert and Katherine Brown (p. 72) state higher figures for the black population. "Compilations from the tithable lists give a total population of 84,000 whites and 60,000 blacks in 1730; 173,304 whites and 119,990 blacks in 1755; and in 1774 Lord Dunmore placed the population at 300,000 whites and 200,000 Negroes."

2. That is, money paid to the Crown or to absentee English landlords for use of the land. Quitrents will be discussed in greater detail later.

3. Despite the labored research of Philip A. Bruce (see Bibliography), the "higher planting class" was composed of persons of respectable but undistinguished lineage. The Woodhouses, the Bacons, the Lees, the Wormeleys and the Washingtons were almost alone from the British knightly class. In fact, Virginia—like Australia later—was a dumping ground for convicts, as authorized by Parliament in 1717. See Morgan (1975), 339.

4. Padover (1952), 23. However, Page Smith ([1976], p. 59) states that the young couple were left 11,000 acres and thirty-five slaves.

5. Jefferson was one of the foremost slaveholders of Virginia. To make a comparison, Robert Carter, whose Nomini Hall on the Potomac River was a top showplace, operated with less than one hundred fifty slaves (Bridenbaugh [1958], chapter 2). Also see Morgan (1975), 4.

6. For representative statements as to the aristocratic structure of Virginia, see the following: J. T. Adams, 62; Bridenbaugh (1958), 8 and 10; Cooper, 21; Morgan (1975), 280; Morison et al., 131; Philbrick, 106; Wertenbaker (1958), 1–142; Louis B. Wright (1940), 2, 39, and 54. On page 39 Wright states, "aristocratic, even oligarchic."

Robert and Katherine Brown (1964) have argued against this view, stating with impressive statistics that there was much opportunity for the common man in Virginia and that cheap land was available. Cooper also writes that by the eighteenth century the "great majority of white southerners owned their own land" (p. 6). There is no contradiction on certain levels. The large speculators who gobbled up huge land tracts through influence and fraud had to sell at competitive prices with land opening up to the west. The white freeholders in Virginia, even on the smaller land parcels, raised their crops by slaves and identified with the larger plantation owners as mutual racists. Even the Browns admit that to the extent Virginia was more aristocratic than a colony such as Massachusetts, it was due to slavery (p. 77). The small farmers had traditionally deferred to the great plantation "superiors" because the former considered the latter their defenders against the British governors, whose responsibility it was to enforce quitrents (Morgan, [1975], 378). And it should not be forgotten that if one subtracts white non-freeholders and women, as well as slaves and Indians, the voting population of Virginia was a small minority.

7. Larabee, 6–8.

8. Philbrick, 106.

9. Wertenbaker ([1942], pp. 318–19) states 65,000 acres. Turner ([1962 reprint], p. 91), states 59,786 acres.

10. Thomas Jefferson preferred to call average whites "rubbish." See Robert and Katherine Brown, 301.

11. McColley, 43.

12. As late as 1810, Governor John Tyler (whose son became the tenth president of the United States) addressed the Virginia legislature: "Commerce is certainly beneficial to society in a secondary degree, but it produces also what is called citizens of the world—the worst citizen in the world."

13. Charles M. Andrews (1959), 156.

14. Mereness, 61.

15. Wertenbaker (1942), 321. Gould has different figures. The apparent discrepancy is due to the fact that in Maryland, unlike Virginia, the large landowners held many properties in different counties rather than one or two enormous estates. Also see Charles A. Barker, 36.

16. Gould, 20.

17. The proprietary charter, though granting royal privileges to the Baltimores, did require the establishment of an assembly, which could not, however, initiate legislation. But "the assembly itself was prevailingly aristocratic in composition" Louis B. Wright (1947), 69.

18. The contradictions of the human mind astound. John Locke, the great advocate of individual liberty, also suggested that children should be set to work at the age of three in order to get them used to labor so they would think of nothing else. See Morgan (1975), 322. John Stuart Mill, like his father before him, was in administrative charge of the East India Company. "Dangerous radicals as they were as far as Europe was concerned, for India they were more tory than the Tories," and "despotism was the only possible system." *The Life of John Stuart Mill,* by Michael St. John Packe, 389.

19. The great profit in rice production lay in labor cost, and slaves were worked at one-quarter the cost of English hired hands. See Land, 64.

20. See summary conclusions of Clowse.

21. Larabee, 11 and 12.

22. Nettels, 522.

23. Ibid.

Chapter 5: The Middle Colonies

1. Beard (1930), 74.

2. Mark, 38.

3. Report of Agent for New York, 1700, *N. Y. Col. Docs.* II.

4. "England, by alienating many of the colonists in her attempts to protect the Indians and their lands, undoubtedly contributed to the growth of revolutionary sentiment" Nammack, x. See also p. 106 for the same reason the Iroquois sided with the British during the Revolution.

5. "The Gentlemen of the Law, both the Judges and the principal Practicioners at the Bar are either, owners, Heirs or strongly connected in family Interest with the Proprietors." Cadwallader Colden, December 6, 1765, *N. Y. Col. Docs.* VII, 796.

6. The Five Nations, five Indian tribes forming a linguistic family—the Mohawks, Oneidas, Onondagas, Cayugas, and Senecas—were joined in the early eighteenth century by the Tuscaroras; the confederated group was then called the Six Nations. Collectively these Indians were known as the Iroquois.

7. Edith Fox, 25.

8. Ibid., 6.

9. Sosin (1967), 49.

10. Flexner (1959), 304–308.

11. Becker, 8 and 9.

12. Mark, 92. Labaree is blunt: "There were no colonies north of the Mason and Dixon line and few south of it so dominated in their political organization and life by a small and privileged class as New York was by its great families" (p. 18). Cadwallader Colden said the New York assembly was no different. In a letter he wrote on September 20, 1764, to the Lords of Trade, Colden stated that he knew of three tracts of land each of which contained over a million acres and, as these tracts were given representation in the assembly, their proprietors automatically had "hereditary membership." The owners of other great patents had enough influence to become the "perpetually" elected representatives. Colden asserted that the assembly in large part was composed of owners of vast tracts and wealthy merchants, and that many of the latter were connected with the landowners by family interest. Cadwallader Colden Papers, III, 77–79.

13. Patricia W. Bonomi debunks the "myth" of oligarchic power. Even she admits, however, that "there is abundant evidence that patrician families played a prominent role in government at all levels" (p. 21). In other scattered references she states that members of the Livingston, Cruger, Philipse, and Schuyler families not only repeatedly served in the legislative branch but also as mayors and aldermen because of their economic power.

14. This was aided by a deliberate restriction on the number of persons who could vote, mainly through property qualifications that disenfranchised white males as well. Becker (p. 11) states that only 20,256 persons, some twelve percent of the New York population, could vote as late as 1771.

15. Morison, Commager, and Leuchtenburg, Vol. 1, 75. James Edward Oglethorpe was a similar bundle of contradictions, Head of the Royal African Company, the greatest English slaving corporation of the eighteenth century, Oglethorpe founded Georgia for the benefit of imprisoned debtors. He forbade slavery in this last of the English colonies in North America. See Woodward (1937), 88.

16. Quoted by Louis B. Wright (1947), 218.

17. Jennings (1984), 318. The entire matter is discussed on pp. 316–24.

18. For a detailed description of this fraud, see Jennings (1984), 325–42.

19. Labaree, 15.

20. Bond (1919), 107.

Chapter 6: The Northern Colonies

1. Bond, (1919), 40–41.
2. Ibid., 41. Also Charles M. Andrews (1967), Vol. 2, 225.
3. James T. Adams (1934), 39.
4. Woodward (1937), 51.
5. Jennings (1975), 477.
6. Ibid., 283–284.
7. Charles M. Andrews (1967), Vol. 2, 2.
8. Akagi, 189.
9. Billington, 81.
10. Akagi, 182.
11. Turner (1962 reprint), 54–61.
12. Bond (1919), 43.
13. Woodward (1937), 54.
14. Charles M. Andrews (1959), 89.
15. The records are extremely vague about the relations of various operating companies in this period. It is not clear whether the Laconia Company was fully independent of, or a subsidiary body to, the Plymouth Company, which at this time had been succeeded by the Council of New England.
16. James T. Adams (1923), 57.
17. New Hampshire Papers, XXIV, XXV and XXVI.
18. Sam Adams, who ranks with Tom Paine and Patrick Henry among the leading radical colonial leaders, was a grantee in this speculation, and speculated in Maine land as well. Sakolski (1966), 27.
19. Labaree, 20.

Chapter 7: The Quitrent Thorn

1. The manor lords in New York also faced tenant revolts, but this was due to high rent as distinguished from quitrent.
2. Barck, 330.
3. Ibid., for all figures quoted.
4. The most detailed discussion of this matter is in Bond (1919), 388–422.
5. Quoted from Andrews's Introduction to Bond (1919), 11.

Chapter 8: The American Child Is Born

1. Charles and Mary Beard (1930) Vol. 1, 126–28. See also Schlesinger, 73.
2. Labaree, 30 and 31.
3. Bridenbaugh (1971), 339.
4. Jensen (1968), 24.
5. Abbott, 30.
6. This was completely true in the southern colonies, mainly true in the middle colonies, and less true in the North, where the merchant interest was stronger than the land interest. But the fortunes of New England were closely bound to the southern provinces, especially through the slave trade, and the elite there operated in a similar manner politically.

7. Including taxes to pay part of the expenses of British soldiers fighting the French on the North American continent. This was a main source of discontent and one that figured as an important cause of the growth of revolutionary sentiment.

PART TWO: LAND AND THE AMERICAN REVOLUTION

Chapter 9: Preamble

1. Though oversimplified, the Tories may be defined as conservatives: the landed aristocracy favoring agriculture, the Church of England, and a strong monarch. The Whigs were liberals, the rising mercantile and industrial interests allied with the untitled gentry and Protestant dissidents. Whigs tended to be pro-American while Tories desired to make the colonies completely subservient to Crown policy.

2. Billington (p. 138) states that at the time of the French and Indian War, there were 1,500,000 settlers in the English colonies compared to 70,000 in the French. Knollenberg (p. 99) writes, "there were probably less than 90,000 whites in the whole of Canada." Lamar and Thompson (p. 137) give figures of 1,250,000 in the English colonies and only 60,000 French.

3. Bailyn (1986), 24.

4. The hyphenated expression "Scotch-Irish" refers to Protestant Scotsmen who settled in the three northern counties of Ireland during the reign of James I, a great many of whom later emigrated to America. Their main settlement was in western Pennsylvania.

5. Indian trade was extraordinarily profitable. According to Max Savelle in *George Morgan: Colony Builder,* a tomahawk worth fifteen shillings in Philadelphia could be exchanged for several otter skins worth eighteen shillings each, or a musket for mink worth many times its value, with no more added expense than the transport to the western Indian country. Naturally the Pennsylvania merchants at Philadelphia and Carlisle did not want to see their flourishing business destroyed.

Chapter 10: The Ohio Company and the French and Indian War

1. To be exact, the Indians did not back the French claim but rather supported the French position for their own reasons. "Indian warriors rallied to the French cause and submitted to French or Canadian officers for a variety of reasons. One has been widely noticed; to wit, that the land hunger of Britain's multiplying colonials frightened Indians in general and convinced them to resist while they could" (Jennings [1988], 189).

2. Kenneth P. Bailey in *The Ohio Company of Virginia* states 100,000 acres; Thomas P. Abernethy in *Western Lands and the American Revolution* states 120,000 acres. Colonel Patton, who moved west to his land, was scalped during the French and Indian War.

3. The assembly in Virginia was called the House of Burgesses, the latter word being derived from the French "bourgeois." Assemblymen were called burgesses.

4. Bailey, 203–205, 208.

Chapter 11: The Proclamation of 1763

1. E. Benjamin Andrews, Vol. 1, 370.

2. James T. Adams (1934), 78.

3. "The Proclamation of 1763 was simply ignored in certain places. In 1774 certain wealthy speculators of Annapolis applied for warrants for new western lands, and the Maryland land office made the concessions. The judges of the land office justified doing this 'by saying that the line had long been disregarded in Maryland' " (Barker, 291).

4. For closer analysis of the threads connecting the Seven Years War, the Proclamation of 1763, the Stamp Act, and the movement toward Revolution, see: Abbott, 27; Cooper, 28–29; DeVoto, 235–36; Lamar and Thompson, 139; and Sosin (1961), 4, 250.

Chapter 12: Evading the Proclamation: The Land Companies

1. Though having the name "company," these land companies were not corporations but, rather, partnerships. They were small groups with exclusive membership; they had no relation to corporations with publicly traded stock. The first corporate land company was the Connecticut Company of 1796, which was awarded the Western Reserve.

2. Livermore (p. 105) writes that the amount was "over £25." Alfred P. James (pp. 183, 184), after making a careful study, states "the gentlemen of the Ohio Company, not necessarily as individuals but as a group, suffered no actual financial losses from their land investments," and concludes that, "the losses were in fact not real but losses of possible speculative profit, losses of expectations not fulfilled. . . ."

3. Shelburne Papers, L, 93–95.

4. Abernethy (1959), 12.

5. Philbrick, 32. John Stuart was no shrinking violet either. A native of Scotland, he settled in South Carolina in 1748 and "accumulated a vast landed property and over 200 slaves, only a very small part of which was obtained before he became Indian Superintendent" (Shaw, 18).

6. Abernethy (1959), 52, 77–78, 90.

7. Ibid., 28.

8. Ibid., 29, quoting Johnson Papers, V, 128–30.

9. Ibid., 30. To be fair to Franklin, it should be noted that he was no worse than other esteemed persons at that time. The English Parliament could be called an auction house or a brothel, depending on one's sensibilities. The king himself bribed and was bribed. The merchants of New England were little different. Corruption in the illicit trade with the French West Indies was a recognized way of life and John Hancock was said to reign as king of contraband.

10. Ibid., 31.

11. Ibid., 33. Also Lewis, on the Treaty of Fort Stanwix.

12. Lord Hillsborough was not as hoodwinked by Sir William Johnson as has been supposed. When asked for an explanation as to why he made the second purchase of Indian lands to the south and west at Fort Stanwix, Sir William, among other reasons, lamely asserted that the Indians had desired it. Hillsborough wrote back ordering him to retrocede the second purchase, ironically adding, "if it could be done without giving them offense" (Report of the Board of Trade, April 25, 1769). Croghan and Johnson also did some private business on the side at Fort Stanwix, acquiring for themselves privately over 100,000 acres, also invalidated by Hillsborough. See Wainwright, 256–58; and Philbrick, 30–31.

13. Sir Nathaniel Wraxall, *Historical Memoirs of My Own Time,* London, 1815.

14. Report of the Board of Trade, April 15, 1772.

15. According to Herbert B. Adams in *Maryland's Influence in Founding a National Commonwealth,* the soiled laurel in this matter goes to the ubiquitous Benjamin Franklin, who persuaded Thomas Walpole in London to serve as the figurehead.

16. Peter Marshall, 723.

17. August 17, 1772. Ricord and Nelson, in *Archives of the State of New Jersey* (Series 1, Vol. X, 377–78); Morison, Commager, and Leuchtenburg (p. 142); and Bailyn ([1986], 29–30) maintain that Lord Hillsborough was opposed to emigration because his large estates in Ireland might be affected by loss of labor. But this is facile economic determination because Lord Dartmouth, who succeeded Hillsborough, and also owned large estates, was head over heels in colonial land speculation.

18. Dartmouth College in New Hampshire is named after Lord Dartmouth.

19. Abernethy (1959), 55.

20. The machinations of the Vandalia shareholders, and the counter voices, are well documented in Sosin (1961), chapter 8, 181–210.

21. Samuel Wharton, who with his brother and family held the largest position in Vandalia, tried to disassociate himself from Franklin after the Hutchinson letters, hoping in vain to keep alive the enormous patent. See Peter Marshall, 735–38.

22. Abernethy (1959), 116.

23. The Earl of Dunmore's family name was Murray, and William Murray was his kinsman. Without doubt the Franks-Gratz group hired him for that reason; probably they considered using the connection from the beginning.

24. Philbrick (p. 34) sums up neatly: "Virginia's last royal governor (John Murray, Earl of Dunmore, father of the king's son-in-law) ignored and suppressed royal orders, both general and personal; recommended approval by the home government of the illegal land purchases, of which he was a secret beneficiary; made grants and permitted surveys specifically prohibited. . . ."

25. Most Virginians opposed this war as they had previously opposed similar action on the part of Dinwiddie. This was especially true of the eastern districts. Patrick Henry now enters from the wings. Henderson ([1920], p. 207) writes: "In shaping his plans Dunmore had the shrewd legal counsel of Patrick Henry, who was equally intent upon making for himself a private purchase from the Cherokees."

26. Thwaites and Kellogg, 93.

27. Thomas Wharton to Thomas Walpole, September 23, 1774, "Letter-Book of Thomas Wharton," in Pennsylvania *Magazine of History and Biography,* Vol. 33, 445.

28. Abernethy (1959), 134.

29. Colonel Henderson must have been very persuasive, for he and his associates later received a similar land grant from North Carolina between the Powell and Clinch rivers in Tennessee.

30. Morison (1965), 173.

31. Alvord (1917), Vol. 1, 213n.

Chapter 13: The Quebec Act of 1774

1. Alvord (1916), 25; also Morison, Commager, and Leuchtenburg, 143. Jensen ([1968], p. 399n) states that the issue is too complex to insist that Britain's western policy drove Virginia into the Revolution, but "to argue that British restrictions had no impact on Virginia opinion is to ignore the evidence."

2. Miller (1943), 373.

3. Sosin (1961), 249; Philbrick, 39; and Jennings (1988), 466.
4. DeVoto, 264.

Chapter 14: The Influence of Land on the Revolution

1. Gipson (1954), 55.
2. Charles M. Andrews (1935), 129–30. It has also been claimed that the British garrisons were quartered in the colonies to intimidate the colonists as well as, or more than, the Indians. Another claim is that these garrisons merely offered a convenient way to keep well-placed officers on the government payroll.
3. For fuller discussion, see Sosin (1961), and especially the massive analysis of these actions in Alvord (1917).
4. Woodward (1937), 114.
5. Williams (pp. 80 and 113) refers to this quote as a buttress to his radical analysis of American history.
6. For a fuller discussion, see Charles M. Andrews (1935), 203; Abernethy (1959), 160–61; and Morgan (1965), 147–65.
7. The southerners also wanted local control of the Episcopal church structure, the conflict which vaulted Patrick Henry to fame.
8. Bridenbaugh (1958), 76-77.
9. Jefferson's *A Summary View of the Rights of British America,* 1774.
10. The writer does not suggest that the English protection of the Indians was based on idealism. It was practical economics, the fear of another Pontiac-like uprising; and the interests of the fur trade.
11. Sosin (1967), 21; Bailyn (1986), 43–49.
12. "For the merchants, the unfolding of the new imperial program involved a very serious interference with their customery trading operations; and during the decade from 1764 to 1774 their constant aim was to effect a restoration of the commercial conditions of 1763" (Schlesinger, 165). Specific references are made to the cities of Boston, New York, Philadelphia, and Newport.

Chapter 15: Some Eminent Patriots

1. Williams (p. 92) states: "In any event, it is difficult to think of Franklin as a scientist if only because he invested so much time and intelligence in land speculation."
2. Boorstin, 161. Also Morris (1973), 23.
3. Williams, 92; same page for reference to "outlaw."
4. Van Doren (1952), 257.
5. Also see Jennings (1988), 258–59.
6. Franklin (1951), xv–xix.
7. Beard (1961), 49, 92, and 93. Abernethy (1959) lists no less than sixty-two references to Franklin's land speculations.
8. Clark, 221. Van Doren ([1938], 399) states 2,000 acres rather than 20,000. All other sources indicate the larger figure; this was probably a proofreading error.
9. Van Doren (1938), 398. Note that Franklin defined "affection and respect of the colonies for a royal government" in terms of the speculators getting grants to huge tracts of western land.

10. Those men among Franklin's colleagues who worked closely with him almost uniformly shared a low opinion of the Pennsylvanian, one quite the contrary to that now held. John Adams wrote, "He has been possessed by the lowest cunning and the deepest hypocrisy I ever met." John Jay, Henry Laurens, and Francis Dana, the other prominent envoys who accompanied Franklin to France, were agreed that "Franklin was lazy, immoral, careless in the discharge of his duties, excessively vain, and too much under French influence." See Page Smith (1962), Vol. 1, 570. Some of these comments may have been due to envy. Perhaps Franklin was also too sophisticated for their provincial minds.

11. According to Bowers (p. 31), "Patrick Henry studied three months [the law] in a cursory fashion." The usual period was one year.

12. Meade (1957), 137.

13. William Wirt, Henry's early biographer, wrote to a friend, ". . . from 1763 to 1789, covering all the bloom and pride of his life, not one of his speeches lives in print, writing or memory. . . . In short, it is verily, as hopeless a subject as men could well desire. I have dug around it, and applied all the plaster of Paris that I could command." Boorstin (p. 358) refers to this letter and boldly states that Wirt "himself concocted" the famous lines. Page Smith ([1976], p. 36) feels the lines are genuine but that "if this be treason, make the most of it" could not be, because a French visitor who was present and made notes did not include the words.

14. Whitaker (1927), 49, 93, 125 and 126.

15. Abernethy (1959), 131.

16. Ibid., 121. Vandalia, its English name, had been rechristened the Indiana Company, its earlier American name, by this time.

17. Malone, 308.

18. James A. James (1912), 115.

19. Patent Book A, 330–33; F, 400–470.

20. Meade (1969), 421.

21. In a later Yazoo speculative purchase, investigation revealed that every member of the Georgia legislature, with one exception, had been bribed to vote for the sale.

22. Meade (1969), 423.

23. Abernethy (1959), 368, To get an opposing view, it is amusing to read Norine D. Campbell's *Patrick Henry: Patriot and Statesman,* published in 1969, long after research indicated Henry's private activities. In the Campbell eulogy, which lifts superficiality to heroic heights, not even the subjects "land" or "speculation" enter the Index, let alone the contents.

24. Colonel Peter Jefferson, Thomas's father, was also surveyor of Albemarle County. Malone (p. 12) categorically states, "Such knowledge [surveying] was immensely useful to any planter and it played an important part in Peter's successful career, as it did in that of George Washington."

25. Dowdey, 221.

26. The most important are those by Bellamy, Butterfield, Cook, Flexner (1969), Hughes, Ritter, and Woodward (1926.)

27. Bellamy, 71.

28. Morris (1973), 48.

29. George Washington to Major Francis Hackett, August 2, 1758. John C. Fitzpatrick, *The Writings of George Washington* (Washington, D.C., 1931-44), Vol. 2, 260–61.

30. Equivalent to $5.9 million, as reported in an article in the *New York Times* dated April 22, 1985, p. A 12.

31. The burning desire that Washington bore for Sally Fairfax is well recorded. When engaged to Martha, he wrote passionately to Mrs. Fairfax that it was she alone whom he loved (Flexner [1969], 41). A psychologist might note that though Mrs. Custis bore four children in her previous brief marriage, she was barren with Washington.

32. Quoted by Woodward (1926), 218.

33. Consul W. Butterfield. Colonel Crawford was tortured to death at the stake by the Indians on June 11, 1782, an episode that shocked the colonials even in that period of mutual brutality. It should be noted, however, that Crawford had a most belligerent history involving Indians. He was active in Pontiac's War on the frontier and was a major in Lord Dunmore's War, a scheme to defraud Indians of their land. It ended with a bloody battle that broke the Shawnees. Crawford commanded the last action, the destruction of two Mingo villages. His service in the Revolution was mainly devoted to fighting the Indians in what is now Ohio.

34. These were part of General Lyman's "Military Adventurers": land claims derived, like those of Washington, from a soldiers' bonus given to troops from the northern colonies who had fought in the Seven Years War.

35. Though this was ten years after the Proclamation forbidding western land purchases, Washington's advertisement guaranteed to prospective purchasers the validity of the sale, "notwithstanding the unsettled counsels respecting a new colony on the Ohio," which is to say, Vandalia. Sosin (1961), 224.

36. Woodward (1926), 222. Also see Sakolski (1957), 55; and Jensen (1968), 387.

37. McDonald ([1985], 94, n78) states without elaboration, "Washington eventually owned upwards of 500,000 acres."

38. Cook, 128.

39. Washington also held improved lots as well as shares in land partnerships.

40. Cook, 134. This would be about $2.5 billion in 1988 dollars! For details on Washington's property, see Ritter, 284. Herbert B. Adams (1885) also made a careful study. Mere listing of the number of acres does not indicate the more significant factor of location, in which choice Washington was equally clever.

Chapter 16: Land Bounties Fueling the Revolution

1. Morison, Commager, and Leuchtenburg, 176. Also Morgan, 1965, quoting David Ramsay's *History of the American Revolution* (1789), 310–325; also quoting Charles K. Adams (1898), 174–75, 177–89.

2. Ibid., 176. Actually, the prize for foot dragging goes to Maryland, where its convention on May 15, 1776, instructed its delegates to oppose any declaration of independence.

3. Gelb, 164. See also Sosin (1967), 102.

4. Gelb, 216.

5. Quoted by Charles A. and Mary R. Beard, "The Agricultural Era," 273.

6. Gelb, 79.

7. Quoted by Gelb, 184. It was the British, not the Americans, who offered freedom to the slaves. See Brodie, 111. As Morris (1967) writes, "It is ironical that no simple event did more to propel the uncommitted Southern planters into the camp of rebellion than Lord Dunmore's call summoning the Negro slaves to the British cause with a promise of freedom." Tongue in cheek, Morris concludes, "Somebody might make out a plausible argument that the British fought to free the slaves and the Americans fought to keep them enslaved"(pp. 74, 75).

8. "The United States," *The Cambridge Modern Library*, Vol. 7, (Cambridge, Mass., 1903), 211. See also Jellison (p. 243), who writes: "There were in those days men of staggering inadequacy occupying key positions within the British government and military establishments. To these men, Americans must forever be indebted, for had it not been for their remarkable deficiencies, the Revolution would doubtless have been crushed within a matter of a few months."

9. This is the minimum figure. Both Channing, Vol. 3, 221, and Nettels, 692, calculate the figure as 250,000 men.

10. Morison, Commager, and Leuchtenburg (p. 180), quoting these figures, conclude: ". . . a disgracefully small number of Americans were willing to do any sustained fighting for their country's cause." Jameson (p. 75) writes that at top strength in 1776 the army, including both Continentals and all state militias, totaled a little less than 90,000 men, about one-eighth of the men of fighting age, and then dwindled to half this number, while in contrast, the ratio was one-fifth in the Civil War. Channing (Vol. 3, 223) agrees with these figures and states that the British had from 60,000 to 200,000 soldiers, depending on the period. Gelb (p. 75) adds that at least a third of the Americans deserted.

11. Charles A. and Mary R. Beard, "The Agricultural Era," 273.

12. Alvord ([1925], p. 6) quite properly ascribed the defeat of England to "the work of a man of genius, the Count of Vergennes." Persuading Louis XVI to support the colonials in order to weaken the British, the French made loans and grants amounting to 47,400,000 livres ($8,752,000), an astronomical sum at that time, while in the same period Congress refused to tax Americans. See Ferguson, 126–28. This was aside from direct military intervention; the turning point of the Revolution was the defeat of Cornwallis at Yorktown, achieved by Washington with more French soldiers and sailors fighting under General Rochambeau and Admiral de Grasse than with his American troops. In large part it was the French people, not the Americans, who paid for the Revolution; indeed the French government went bankrupt short years later. The Dutch also lent the great sum of $2,000,000 in 1782, when it became apparent that the American cause was winning.

13. Quoted by Page Smith (1962), 288.

14. Sosin (1967), 135.

15. Morison, Commager, and Leuchtenburg, 181.

16. Quoted by Jennings (1988), 63.

17. There are many scattered references to these facts. See among them Nettels, 684 and 691; E. S. Morgan (1975), 385; and Morison, Commager, and Leuchtenburg, 181.

18. Tom Paine, at the end of his life, came to the conclusion that the pattern of speculation, which involved taking over the veterans' warrants for a few cents on the dollar and then funding at full value the discounted paper, was deliberately plotted by the Federalist party leaders. This, with his similar comments about Washington, was paranoia.

Chapter 17: The Articles of Confederation and Western Land

1. Most historians write of "conservative" and "radical" factions, but this writer believes that "popular" is more fitting than "radical." The patriotic conservatives, men such as George Washington and John Adams, were as zealous in the prosecution of the war as were the so-called radicals. We can note briefly the nature of the popular leaders. Willie Jones of North Carolina, a great planter, was one of the largest slaveholders in the state. Christopher Gadsden, the firebrand of South Carolina, was a rich merchant with many slaves, who rejected universal suffrage and became a devoted Federalist after the war. John

Hancock of Massachusetts, first as a contrabandist and then as a privateer, waxed very rich and developed an amiable sickness that indisposed him whenever a crucial vote was needed. Sam Adams of Massachusetts receded as a constructive force after the war started. Patrick Henry has already been discussed. The difference between these men and the conservatives is not great enough to denote them as radical in any accepted sense.

2. In the case of New York, the treaties involved the Iroquois giving away land belonging to other tribes. The case for Massachusetts was dubious, and indeed never much pressed. Connecticut's claim rested on an absurdity. When Governor Winthrop went to England to ask for an extension of Connecticut westward, King Charles asked him the distance between Connecticut and the Pacific Ocean. Winthrop said that from the hills of western Connecticut one could faintly see the water, and the king, thinking the request reasonable, complied. The main tension caused in these three claims was Connecticut's insistence on owning the Wyoming Valley of Pennsylvania.

3. Jensen (1940), 151 and 153.

4. The landed states of the North, with the partial exception of Connecticut, gave up their claims earlier to make way for a settlement. They opposed the claims of the land companies with less vigor, in some cases because of share participation.

5. In this connection it is worth quoting from a letter George Mason of Virginia wrote to his friend Patrick Henry on May 6, 1783, as the war ended and some members of Congress felt pre-war debts to Britain should be honored: "If we are to pay the debts due to the British merchants, what have we been fighting for all this while?" William W. Henry, *Patrick Henry: Life, Correspondence and Speeches*, Vol. II, 187.

6. Lewis, 205.

7. Ibid., 217 and 222.

8. Abernethy (1959), 143.

9. Lewis, 159.

10. Ibid., 160.

11. Ibid., 161. Also Abernethy (1959), 121.

12. Lewis, 219.

13. Jensen (1940), 210.

14. Abernethy (1959), 228.

15. Jensen (1962), 44. Also see Lewis, 226.

16. As will be discussed, the Adamses of Massachusetts and the Lees of Virginia had formed a "Junto," or working combination, that was usually directed against the conservative mercantile power of the middle provinces. For this reason, and with certain pretensions to western land on the part of Massachusetts, based on her original charter, she, carrying most of New England with her, did not take a sharp stand against Virginia.

17. Morison (1965), 278.

18. Livermore, 93; Henderson (1920), 113; and Morison (1965), 278.

19. Abernethy (1959), 244.

20. The actual deed to the Northwest Territory was not conveyed to Congress by Virginia until March 1, 1784. The land companies fought a desperate rearguard action. The events described in this paragraph have been condensed for clarity and are not in sequential order, but do not violate the spirit of what actually occurred. Right to the end Maryland and New Jersey dissented, and insisted on honoring the Indian grants to the land companies, including the final committee report made on September 13, 1783. For those interested in a detailed analysis, the best study is that of Lewis, 225–65.

PART THREE: LAND SPECULATION IN THE SOUTHERN STATES

Chapter 18: George Rogers Clark

1. Illinois Historical Collections, VIII, 9.

2. Abernethy (1959), 193–202.

3. At this early time, before the flowering of the popular wing in Virginia politics, which opposed the land companies (as mentioned before), there was no thought that Virginia would contest private titles as long as the area came under the state's jurisdiction.

4. J. A. James (1928), 114 and 115.

5. It will be recalled that George Croghan was a founder of the Indiana Company.

6. Abernethy (1959), 199.

7. Alvord ([1916], pp. 34–36) points out that Clark's conquest only involved "a small part of the northwest . . . approximately the southern half of what is now the state of Illinois," and that "Virginia had really only weakened the hold of the mother country on a small corner of the disputed territory." He further states that the first boundaries proposed by Franklin at the peace treaty meeting, including all of Canada as well as the Northwest Territory, were not based on Clark's campaign but rather on a reunion of the two English-speaking peoples against a resurgent France.

8. Philbrick, 58.

9. Clark's powers as a naturalist and amateur archaeologist were praised by both Jefferson and Audubon. As to the exact number of slaves Clark owned, they were twenty-four at his death (Bodley, 337n.); and since his wealth declined, it can be presumed they were more at this time. Like Jefferson and Henry, Clark's enthusiasm for liberty never extended to include slaves.

10. T. Roosevelt, *Winning of the West*, Vol. 4, 163.

11. Bodley, 343.

12. Affaires Etrangères, Correspondence Politique, Etats-Unis, XLVI, XLVII, XLVIII, and L. Library of William S. Mason, Evanston, Illinois).

13. J. A. James (1928), 421.

14. Jefferson's "Conversations with Genêt," *Report of the American Historical Association* (1896), Vol. 1, 984–85.

15. Fearing for his head, Genêt refused to return to Paris. Marrying the rich daughter of Governor Clinton of New York, he settled down to a good burgher's life.

16. J. A. James (1928), 457.

17. Bodley, 366.

18. DeVoto, 338. It should be noted that the biographies of Clark written by both Temple Bodley and John Bakeless are hero worshipping. Bakeless in particular presents Clark without freckles or warts; only three references in the entire book are made to land grants, as though land had nothing to do with his motives.

Chapter 19: The American Settlement of Kentucky

1. The figure before 1775 comes from Abernethy (1959), 110. The 1781 figure is quoted by J. A. James ([1928], p. 185) with Temple Bodley in accord. The 1783 estimate also comes from James (p. 322); but Philbrick (p. 91) claims the population did not rise to this figure until 1785. The 1788 quotation is from Abernethy (1959), 352.

2. Bakeless, 257.

3. Draper MSS, 14 S 31. Also quoted by J. A. James (1928), 183.

4. American State Papers, *Public Lands,* Vol. 1, 122.

5. There were several block allotments of precisely 157,722 acres. Apparently this is a very large but recognized unit in surveying measurement.

6. January 24, 1780. *Clark Papers,* 384. Quoted by J. A. James (1928), 182.

7. Regarding this episode, Hamilton wrote an odd statement in a pamphlet issued in 1797 titled *Observations on Certain Documents . . . Written by Himself:* "The charge against me is a connection with one James Reynolds for purposes of improper pecuniary speculation. My real crime is an amorous connection with his wife for a considerable time, with his privy and connivance, if not originally brought on by a combination between the husband and wife with the design to extort money from me."

8. Listed under "Patrick, Henry" is an additional 13,000 acres. This may have been a clerk's error.

9. Clark must have picked up more through dummies, or acquired additional acres later, for the total he sold over the years was greater than this amount.

10. Like the Hites, the Shelbys were actual settlers and not absentee speculators. Isaac Shelby might be considered a freak in that he did not use political office for personal profit. He is on record for refusing to take part in Indian conferences forcing the helpless natives to give up their land "because he disapproved of the way his colleagues made use of their official position to engage in private speculations" (Abernethy [1959], 262).

11. Among the top Pennsylvanians speculating in Kentucky, only the Gratz family, of the Jewish faith, seems to have put down deep roots. Michael Gratz's son, Benjamin, a lieutenant in the War of 1812, settled in Lexington, Kentucky, and married the daughter of Colonel Nathaniel Gist of the Revolution, a descendant of Christopher Gist, surveyor for the Ohio Company and one of the first white men to explore Kentucky. The Gratz children were brought up as Christians and one of the daughters married Thomas Clay, grandson of Henry Clay.

12. James Madison's father, of an old landed family, had the same name and this may have been a speculation of the older Madison.

13. F. J. Turner, "Western State-Making in the Revolutionary Era," Vol. 2, *American Historical Review* (1896).

Chapter 20: The Land Claims of Spain Southwest of the Alleghenies

1. Jensen (1940), 219.

2. Whitaker (1927), 11.

3. Ibid., 9.

4. Ibid., 21 and 26.

5. Ibid., 24.

6. Turner (1962), 159; and Nevins, 554–56 and 660.

7. Jensen (1940), 163 and 164.

8. Nevins, 602.

9. Wecter, 106.

10 Nevins, 548.

11. Ibid., 551.

12. *The Federalist Papers,* No. 46, see Edward M. Earle.

13. Jensen (1940), 173.

14. Padover ([1958], p. 9) writes of Hamilton that ". . . his foreign birth played a not inconsiderable role, for it gave him the kind of perspective most native Americans still lacked."

15. Woodward (1937), 248. Abernethy ([1967], p. 200) quotes various sources indicating that the freight rate across the mountains to Nashville during this period was $10 per hundred pounds.

16. Whitaker (1927), 52–53.

17. Ibid., 161.

18. Congress's Treaty of Hopewell, which its commissioners had negotiated with the Cherokee in December, 1785, guaranteed to the Indians land that North Carolina considered its own. This treaty alienated land speculators and frontiersmen throughout the South. One way Congress recouped the confidence of these failing patriots was to scrap the Hopewell treaty in 1791 and force the harried Indians to cede more land. William Blount, whom we will meet shortly, negotiated on behalf of the United States.

Chapter 21: ¡ Viva el General Jaime Wilkinson!

1. Jacobs, 240.

2. Humphrey Marshall, 165.

3. Abernethy (1959), 299.

4. Anne Biddle, his wife, was cousin to Nicholas Biddle, later president of the Second Bank of the United States.

5. Bodley, 313.

6. Ibid., 329.

7. Abernethy (1959), 353.

8. Seven thousand dollars seems a small sum at the present time. To give an idea of how much it was then, the salary of Alexander Hamilton as secretary of the treasury was $3,500 a year.

9. Jacobs, 214.

10. For a fuller discussion, see Whitaker (1927), 185–209.

11. Sakolski (1966), 119.

12. Archivo General de Indias (Seville), *Papeles de Cuba,* bundle 2374, December 15, 1792.

13. Jacobs, 219.

14. Morrison to Wilkinson, *Wilkinson Papers* III, Chicago Historical Society, Chicago, Illinois.

15. There were many American adventurers operating in Mexico at this time with the same aim. Among these *empresarios,* or promoters, only Stephen F. Austin was successful. Austin's view of Mexicans can be summarized by a brief quotation from a letter he wrote: "The majority of the people of the whole nation, as far as I have seen them, want nothing but tails to be more brutes than apes" (S. F. Austin to J. E. B. Austin, "Austin Papers," *Annual Report American Historical Association,* 1919, Vol. II, Part 1, 531).

16. As recent a writer as Francis S. Philbrick insists that Wilkinson should be viewed according to the values of his time and not from those of later nationalism. "Treason against the United States shall consist only in levying war against them, or in adhering to their enemies," Philbrick quotes from the Constitution, adding that the latter phrase only refers to a time of war. His final conclusion is that Wilkinson was motivated by the desire to prolong his Spanish pension. (See Philbrick, 176–82 and 200). Curiously, Philbrick does

not address the question why Wilkinson, as a top American military officer, should have continued to accept a pension from a foreign government conspiring to separate a part of the country from the Union.

Chapter 22: Colonel George Morgan's New Madrid

1. Hutchins, who had met Morgan in the Illinois country when they were both young men, became a noted scientist and was later official geographer for the United States.
2. Savelle, 203.
3. Archivo Historico Nacional, Madrid, 3894, Morgan to Gardoqui, August 30, 1788.
4. MSS Madison Papers, 80.
5. Wilkinson was the only American who went along with the Spanish obsession that all colonists in Louisiana must embrace the Catholic faith. See also Jacobs, 95.
6. Archivo Historico Nacional, Madrid; Gardoqui to Floridablanca, March 4, 1789, 3893; Wilkinson to Miró, February 14, 1789, 3888.
7. Savelle, 221.
8. Morgan to Gardoqui, February 24, 1791. Mrs. A. G. Happer Collection (Washington, Penn.). Quoted by Savelle, 228.
9. Rowland, 341.

Chapter 23: William Blount, John Sevier, and Tennessee

1. Abernethy (1967), 47.
2. Masterson, 141.
3. This James White is not to be confused with Dr. James White, the Spanish agent whose role will shortly be discussed.
4. Abernethy (1967), 54.
5. Masterson, 141.
6. Daniel Boone was such a bumbler he even lost his original 9,879 Kentucky acres as well as the 27,000 acres taken up in the names of his brother, Squire Boone, and the Boone children, because of improper filing. He went to work for Richard Henderson "to recruit his shattered circumstances" (A. Henderson [1913], 104). At the age of sixty-five he settled in Spanish Louisiana, renouncing his American citizenship in return for a grant of 840 acres. There he was appointed a magistrate in 1800 and served until Louisiana became American territory, whereupon he moved west again.
7. The measure of William Blount can be taken from a letter he wrote on January 7, 1782, to his brother John Gray Blount: ". . . if it is possible . . . have it [a land claim] condemned in Georgia either by Party, Bribery, or in any other way" (John Gray Blount MSS, North Carolina Historical Commission [Raleigh]).
8. Philbrick, 85.
9. In 1977, almost two hundred years later, the completion of the Tennessee Tombigbee Waterway, a canal connecting the two rivers, was authorized by President Jimmy Carter of Georgia. The fulfillment of this measure cost the American taxpayers over $3 billion. Special interests, operating on the national level exactly as men like William Blount did centuries before on the state level, pushed through this pork-barrel deal.
10. Henderson (1920), 198.
11. Whitaker (1926), 366.
12. Ibid., 368.

13. Ibid., 369. Also s ⊕Abernethy (1959), 289. Emphasis is in the original letter.

14. Draper MSS (State Historical Society of Wisconsin), XI DD 78a.

15. Abernethy (1959), 289. Blount willed the commissioners well: "an agreeable Journey and greate choice and great plenty of Chickamogga Squaws" (Ibid., 289).

16. Named after Benjamin Franklin. The new "state" was also referred to as Frankland or Land of the Free.

17. Draper MSS, 7 XX, 17–18.

18. Jensen (1950), 333.

19. Draper MSS, 4 XX 18a, July 12, 1786.

20. State Records of North Carolina, XVIII, 608. Anthony Bledsoe to Governor Caswell, May 12, 1786.

21. Georgia offered to each volunteer from Franklin in this war one and one-half square miles of land as bounty on the "Bent," or Muscle Shoals, hunting grounds—important not only to the Creeks, but the Cherokees and Shawnees as well. This was much like what is now called a leveraged buyout, where in making a purchase, a group borrows money and then, after the closing, repays the money from the funds of the company acquired or through liquidation of its parts.

22. Henderson (1917), 232.

23. Whitaker (1925), 160.

24. Whitaker (1926), 379.

25. Archivo General de Indias (Seville), 86-6-17, White to Ezpeleta, Havana, December 24, 1788, trans. No. 2 *reservado,* December 29; and Ezpeleta to Valdés, No. 2 *reservado,* December 29, 1788. Among the usual ironies of history, John Sevier was of Huguenot origin and his people had fled France rather than live under Catholic oppression.

26. Gayarré, 262.

27. Abernethy (1967), 91–102.

28. White moved to Louisiana in 1799—before it was transferred to the United States —another example of his Spanish connection. There he became the first judge of southwestern Louisiana after the transfer. His son, Edward Douglas White, became governor of Louisiana; his grandson was even more distinguished. Edward Douglas White, Jr., became chief justice of the U.S. Supreme Court.

29. Whitaker (1927), 120–22.

30. Masterson, 298.

31. Abernethy (1967), 171–78. It was during this scandal that Andrew Jackson made his first signal appearance on the Tennessee stage.

32. John Sevier was from Watauga, the outlying western settlement of North Carolina, and was second in command when the Cherokees, who took the British side during the Revolution, besieged the town garrison for six weeks. This experience must have so seared him that he developed a psychopathic hatred for Indians, much like Tom Quick in western Pennsylvania some twenty years before who, on seeing his father killed by an Indian, became a man so sick that he only existed to murder as many Indians as he could—men, women, or children, it did not matter. Quick and Sevier were extreme types, but the outer western frontier always at bottom glorified the Indian killer.

Chapter 24: The Yazoo Land Frauds of Georgia

1. Haskins, 66. Sakolski ([1966], p. 126) uses these same figures. Whitaker ([1927], p. 129) states a smaller total acreage. Livermore (p. 148) introduces a fourth company, the

Georgia, in this earlier grant, but Haskins specifically notes, "When it [the bill] reached the House, there appeared another set of petitioners, the Georgia Company. . . . Efforts to insert this company among the other applicants failed. . . ."

2. It was later, as a result of negative publicity, that the Georgia legislature passed a resolution commanding the state treasurer to accept only specie in settlement of state debts. This caused most of the difficulties to be described.

3. Haskins, 68.

4. Gayarré, 276 and 282.

5. Haskins, 69.

6. Gayarré, 273.

7. Haskins, 69.

8. Gayarré, 293-300.

9. Haskins, 72. Also see Whitaker (1927), 126-39.

10. Haskins, 78-79; Whitaker (1927), 144; and Livermore, 150. Henry was not alone in this matter. The net profit for speculators in these certificates has been estimated at $40 million, which, according to Charles Beard, was about one-tenth of the whole value of the taxable land in the United States at that time. W. E. Woodward states that nearly half of the U.S. representatives and a majority of the U.S. senators, by purchasing depreciated certificates beforehand, made money on this one piece of legislation. George Washington also profited handsomely.

11. Jefferson to Washington, April 24, 1791. Jefferson's *Writings*, iii, 251.

12. Harper, brother-in-law to Alexander Hamilton, was a close colleague of Robert Morris, and the two were involved in other speculations. It was Harper who in 1796 published in London the prospectus of the North American Land Company, adding as *Observations* his comments on the value of southern pine-lands in order to interest English investors. Harper had earlier speculated in Illinois and Wabash company shares. He became a Federalist leader in Congress under President Adams.

13. Francis Watkins to Patrick Henry, March 7, 1795, Henry MSS.

14. Philbrick (p. 192) even doubts this: "Every member of the legislature with a simple exception (according to him) was bribed." It has also been stated that he was sick at the time of the vote.

15. Haskins, 84.

16. Ibid., 88. Quoted from *Travels* of La Rochefoucauld-Liancourt, II, 480.

17. Granger was also speculating in lands of the Western Reserve.

18. Ibid., 94.

19. Henry Adams, 119.

20. That is, those who had initially bought land from the original grantees.

21. Haskins, 103.

PART FOUR: LAND SPECULATION IN THE NORTHERN STATES

Chapter 25: The Northwest Territory

1. Hinsdale, (p. 270) states that the Northwest Territory contained 265,878 square miles. The reason for the greater size is that he includes the part of Minnesota east of the Mississippi River and north to the Canadian frontier.

2. This violation was not so unjust because the Americans, who agreed to press for indemnification of unpaid debts to English merchants, did not conform to their pledge either.

3. Jefferson himself was finally swayed by the desperate need for money and changed the 1784 final draft accordingly. Hibbard, 33.

4. Quoted by Havighurst (1956), 96, and Treat (1967), 28. As has been noted, Washington grew enormously in moral stature from his early predatory years. Referring to the Virginia system of skimming off the best lands through political contacts, Washington wrote at this time: "Sparse settlements . . . whilst it opens a large field to land jobbers and speculators, who are prowling about like wolves in many shapes, will injure the real occupiers and useful citizens and consequently the public interest" (quoted by Hibbard, 33).

5. Robbins, 9.

6. Tatter, 170.

7. Ibid., 178.

8. Hibbard, 56.

9. Ogg, 98.

10. Freund, 18.

11. O'Callaghan, 167. Hutchinson (p. 157) agrees and adds, "most of them not veterans," but quotes a much smaller total acreage in the District. Jonathan Dayton, a key man in the Symmes purchase (to be discussed), was by far the largest speculator. He filed warrants for about one-sixteenth of the whole area. Philbrick (p. 125) makes the astounding statement in brackets, without footnote or further clarification: "It has been said that title to all of Ohio passed through one or more of six hands."

12. Robbins, 17. Hibbard (p. 41) states that after reducing the figures for forfeiture due to nonpayment, 72,974 acres were sold initially in 1787. Treat ([1967], p. 376) agrees. The difference between the figures may be due to the inclusion of Ohio Company sales in the latter.

13. Sakolski (1966), 181–83, and Bond, 299–302. St. Clair was also unpopular with the Jefferson faction because of his extreme Federalist views.

14. In a tragic end for a man basically honorable—for though a land speculator, unlike many others in his position, St. Clair did not pervert his authority to grab land for himself—St. Clair eked out a forlorn existence until he died a destitute old man in 1818. All his property had been seized by creditors, and he was reduced to selling corn meal and dried apples from a tavern he ran in western Pennsylvania.

15. Treat (1967), 399. Hibbard (p. 11) and Hinsdale (p. 291) claim 4,204,800 acres. Hutchinson (p. 196) states "about 3,900,000 acres." The difference might be due to the inclusion of the Clark grant and some other special adjustments later.

16. The entire Virginia Reserve was a speculator's paradise built on a dubious base. Virginia's claim that the Kentucky tract was not sufficient to compensate her soldiers was never proven, but Congress finally "acquiesced in a condition which could not be undone without creating chaos" (Hutchinson, p. 9 of Abstract).

17. Hutchinson, 195.

18. Book 141, *Alphabetical List of Patentees,* General Land Office, Department of the Interior, Washington, D. C.

19. The final total after survey was 3,450,753 acres, including the Fire Land Tract. Whittlesey, 257. As to the maneuvers before the sale, see Sakolski (1966), 120–21. Livermore (p. 179) summarizes: "The final sale was made to an association that was essentially a combination of the various competing groups, which had agreed among themselves to make this price their maximum."

20. Philbrick, 310.

21. Amusingly, the easy road of entry to the Western Reserve was the "Pittsburgh Pike," built by the British General Forbes during the French and Indian War through western Pennsylvania and which, because it bypassed Virginia, threw the young George Washington into such great despair.

22. Carpenter, 178.

23. Ibid., 195.

Chapter 26: The Ohio Company and the Scioto Associates

1. Not to be confused with the earlier 1748 Ohio Company formed in Virginia before the Revolution.

2. Livermore (p. 137) states that 817 shares were actually paid up, of which less than one-third were held by emigrants to the land acquired.

3. Treat (1967), 51; Hibbard, 49; Charles and Mary Beard, Vol. 1, 511; Bond (1934), 279; and Robbins, 11. Each of these sources agrees that the price paid for the land netted the government eight to nine cents per acre in specie. The initial payment of $500,000 was in U.S. debt certificates "then worth anywhere from $60,000 to $130,000" according to Sakolski (1966), 104. This is between twelve and twenty-six cents an acre. Part of this difference may be explained by the tender of military warrants, which was allowed up to one-seventh of the total cost; it may also be that there was no exact proportion of the first payment to the total acreage involved.

4. Duer, a close friend of Alexander Hamilton, was appointed assistant secretary when, after Washington was inaugurated president two years later, Hamilton became secretary of the treasury. Alexander Hamilton, who usually avoided land speculation, bought five and half shares of Ohio Company stock. Because of the secrecy involving the principals of Scioto (which will soon be discussed), we do not know if Hamilton took a position there as well.

5. Sakolski (1966), 102. Treat (1967), 49.

6. Figure quoted by Sakolski (1966), 103. Philbrick (p. 124) writes that $143,000 was advanced. Livermore, (p. 138) agrees.

7. Havighurst (1956), 137.

8. Charles and Mary Beard, Vol. 1, 512.

9. Morison, 300.

10. The southern congressmen accepted the antislavery provision provided fugitive slaves would be returned, This is often quoted as an example of their patriotic idealism. The truth may be somewhat different. Congressman William Grayson of Virginia, a foremost land speculator and stockholder in the old Indiana Company, admitted that the southern delegates agreed to the clause "for the purpose of preventing Tobacco and Indigo from being made on the N.W. side of the Ohio as well as for several other political reasons" (Grayson to James Monroe, August 8, 1787. Burnett, Vol. 8, 632). To Cutler more than Jefferson goes the credit for insisting on no slavery: "Exclude slavery forever . . . and we will buy your land and help you pay your debts, allow it to enter and not a penny will we invest" (Brown [1938], 14).

11. The Scioto Associates divided their interest into thirty equal shares. Thirteen were taken by Duer and his assignees, four were set aside for foreign interests, and the other thirteen went to Cutler, Sargent, and their assignees (Davis, 139). See also Brown (1938), 13; Hibbard, 48; Sakolski (1966), 106; and Treat (1967), 58. The positions taken by Cutler

and Sargent in Scioto do not exactly fit the patriotic paeans often given them in history books. They each kept a share and assigned the other shares to colleagues like Parsons, Tupper, Putnam, Royal Flint, and Joel Barlow (Davis, 140).

12. William Duer was astonishingly frank about this fraud. When later pressed for a clearer background on Scioto by French investors, he is quoted as having said: "The persons who held these shares were for the most part those who had much influence in the formation of the Company of the Ohio at Marietta, or in the Legislative or Executive Branches of the Government" (Davis, 231). Since Colonel Duer kept no minutes or records, we will never know precisely who participated. Curiously, Davis (p. 145) seems to see nothing wrong with an arrangement whereby executive and legislative members of the U.S. government make money from inside information and influence: "Yet in the project of the Scioto associates there was nothing illegitimate, from public or private standpoint." Later he modifies this position, but never explicitly condemns these self-seekers. Livermore (p. 139) agrees with Davis.

13. In 1790 Playfair absconded with the remainder of the sales money received at the Paris office.

14. Havighurst (1956), 152.

15. Davis, 216.

16. Havighurst ([1956], p. 161) states that Barlow lived till 1824 when "he went to Poland on a mission for the French government" and died near Cracow. This is contrary to all other sources.

17. It should be noted that like certain assigned prisons at the present time for high-class white-collar prisoners, these debtor prisons varied greatly in facilities. Some were quite liveable.

Chapter 27: John Cleves Symmes and the Miami Purchase

1. Dayton, together with Governor St. Clair of the Northwest Territory; Israel Ludlow, the land surveyor for the Miami Purchase; and General Wilkinson, later purchased from Symmes a part of his tract on which the city of Dayton was laid out.

2. Symmes expected a 400 percent profit. In correspondence with a friend, he saw a fortune for "the lucky speculator who should buy lands from Congress for five shillings an acre and sell it to the immigrants at twenty" (quoted by Hibbard, 51).

3. McDonald, (1975), 53.

4. Symmes settled at North Bend, at the farthest northern sweep of the Ohio west of the Kanawha River. This was twelve miles below what became the site of Cincinnati. Amusingly, North Bend was not made the capital due to a love affair between the commanding officer of the American troops (quartered to protect the settlers) and the wife of a settler who lived at the other town; the officer therefore transferred the garrison to be close to his paramour.

5. Sakolski (1966), 114.

6. Symmes had a certain peculiar justice in his position. The original contract was for a million acres but final surveys indicated the tract contained a much smaller amount. Symmes expected that Congress would honor the terms of the original contract but a change of sentiment in that body, forced by agitation against very large private grants, made it refuse him a patent on more acreage. On the other hand, to balance the equation, through the political influence of Dayton, the percentage of the purchase payment allowed in military warrants, which could be bought at great discount, was increased. As to the final acre-

age received by Symmes, Treat ([1967], p. 61) states 248,540 acres, Hutchinson (p. 94) claims 272,540 acres, while Havighurst ([1956], p. 100) writes "a third of a million acres."

   7. Havighurst (1956), 100.

Chapter 28: Tecumseh: The View from the Other Side

   1. Jennings (1988), 479.

   2. Quoted by Havighurst (1956), 43. Also Edmunds, 189.

   3. This is the usual version. Havighurst ([1956], p. 22 and [1966], p. 127), states that Tecumseh's father was killed at Point Pleasant, with which Edmunds (p. 29) agrees. There seems to be no universal agreement on the family background of Tecumseh. Van Every (p. 19) even denies Tecumseh's mother was a Creek, but rather "a Cherokee living with the Creek."

   4. Josephy, 140. It is useful to keep in mind that some 7,000 whites, mainly French-Canadians, already dwelt in the Northwest Territory before the passage of the Ordinance. They rarely had trouble with the Indians. It was the swarming immigration and the blatant racism of the Americans that caused the Indian wars north of the Ohio.

   5. Tecumseh came from an unusually large Indian family, with four brothers.

   6. Bond (1934), 246.

   7. "Harrison reported that when there were only six hundred warriors on the Wabash, the annual consumption of whisky there was six thousand gallons, and that killing each other in drunken brawls had 'become so customary that it was no longer thought criminal' " (Ogg, 134). Though it was against official government policy to sell liquor to the Indians, Acting Governor Winthrop Sargent authorized three traders at Vincennes to do so (Bond, 245). Due to the same factors of lack of self respect and loss of hope, by substituting "blacks" for "Indians" and "crack" for "whiskey" and "pushers" for "traders," we have described black youth in the major urban centers today.

   8. Quoted by Josephy, 147. A major economic factor often overlooked is that by 1797 the supply of pelts declined. Many Indians depended entirely on the fur trade to support their families. As Edmunds (p. 25) notes, "a social organization that venerated hunters and warriors broke down under new conditions that afforded little opportunity for either role."

   9. Edmunds states that before the defeat of the Indians at Tippecanoe, the Prophet's influence was greater than that of his older brother. This is a rather unique point of view.

   10. Pontiac, in 1763, had temporarily united eighteen tribes in his war against encroaching settlers. Tecumseh, however, was the first Indian to preach the brotherhood of all red men.

   11. Josephy, 131.

   12. From this point in time we know that without Creek and Cherokee participation in the South and the Iroquois in the North, any hope of a Pan-Indian confederation east of the Mississippi was doomed.

   13. It is known that Harrison not only despised Indians but also worked for the introduction of slavery into the Indiana Territory. See Bond (1954), 154–57, 174–77. But the legion of naive admirers of Jefferson's idealism may be interested in extracts from a confidential letter about the Indian question that the president sent to Governor Harrison of the Indiana Territory: "We shall push our trading houses and be glad to see the good and influential individuals among them run into debt. . . . When these debts get beyond what the individuals can pay, they will be willing to lop them off . . . by a cession of lands" (Jefferson to Harrison, Esarey, *Harrison Letters,* Vol. I, 69–73). This is the same man who

bitterly wrote in earlier days how the debt of Virginia planters to the English factors was driving the colonials to Revolution. Harrison, while still young, actually felt guilty about his role. In a letter dated July 15, 1801, he wrote: "Whether something ought not to be done to prevent the reproach which will attach to the American character by the extermination of so many human beings I beg leave most respectfully to submit to the Consideration of the President" (Ibid.). But Jefferson was not interested, and within a decade Harrison also got over his fit of humanity.

14. Bond, 255.

15. Ibid., 262–63.

16. Josephy, 157.

17. The Americans thought that Tecumseh was an English agent. Documentary evidence indicates that the reverse was true and that the British government, fearful of losing the very profitable fur trade, discouraged Tecumseh's agitation.

18. Josephy, 161.

19. George Catlin, the famous artist of the West, painted his portrait when visiting the tribes in Kansas in 1832.

20. Josephy, 162–63.

21. Auxiliary Indian warriors also fought with Harrison. The Indians never heeded the fable of the eagle who was shot to earth by the arrow feathered with one of its own plumes. The Oneidas and the Tuscaroras were the two tribes of the Iroquois Six Nations who supported the colonials during the Revolution. It made no difference; in 1785 and 1788 they, too, except for small reservations, were forced to cede their land. In 1812, Tarhe, the Wyandot war chief, fought with Harrison in the American invasion of Canada, and the Wyandots also lost their land. The Cherokees fought with Andrew Jackson against the Creeks in the War of 1812, and indeed won for him the victory at Horseshoe Bend (Van Every, 22). Again it made no difference: President Jackson, almost a quarter century later, acquiesced in their expulsion as well.

22. Havighurst (1946), 141.

23. Philbrick, 284. It was the royalist British and not the democratic Americans who tried to create an Indian country. One of the points on the English agenda when they met with the Americans in the summer of 1814 at Ghent to negotiate an end to the War of 1812 was that the treaty of peace must embrace a land for their Indian allies, a buffer state between Canada and the United States. It was only in October, when tensions with Britain's allies at the Congress of Vienna were building up over the European settlement after Napoleon's defeat and the economic cost of continued warfare became evident, that England abandoned its Indian allies. See Engelman, "The Peace of Christmas Eve," in Dobell, *A Sense of History,* 136–53.

24. Quoted by Padover (1958), 444.

Chapter 29: The Allen Clan and Vermont

1. Sakolski (1966), 27. Fox (p. 163) states 70,000 acres. Duane must have partnered these land deals with his brother-in-law William Livingston, who became the first governor of New Jersey in 1776, after retiring to that state from New York. This deduction is made because Livingston was not mentioned among the original New York speculators but stated at the time of the Constitutional Convention that his estate had dwindled due to "currency depreciation and the confiscation by Vermont of the extensive holdings he had there"

(McDonald [1975], 53). Duane went on to become the first mayor of New York City, and was later appointed by President Washington the first U.S. Circuit Court judge.

2. Cochran, 86.

3. The historian Irving Mark (p. 15) who stresses the economic aspect of social movements in a broad concept, suggests that the Vermont civil commotion was the last stage in a series of violent outbreaks of tenant farmers against their landlords. The violence began in the province of New York before 1750 in Dutchess County and engulfed Westchester and Albany counties, reaching a climax in 1766 and then began spreading again.

4. The presiding judge in the first trial of ejectment [ejecting the settlers with New Hampshire land titles], whose decision was in favor of the New York claims, was Robert Livingston, one of the New York grantees of the land in question (Holbrook, 43).

5. It should be emphasized that Seth Warner, not Ethan Allen, was elected and led the Green Mountain Regiment for over five years during the Revolution until brought down by ill health caused by his many campaigns. Probably the greatest Vermont patriot, he never fell under suspicion of treason during the entire period to be discussed, when Ethan and Ira Allen dealt with the enemy.

6. The Allens had come from Connecticut as grown men and first called the region New Connecticut. Ethan Allen left Connecticut because he was in constant trouble with the law over his swearing, drinking, and brawling. His first stop was Northampton, Massachusetts, from which he was ordered to leave by the selectmen for his rowdiness. He probably would have ended up as an obscure town lush killed in a brawl in frontier New England if it were not for the opportunity rising out of the New York-New Hampshire land grant tensions.

7. Revised Morison edition. Morison, Commager, and Leuchtenburg, Vol. 1, 223.

8. Dixon R. Fox, 170.

9. Livermore, 130.

10. Pell, 75; Mark, 193. Quoted by Livermore, 131.

11. When Ira Allen applied for a loan in Boston in February 1794, he brought with him an attested statement that his Vermont real estate was worth £90,000. The value of the pound at that time being $3.34, this amounted to over $300,000, an enormous sum for the period. Wilbur, Vol. 2, 47 and 57.

12. Holbrook, 142.

13. The source for this famous line is Ethan Allen himself and stands in the same dubious bracket of mythology as Patrick Henry's "Give me liberty or give me death."

14. Pell, 156.

15. Jellison, 235. Washington was also pressing Congress to decide the Vermont question because so many deserters from the army fled to Vermont, where there was no danger of arrest. "He feared that if something was not done most of his troops would be found living in the Green Mountains" (Holbrook, 182).

16. William Smith ended up as chief justice of the Province of Quebec. James DeLancey and Isaac Low also became prominent Loyalists. It has been claimed that James Duane and Robert Livingston, both dyed-in-the-wool conservatives, went through many pangs before opting for independence.

17. Fox, 172; Wilbur, Vol. 1, 168.

18. Quoted by Jellison, 285. After weighing all the evidence, Jellison (p. 248) flatly states, ". . . new discoveries have been made in the British archives which leave absolutely no room for doubt: Ethan and his Arlington friends were bent on delivering Vermont to the enemy." Reading extracts from this correspondence, one can only conclude that the

double talk of Ethan Allen and some of the other top Vermont leaders ranges from hypocritical to disgusting. Sosin ([1967], p. 98) writes that the Allen faction had become convinced by 1780 that separate political status was the only sure way to secure their property, the prime motive.

19. Pell, 233.

20. Ethan Allen's oldest child by his young second wife became a nun. She was so recognized for her piety that a Catholic hospital in Vermont was named after her (Holbrook, 258). Thus was the success at home of the thirsty deist. It should also be noted that Allen got most of his deist ideas from a neighbor, Dr. Thomas Young, who had already died and to whom Ethan gave no credit.

21. Pell, 262.

22. Ebenezer Allen speculated elsewhere as well. He was one of eight partners who made a contract with some local Indian chiefs to buy the whole peninsula of Michigan immediately after General Wayne's victory at Fallen Timbers. Attempting to bribe influential members of Congress to assent, the deal was exposed and cancelled (Havighhurst [1956], 90).

23. Thompson, 109–110. Sosin (1967), 26.

24. This was a commercial enterprise unrelated to Vermont patriotism. Muskets with bayonets at the time sold for about fourteen dollars. He hoped to buy ten thousand and sell them in Vermont at a profit of five dollars each through his political contacts, netting $50,000 profit. See Wilbur, Vol. 2, 77.

PART FIVE: FEDERALISM AT THE HELM

Chapter 30: The United States Constitution and Land Speculation

1. Forrest McDonald ([1975], p. 87) includes other delegates whose primary interest concerned "farming or other realty interests." They are Caleb Strong of Massachusetts, Oliver Ellsworth of Connecticut, and George Reed and Jacob Broom of Delaware. He adds that James McHenry of Maryland, retired at the time of the convention, had an estate that "consisted primarily of realty" (p. 88). Adding these five names to the list would mean that over 70 percent of the delegates fell into the real estate category. Excluded as well is Alexander Hamilton, though he owned five-and-a-half shares of Ohio Company stock; and Nicholas Gilman of New Hampshire, who Beard ([1961], p. 151) has listed among the land speculators without clear evidence. Also eliminated is James Madison, whose father was a leading plantation owner with speculative interests in western land.

2. Patrick Henry, who knew his southern peers very well, used a cogent argument when later fighting for Virginia to turn down the Constitution: ". . . the danger of such a government is, to my mind, very striking . . . they may, if we be engaged in war, . . . liberate every one of your slaves" (W. W. Henry, Vol. 2, 401).

3. One of the hidden threads behind the fight of certain high-placed New Yorkers against the Constitution was their disgust with the Confederation Congress for not coming out in their favor during the New York-Vermont dispute, which meant such great losses to these land speculators. (McDonald [1975], 290). This point may be overstated, however, since James Duane and John Jay, both badly hit by the loss of their lands ceded to Vermont, were in favor of the Constitution.

4. Earle, Intro., viii.

5. Bennett, 6 and 7 (see also the fifth letter, [pp. 33–35]). In a brilliant prophecy (eighteenth letter, p. 130), the writer warns that in forming a strong central government with such extensive powers, the central city (which became Washington, D.C.) would end up a filthy sewer.

6. Morison (1965), 312. Morison adds, ". . . there is little doubt that the Antifederalists would have won a Gallup poll."

7. Among the battery of acclaimed historians who have supported Beard's thesis in general outline, as distinct from specific categories of analysis, are: William E. Dodd, Edward Channing, Max Farrand, Walter Lippmann, Harold U. Faulkner, Albert Jay Nock, Samuel Eliot Morison, Henry Steele Commager, Arthur M. Schlesinger, Thomas P. Abernethy, Vernon L. Parrington, W.E. Woodward, E. James Ferguson, and Merrill Jensen.

8. Beard (1961), 151.

9. See Earle, pages 16 and 153 for essays three and twenty-five respectively. Hamilton in the seventh essay also refers to the British territory ceded to the Americans in the West and states that without a strong union disputes among the states as to which one owned what piece of land would be a major source of strife.

10. Beard (1961), 23.

11. McDonald, 395.

12. Ibid., 129.

13. Ibid., 205. The case of North Carolina is complex. The western districts were the center of the Regulator movement, the sole massive eighteenth-century uprising against legal authority in the colonies. The westerners hated the seaboard aristocrats, and in particular Federalists like William Blount, involved in their suppression. Whatever the coastline counties did, under the influence of these local aristocrats, was opposed by the back country. Besides, Willie Jones, the libertarian leader, campaigned on a letter from his friend Thomas Jefferson, which stated that a second convention should be held assuring a bill of rights, rather than trusting to a promise of later amendments. See Morison ([1965], p. 195) on this matter as well.

14. Ibid., 263.

15. Quoted by Beard (1961), 147.

Chapter 31: Federalism and the Final Frenzy of Land Plunging

1. Quoted by Oberholtzer, 220.

2. Morison (1965), 313, 314.

3. Miller (1960), 125.

4. Quoted in order: from Parrington, Vol. 1, 300; and from Padover (1958), 423, 430, and 432.

5. Miller (1960), 108.

6. Ibid., 79.

7. J. T. Adams (1934), 135.

8. John Adams made a mistake in his diary, thinking that Sarah's father was Peter Livingston, William's older brother. See page 150, *The Founding Fathers, John Adams, A Biography in His Own Words,* ed. by James Bishop Peabody, 1973.

9. *The Duane Papers,* Vol. V, 164. (Collections of the New York Historical Society, 1890).

10. Sakolski (1966), 69. The same attitude is a strong influence at the present time on Japanese land and building purchases in the United States.

11. Wagner, 125.

12. Sumner, Vol. II, 278.

13. Oberholtzer, 326.

14. Wade, 40 and 41.

15. Ibid., 46.

16. Miller (1960), 176.

17. Ibid.

18. Wiltse, 3. William Miller (p. 9) states that the output of cotton in 1800 (as distinct from the export) was more than thirty-six million pounds.

19. Jefferson, the great imperialist, thought even beyond. He wrote the following in 1801: "It is impossible not to look forward to distant times, when our rapid multiplication will . . . cover the whole northern, if not the southern continent" (see William Miller, 144).

Chapter 32: The Strange Case of Robert Morris

1. Whether Robert Morris financed the Revolution or the Revolution financed Morris is an old controversy with sharp partisans on both sides. However, there is no question that the firm of Willing, Morris and Co., in which Morris was the most active partner, was by 1775 one of the leading commercial houses in Philadelphia (see Ver Steeg [1954], 4 and 5). Most of the abusive stories about Morris started with William Lee and, repeated by the Lee-Adams faction in Congress, became accepted by repetition.

2. Ferguson, 77.

3. McDonald, (1975), 54.

4. Oberholtzer, 295.

5. *Journal of William Maclay*, 147.

6. For an analysis of Morris's role, see Sumner, Vol. II, 175, 238–44. See also Sakolski ([1966], pp. 149–50) with some discrepancy as to details.

7. Ferguson, 258.

8. Soderstrom, Swedish consul, received this land for unknown services rendered. Sumner, Vol. II, 294.

9. Sumner, Vol. II, 258. Sakolski (1966), 59.

10. The writer is indebted to Barbara A. Chernow, (pp. 48–55; 61–72) for the only clear analysis of the details of these transactions. Since her book was published in 1974 and devoted exclusively to Morris's role as a land speculator in the years 1790 to 1801, the assumption is that her analysis overrides the rather muddy ones of earlier authors. For other reports, some involving varying figures, see Sumner, Vol. II, 260–63; Livermore, 207; and Sakolski (1966), 58–62.

11. An amusing aspect of these sales to the Dutch was that New York state law prohibited land sales to aliens, and thus these Dutch purchases were illegal. In 1798, largely through the influence of Aaron Burr, who was bribed (Sakolski, [1966], 80), the statute was amended to make legal these purchases.

12. It came to light in 1795 that Morris had sold several parts of these lands to other parties. When faced with a lawsuit, Morris claimed that particular sale was an "innocent Transaction" (Chernow, 72). Other similar suits then were filed; they became one of the factors leading to Morris being sent to debtor's prison.

13. "Nicholson inserted fictitious names on depreciation and donation lists or paid others to buy certificates for him from soldiers who were unaware of the value of the

land. After the speculators had acquired the certificates, the surveyors awarded them only the best tracts." (Chernow, 93).

14. Sumner, Vol. II, 246. Sakolski ([1966], p. 161) states a sale of fewer lots at a somewhat lower profit ratio.

15. Both Chernow (pp. 137–40) and Sakolski ([1966], p. 159) agree that the syndicate purchased a total of 7,235 lots. Sumner (Vol. II, 247) then states that they sold 769 lots, reducing the total to 6,466 lots. When Greenleaf was bought out, he assigned with the sale of his position another 1,316 lots, bringing the total owned by Morris and Nicholson to 7,788 lots minus 25 lots reserved as an adjustment to Greenleaf. Despite internal contradiction in these figures—for Sumner previously wrote that half the original purchase of 6,000 lots was sold—the writer quotes what has been written by authors who have analyzed these deals.

16. Chernow (p. 129) points out that most government officials, until forced by law in 1800 (by which time Morris was bankrupt), refused to live in the federal district.

17. Thomas (p. 26) states: "The president had a double ax to grind. Not only had he put money into land all over the city, but he also had invested in a canal company which schemed to make the Potomac the principal artery of trade between the Atlantic Seaboard and the West. The growth of the City of Washington was a prerequisite to the success of both ventures." Sakolski ([1966], p. 160), agrees. Hutchinson (p. 78), adds that "he [Washington] had 30,000 acres on the Ohio and Great Kanahwa Rivers which he was anxious to lease and the new settlements in the neighborhood would increase their value."

18. Vesting title in a trust was a favorite method during that period to avoid personal judgment in case of bankruptcy.

19. Sakolski (1966), 38. Actually, in the 1790s Morris and Nicholson formed six different land companies to market their enormous land holdings, the Asylum Company and the North America Land Company being the best known. The other four collapsed before they ever got off the ground (Chernow, 104).

20. Oberholtzer, 313.

21. Ibid., 323. Chernow (p. 180) sums up nicely: "In effect, the two Pennsylvanians were trying to sell shares in a land company to creditors, even though the land they were peddling was already mortgaged as security for their debts."

22. Custis, 326.

23. Quoted by Wagner, 124.

24. Sumner, Vol. II, 281. Chernow (p. 193) agrees. Livermore (p. 168) states $1,500,000.

25. Oberholtzer, 350; Wagner, 130.

26. McDonald (1975), 57: ". . . he was, in terms of personal property, the richest man in America."

Chapter 33: James Wilson: A Morality Tale

1. Page Smith (1956), 45.

2. Sumner, Vol. I, 232. Sumner also states other possible reasons for the attack, which "Wilson and his friends repelled," but this is the usual explanation. Smith ([1956], pp. 133–39) describes in detail the incident, perhaps unique in its resemblance to European revolutionary activity.

3. Page Smith (1956), 160.

4. Ibid., 163.

5. Sakolski (1966), 62. Oberholtzer, 208.

6. Page Smith (1956), 373.

7. Ibid., 375.

8. An ultimate irony is that Wilson's Pennsylvania lands, like those of Washington, became among the most valuable in the United States. He owned, among other tracts, 21,000 acres of the Great Schuykill coal field. Less than a century later, 11,000 acres of another tract sold for $3,000,000.

9. Page Smith (1956), 387.

10. Miller (1960), 256.

Chapter 34: Summary

1. Cochran, 61 and 62; Morison (1965), 295; and Nettels, 683 and 684.

2. Alden, 337–338; Ferguson, 284–85, 329–30; John C. Miller (1960), 121; and Woodward (1937), 225 and 239.

3. Quoted by Jensen (1950), 279.

4. Quoted by Williams, 179.

Selected Bibliography

Abbott, Wilbur C. *New York in the American Revolution.* New York and London, 1929.

Abernethy, Thomas P. *Western Lands and the American Revolution.* New York, 1959.

———. *From Frontier to Plantation in Tennessee: A Study in Frontier Democracy.* University, Ala., 1967. Reprint.

Adams, Henry. *History of the United States of America During the First Administration of Thomas Jefferson.* Vol. 1, Reprint, 1962.

Adams, Herbert B. *Maryland's Influence in Founding a National Commonwealth. Or the Accession of Public Lands by the Old Confederation.* Baltimore, 1877.

———. *Maryland's Influence upon Land Cessions to the United States, with Minor Papers on George Washington's Interest in Western Lands.* Baltimore, 1885.

Adams, James T. *Revolutionary New England, 1691–1776.* Boston, 1923.

———. *The Epic of America.* Boston, 1934.

Adams, John. *The Founding Fathers: John Adams, A Biography in His Own Words.* New York, 1973.

Akagi, Roy H. *The Town Proprietors of the New England Colonies.* Philadelphia, 1924.

Alden, John R. *The South in the Revolution: 1763–1789.* Austin, Tex., 1957.

Alvord, Clarence W. "Virginia and the West; An Interpretation." *The Mississippi Valley Historical Review* 3 (June, 1916): 19–39.

Alvord, Clarence W. *The Mississippi Valley in British Politics: A Study of the Trade, Land Speculation, and Experiments in Imperialism Culminating in the American Revolution.* 2 vols. Cleveland, 1917.

———. "Lord Shelburne and the Founding of British-American Goodwill," *The British Academy,* The Raleigh Lecture on History, London, 1925.

Ambler, Charles H. *George Washington and the West.* Chapel Hill, N.C., 1936.

Andrews, Charles M. *The Colonial Background of the American Revolution: Four Essays in American Colonial History.* New Haven, Conn., and London, 1935.

———. *Our Earliest Colonial Settlements, Their Diversities of Origin and Later Characteristics.* Ithaca, N.Y., and London, 1959.

———. *The Colonial Period of American History,* Vols. 2, 3, and 4. New Haven, Conn., and London (Ninth Printing), 1967.

Andrews, E. Benjamin. *History of the United States.* Vol. 1, New York, 1913.

Axtell, James. *The European and the Indian: Essays in the Ethnohistory of Colonial North America.* New York and Oxford, 1981.

———. *The Invasion Within: The Contest of Cultures in Colonial North America.* New York and Oxford, 1985.

Bailey, Kenneth P. *The Ohio Company of Virginia.* Glendale, Calif., 1939.

Bailyn, Bernard. *The Origins of the American Revolution.* Cambridge, 1967.

———. *Voyagers to the West: A Passage in the Peopling of America on the Eve of the Revolution.* New York, 1986.

Bakeless, John. *Background to Glory: The Life of George Rogers Clark.* Philadelphia and New York, 1957.

Barck, Oscar T., Jr., and Hugh T. Lefler. *Colonial America.* New York and London, 1968.

Barker, Charles A. *The Background of the Revolution in Maryland.* New Haven, Conn., 1940.

Barker, Eugene C., ed. *The Austin Papers.* 3 vols. in 4. Washington, D.C., 1924–1928.

Barlow, Joel. *The Vision of Columbus: A Poem in Nine Books.* Hartford, Conn., 1787.

———. *The Columbiad: A Poem.* Philadelphia, 1807.

Beard, Charles A. *An Economic Interpretation of the Constitution of the United States.* New York, 1913. Reprint, 1961.

———., ed. *The Enduring Federalist.* New York, 1948.

Beard, Charles A. *The Economic Basis of Politics and Related Writings.* Compiled and annotated by William Beard. New York, 1957.

Beard, Charles A. and Mary R. *The Rise of American Civilization.* New York, 1930.

Becker, Carl L. *The History of Political Parties in the Province of New York, 1760–1776.* Madison, Wis., 1960.

Bellamy, Francis R. *The Private Life of George Washington.* New York, 1951.

Bennett, Walter H., ed. *Letters from the Federal Farmer to the Republican.* University, Ala., 1978.

Bernstein, Richard B., and Kym S. Rice. *Are We to Be a Nation? The Making of the Constitution.* Cambridge, Mass., and London, 1987.

Billington, Ray A., and Martin Ridge. *Westward Expansion: A History of the American Frontier.* 5th ed. New York and London, 1982.

Blount, John Gray. Manuscript. North Carolina Historical Commission. Raleigh (unpublished).

Bodley, Temple. *George Rogers Clark, His Life and Public Services.* Boston, 1926.

Bond, Beverley W., Jr., *The Quit-Rent System in the American Colonies.* New Haven, Conn., and London, 1919.

———. *The Correspondence of John Cleves Symmes, Founder of the Miami Purchase.* New York, 1926.

———. *The Civilization of the Old Northwest: A Study of Political, Social, and Economic Development, 1788–1812.* New York, 1934.

Bonomi, Patricia U. *A Factious People: Politics and Society in Colonial New York.* New York and London, 1971.

Boorstin, Daniel J. *The Americans, the National Experience.* New York, 1967.

Bowers, Claude G. *The Young Jefferson: 1743–1789.* Cambridge, Mass., 1945.

Bridenbaugh, Carl. *Seat of Empire: The Political Role of Eighteenth-Century Williamsburg.* Williamsburg, Va., 1958.

———. *Cities in the Wilderness: The First Century of Urban Life in America, 1625–1742.* New York, 1971 (Reprint).

Brodie, Fawn M. *Thomas Jefferson, an Intimate History.* New York, 1974.

Brown, Milton W. *American Art to 1900.* New York, 1977.

Brown, Robert E. "Manasseh Cutler and the Settlement of Ohio 1788." Marietta College Press, Marietta, Ohio (1938): 3–19. Offprint.

———. *Charles Beard and the Constitution, a Critical Analysis of "An Economic Interpretation of the Constitution."* Princeton, N.J., 1956.

Brown, Robert E., and B. Katherine. *Virginia 1705-1786: Democracy or Aristocracy?* East Lansing, Mich., 1964.

Bruce, Philip A. *Social Life in Virginia in the Seventeenth Century: An Inquiry into the Origin of the Higher Planter Class.* Lynchburg, Va., 1927.

————. *The Virginia Plutarch.* 2 vols. Chapel Hill, N.C., 1929.

Brumbaugh, Gaius M. *Revolutionary War Records: Volume 1, Virginia.* Baltimore, 1967.

Burnett, Edmund C., ed. *Letters of Members of the Continental Congress.* 8 vols. Washington, D.C., 1921-1936.

Burney, James, *History of the Buccaneers of America.* London, 1902.

Butterfield, Consul W., ed. *The Washington-Crawford Letters.* Cincinnati, Ohio, 1877.

Butterfield, Roger. *The American Past: A History of the United States from Concord to the Great Society.* 2d ed. New York, 1966.

Call, Daniel, ed. *Report of Cases Argued and Adjusted in the Court of Appeals of Virginia.* Richmond, 1854.

Campbell, Mildred. *The English Yeoman Under Elizabeth and the Early Stuarts.* New Haven, Conn., and London, 1942.

Campbell, Norine D. *Patrick Henry: Patriot and Statesman.* New York, 1969.

Carpenter, Helen M. "The Origin and Location of the Firelands of the Western Reserve." *The Ohio State Archaeological and Historical Quarterly* 44, no. 2 (April 1935): 163-203.

Channing, Edward. *The History of the United States.* 6 vols. Vol. 3. New York, 1905-1925.

Chernow, Barbara A. *Robert Morris: Land Speculator, 1790-1801.* New York, 1974.

Cheyney, Edward P. *European Background of American History: 1300-1600.* New York and London, 1904.

Clark, Ronald W. *Benjamin Franklin, A Biography.* New York, 1983.

Clowse, Converse D. *Economic Beginnings in Colonial South Carolina, 1670-1730.* Columbia, S.C., 1971.

Cochran, Thomas C. *New York in the Confederation: An Economic Study.* Philadelphia, 1932.

Coe, Michael, Dean Snow, and Elizabeth Benton. *Atlas of Ancient America.* New York and Oxford, 1986.

Commager, Henry Steele. *Jefferson, Nationalism, and the Enlightenment.* New York, 1975.

Conway, Moncure D., ed. *The Writings of Thomas Paine*. 3 vols. New York, 1894.

Cook, Roy B. *Washington's Western Lands*. Strassburg, Va., 1930.

Cooper, William J. *Liberty and Slavery: Southern Politics to 1860*. New York, 1983.

Countryman, Edward. *The American Revolution*. New York, 1985.

Cronon, William. *Changes in the Land: Indians, Colonists, and the Ecology of New England*. New York, 1983.

Custis, George W. *Recollections and Private Memoirs of Washington*. New York, 1860.

Daniels, Jonathan. *Ordeal of Ambition: Jefferson, Hamilton, Burr*. Garden City, N.Y., 1970.

Davidson, Marshall B. *Life in America*. Vol. 1. Boston, 1951.

Davis, Joseph S. *Essays in the Earlier History of American Corporations* Vol. 1, New York, 1917. Reprint 1965.

DeVoto, Bernard. *The Course of Empire*. Boston, 1952.

Dillon, Dorothy R. *The New York Triumvirate: A Study of the Legal and Political Careers of William Livingston, John Marion Scott, William Smith, Jr.* New York, 1949.

Dowdey, Clifford. *The Great Plantation: A Profile of Berkeley Hundred and Plantation Virginia from Jamestown to Appomattox*. New York and Toronto, 1957.

Drake, Sir Francis [nephew]. *Sir Francis Drake Revived: Calling Upon this Dull or Effeminate Age, to Follow His Noble Steps for Gold and Silver*. New York, 1919 (reprint).

Driver, Harold E. *Indians of North America*. 2d ed. Chicago, 1969.

Duane, John, ed. *New Materials for the History of the American Revolution*. New York, 1889.

Dulany, Daniel. *Consideration on the Propriety of Imposing Taxes in the British Colonies, for the Purpose of Raising a Revenue, by Act of Parliament*. London, 1766.

Earle, Edward M. Introduction to *The Federalist : A Commentary on the Constitution of the United States. From the Original Text of Alexander Hamilton, John Jay, James Madison*. The Modern Library, N.Y., n.d.

Eckenrode, Hamilton J. *The Revolution in Virginia*. Hamden, Conn., 1964.

Edmunds, R. David. *The Shawnee Prophet*. Lincoln, Neb., and London, 1983.

Egleston, Melville. *The Land System of the New England Colonies*. Baltimore, 1886.

Engelman, Fred L. "The Peace of Christmas Eve." In *A Sense of History: The Best Writing from the Pages of American Heritage*, introductory note by Byron Dobell. New York and Boston, 1985.

Failor, Kenneth M., and Eleanor Hayden. *Medals of the United States Mint.* Washington, D.C. n.d.

Ferguson, E. James. *The Power of the Purse: A History of American Public Finance, 1776-1790.* Chapel Hill, N.C., 1961.

Fisher, Joseph. *The History of Landholding in England.* New York, 1881.

Fiske, John. *The Critical Period of American History, 1781-1789.* Boston and New York, 1901.

Flexner, James T. *Mohawk Baronet: Sir William Johnson of New York.* New York, 1959.

———. *Washington the Indispensable Man.* Boston and Toronto, 1969.

Fox, Dixon R. *Yankees and Yorkers.* New York and London, 1940.

Fox, Edith. *Land Speculation in the Mohawk Country.* Ithaca, N.Y., 1949.

Franklin, Benjamin. *The Autobiography.* New York, 1951 (reprint). With an Introduction by Carl Van Doren.

[Franklin, Benjamin]. *The Interest of Great Britain Considered, With Regard to her Colonies, and the Acquisitions of Canada and Guadaloupe . . . ; Observations Concerning the Increase of Mankind, Peopling of Countries.* London, 1760.

Freund, Rudolf. "Military Bounty Lands and the Origins of the Public Domain." *Agricultural History* 20 (1946): 8–18.

Gayerré, Charles. *History of Louisiana.* Chapter 3: "The Spanish Domination." New Orleans, 1885.

Gelb, Norman. *Less Than Glory.* New York, 1984.

Gipson, Lawrence H. *The Coming of the Revolution, 1763-1775.* New York, 1954.

———. *The British Isles and the American Colonies (The Southern Plantations, 1748-1754).* New York, 1958.

Godbold, E. Stanley, Jr., and Robert H. Woody. *Christopher Gadsden and the American Revolution.* Knoxville, Tenn., 1982.

Goodpasture, Albert V. "Dr. James White. Pioneer, Politician, Lawyer." *Tennessee Historical Magazine* 1 (n.d.): 282–291.

Gould, Charles P. *The Land System in Maryland, 1720-1765.* Baltimore, 1911.

Hakluyt, Richard. *Divers Voyages Touching the Discovery of America and the Islands Adjacent.* London, 1850 (reprint).

Hakluyt, Richard. *Discourse on Western Planting.* Cambridge, 1877 (reprint).

Harper, Robert G. "Observations." Prospectus of *North American Land Company.* London, 1796.

Harrel, Isaac S. *Loyalism in Virginia: Chapters in the Economic History of the Revolution.* Durham, N.C., 1926.

Harris, Marshall. *Origin of the Land Tenure System in the United States.* Ames, Iowa. 1953.

Haskins, Charles H. "The Yazoo Land Companies." *Papers of the American Historical Association* 5 (1891) : 395–437.

Hatcher, Harlan. *The Western Reserve: The Story of New Connecticut in Ohio.* Cleveland and New York, rev. ed.; 1966.

Havighurst, Walter. *Land of Promise: The Story of the Northwest Territory.* New York, 1946.

———. *Wilderness for Sale: The Story of the First Western Land Rush.* New York, 1956.

Hayes, Edward. *Sir Humphrey Gilbert's Voyage to Newfoundland.* New York, 1910 (reprint).

Henderson, Archibald. "The Creative Forces in Westward Expansion: Henderson and Boone." *American Historical Review* 20 (1913): 86–107.

———. "The Spanish Conspiracy in Tennessee." *Tennessee Historical Magazine* 3, no. 4 (1917): 229–243.

———. *The Conquest of the Old Southwest: The Romantic Story of the Early Pioneers into Virginia, the Carolinas, Tennessee, and Kentucky, 1740–1790.* New York, 1920.

———. "Dr. Thomas Walker and the Loyal Company of Virginia." *Proceedings of the American Antiquarian Society.* New Series 41 (April 15, 1931–Oct. 21, 1931). Worcester, Mass.

Hibbard, Benjamin H. *A History of the Public Land Policies.* Madison, Wis., 1924. 1965 (reprint).

Hinsdale, Burke A. *The Old Northwest.* Boston, 1899. Reprint 1975.

Holbrook, Stewart H. *Ethan Allen.* New York, 1946.

Hughes, Rupert. *George Washington, the Rebel and the Patriot.* 3 vols. New York, 1926–1930.

Hutchinson, William T. *The Bounty Lands of the American Revolution in Ohio.* New York, 1979.

Jacobs, James R. *Tarnished Warrior, Major-General James Wilkinson.* New York, 1938.

James, Alfred P. *The Ohio Company: Its Inner History.* New York, 1959.

James, James A., ed. *George Rogers Clark Papers, 1781–784.* Collections of the Illinois State Historical Library 8, Virginia Series 3, Springfield, Ill., 1912.

———. *The Life of George Rogers Clark.* Chicago, 1928.

James, James A.. "Oliver Pollock, Financier of the Revolution in the West." *Mississippi Valley Historical Review* 16 (n.d.): 67–80.

James, King I. [First] Charter of Virginia. New York, 1910 (reprint).

Jameson, J. Franklin. *The American Revolution Considered as a Social Movement.* Princeton, N.J., 1926.

Jefferson, Thomas. *Autobiography.* With an Introduction by Dumas Malone. New York, 1959.

Jellison, Charles A. *Ethan Allen, Frontier Rebel.* Syracuse, N.Y., 1969.

Jennings, Francis. *The Invasion of America: Indians, Colonialism, and the Cant of Conquest.* Chapel Hill, N.C., 1975.

———. *The Ambiguous Iroquois Empire: The Covenant Chain Confederation of Indian Tribes with English Colonies from Its Beginnings to the Lancaster Treaty of 1744.* New York and London, 1984.

———. *Empire of Fortune: Crowns, Colonies, and Tribes in the Seven Years War in America.* New York and London, 1988.

Jensen, Merrill. *The Articles of Confederation: An Interpretation of the Social-Constitutional History of the American Revolution, 1774–1781.* Madison, Wis., 1940.

———. *The New Nation: A History of the United States during the Confederation, 1781–1789.* New York, 1950.

———. *The Founding of a Nation: A History of the American Revolution, 1763–1776.* New York, London, and Toronto, 1968.

Jillson, Willard R. *The Kentucky Land Grants.* Filson Club Publications Vol. 33. Louisville, Ky., 1925.

Johnson, Cecil. "Expansion in West Florida, 1770–1779." *Mississippi Valley Historical Review* 20 (n.d.): 481–96.

Johnson, Gerald W. *American Heroes and Hero Worship.* New York and London, 1943.

Jones, Alice H. *Wealth of a Nation to Be.* New York, 1980.

Josephy, Alvin M., Jr. *The Patriot Chiefs: A Chronicle of American Indian Leadership.* New York, 1961.

King, Gregory. *Natural and Political Observations and Conclusions upon the State and Conditions of England, 1696.* Reprinted by George Chalmers, London, 1804.

Knollenberg, Bernhard. *Origin of the American Revolution, 1759-1766.* New York, 1960.

Labaree, Leonard Woods. *Conservatism in Early American History.* New York, 1948.

Lamar, Howard, and Leonard Thompson, eds. *The Frontier in History: North America and South Africa Compared.* New Haven, Conn., and London, 1981.

Land, Aubrey C., ed. *Bases of the Plantation System.* New York; Evanston, Ill.; and London, 1969.

Las Casas, Bartolome de. *Regionum Indicarum Per Hispanos olim devastarum accuratissima descriptio.* Heidelberg, 1664.

Leach, Douglas E. *The Northern Colonial Frontier, 1607-1763.* New York, 1966.

Leon-Portilla, Miguel, ed. *The Broken Spears: The Aztec Account of the Conquest of Mexico.* Boston, 1962.

Lewis, George E. *The Indiana Company, 1763-1798.* Glendale, Calif., 1941.

Library of Congress, Spanish transcripts. *Archivo General de Indias. Papeles procedentes de la isla de Cuba,* legajo 198.

Livermore, Shaw. *Early American Land Companies: Their Influence on Corporate Development.* London, 1939.

Locke, John. *Second Treatise on Civil Government.* London and New York, 1924 (reprint).

Maclay, William. *The Journal of William Maclay, United States Senator from Pennsylvania, 1789-1791.* New York, 1927.

Malone, Dumas. *Jefferson and His Time. Vol. 1. Jefferson the Virginian.* Boston, 1948.

Marcus, Jacob R. *Early American Jewry: The Jews of Pennsylvania and the South, 1655-1790.* Vol. 2. Philadelphia, 1953.

Mark, Irving. *Agrarian Conflicts in Colonial New York, 1711-1775.* New York and London, 1940.

Marshall, Humphrey. *The History of Kentucky.* Vol. 1. Frankfort, 1824.

Marshall, Peter. "Lord Hillsborough, Samuel Wharton and the Ohio Grant, 1769-1775." *English Historical Review* 80 (1965): 717-39.

Masterson, William H. *William Blount.* Baton Rouge, La., 1954.

Mather, Increase. *A Brief History of the Warr With the Indians in New-England.* Boston, 1676.

Mayo, Laurence S. *John Wentworth, Governor of New Hampshire, 1767-1775.* Cambridge. 1921.

McColley, Robert. *Slavery and Jeffersonian Virginia.* Urbana, Ill., 1964.

McDonald, Forrest. *We the People: The Economic Origins of the Constitution.* Chicago, 1958. Reprint 1975.

———. *E Pluribus Unum: The Formation of the American Republic, 1776–1790.* 2d ed. Indianapolis, 1979.

———. *Novus Ordo Seclorum: The Intellectual Origins of the Constitution.* Lawrence, Kan., 1985.

Meade, Robert D. *Patrick Henry: Patriot in the Making.* Philadelphia, 1957.

———. *Patrick Henry, Practical Revolutionary.* Philadelphia and New York, 1969.

Meltzer, Milton. *Milestones to American Liberty: The Foundations of the Republic.* New York, 1961.

Mereness, Newton D. *Maryland as a Proprietary Province.* Cos Cob, Conn., 1968.

Miller, John C. *Origins of the American Revolution.* Boston, 1943.

———. *The Triumph of Freedom.* Boston, 1948.

———. *The Federalist Era, 1789–1801.* New York, 1960.

Miller, William. *A History of the United States.* New York, 1958.

Morgan, Edmund S. *The Birth of the Republic, 1763–1789.* Chicago, 1956.

———. *The American Revolution: Two Centuries of Interpretation.* Englewood Cliffs, N.J., 1965.

———. *American Slavery, American Freedom: The Ordeal of Colonial Virginia.* New York, 1975.

Morison, Samuel E., ed. *Journals and Other Documents on the Life and Voyages of Christopher Columbus.* New York, 1963.

———. *The Oxford History of the American People.* New York, 1965.

Morison, Samuel E., Henry S. Commager, and William E. Leuchtenburg. *The Growth of the American Republic.* Vol. 1, 7th ed., New York and Oxford, 1980.

Morris, Richard B. *The American Revolution Reconsidered.* New York; Evanston, Ill.; and London, 1967.

———. *Seven Who Shaped Our Destiny: The Founding Fathers as Revolutionaries.* New York; Evanston, Ill.; San Francisco; and London, 1973.

———. *The Forging of the Union, 1781–1789.* New York, Cambridge, Philadelphia, etc., 1987.

Myers, Gustavus. *History of the Great American Fortunes.* New York, 1937 (reprint).

Nagel, Paul C. *Descent from Glory: Four Generations of the John Adams Family.* New York and Oxford, 1983.

Nammack, Georgiana C. *Fraud, Politics, and the Dispossession of the Indians: The Iroquois Land Frontier in the Colonial Period.* Norman, Okla., 1969.

Nettels, Curtis P. *The Roots of American Civilization, A History of American Colonial Life.* 2d ed. New York, 1963.

Nevins, Allan. *The American States During and After the Revolution (1775-1789).* New York, 1924.

Nichols, Jeannette P., and Roy F. Nichols. *The Republic of the United States, A History.* Vol. 1. New York and London, 1939.

Oberholtzer, Ellis P. *Robert Morris, Patriot and Financier.* New York, 1903.

O'Callaghan, Jerry A. "The War Veteran and the Public Lands." *Agricultural History* 28 (1954): 163–68.

Ogg, Frederic A. *The Old Northwest: A Chronicle of the Ohio Valley and Beyond.* New Haven, Conn., 1919.

Packe, Michael St. John. *The Life of John Stuart Mill.* New York, 1954.

Padover, Saul K., ed. *The Complete Jefferson, Containing His Major Writings, Published and Unpublished, Except His Letters.* New York, 1943.

————. *Jefferson.* New York, 1952, Abridged.

————. *The Mind of Alexander Hamilton.* New York, 1958.

Parish, John C. "The Intrigues of Doctor James O'Fallon." *Mississippi Valley Historical Review* 17 (n.d.): 230–63.

Parrington, Vernon L. *Main Currents in American Thought: An Interpretation of American Literature from the Beginnings to 1902.* Vol. 1, New York, 1927.

Pasqualigo, Lorenzo. *Letter from Lorenzo to His Brothers Alvise and Francesco.* Calendars of State Papers 1, No. 752, Venice. New York, 1910 (reprint). [John Cabot's Discovery of North America.]

Peden, William, ed. *Notes on the State of Virginia,* by Thomas Jefferson. Chapel Hill, N.C., 1955.

Pell, John. *Ethan Allen.* Boston and New York, 1929.

Penn, William. *A Brief Account of the Province of Pennsylvania.* London, 1681. Boston (reprint), 1924.

Philbrick, Francis S. *The Rise of the West: 1754-1830.* New York, 1965.

Priest, William. *Travels in the United States of America: Commencing in the Year 1793, and Ending in 1797.* London, 1802.

Quaife, Milo M. *The Preston and Virginia Papers of the Draper Collection of Manuscripts.* State Historical Society of Wisconsin, Calendar series, 1, Madison, 1915.

Raleigh, Sir Walter. *The Discovery of Guiana.* New York, 1910 (reprint).

Ramsay, David. *The History of the American Revolution.* Philadelphia, 1789.

Recinos, Adrían and Delia Goetz, trans. *The Annals of the Cakchiquels.* Norman, Okla., 1953.

Reese, Richard T. *Colonial Georgia: A Study in British Imperial Policy in the Eighteenth Century.* Athens, Ga., 1963.

Ricord, Frederick W., and William Nelson, eds. *Archives of the State of New Jersey,* first series, IX-X. Newark, 1886.

Ritter, Halsted L. *Washington as a Businessman.* New York, 1931.

Robbins, Roy M. *Our Landed Heritage: The Public Domain, 1776-1936.* Lincoln, Neb., 1962.

Rogers, James E. Thorold. *The Economic Interpretation of History.* London, 1888.

Roosevelt, Theodore. *Winning of the West.* New York, 1889.

Rowland, Kate M. *The Life of George Mason.* New York, 1892.

Sakolski, Aaron M. *The Great American Land Bubble.* New York, 1932. Reprint 1966.

———. *Land Tenure and Land Taxation in America.* New York, 1957.

Sale, Kirkpatrick. *The Conquest of Paradise: Christopher Columbus and the Columbian Legacy.* New York, 1990.

Savelle, Max. *George Morgan: Colony Builder.* New York, 1932.

Schlesinger, Arthur M. *New Viewpoints in American History.* New York, 1922. Reprint 1948.

Shaw, Helen L. *British Administration of the Southern Indians, 1756-1783.* Lancaster, Penn., 1931.

Sheehan, Bernard W. *Seeds of Extinction: Jeffersonian Philanthropy and the American Indian.* Chapel Hill, N.C., 1973.

———. *Savagism and Civility: Indians and Englishmen in Colonial Virginia.* Cambridge, London, and New York, 1980.

Skinner, Constance L. *Pioneers of the Old Southwest: A Chronicle of the Dark and Bloody Ground.* New Haven, Conn., 1921.

Smith, Henry N. *Virgin Land: The American West as Symbol and Myth.* New York, 1957.

Smith, [Captain] John. *The Generall Historie of Virginia, New England and the Summer Isles.* Facsimile edition, New York, 1966.

Smith, Page. *James Wilson: Founding Fathers 1742–1798.* Chapel Hill, N.C., 1956.

———. *John Adams.* 2 vols. New York, 1962.

———. *Jefferson: A Revealing Biography.* New York, 1976.

Sosin, Jack M. *Whitehall and the Wilderness: The Middle West in British Colonial Policy, 1760–1775.* Lincoln, Neb., 1961.

———. *The Revolutionary Frontier, 1763–1783.* New York, Chicago, San Francisco, Toronto, and London, 1967.

Soule, George. *Economic Forces in American History.* New York, 1952.

Spencer, Charles W. "The Land System of Colonial New York." In *Proceedings of the New York State Historical Association* 16.

Sumner, William G. *The Financier and the Finances of the American Revolution.* 2 vols. New York, 1891.

Sullivan, James, and Alexander C. Flick, eds. *The Papers of Sir William Johnson.* 8 vols. Albany, N.Y., 1921–1933.

Sutton, Imre, ed. *Irredeemable America: The Indians' Estate and Land Claims.* Albuquerque, N.M., ca., 1985.

Sydnor, Charles S. *Gentlemen Freeholders: Political Practices in Washington's Virginia.* Chapel Hill, N.C., 1952.

Tatter, Henry. "State and Federal Land Policy During the Confederation Period." *Agricultural History* 9 (1935): 176–86.

Tawney, Richard H. *Religion and the Rise of Capitalism: A Historical Study.* London, 1944.

Thayer, Theodore. *Nathanael Greene: Strategist of the American Revolution.* New York, 1960.

Thomas, Dana L. *Lords of the Land.* New York, 1977.

Thompson, Daniel P. "Ira Allen." *Proceedings of the Vermont Historical Society,* 1907–1908.

Thwaites, Reuben G. *Daniel Boone.* New York, 1903.

Thwaites, Reuben G., and Louise P. Kellogg, eds. *Documentary History of Dunmore's War, 1774.* Madison, Wis., 1905.

Treat, Payson J. "Origin of the National Land System under the Confederation," *American Historical Association Report* 1 (1905): 231–39.

———. *The National Land System, 1785–1820.* New York, 1910. Reprint 1967.

Tuchman, Barbara W. *The First Salute.* New York, 1988.

Turner, Frederick J. *The Frontier in American History.* New York, 1920. Reprint 1962.

———. "Western State-Making in the Revolutionary Era." *American Historical Review* (1896): Part I: 70–87; Part II: 251–69.

Tyler, Moses C. *Patrick Henry*. Boston and New York, 1887.

Van Doren, Carl. *Benjamin Franklin*. New York, 1938. Also, reprint 1952.
Van Every, Dale. *Disinherited: The Lost Birthright of the American Indian*. New York, 1966.
Vaughan, Alden T. *New England Frontier: Puritans and Indians, 1620–1675*. Boston and Toronto, 1965.
Ver Steeg, Clarence L. *Robert Morris, Revolutionary Financier*. Philadelphia, 1954.
———. *The Formative Years, 1607–1763*. New York, 1964.
Virginia Historical Society. *Executive Journal of the Council of Virginia, 1740–1752*. Richmond (copy from the Public Record Office, London).

Wade, Richard C. *The Urban Frontier: The Use of Western Cities, 1790–1830*. Cambridge, 1959.
Wagner, Frederick. *Robert Morris: Audacious Patriot*. New York, 1976.
Wainwright, Nicholas B. *George Croghan, Wilderness Diplomat*. Chapel Hill, N.C., 1959.
Ward, A. W., G. W. Prothero, and Stanley Leathes, eds. *Cambridge Modern History*. Vol. 7, "The United States." Cambridge, 1903.
Washburn, Wilcomb E. *The Effect of Bacon's Rebellion on Government in England and Virginia*. Washington, D.C. Smithsonian Institution. U.S. National Museum Bulletin 225.
———. *Red Man's Land/White Man's Law: A Study of the Past and Present Status of the American Indian*. New York, 1971.
Weaks, Mabel C. *The Preston and Virginia Papers of the Draper Collection of Manuscripts*. State Historical Society of Wisconsin, Calendar series, II. Madison, Wis., 1915.
Wecter, Dixon. *The Hero in America: A Chronicle of Hero-Worship*. New York, 1972.
Wertenbaker, Thomas J. *The Old South: The Founding of American Civilization*. New York, 1942.
———. *The Shaping of Colonial Virginia, Volume 2: The Planters of Colonial Virginia*. New York, 1958.
Wharton, Thomas. "Selections from the Letter-books of Thomas Wharton of Philadelphia, 1773–1783." *The Pennsylvania Magazine of History and Biography* 33.
Whitaker, Arthur P. "Spanish Intrigue in the Old Southwest: An Episode, 1788–1789." *Mississippi Valley Historical Review* 12, no. 2 (1925):155–76.

Whitaker, Arthur P. "The Muscle Shoals Speculation, 1783–1789," *Mississippi Valley Historical Review* 13 (1926): 356–86.

———. *The Spanish American Frontier: 1783–1795.* Boston, 1927. 1970 edition.

Whittlesey, Charles. *Early History of Cleveland, Ohio.* Cleveland, 1867.

Wilbur, James B. *Ira Allen, Founder of Vermont, 1751–1814.* 2 vols. Boston, 1928.

Williams, William A. *The Contours of American History.* Cleveland and New York, 1961.

Wiltse, Charles M. *The New Nation: 1800–1845.* New York, 1961. Reprint 1981.

Woodward, W. E. *George Washington: The Image and the Man.* New York, 1926.

———. *A New American History.* New York, 1937.

Wright, Fletcher W., ed. *The Federalist.* By Alexander Hamilton, James Madison, and John Jay. Cambridge, 1961 (reprint).

Wright, Louis B. *The First Gentlemen of Virginia: Intellectual Qualities of the Early Colonial Ruling Class.* San Marino, Calif., 1940.

———. *The Atlantic Frontier: Colonial American Civilization [1607–1763].* New York, 1947.

Wright, Louis B., and Marion Tinling, eds. *The Secret Diary of William Byrd of Westover, 1709–1712.* Richmond, 1941.

Zinn, Howard. *A People's History of the United States.* New York, 1980.

Index